The LORD's Service

The LORD's Service

A Ritual Analysis of the Order, Function,
and Purpose of the Daily Divine Service
in the Pentateuch

ROBERT D. MACINA

Foreword by John W. Kleinig

◆PICKWICK *Publications* · Eugene, Oregon

THE LORD'S SERVICE
A Ritual Analysis of the Order, Function, and Purpose of the Daily Divine Service in the Pentateuch

Copyright © 2019 Robert D. Macina. All rights reserved. Except for brief quotations in critical publications or reviews, no part of this book may be reproduced in any manner without prior written permission from the publisher. Write: Permissions, Wipf and Stock Publishers, 199 W. 8th Ave., Suite 3, Eugene, OR 97401.

Pickwick Publications
An Imprint of Wipf and Stock Publishers
199 W. 8th Ave., Suite 3
Eugene, OR 97401

www.wipfandstock.com

PAPERBACK ISBN: 978-1-5326-6193-8
HARDCOVER ISBN: 978-1-5326-6194-5
EBOOK ISBN: 978-1-5326-6195-2

Cataloguing-in-Publication data:

Names: Macina, Robert D., author. | Kleinig, John W., foreword writer

The LORD's service : a ritual analysis of the order, function, and purpose of the daily divine service in the Pentateuch / Robert D. Macina, with a foreword by John W. Klein.

Description: Eugene, OR: Pickwick Publications, 2019 | Includes bibliographical references and index.

Identifiers: ISBN 978-1-5326-6193-8 (paperback) | ISBN 978-1-5326-6194-5 (hardcover) | ISBN 978-1-5326-6195-2 (ebook)

Subjects: LCSH: Bible—Old Testament—Rites and ceremonies | Sacrifice—Biblical teaching | Worship in the Bible | Public worship in the Bible | Bible—Pentateuch—Criticism, interpretation, etc.

Classification: BS1199.W76 M11 2019 (paperback) | BS1199.W76 (ebook)

Manufactured in the U.S.A.   04/18/19

For Tracy, my dear wife and beloved soulmate,
with joy and gratitude!

"The heart of her husband trusts in her, and he has no lack of gain.
She brings good to him and no evil, all the days of her life."
Proverbs 31:11–12

"You shall make a distinction, between the holy and the common, and between the unclean and the clean."

Leviticus 10:10

Contents

List of Figures | ix
Foreword by John W. Kleinig | xi
Preface | xv
Scripture Abbreviations | xix

1 Prologue | 1

2 The Practical Order of the Daily Divine Service | 24

3 The Ritual Function of the Daily Divine Service | 68

4 The Theological Purpose of the Daily Divine Service | 178

Bibliography | 203
Index of Ancient Sources | 209
Index of Subjects | 223

Figures

Figure 1. The sequential order of the daily divine service. | 66
Figure 2. The tabernacle ground plan. | 81
Figure 3. The camp of Israel. | 81
Figure 4. The tent of meeting and the courtyard. | 99
Figure 5. The altar and its north side. | 112
Figure 6. The rite of atonement. | 116
Figure 7. The relation of the blood rite to the three ritual spheres. | 120
Figure 8. The ritual locations of the incense rite. | 137
Figure 9. The burning rite at the altar. | 153
Figure 10. The ritual locations of the blessing rite. | 163
Figure 11. The location of the meal rite. | 174
Figure 12. Unauthorized approach. | 181
Figure 13. Authorized mediation. | 181
Figure 14. The Levitical barrier between the Israelites and the tabernacle. | 182
Figure 15. The theological purpose of the main parts of the system of ritual acts. | 185
Figure 16. The theological and anthropological systems. | 188
Figure 17. The LORD's means of purification and sanctification through the system of ritual materials. | 189
Figure 18. The states of the rites of passage. | 191
Figure 19. The purification rites of passage. | 192
Figure 20. The sanctification rites of passage. | 192
Figure 21. The states of the divine service's complex rite of passage every morning and evening. | 192
Figure 22. The stages of rites of passage | 192

Figure 23. The stages of the daily service's complex rite
of passage every morning and evening | 193

Figure 24. Israel's status in relation to the stages of the divine service
according to the complex rite of passage every morning and
evening. | 193

Figure 25. Grades of holiness "before the LORD." | 196

Figure 26. Holy and common, unclean and clean locations. | 197

Figure 27. The centrality of the most holy place in the system of ritual
locations. | 197

Figure 28. The daily system of purification and sanctification
from desecration and defilement. | 200

Foreword

WE ALL HAVE OUR intellectual blind spots. That, sadly, is all too often the case even with scholars, who necessarily have a narrow focus in their specialized studies and a firm commitment to their theoretical presuppositions. These blind spots prevent them and us from seeing something that lies in plain view before our very eyes. Or, if we see it, we overlook and discount what is there, because it should not be there, or else, more commonly, because it is held to be of little or no importance, like a smudge on our spectacles. We disregard that matter because it does not fit in with our personal prejudices and our mental preconceptions.

If we want people to see what their preconceptions otherwise prevent them from seeing, it is not enough to describe what has been overlooked, because that does nothing for their blind spots. Two things are required for them to understand what is obscured and hidden from them. On the one hand, what they fail to see must be explained for them within their own frame of reference, like the translation of words in a foreign language into their own language. On the other hand, their frame of reference with its concomitant mentality, the way of imagining, thinking and feeling that corresponds with it, must be expanded and reconfigured, so that they can grasp and receive what they have as yet not been able to see and appreciate.

As far as I am concerned the best Biblical scholars do just that. These groundbreaking scholars do not just repeat what has already been said and confirm what is already known; they open up our eyes and our minds to comprehend and appreciate what has previously been overlooked and disregarded because it has made little or no sense to its readers. They perform a kind of mental surgery by their removal of a blind spot from our minds, like a cataract from our eyes. An instance of this for me was Gerhard von Rad's monograph on "Wisdom in Israel." It opened up that approach to the world and its view of human life which produced the book of Proverbs and the other wisdom literature in the Old Testament.

The removal of a blind spot opens up new vistas for investigation and provides new insights for the enrichment of understanding. To be sure, such scholarship does not have the final word to say on the matter for study, for that can never be. Instead, it enables those who enter a new place by the door that it has opened, to see it from inside and explore it for themselves. In that way their minds are enlarged and their capacity for understanding is enhanced. They see what they had previously been unable to see. Like a blind person who has gained sight, they perceive what they experience in a new way and have a bigger, better picture of the world before them.

My former student, Robert Macina, has done just that in his groundbreaking investigation of the divine service in the Pentateuch. To be sure, he, like every Biblical scholar, builds on the work of other scholars who have been working to remove similar blind spots in the interpretation of the priestly material in the Pentateuch. These blind spots have to do with the lack of insight into the nature and purpose of the ritual legislation in the Pentateuch. Two such blind spots are a contempt for ritual in general and for the sacrificial ritual in ancient Israel in particular.

The lack of attention to the ritual legislation in Exodus, Leviticus, and Numbers is surprising, given that it lies at the heart of the Pentateuch. The whole of Exodus 25 to Numbers 10:10 reports God's institution of ritual enactments for Ancient Israel. Even more are given before and after that. Testimony to its importance is found in the rest of the Old Testament and the whole Jewish tradition up to the Mishnah and the Talmud. Yet despite the overwhelming evidence for its importance, scholars tend to belittle it, or dismiss it out of hand. Ritual enactments are regarded, by and large, as primitive, superstitious, empty mumbo jumbo, and the range of rites that are legislated in the Pentateuch are treated piecemeal as curiosities with minimal coherence and little ongoing significance, or as a kind of charade for the inculcation of moral or spiritual ideas. But in themselves they are held to have no intrinsic value, because they do nothing that could not be done better by other more pertinent means.

While some scholars, such as the social anthropologist Mary Douglas have addressed the contempt for ritual among intellectuals and much of Western society since the Enlightenment, other Biblical scholars, such as Haran and Milgrom, have made good sense of many aspects of ritual legislation in the Pentateuch and the symbolic social and religious world view that these rites embody. Macina advances their studies by his close ritual analysis of the daily service that was enacted as the main public ritual enactment for Israel as God's people. It revolved around the burning of incense and the presentation of a burnt offering each morning and evening. He builds his case mainly on the legislation for the divine service in Exodus 25:1–31:10

and the account of its inaugural enactment in Leviticus 9. In his view the daily offering was a single, complex service that was performed in seven stages, each with its own coherence and indispensable function, and each as an important part of a whole sequence of acts which all made their unique contribution to the common purpose of the whole service. Most significantly, he argues that God had instituted the whole service for him to meet with his people at the sanctuary to purify, sanctify and bless them. That divine purpose determined the order of the service and the function of each part of it. The loss of it meant that Israel lost assured access to God's gracious presence and the blessings that came from his residence with them.

In itself this careful, meticulous study succeeds in making good sense of the daily service and all its parts. Yet it does even more than that. It helps us to understand why the performance of that service, first at the tabernacle and then at the temple in Jerusalem, was so significant in the life of Israel in the pre-exilic period, as is evident even from a cursory reading of its history from Joshua to Chronicles, as well as in the life of Israel after the exile, as is evident from the focus on it in Ezra–Nehemiah and 1–2 Maccabees. It also helps Christian readers to understand why Paul includes the divine service in Romans 9:4 in the seven-fold legacy of the church from the Old Testament, as well as why Hebrews regards the service of worship in the church as both a partial continuation and the complete fulfillment of what was established for Israel in the Pentateuch.

Macina's study provides a great service for the discerning readers of the Pentateuch who wish to make sense of it in all its parts. It helps to remove some of the blind spots that bar access to the significance of its ritual legislation for the divine service and helps them to appreciate its theological purpose and relevance. It helps Jews and Christians to understand what they receive from God by the performance of the Aaronic benediction.

John W. Kleinig, PhD
Professor Emeritus
Australian Lutheran College, University of Divinity
Adelaide, South Australia

Preface

THIS BOOK IS THE product of a long journey that began with my Holy Baptism as an infant and that has continued throughout my life as I have heard, learned, studied, taught, and preached the Holy Scriptures as well as received and administered Holy Absolution and Holy Communion in the divine service of the Church. It is within this ecclesial context and from this perspective that I have studied the Bible, which remains for me the only divine source and guide for Christian faith, love, and life. Thus, my research of the Scriptures has not merely been an academic exercise, but chiefly a Spiritual journey.

Moved by the Holy Spirit, one might say, I was urged to enter into formal theological education in undergraduate school, where I obtained a working knowledge of Biblical Greek and Hebrew. I then continued on to Concordia Theological Seminary, Fort Wayne, to prepare for service in the Holy Ministry. The Master of Divinity degree provided the opportunity for me to major in New Testament. My Master of Sacred Theology studies initiated the challenge of looking at how the Old and New Testaments relate to each other. At the same time as my formal theological education, I intensely appreciated the chapel services at the seminary. This formative period along my Spiritual journey was one of great joy, in which class lectures often resembled fervent preaching and chapel sermons revealed deep theological insights.

Every one of my teachers at the seminary was helpful on this path, yet there are a few who were most influential to me. Arthur Just, who was also the dean of chapel, taught me Luke, Acts, and Hebrews from an eschatological liturgical point of view. David Scaer introduced me to the Gospel of Matthew and the Synoptic Gospels from the Christological, sacramental perspective. William Weinrich showed me the mysteries of the Gospel of John and the Epistle of 1 John through the matrix of several early Church fathers; and he guided me through my MDiv thesis on St. Paul's understanding of apostolicity. Dean Wenthe opened my eyes to see Christ in every book of the Hebrew Bible and taught me to discern the typological connections between the Old and New Testaments. Each of these professors demonstrated an organic connection between theology and practice within the Church. I also met a kindred spirit of these men who happened to be a guest speaker from Australia at an exegetical symposium at the seminary, who would later impress upon me that all good theology is practical. He was John Kleinig, who a decade and a half later would become my doctor-father and supervisor for the study that resulted in this book. These, and many other teachers, have inculcated within me a deep appreciation for the theology and practice of the divine service as it is prescribed and described in the Sacred Scriptures. Their influence has remained in my scholarship and in my ministry.

After serving many years as a parish pastor and teaching Bible classes, I came to realize that my knowledge of the Old Testament needed expanding. So, I began studying and teaching the Pentateuch in our main Bible class at Church. We covered all of Genesis and were coming to the end of Exodus when I received an advertisement from Concordia Theological Seminary for a continuing education course on Leviticus, taught by John Kleinig. I attended the course in Fort Wayne and it changed my life! The book of Leviticus, which portrays most of the elements of the divine service in the Old Testament, was opened for me thanks to Kleinig's instruction as well as his commentary on Leviticus. Just as significant as the course, is the fact that John and I began a relationship and, over the following year and a half, corresponded about various texts that I was teaching in Bible class. An eagerness to learn more about the divine service in the Pentateuch was growing inside of me.

My journey would take a turn when, a short time later, I began doctoral studies at Australian Lutheran College, Adelaide with Dr. Kleinig as the supervisor of my dissertation. At my initial visit to discuss the scope of my study, he indicated that there was a need for additional scholarship on the daily divine service in the Pentateuch. The topic was perfect; and I have never tired of it!

At the commencement of my research, I expected to find a correlation between the Old Testament divine service and the traditional liturgies of the Church. However, it did not take long to discover that there is almost no correlation whatsoever. This is due to the divine service in the Pentateuch not having a spoken service; there was no verbal liturgy at all. The divine service that God established for ancient Israel in the Old Testament involved almost entirely unspoken ritual acts. The only part of the service that was spoken according to the Pentateuch was the Aaronic benediction from

Numbers 6:24–26. That blessing is used in many of the historic liturgies of the Church, but this hardly constitutes a correlation between the broader service in the Old Testament and the spoken service of the New Testament. Still, there is a correlation; it is not one of speaking but of ritual acts.

This study has resulted in the discovery of the theological purpose of the daily divine service in ancient Israel. Through the ritual acts that were carried out at the Tabernacle every morning and evening, God acted upon his people to purify them, sanctify them, and bless them. This was the purpose for which God instituted the divine service in the Old Testament; and it is this same reason why the Church in the New Testament continues its ritual acts that were instituted by Christ. In truth, there is only one divine service, the ongoing heavenly angelic praise of the Holy Father, Holy Son, and Holy Spirit as indicated in Isaiah 6 and Revelation 4. Thus, whether it was the ritual acts at the Tabernacle or it is the rites of the Church, the divine service is enacted to give God's people access to his purifying, sanctifying, and blessing presence. Although this study does not extend beyond the focus of the Pentateuch, recognizing this ritual correlation between the divine service of the Old Testament and that of the New Testament gives the reader an insight into the unified theological purpose of both.

Special thanks must go to the many people who have been with me on this journey that has resulted in the completion of my scholarship on this topic and the production of this book. First and foremost, I thank my doctor-father, John Kleing, who suggested this fascinating area of study, introduced me to ritual analysis as a method of interpretation, insisted on excellence in composition, and has both challenged and encouraged me as a scholar, a pastor, and in my personal life. I am very grateful for the careful examination and thoughtful comments by the readers of my Ph.D. dissertation, Joel Humann and Christopher Mitchell. I thank the professors at Australian Lutheran College who were directly involved with my doctoral studies. Jeff Silcock served as the dean of postgraduate studies and taught me more fully the German language. Stephen Haar instructed me in Research Methods and examined my Greek competency. Peter Lockwood administered and graded my Hebrew exam. In addition, several other professors befriended me and offered helpful questions, suggestions, and discussions for which I thank Andrew Pfeiffer, Gregory Lockwood, Dean Zweck, and Stephen Pietsch. I am most thankful to University of Divinity in Kew, Victoria, Australia for conferring upon me the Doctor of Philosophy degree as a result of this research project.

Most especially, I am grateful to my wife and children for supporting me and traveling together with me on this journey. At times along the way they struggled, and most difficult were the two or three week periods when

I traveled to Australia leaving my wife alone to take care of our three young children. When I was at home, I often sacrificed our time together so that I could read, write, and spend countless hours at the library. I am ever grateful to my children, Daniel, Mark, and Rebekah for maintaining their love, joy, and understanding, during the years of my work on this project. Above all, I thank Tracy, my dear wife and beloved soulmate, who has traveled this journey with me for more than three decades. I owe her a great debt of gratitude for being our primary provider throughout the many years of my undergraduate studies and seminary education. She has encouraged me and has always shared in the goal of completing the work necessary for the production of this book. I thank God for her!

March 25, 2019
Annunciation of Our Lord

Scripture Abbreviations

OLD TESTAMENT:

Gen	Song
Exod	Isa
Lev	Jer
Num	Lam
Deut	Ezek
Josh	Dan
Judg	Hos
Ruth	Joel
1–2 Sam	Amos
1–2 Kgs	Obad
1–2 Chr	Jonah
Ezra	Mic
Neh	Nah
Esth	Hab
Job	Zeph
Ps	Hag
Prov	Zech
Eccl	Mal

NEW TESTAMENT:

Matt	1–2 Cor
Mark	Gal
Luke	Eph
John	Phil
Acts	Col
Rom	1–2 Thess

1–2 Tim
Titus
Phlm
Heb
Jas

1–2 Pet
1–2–3 John
Jude
Rev

APOCRYPHA

Tob
Jdt
Add Esth
Wis
Sir
Bar
1–3 Esd

Ep Jer
Sg Three
Sus
Bel
1–2 Macc
3–4 Macc
Pr Man

1

Prologue

AFTER THE EXODUS OF the ancient Israelites from Egypt, they camped at Mount Sinai where the LORD[1] called Moses to come to the top of the mountain, which was covered by a cloud filled with the LORD's glory (Exod 24:12–17).[2] On top of that mountain during a period of forty days and forty nights the LORD revealed to Moses his plans for constructing a tabernacle as his dwelling place on earth and prescribed the main rites that the Israelites would enact in it (Exod 24:18–31:18).[3] This legislation includes ritual activities that must be carried out daily, every morning and every evening at the tabernacle. Smoking up burnt offerings and burning incense form the basic acts that the LORD commanded to be performed every day at his earthly dwelling place (Exod 29:38–42; 30:7–8). Additional enactments were prescribed for the daily service after the tabernacle had been erected and the LORD established his residence there (Exod 40:34–38; Lev 1:1). The rites and ritual activities of that daily divine service are the focus of this book.

The daily service of ancient Israel with all of its correlated ritual acts has been almost entirely ignored by modern scholarship. Analyses of its various components are often given in great detail, but these tend to be

---

1. Throughout this book, the divine name, יהוה, is usually rendered LORD unless it is necessary to use the Hebrew word itself or its transliteration, YHWH.

2. The biblical references are the chapter and verse numbering in the Masoretic Text. Where the chapter and/or verse numbering is different in the modern English translations, these are marked in brackets, e.g., [6:15].

3. In this book, a *rite* is understood as a discrete religious enactment consisting of a number of correlated acts, while *ritual* is used as a comprehensive, generic term for a form, system, or class of such activity.

piecemeal. No contemporary study has attempted to reconstruct the entire daily service, examine the function of all of its rites, and determine its divine purpose on the basis of the Pentateuch. This neglect is astounding, especially if one considers the centrality of the ritual system of ancient Israel as it is consistently portrayed throughout the biblical writings. Perhaps scholarship in this area has been lacking due to the difficulties of doing so. Nowhere does the Pentateuch spell out the entire order of the daily service, much less explain the function of its parts and its theological purpose. Rather, it presents the daily service in pieces rather than as a whole. Attempts at reassembling the daily divine service is like trying to find hidden pieces of a puzzle before determining where they must be placed. This is no easy task! There is, however, enough evidence in the Pentateuch and other sources to reconstruct the basic order of the daily divine service, examine its ritual function, and determine its divine purpose. I aim to stimulate a renewed interest in and shed new light upon a topic that has bewildered scholars.

CATEGORIES OF BURNT OFFERINGS

Without a general knowledge of the entire daily service, scholars frequently fail to recognize, on the one hand, the organic connection between the various kinds of offerings and, on the other hand, a distinction between the functions of the same kinds of offerings for different circumstances. The daily public burnt offerings must be distinguished from the occasional public burnt offerings and from individual burnt offerings. The public daily burnt offering was offered every day of the year in the morning and in the evening (Num 28:1–8). Public burnt offerings were also prescribed for other regular occasions (Num 28:9–39). They were presented in addition to the daily burnt offering every Sabbath, on the first day of every month, and at special times of the year, such as Passover, Pentecost, the Day of Acclamation, the Day of Atonement, and in the Feast of Tabernacles. Any Israelite could also present individual burnt offerings any time they desired as a personal devotion to God (Lev 1:1–17). In addition, other kinds of offerings, such as peace, sin, and guilt offerings, that were burned on the altar should not be incorrectly referred to as "burnt offerings." Only small portions of these offerings were smoked up, however, while burnt offerings were entirely incinerated. I limit the term *burnt offering* [עֹלָה] only to those offerings that are burned completely.[4] Even though all of the offerings of the

---

4. For an overview of the Hebrew word עֹלָה and its use in ancient Israel's cultus see Kellermann, "עֹלָה," 96–113.

entire ritual system were coordinately enacted, in this book I only examine the public daily burnt offering and the other ritual activities that were conducted every day.

THE FOUNDATION OF ISRAEL'S PERPETUAL DIVINE SERVICE

The present study is based on data from the ritual sections in the Pentateuch. These areas in Exodus, Leviticus, and Numbers are examined to determine the practical order, the ritual function, and theological purpose of the daily divine service in ancient Israel.

The texts in the Pentateuch that deal with the daily service may be divided into three categories. First is the primary prescriptive source, which consists of Exod 25–30. Since this legislation was given by God to Moses on Mount Sinai, it may be viewed as the foundational regulation which establishes Israel's performance of the rites and activities at the tabernacle. This section of the Pentateuch is the most important among the three main sources because, on the one hand, it is the first place where the Pentateuch prescribes Israel's rites and, on the other hand, because the other sections presuppose it and build upon it. The next significant legislation for the daily divine service is the secondary prescriptive material found in Lev 6:1–16 [8–23]; 24:1–9; Num 6:22–27; 10:1–10; and 28:1–8. The LORD did not give these regulations to Moses on Mount Sinai but at the tabernacle after its construction. They may, therefore, be understood as supplementary prescriptions for the daily divine service. The final category of the Pentateuch that provides information about the daily service is the descriptive material in Exod 40:1–35 as well as Lev 8–9. Whereas the prescriptive sources record the institution of the ritual acts of ancient Israel, the descriptive sources tell how they enacted what had been previously legislated. The prescriptive and descriptive texts in the Pentateuch provide the foundation for this study.

The Pentateuch employs three different technical terms to indicate that certain parts of the divine service are intended to be performed perpetually as founded by the LORD through Moses. First, there is the legislation for *future generations* [לְדֹרֹתָם/לְדֹרֹתֵיכֶם].[5] Not only were Moses and his

---

5. The related terms לְדֹרֹתָם/לְדֹרֹתֵיכֶם, *for your/their generations*, are used in the Pentateuch to indicate those things that are not merely a one-time occurrence but which must be carried out perpetually from one generation to the next. Freedman and Lundbom claim that the concluding formula in Num 35:29 includes the entire ritual legislation in the Pentateuch as instructions for all the generations of Israel (Freedman and Lundbom "דּוֹר," 178–79).

contemporaries to carry out the regulations for the ritual system in their own time, all of the descendants of Israel were obligated to keep performing the divine service throughout their generations. Every generation of the Israelites must conduct the main parts of the daily divine service (Exod 27:21; 29:42; 30:8, 21; Lev 6:11 [18]; 24:3; Num 10:8) as well as observe services at feast times throughout the year and follow the stipulations for the entire ritual system (Exod 12:14, 17, 42; 16:32–33; 30:10, 31; 31:13, 16; 40:15; Lev 3:17; 7:36; 10:9; 17:7; 21:17; 22:3; 23:14, 21, 31, 41, 43; Num 9:10; 15:14–15, 21, 23, 38; 18:23). The second technical term is Israel's *perpetual ritual statutes* [חֻקַּת עוֹלָם].[6] These, like the first term, apply to the ongoing enactment of the daily divine service (Exod 27:21; 28:43; Lev 24:3; Num 10:8) and to other occasions and conditions (Exod 12:14, 17; 29:9; Lev 3:17; 7:36; 10:9; 16:29, 31, 34; 17:7; 23:14, 21, 31, 41; Num 15:15; 18:23). They are the ritual ordinances that the LORD commanded to be kept ceaselessly from the time of their institution onward. The final term concerns the *perpetual ritual provisions* [לְחָק־עוֹלָם].[7] One of the reasons the LORD established the divine service was to provide for his people (Exod 12:24), his priests (Exod 29:28; 30:21; Lev 6:11 [18]; 7:34; 10:15; 24:9; Num 18:8), and for their families (Num 18:11, 19). The perpetual ritual provisions were also part of the daily divine service (Exod 30:21; Lev 6:11, 15 [18, 22]). These three terms are used in the Pentateuch to ensure that the divine service and the entire ritual system must be observed in perpetuity throughout the generations of the Israelites.

An examination of the aforementioned technical terms reveals that there are four interconnected parts of the divine service that were instituted for the *perpetual* [עוֹלָם] observance of the Israelites. The first involves the daily service and its ritual acts that were required to be performed *regularly* [תָּמִיד].[8] The lamps inside the tent of meeting must be tended and lit (Exod 27:21; Lev 24:3), the burnt offering of an unblemished yearling male lamb must be smoked up at the outer altar (Exod 29:42; Num 15:14, 15), fragrant incense must burn in the holy place (Exod 30:8), the bread offering of the high priest must be smoked up on the altar (Lev 6:15 [22]), and the priests

---

6. The phrase חֻקַּת עוֹלָם, *perpetual ritual statutes*, has to do with required ceremonies that the priests are obligated to carry out repeatedly. This kind of legislation establishes ritual acts for their continued performance from then on (Ringgren, "חָקַק," 143–45).

7. לְחָק־עוֹלָם, *perpetual ritual provisions*, refer to the parts of the offerings that are assigned to the priests as their legal allotted portion. The prescriptions in the Pentateuch that use this terminology spell out the ongoing obligation of the Israelites to provide for the livelihood of the priest (Ringgren, "חָקַק," 144).

8. The Hebrew term for ritual acts that must be performed regularly or daily is תָּמִיד. This is the name by which the daily divine service was called later in Daniel (8:11–13; 11:31; 12:11) and in the *Mishnah*. This term is discussed further in chapter 2.

must sound the silver trumpets over the offerings (Num 10:8). The LORD instituted each of these ritual acts to be performed throughout the generations of the Israelites.

The second has to do with the priesthood that the LORD instituted to serve on behalf of Israel and for their benefit. The priests are required to *regularly* [עוֹלָם] wear their vestments at the tabernacle (Exod 28:43), conduct the divine service (Exod 29:9), refrain from drinking alcoholic beverages while they are serving at the sanctuary (Lev 10:9), and bear the iniquity of the Israelites along with their fellow Levites (Num 18:23). They were also responsible throughout their *generations* [לְדֹרֹתָם/לְדֹרֹתֵיכֶם] for excluding blemished priests from presenting offerings (Lev 21:17) and ritually impure priests from serving at the tabernacle (Lev 22:3). The priests were responsible for keeping these regulations throughout the history of Israel.

The third concerns the *perpetual* [עוֹלָם] observance of the ritual calendar in each successive *generation* [לְדֹרֹתָם/לְדֹרֹתֵיכֶם]. The Israelites are commanded to not fail to keep the Sabbath (Exod 31:13, 16), observe the Passover and Feast of Unleavened Bread (Exod 12:14, 17, 42; see Num 9:10), offer the first fruits of their produce and commemorate the Feast of Pentecost (Lev 23:14, 21), uphold the Day of Atonement (Exod 30:10; Lev 16:29, 31, 34; 23:31), celebrate the Feast of Tabernacles (Lev 23:41, 43), and keep the year of Jubilee (Lev 25:30). All the Israelites throughout their generations were responsible for observing the ritual calendar perpetually.

The last part involves the *perpetual* [עוֹלָם] legislation that is specifically for the Israelite laity. They are prohibited from eating fat or blood from animals (Lev 3:17). The Israelites are required to give the priests their portion of peace offerings (Lev 7:36). They must present their offerings at the tabernacle rather than anywhere else (Lev 17:7). The laity is prohibited from eating bread from new grain before they present their first fruits at Pentecost (Lev 23:14). They are prohibited from working on Pentecost (Lev 16:29, 34; 23:21) and on the Day of Atonement (Lev 23:31). The Israelites are required to fast on the Day of Atonement (Lev 16:29). They must celebrate the Feast of Tabernacles for seven days (Lev 23:41). Finally, the Israelites are required to purify themselves from ritual uncleanness with the water for cleansing from the ashes of a red heifer (Num 19:10, 21). The LORD commanded the laity to observe these ritual decrees without ceasing.

It is clear from the ritual legislation regarding each of these overlapping parts of the divine service that the LORD instituted them for Israel to observe in perpetuity.

There is evidence for the perpetual enactment of the daily divine service in texts outside of the Pentateuch. After Joshua led the community of Israel across the Jordan River into the land of Canaan, they gathered at

Shiloh and erected the tabernacle (Josh 18:1). Since the LORD was present there (Josh 18:10; 19:51; Judg 18:31), the Israelites carried out the divine service in Shiloh (Judg 21:19; 1 Sam 1:3; 2:13–17). The tabernacle also resided in Shechem for a while and the divine service conducted there (Josh 24:1, 25–26). Following this, the tent of meeting was set up at Gibeon and the regular service enacted in that place even though some time later the ark was removed from it and placed in a different tent in Jerusalem (1 Kgs 3:4; 1 Chr 16:39; 21:29; 2 Chr 1:3–6, 13). After the temple in Jerusalem was constructed, the ark of the testimony, the disassembled tabernacle, and its furniture were brought to the temple and placed inside it. From then on the priests conducted the LORD's ministry there (1 Kgs 8:1–13; 62–66; 12:27; 1 Chr 16:39–40; 22:19; 2 Chr 2:4; 3:1; 5:7–14; 7:1–11; 29:35; 30:1, 15). Likewise, the divine service was re-established after the Israelites returned from exile and the temple was rebuilt in Jerusalem (Ezra 1:2–11; 3:2–6; 6:22; Neh 10:28–39; Sir 50:5–21). Most importantly, after the exile the Israelites turned to the Pentateuch to discover how to perform the divine service and to justify why they enacted it. They did not merely regard the Pentateuch as a historical account or legislation only for the tabernacle in the desert; they believed it to be a canonical template for the enactment of the divine service in the first and second temples in Jerusalem (1 Chr 6:49; 16:39–40; Ezra 3:2–6; Neh 10:29). It may be concluded, therefore, that the divine service was conducted as intended across the generations in ancient Israel according to the LORD's institution of it in the Pentateuch.

SUMMARY OF SCHOLARSHIP

It is difficult to categorize those scholars who have written about the daily divine service in ancient Israel. This is because of two main reasons. On the one hand, very few scholars have shown much interest in the order of the daily service. On the other hand, hardly any of them have focused on the entire daily service and have mainly examined its individual parts. I, therefore, have had to comb through vast amounts of material in an effort to find data that is relevant to this topic. After examining this array of scholarship, it has been difficult to classify how various scholars have dealt with this topic. In part, this is due to the fact that these scholars do not all approach their study of the Pentateuch from the same perspective. Researchers approach the topic with different presuppositions and use different methods by which they come to their conclusions.[9] Despite that, however, they, by and large,

---

9. See, for example, Haran, *Temples and Temple Service*, v–vii.

have examined the divine service from three fundamental perspectives: the narrative, the critical, and the ritual.

Narrative scholarship shows little interest in the ritual function or theological purpose of the daily divine service, although it does attempt to examine the service as a whole rather than merely its parts. These scholars recognize the Law of Moses as the legal basis for the establishment of the divine service and are content to write detailed descriptions of its ritual activities.

One of the foundational works for this view is the *Mishnah's Tamid*, which describes the daily service at the second temple in Jerusalem. Even though the ritual practice at the second temple was most likely not identical with the worship at the tabernacle, the *Tamid* offers insights about how the legislation for the divine service was understood and enacted in the second temple before its destruction in 70 AD. It portrays two chief things. First, the daily service that was performed at the temple is based on the ritual law in the Pentateuch. Although the *Tamid* does not quote the Scriptures, scholars with a working knowledge of the ritual texts in the Pentateuch will recognize that its writers are thoroughly familiar with the biblical basis for the ritual activities of the regular daily service and constantly interact with them. Second, it was written to preserve and pass on to future generations a description of the procedures for the daily service if the temple is ever rebuilt (*Tamid* 7:3).[10] This document at first appears to be a prescriptive text but since the temple no longer exists it is a description of the service that was once enacted there. The *Tamid* in the *Mishnah* is instructive for the current topic because, on the one hand, much of it is relevant for reconstructing the order of the daily service and, on the other hand, it assumes that the daily service was divinely instituted according to the ritual laws in the Pentateuch. The *Tamid* is entirely descriptive and offers no theological analysis of the service or its parts.

The medieval commentator, Maimonides, bases his account of the daily divine service on its legislation in the Pentateuch. He employs sets of positive and negative commands from the ritual law to prove the divine authority of the daily service. Interestingly, however, he quotes the *Mishnah* verbatim in most of his comments about the divine service. It appears that Maimonides tries to supply the Scriptural basis for the *Mishnah's Tamid*, since that document assumes such a basis without stating it (*Code* 6:1–6). Like the *Mishnah*, Maimonides does not examine the daily service to tell of its significance, function, or purpose. He merely narrates how the service must be enacted.

---

10. See Blackman, *Kodashim*, 496.

Edersheim builds on the previous two works. Although he relies heavily upon Maimonides, his writing more closely resembles the *Mishnah* in its descriptive approach. Edersheim moves beyond the previous two examinations by interpreting the typological and symbolical meaning of the rites of the daily service. He fails, however, to discuss the ritual function or theological purpose of the service. Like other narrative scholars, he does not ask why the service and its ritual acts must be performed or what God accomplishes through them. Rather, he is primarily interested in describing the daily divine service as it occurred at the second temple.[11]

Narrative scholarship assumes the Mosaic authorship of the Pentateuch and is not concerned about questions of its historicity. Rather, these scholars are satisfied to describe the daily divine service as if it is sufficient to know *how* it is enacted rather than *why*.

Critical scholars show little interest in what the rites of the daily divine service do or accomplish on a practical level. Their scholarship tends to focus on the isagogical issues related to the Pentateuch as well as analyzing the ritual texts developmentally rather than rites as such or how they were to be enacted, and why.

Whereas narrative scholars assume the Mosaic authorship and divine authority of the Pentateuch, critical scholars, such as Wellhausen, hold just the opposite view. Wellhausen believes that the priestly tradition in the Pentateuch postdates Moses and is a construct of Jewish priests after the Babylonian captivity. His main thesis is that the Law of Moses is not the starting point for the history of ancient Israel but it is rather the history of post-exilic Judaism, which he understands as a distinct religion from the pre-exilic Yahwism of Israel. This is a complete rejection of the narrative assumption that the daily service was divinely instituted. Wellhausen asserts that the corporate service in the Old Testament was an abrogation and institutionalization of the more free and individualistic worship of Israel's early period. Those offerings and sacrifices that were once given to the deity in joyful celebration have become obligatory acts of atonement under the priesthood so that they can provide for their own livelihood. Although Wellhausen acknowledges that daily public offerings may have existed in the pre-exilic period, he holds that freewill private offerings held much more prominence than the "later" period of the Mosaic Law, which requires public offerings for the daily service. He laments that the spontaneity of individual offerings has been replaced with the monotonous seriousness of daily congregational

---

11. See Edersheim, *Temple*, 5–12, 105–22, 140–73.

offerings. Since Wellhausen rejects the divine institution of the daily service he shows little interest in examining its function or purpose.¹²

Baxter objects to Wellhausen's views about the historical development of the Pentateuch. He claims that Wellhausen violates the principles of higher criticism and true scientific study of the text by replacing them with entirely unsubstantiated opinions. True critical scholarship, he maintains, is not based on a person's own imaginations but upon the object of its examination, which in this case is the Pentateuch. Thus, Baxter takes Wellhausen to task point by point to disprove all of his assertions. In so doing, however, Baxter does not offer any new insights into the daily service of ancient Israel. Rather, he practically re-establishes the narrative position by defending the Mosaic authorship of the Pentateuch and the divine institution of the ritual system. He holds that the divine service does not drive a wedge between the individual and the corporate offerings, as Wellhausen holds, but, on the contrary, affirms the proper place of both of them based on the ritual laws in the Pentateuch. Those offerings that were originally enacted by individuals were later incorporated into the public divine service to establish the Israelites as a priestly community. Corporate worship does not take away the freedom and spontaneity of the individual but enhances them. Although Baxter effectively challenges the stated positions of Wellhausen about the daily service as portrayed in the Pentateuch, he too falls short of examining the ritual function and theological purpose of the divine service. By his own admission, his sole task is to refute the claims of Wellhausen so as to reaffirm that the foundation for scientifically and critically analyzing the Pentateuch is in the divine authority of the Scriptures rather than in a person's own ideas.¹³

Von Rad holds that the Pentateuch was compiled from various oral and written sources and edited late in Israel's history but he believes that its creedal forms are drawn from early periods. He denies that the Pentateuch originally consisted of a well-thought-out ritual system but rather that it portrays a later systematic categorization of different kinds of offerings. Although he inquires about the function of the different kinds of offerings, von Rad does not deal specifically with the daily divine service. He determines that the offerings of the Israelites may accomplish three distinct things. They can function either as a gift, or as the means of atonement, or as recognition of communion between two or more parties, but he does not rule out that on some occasions the offerings may perform more than one function at a time. Von Rad is sharply critical of any magical notion or ritual

---

12. See Wellhausen, *Prolegomena*, v–x, 1–13, 17, 34–82, 150–67.
13. See Baxter, *Sanctuary and Sacrifice*, vii–xv, 83–129, 287–434, 464–506.

function, which he also designates as a "dynamistic" understanding of the world. In this view, humans see themselves in relation to other things in the world and they strive to maintain their status with them through objects by which they influence those around them including the deity. Von Rad claims that the Pentateuch supersedes any notion of magic by emphasizing the moral responsibility of individuals. He does, however, acknowledge the saving aspect of the offerings of Israel. He objects to the neo-Protestant suspicion that the offerings are effective simply by enacting them, *opera operata*, and states that they become saving events because the divine word is added to them. Although he makes a limited effort to analyze the ritual function and theological purpose of the offerings, von Rad's chief interest lies in their theological meaning. He believes that more important than what the offerings do is what they mean; the theological ideas expressed by the offering and the reasons for offering it are far more significant than what they actually accomplish. Thus, von Rad holds that a distinction must be made between the basic idea of an offering and the reason for its performance. For him, the significance of the offering and the motive for offering it are its most important spiritual aspects, not the act itself. So von Rad offers many new insights about the cultus of Israel, but his views lead to a dead end because they focus on the meaning of rites instead of what they accomplish ritually.[14]

Eichrodt challenges the conclusions of historical-critical scholarship, such as that of Wellhausen, by insisting that developments in the ritual system of Israel must coincide with its history. On the one hand, he claims that overemphasizing the historical development of the Pentateuch has led to a diminishment of the meaning of the texts and the rites they describe. Thus, such developmental analysis must be replaced with systematic synthesis to properly interpret the religious phenomena of the Old Testament in their deepest significance. On the other hand, he is critical of the methodology employed by some scholars who coordinate proof-texts with an extensive system of typology for the purpose of demonstrating a coherence of dogmatic instruction by the various biblical writers. As opposed to this, Eichrodt prefers a systematic approach, which is dominated by a covenant theology that holds up the relationship of Israel with God as the central focus of the Old Testament. Because of this, all of the ritual laws in the Pentateuch are subservient to the covenant. Furthermore, he believes that rites of ancient Israel are significant in two separate areas of human life. One is in the emotional life of the spirit within the individual and the other is in the physical and corporate social life of a human being. He acknowledges that

---

14. See von Rad, *Old Testament Theology*, v–vii, 3–14, 34–35, 102, 187–90, 232–62.

the ritual acts of Israel are mediums of divine power through which God's blessing is communicated to them. Yet, he denies that such effectiveness is due to magic. Eichrodt's main interest lies in determining the symbolic significance attached to the ritual act, as if the outward enactment were primarily a means of entry into the human spirit that animates them. The outward act affects the physical existence of people, while the meaning of the act affects their inner being. He does not believe, however, that God always influences either the outward or the inward human being through every kind of ritual activity. In addition, Eichrodt holds that there are four ideas that the Old Testament conveys about the ritual system: feeding, gift, communion, and atonement. Of these four, he only sees the communal offerings as divine gifts to humans, and this is merely because of God's declaration of grace pronounced by the priest. Eichrodt's sole mention of the daily divine service refers to it as an offering of human gifts to God, leaving out the remaining three notions about feeding, atonement, and communion. While Eichrodt significantly advances Old Testament scholarship toward the recognition of the function of its ritual system, he fails to acknowledge that the daily service is chiefly an act of God upon humans or that it affects the whole of them, both their inner and outer beings. Although he moves critical scholarship beyond investigations of the historical development of Old Testament texts to delve into their deeper significance, he still comes short of a full blown analysis of the ritual system of ancient Israel.[15]

Since critical scholars mostly focus on the meaning of ritual texts instead of on what rites do or accomplish ritually, they show little interest in offering detailed analyses of the regular divine service in ancient Israel. This can result in generalizations that place ritual activities into broad categories without recognizing that the same ritual acts often have different functions when they are enacted at different times and in different contexts. One such failure of distinction is between the corporate burnt offering in the daily service and a burnt offering of an individual or one offered corporately at another time in the ritual calendar. Each of these specific offerings functions differently within the ritual system and vary in what God accomplishes through them. If the only concern, however, is what a burnt offering means or signifies then discussion and analysis of its ritual function and theological purpose will be lacking. This is the void in ritual studies left by critical scholarship.

---

15. See Eichrodt, *Theology of Old Testament*, 11–19, 25–35, 73, 98–177, 419–24, 512–20.

Ritual biblical scholars analyze the rites that are described in the Pentateuch and other biblical writings. Most of these scholars have been heavily influenced by anthropological ritual analysts, such as Douglas, van Gennep, and Turner,[16] and have borrowed methods of ritual interpretation from them. In anthropology, however, ritual analysts have traditionally conducted field studies to observe the rites and ceremonies within a particular culture or society that they intend to analyze. Since the daily divine service in ancient Israel is no longer enacted, ritual analysts can only examine its rites based on the written accounts in the biblical texts. Thus, biblical ritual scholars are chiefly concerned with analyzing the ritual acts legislated or described in the Scriptures rather than examining the development of the texts that portray them. The Pentateuch and other Old Testament writings are usually taken at face value by biblical ritual scholars since they are the primary sources for analyzing the ritual system of ancient Israel.

Haran is the most important scholar who has examined the ritual activities inside the tabernacle in the daily divine service. More than anyone else, he has laid the foundation for discovering the function of all of the acts performed by the high priest in the holy place at the incense altar, lampstand, and table. This is due primarily to his belief that the rites inside the tabernacle are more holy than those performed in the courtyard at the font and altar for burnt offering. He holds that the closer to the ark of the testimony that ritual acts are conducted the more sacred they are, and the further away from the ark the less sacred they are. Thus, while the ritual activities at the lampstand and the table are more holy than those at the font or outer altar, burning the spiced incense in the holy place every morning and evening is the most sacred act that is conducted in the daily divine service. One of Haran's most insightful and groundbreaking observations is that the ornate vestments of the high priest are not merely garments with which he clothes himself in preparation to perform his sacred tasks, but that wearing the various parts of the vestments comprises ritual acts. Bearing the names of the tribes of Israel on his shoulder pieces and on his breastplate accomplish something ritually, as do the Urim and Thummim as well as the bells and pomegranates on his robe and, most especially, the golden crown with the divine name on his head. The ritual acts that are conducted every day inside the holy place function as part of the daily divine service. Haran, however, does not entirely abandon either the discussion about historical development or the emphasis on meaning by critical scholarship; he spends much time discussing the symbolism and significance of the rites in the daily service. Rather than viewing it as actions of God toward his people,

---

16. These scholars are discussed later in the book.

Haran understands the rites of the divine service as means to provide for the "needs" of God. Although, in my opinion, Haran does not altogether accurately interpret the ritual acts of the daily service inside the tabernacle, the magnitude of his scholarly contribution to ritual studies and specifically to the daily divine service of ancient Israel cannot be diminished. His work is of the greatest significance for this area of scholarship.[17]

Milgrom has laid the foundation for biblical ritual studies that pertain to the daily ritual activities primarily at the altar for burnt offering in the courtyard.[18] Although he identifies himself as a critical scholar, his extensive analysis of the ritual system of ancient Israel has pioneered new interest in ritual studies. Milgrom's synchronistic approach seeks to view the rites of Israel systemically by how they organically relate to one another. Ritual acts can have more than one meaning and perform more than one function. They are multi-faceted. This leads him to conclusions that are very different from the systematic approach of placing its rites into specific categories. He disagrees with some critical scholars who dismiss the ritual texts in the Pentateuch as meaningless, and he is willing to examine and expound these texts in detail. His main thesis is that the ritual acts of ancient Israel function ethically. Milgrom's interpretation of them, therefore, tends to probe their symbolic value. He notes that anthropology has taught how cultures and societies express and preserve their values ritually. Whereas words can easily be forgotten, the repetition of ritual acts ensure the endurance of what they teach symbolically because they are visual and participatory, being reinforced with each enactment. Rites, he claims, must signify something beyond themselves. The ritual system, therefore, is a system of meaning that reveals a web of values that not only model how people must relate to God and to one another, but actually help them to do so. Milgrom does not believe that rites exercise magical power by which the priests and people of Israel are able to manipulate God or others. For example, the system of purity is not meant to deal with the demonic power of impurity, but rather aims to curb the free will of the Israelites and promote their obedience to God. Thus, Israel is not caught between God and demonic forces; they deal with God alone at his sanctuary, which symbolizes his presence among them. Their daily offerings, therefore, serve as gifts to God with several and complex purposes, including propitiation, expiation, devotion, and possibly many others. For Milgrom, the offerings are always gifts that the Israelites

---

17. See Haran, *Temples and Temple Service*, v–viii, 1–12, 58–275.

18. Milgrom analyzes the ritual acts associated with the lampstand and the table in the holy place in his commentaries on Lev 24, but this examination is limited in comparison with his study of the activities at the outer altar (Milgrom, *Leviticus 23–27*; *Leviticus: Ritual and Ethics*).

offer to God and not gifts that God gives to them. If atonement results from offerings, then it is because the Israelites have shown their devotion to God by giving him their gifts. He believes that the offerings summon God to help them but, unlike in other cultures, their offerings do not feed him, or assimilate the life force of animal victims into the people, or effect communion between the Israelites and God. Their ritual system functions ethically to instruct what the people of God must do in accordance with his will. Although Milgrom's approach to biblical studies is mainly from a critical perspective, his extensive examination of the rites at the outer altar in the daily divine service places him among the most important contemporary ritual scholars.[19]

Levine has challenged commonly held ideas about the functional nature of the ritual activities in the divine service. Whereas other scholars have rejected the notion of magic in the ritual system of ancient Israel, Levine has embraced it. He thinks that there are different kinds of magic, both good and bad, that can accomplish their intended purposes. While he condemns magic that is used for evil, he maintains that the ritual acts that God has instituted function magically for the good of his people. For Levine, magic is another way to refer to the potent effects of ritual functions. In opposition to some critical scholars, such as Kaufmann, who claim that Israel's rites mostly concern their covenant relationship with God,[20] Levine holds that in the daily service and other times at the sanctuary ritual activities ward off demonic powers. He further explains his position with an example of one of the main enactments in the daily service. The manipulation of blood at the sanctuary brings about the ritual purification of the Israelite community by removing from them evil forces that are opposed to God. Levine holds that the objection by scholars to the use of magic in the divine service usually centers on an overemphasis of monotheism. It is believed that if there is only one God, then he is the only spiritual force with whom people must interact. Demons and the deities of pagans are nonexistent, it is argued. Levine points out that the Hebrew Bible nowhere states that there is no other power of any sort except for the God of Israel. There are statements about the LORD being the only true deity who created the universe, who was victorious over other gods such as those of the Egyptians, who works great wonders and acts of deliverance and healing, and who knows all things; but nowhere does the Old Testament declare that the LORD's rule is completely without opposition from other supernatural forces. Evil powers exist, yet God is

---

19. See Milgrom, *Studies in Cultic Theology*, 75–84, 104–18; *Leviticus 1–16*, 1–67, 378–400, 440–57; *Leviticus 23–27*, 2080–2101; *Leviticus: Ritual and Ethics*, xi–xiii, 1–6, 62–69, 288–91.

20. See Levine, *In the Presence*, 77–91.

capable of controlling them for his own purposes and employs his agents to exercise his authority over them through the ritual acts that he has instituted. Levine explains that the Old Testament is not opposed to all forms of magic, but only to certain varieties of it, such as divination and sorcery. The four explicit statements against magic in the Pentateuch (Exod 22:7; Lev 19:26–28; 20:6; Deut 18:9–11) all exclude prohibitions against apotropaic and prophylactic magical activities. While magic that harms another person is forbidden, magic in the form of ritual acts and those that benefit the health of a person are employed according to the word of God. As a force of God, magic does not contradict the biblical conception of monotheism. Therefore, ritual impurity is not merely a moral defect but rather a demonic power that may only be purged with divinely established enactments of purification. Although his main contribution to ritual biblical scholarship rests in his views of magic, Levine also emphasizes the order of ritual activities within the divine service and he especially investigates how they function in relation to each other. His belief, however, that the ritual activities of the Israelites are primarily human actions in obedience to God, prevents him from investigating the theological purpose of the divine service and what God accomplishes for his people through it. The chief value of his ritual research is his elevation of the functional aspect of the ritual activities in the divine service of ancient Israel.[21]

Kleinig has promoted an integrative approach to analyzing the ritual system of ancient Israel more than any other modern scholar. He has contributed to ritual studies by identifying four interrelated components of the daily service of ancient Israel: its divine institution, its sequential order, its ritual function, and its theological purpose. First, Kleinig holds that all of the activities in the divine service are instituted by God through his authoritative word that he spoke to the Old Testament lawgiver, Moses. Unlike many of the critical scholars, who hold that a specific class of Israelite people invented the corporate ritual system late in Old Testament history, he believes that the divine service was authorized and instituted by God. Although Kleinig maintains that the Pentateuch may have been compiled and canonized after the Babylonian exile, nonetheless its contents are divinely authoritative and were part of the oral tradition that began with God speaking to Moses at Sinai and then to both Moses and Aaron at the tabernacle. Second, Kleinig observes that the rites of ancient Israel follow a prescribed sequence. The order of the daily service and all the parts of the ritual system follow a basic pattern that often specifies their function and purpose, even

---

21. See Levine, *In the Presence*, 3–8, 20–52, 77–91; *Leviticus*, xi–xli, 9–14, 34–39, 164–66; *Numbers*, 370–75, 395–403.

though the biblical text does not explicitly state them. It is important to determine the correct sequence to ascertain the implied significance, function, and purpose of the service. Kleinig is the only modern scholar who has written about the order of the daily divine service and has attempted to reconstruct its sequence, although he has not taken the opportunity to extensively examine the ritual function and theological purpose of all of its parts. Third, Kleinig emphasizes, not merely the meaning of the rites in the divine service, but more importantly their functions. To find out what rites do, he identifies five main areas of investigation: the ritual agents involved in the service, the ritual activities that are enacted and in what order, the ritual materials utilized in the performance of the ritual acts, the occasion or time of their enactments, and the locations where they take place. These components are interrelated and aid in properly analyzing the parts of the divine service to determine their functions within it. Fourth, Kleinig has introduced a topic of ritual investigation that is mostly lacking in other scholars, the theological purpose of the service and all of its rites. Whereas some scholars have focused on the divine institution or order of at least some of the parts of the service, and other scholars have advanced an interest in how rites function, Kleinig is the first to seriously inquire about what God does or accomplishes through the divine service. Most scholars assume that the purpose of a rite is for someone to do something for God. Kleinig, however, holds that God instituted Israel's ritual system, established its sequential order, and spelled out its ritual functions for theological purposes. The objective of the divine service is for God to do something to or for his people. Kleinig classifies them under five main headings: atonement, acceptance, approval, blessing, and provision. By his integrative analysis of the divine institution, sequential order, ritual function, and theological purpose of the divine service, Kleinig has opened up new areas of research that require further exploration.[22]

Ritual biblical scholars investigate the activities in the divine service of ancient Israel from different perspectives and with varying results. They hold in common, however, the desire and interest to examine the rites that are described in the Bible. Unlike some scholars, who think that the corporate divine service in the Old Testament is meaningless and unimportant for the religious experiences of individuals, ritual scholars appreciate the significance and function of its ritual system. This book stands in that trend, yet its focus is not on the meaning of rites but on what God does and accomplishes for his people through them.

---

22. See Kleinig, "Witting or Unwitting Ritualists"; "Sharing God's Holiness"; "Blood for Sprinkling"; *Glory and Service*; *Lord's Song*; *Leviticus*, 1–18, 20–24, 141–57, 512–18.

The Pentateuch asserts that the daily divine service was instituted by God and that it followed a set order with specific functions so that he could accomplish his purposes through its ritual activities. Furthermore, the daily divine service was foundational to and integrated with all of the other occasional rites that the Israelites were required to perform. Thus, the daily service can hardly be unimportant or insignificant for the worshipping community of Israel. Yet, most Old Testament scholars have paid little attention to the daily service as a whole. Apart from inquiries by Kleinig as well as passing observations by Haran, Levine, and Milgrom, no scholars have yet investigated the Pentateuch to reconstruct the sequence of rites in the daily divine service of ancient Israel, to determine its ritual functions, and to ascertain what God accomplished through them. That is the aim of this book.

PRESENT STUDY AND ITS ORGANIZATION

The present study seeks to answer: what was the order of ancient Israel's divinely instituted public daily service, its ritual function, and its theological purpose? This question assumes four things. First, there was a daily public divine service in ancient Israel. Second, God instituted all the ritual activities performed in the service. Third, it followed a set order, though with variations for festivals and other occasions. Fourth, God accomplished his purposes through it. These assumptions are based on the data from the ritual texts in the Pentateuch. In this book, I neither analyze the origin of the Pentateuch nor its historical development. Rather, the content of the canonical texts are synchronically examined to determine the order, function, and purpose of the rites performed in the daily divine service of ancient Israel.

The ritual legislation in the Pentateuch authorizes the public daily burnt offering as well as occasional public and individual offerings, which could only be offered in connection with the daily service. Occasional offerings include burnt, sin, guilt, and peace offerings. An Israelite presents them either at various times within the ritual calendar, or as consequences of ritual impurity or desecration. People normally present individual burnt and peace offerings any day immediately following the morning public burnt offering, and never after the evening offering. The priests conduct the rites for the regular burnt offering twice per day. They offer two yearling male lambs without blemish, one in the morning and the other in the evening. The daily burnt offering incorporates three additional offerings with each lamb: an offering of fine wheat flour mixed with oil and salt, with a token portion of frankincense on top of it, the daily bread offering of the high priest cooked in oil, with salt and frankincense added on top, and a drink offering of wine. In addition to the ritual acts performed at the altar for burnt offering in the courtyard, the priest performs duties in the holy place, such as burning incense, and tending or lighting the lamps. Since legislation for all the parts of the daily divine service is not found in only one pericope in the Pentateuch, a number of passages must be examined to determine the order, function, and purpose of the service.

The ritual sources in the Pentateuch fall into two basic categories. Levine has identified them with his insightful distinction between *prescriptive* and *descriptive* ritual texts. A prescriptive text institutes ritual activities. Descriptive texts describe the activities after someone performs them. Levine argues that one must always treat the ritual sources in the Bible, especially the Pentateuch, either as divine command presented prescriptively, or as an event presented in narrative form descriptively.[23] His student, Rainey, expands on this distinction between prescriptive and descriptive ritual texts. He further divides the prescriptive category into *legislative* and *prophetic*, and the descriptive category into *narrative* and *formulaic*.[24] The legislative are mostly found in the Pentateuch, while the prophetic are contained in the prophets, especially Ezekiel. A point of discrepancy exists between Rainey and his teacher in that Levine identifies Lev 6:1 [8]–7:38 as prescriptive, while Rainey views it as descriptive. I hold that Rainey has misidentified this text, a criticism that Levine has made about other scholars too.[25] The prescriptive texts authorize and institute the ritual activities, while the descriptive texts explain how the agents carry out what God instituted. In addition, other sources outside the Pentateuch shed further light on the sequential order, ritual function, and theological purpose of the daily divine service. Yet, the basis for the present study remains in the prescriptive and descriptive passages in the Pentateuch.

---

23. See Levine, "Descriptive Tabernacle Texts." Trudinger appears to employ the distinction between prescriptive and descriptive ritual texts, but he does not limit these categories to Biblical texts (Trudinger, *Psalms of the Tamid Service*, 29–34).

24. See Rainey, "Order of Sacrifices." Levine mentions this distinction between two kinds of descriptive texts, but gives no further explanation of *formulaic* ritual texts (Levine, "Descriptive Tabernacle Texts," 313). Since Rainey's article primarily examines the distinction between the legislative and prophetic *prescriptive* texts, he provides no further explanation for Levine's *formulaic* category.

25. See Rainey, "Order of Sacrifices," 487; Levine and Hallo, "Offerings," 17–18.

METHODOLOGY

My methodology for interpreting the daily divine service in the Pentateuch is ritual analysis. Ritual scholars engage in ritual analysis in different ways.[26] Some of them employ ritual analysis to understand rites within communities culturally, such as van Gennep[27] and Turner,[28] while others, such as Haran[29] and Milgrom,[30] use it as a tool to explain a theology that a person or group expresses ritually. Some scholars utilize ritual analysis as a hermeneutical tool for understanding how rites shape society, such as Douglas,[31] while others employ it to determine the theological purpose of the rites prescribed in biblical ritual texts, such as Klingbeil[32] and Kleinig.[33] I build on the work of each of these scholars, yet my specific methodology is a form of *theological* ritual analysis

Van Gennep has influenced many scholars through his form of analyzing ritual activities. He holds that rites of passage have three stages, separation, transition, and incorporation, through which people move from one condition or status to another.[34] Furthermore, van Gennep applies ritual

---

26. Ritual analysis as developed by anthropologists normally interprets rites either by observation of ritual activity or data collected from observing rites. Since ancient Israel's ritual system is no longer enacted, its rites can only be analyzed by examining the prescriptive and descriptive texts from the Old Testament and the writings of other traditions. Old Testament scholars have applied this method of interpretation by borrowing techniques from various approaches in anthropology. For an extensive survey of ritual scholars and their teachings, see Bell, *Ritual*.

27. See van Gennep, *Rites of Passage*.

28. See Turner, *Ritual Process*.

29. See Haran, *Temples and Temple Service*.

30. See Milgrom, *Leviticus: Ritual and Ethics*.

31. See Douglas, *Purity and Danger*; *Natural Symbols*.

32. See Klingbeil, *Bridging the Gap*.

33. See Kleinig, *Lord's Song*; *Leviticus*.

34. See van Gennep, *Rites of Passage*, 21. Turner does not describe them as transitional stages but as *states* of transformation (Turner, *Ritual Process*, 94). He proposes that rites have a dramatic structure, a plot, with a linear movement from one state of being to another. He challenges the ritual theorists—such as Eliade, *Sacred and Profane*—who treat rites in terms of circular imagery, and he holds that the movement from one rite to another is irreversible (Turner, "Social Dramas," 161–63). For a succinct summary of Turner's position of the three states, see Grimes, *Ritual Criticism*, 176–77. Douglas proposes that the transition from one state to another is hazardous because initiates die to their old life and are reborn to a new one (Douglas, *Purity and Danger*, 119–20). Kavanagh applies Turner's concept of transformation from anti-structure, through *liminality*, and into *communitas* to the passing from death to life (Kavanagh, *Elements of a Rite*, 199–200).

analysis only to rites of passage.[35] My argument is that one may employ the three stages in a more general sense. Ritual acts generally involve three stages: a beginning, middle, and an end. I designate the three stages of the daily divine service of ancient Israel as initial rites, central rites, and concluding rites.

Douglas,[36] Milgrom,[37] and Bell[38] understand rites *systemically*. They distinguish between a system*ic* and a system*atic* means of interpreting them. A system*atic* approach classifies ritual enactments into categories under certain headings.[39] System*atically*, all burnt offerings purportedly have the same characteristics, function, and purpose. A system*atic* method of interpretation fails to recognize that within a ritual category there may be several distinct uses of a rite to perform different functions. System*ically*, however, the daily public burnt offering presented by a priest performs a different function than a private burnt offering brought by an Israelite layperson. The priests offer the public burnt offering on behalf of the entire nation of Israel, while they offer the individual burnt offering on behalf of the one who presents it. This system*ic* approach understands that in any given ritual system, each rite functions in relation to other rites. They function as parts of an organic whole, just as the circulatory, nervous, digestive, and respiratory systems of a human body work together.

The rites that make up the divine service also function relationally to one another within a ritual system. The ritual system of Israel consists of everything related to the divine service, including the entire ritual calendar with its daily, weekly, monthly, yearly, seasonal, and occasional rites. This system is comprised of sub-systems, such as the various burnt offerings with their accompanying grain and drink offerings, the peace offerings, the sin

---

35. Kleinig recognizes that ritual acts both constitute and maintain communities by founding new communities, initiating people into existing communities, integrating people with each other, and ordering the operation of communities (Kleinig, "Witting or Unwitting Ritualists," 15). Gorman identifies three kinds of rites: founding, maintenance, and restoration rites (Gorman, *Ideology of Ritual*, 53–55).

36. See Douglas, *Purity and Danger*.

37. See Milgrom, *Numbers*.

38. See Bell, *Ritual*.

39. Douglas claims that the modern systematic approach (such as that of Tigay, *Deuteronomy*, 450) imposes a foreign interpretation on ritual activity. She maintains that scholars of the Pentateuch do well when they recognize the organic coherency and correlation of the texts of each book (Douglas, *Leviticus as Literature*, 51). Douglas employs ritual analysis to interpret how rites function socially, but does not appear to be interested in how they function theologically. Milgrom refuses to divide the whole of ritual systems into parts to try to determine their meaning apart from it; all the parts of a ritual system must be interpreted in view of one another (Milgrom, *Numbers*, xii).

offerings, and the guilt offerings. The sub-systems contain the distinct rites within the daily divine service, including all the activities within each one. Thus, a systemic method of ritual analysis takes into account every aspect of the entire ritual system.

The ritual system of ancient Israel functions like the solar system, especially the relation of the sun to the earth and the moon. The sun distinguishes night from day by the rotation of the earth, season from season by the tilt of its poles and year from year by the circuit of the earth around it, just as by its relation to the moon it marks out month from month and week from week on earth. Like the solar system, the ritual system is multi-dimensional. The daily divine service within the ritual system may be compared to the sun within the solar system. The daily service corresponds to the morning and evening rites, daily, to the Sabbath rites, weekly, to the new moon rites, monthly, and to specific days of certain months, yearly. It is also tied to the specific times of the year, seasonally. The daily divine service is the regular rite to which all other rites are oriented, like the sun is to the earth and the moon. In addition, the solar system is organically connected with the ritual system to such an extent, that the solar and lunar cycles, together with polar alternation, regulate the ritual calendar.

Since the daily divine service is the foundation for the function of the entire ritual system, its sequence is vital to everything that occurs at the sanctuary. So in this study I examine the daily service to determine by whose authority, to or with whom, who performs its acts, by means of which materials, when, where, and for what purpose each rite within the service is performed. This examination focuses on the smallest components of each rite: institution, agents, acts, materials, time, location, and purpose. After analyzing these, I inquire about the theological purpose of each rite and of the daily service as a whole.

In sum, this book is an investigation into the daily divine service of ancient Israel according to the ritual legislation in the Pentateuch. The service as a whole is examined in terms of the morning offering and the evening offering, each consisting of three main stages: initial rites, central rites, and concluding rites. I analyze the extent to which the rites of the daily divine service function to accomplish the intended purpose of God as evidenced from his authorization of them. Within this theological framework the practical order and its ritual function are critically investigated to determine the divine purpose of the daily divine service according to the Pentateuch.

PRESENTATION

This analysis of the daily divine service in ancient Israel is carried out in three stages.

Chapter 2 examines the order of the entire service based on the evidence from the prescriptive and the descriptive texts in the Pentateuch. I state my assumptions about the order of the service and identify problems in determining the sequence of each rite with its basic ritual activities. The bulk of the chapter investigates the placement of the rites in relation to each other, and argues for a probable order for the morning and evening offerings. It includes a detailed diagram of the order of the daily service illustrating all of its parts. This chapter concludes with a summary that ties all the rites together as a cohesive unit within the broader order of the service for the entire day.

The third chapter probes the divine institution, the ritual function, and the theological purpose of each rite with its ritual activities within the daily divine service. To ascertain the function of each enactment, I inquire by whose authority, who is involved in the rite, what physical substances are utilized, when it is performed, where the rites take place, and the outcome that it accomplishes. My intent in this chapter is to answer these questions by examining the texts in the Pentateuch that provide evidence for determining the institution, agents, acts, materials, time, location, and purpose of each rite. Rites do something; they function to accomplish their purposes within the context of the whole service.

The fourth chapter studies the theological purpose of the entire daily service. I assume that God institutes the daily divine service to accomplish his own purposes, not only through each of its rites, but also through the whole service. Problems occur trying to determine these purposes, since they are not always expressly stated. To ascertain what God achieves in the daily divine service I review its system of ritual agents, its system of ritual acts, its system of ritual materials, its system of ritual times, and its system of ritual locations.

In summary, chapter 2 determines the ritual sequence; chapter 3 ascertains what the rites and ritual activities do in the service, and chapter 4 draws conclusions about what God achieves through the public daily divine service. In anthropological terms, chapter 2 deals with the ritual *structure*, chapter 3 involves the ritual *function*, and chapter 4 concerns the ritual *symbol*.[40] In linguistic terms, chapter 2 is an analysis of the *pragmatics* of the di-

---

40. Searle broadly defines rites from three perspectives, regardless of the discipline. *Formal*, sometimes referred to as structural, definitions seek to differentiate formal ritual activity from other kinds of behavior. This understanding claims that rites are

vine service, chapter 3 its *syntax*, which also comprehends *morphology*, and chapter 4 its *semantics*.[41] So then, the Pentateuch is analyzed to discover the practical order of the daily divine service in ancient Israel, after which its ritual function will be examined and its theological purpose determined.

---

repetitive, prescribed, rigid, and stereotyped. *Functionalist* definitions of ritual activities see them in terms of the functions and purposes they serve in human life. Psychologists focus on the needs of individual people, while sociologists and anthropologists analyze the way ritual activities serve collective needs. Religious rites enable people, collectively and individually, to recognize that the realms of faith and experience are synonymous. *Symbolic* definitions of rites entail their meaning, often with various levels conveying multiple meanings (Searle, "Ritual," 11–12).

41. Klingbeil, *Bridging the Gap*, adapts linguistic terminology to explain his theory of ritual analysis, which is that rites function similar to a language. The smallest units of a language are the parts of words, including their formation, its *morphology*. Words organize into parts of a language, such as its subject, verb, and objects, and they function together in a sentence structure, its *syntax*. Sentences function in relation to other sentences in the context of paragraphs within the environment of either speaking or writing. This is the practical aspect of a language, its *pragmatics*. Words, sentences, and paragraphs, including the signs and symbols they represent, function together within a language to express meaning, its *semantics*. I recognize that these linguistic categories may be employed to describe the rites in the divine service. The ritual system consists of sub-systems, such as each of the seasonal, yearly, monthly, weekly, and daily rites. These compose an order that builds on the daily service and is inseparable from it. The ritual order of the daily service consists of two parts, the morning and evening offerings, each made up of initial rites, central rites, and concluding rites. The order is akin to *pragmatics*. Within the basic order, each rite includes all the distinct ritual activities performed in a sequence. The interaction of each ritual activity within the order is similar to *syntax*. Each rite also consists of ritual components: by whose authority (institution), to or with whom, who (agents) does what (acts), by means of what (materials), when (time), where (location), and why (purpose). These components are analogous to *morphology*. All the rites of a sub-system function together for a reason and with a purpose, which corresponds with *semantics*. I believe that the daily divine service of ancient Israel functions within an ordered ritual system for a theological purpose.

2

The Practical Order of the Daily Divine Service

WHAT IS THE PRACTICAL order of the daily divine service of ancient Israel according to the ritual sections in the Pentateuch? To answer this question, I analyze the rites of the daily service by investigating two kinds of texts from Exodus, Leviticus, and Numbers: the prescriptive texts and the descriptive texts.[1] The prescriptive texts prescribe the rites and ritual activities that must be performed. The descriptive texts indicate how they are to be performed. Both kinds of texts usually indicate when the priests should do them in relation to the other rites; but no one passage describes the exact sequence for all of the rites. Thus, the evidence from the Pentateuch is like a mosaic. All the rites relate to one another and must fit together correctly in order to reveal the full picture. Furthermore, determining the order of the daily service is like trying to reconstruct the mosaic with some of the pieces missing. Fortunately, a few texts exist outside the Pentateuch that give evidence about some of the missing pieces and how they fit together. These sources help to reconstruct the probable order for the daily divine service of ancient Israel.

Three assumptions guide my analysis of the order of the public daily service. First, the daily service consists of all the rites and ritual activities performed throughout the entire day. This includes everything that the priests do at the tabernacle beginning in the morning of one day and ending in the morning of the next day. Second, the daily service is composed of two parts: the morning rites and the evening rites. Neither the morning rites nor

---

1. See Levine, "Descriptive Tabernacle Texts"; Rainey, "Order of Sacrifices."

the evening rites by themselves constitute the entire daily divine service. One must consider both of them together, to determine the sequential order of the whole service. Third, the morning and evening services consist of seven rites performed in each of them. The fire is stoked to produce coals, the materials are presented for the offerings, the blood from the victim is splashed against the altar, the incense is burned in the holy place, the burnt offering is turned into smoke on the altar, the Aaronic benediction is proclaimed, and the bread made from the cereal offering is eaten. Each rite proceeds with a set sequence of ritual activities. The ritual acts in the morning are not always identical with those in the evening, but their order is the same.

The exact order and sequence of each part of the service cannot be determined with equal certainty. While some are quite evident, others are less so. The most definite are the blood, the incense, and the burning rites. With the exception of a slight variation in the procedure inside the tent of meeting, all the activities for these three parts of the service are identical in both the morning and the evening. These form the heart and center of the daily divine service. Without each of these three rites, the daily service would not achieve its purpose as given by the LORD. It is also relatively certain that the priests enact the fire and presentation rites to prepare for the ones that come after them. As a matter of common sense, without the fire, nothing can be burned, and without presenting the materials, nothing can be offered. The blessing and meal rites are the least certain. There is some evidence for more than one blessing on other occasions in the religious calendar of Israel, but it is difficult to prove this about the daily service. Furthermore, the Pentateuch never prescribes when the priest must bless the people, only the words with which to bless them. Likewise, the Pentateuch gives few details about the meal of the priests, but it makes little sense if the priests perform this rite anytime other than at the end of the service. Although there is some uncertainty about the exact sequence of ritual acts, my analysis of the Pentateuch provides firm evidence for a probable order of the daily divine service of ancient Israel.

THE INITIAL RITES

The Fire Rite

The fire rite is one of two initial parts of the daily service. It is also the first of the seven rites that are conducted twice per day in the morning and in the evening. It consists of several ritual activities that are prescribed by the

LORD in the Pentateuch. Descriptions of services from other sources, such as the ordination of the priests, the Day of Atonement, and the daily service at the temple in Jerusalem, bear witness to a set sequence of activities for maintaining the fire on the altar in the daily service at the tabernacle. Although there is a variation between the ritual activities in the morning and in the evening, the sequence is the same. As the first enactment in the daily service, the fire rite is essential to all the others that it precedes.

The main parts of the fire rite for the daily service are prescribed in Lev 6:1–6 [8–13]. Every morning the priests must remove the ashes from the offerings of the previous day and add wood to the altar for burnt offering. Since the LORD charges the priests three times not to ever let the fire go out, especially during the crucial procedure of removing the ashes and adding wood, it makes the most sense that they would do this at the beginning of the day. Without the fire, none of the materials can be smoked up to the LORD on the altar. The fire rite almost certainly precedes the presentation rite and all the others following it. This regulation is for the *morning* fire rite only. What about the one for the evening?

The Pentateuch provides no prescription for the removal of ashes at any time other than the morning. Thus, we may assume that the priests do not remove ashes in the evening fire rite. Yet, do they add wood? The priests must add wood to the altar for every burnt offering, whether it is for an individual or the public (Lev 1:7, 12).[2] The same does not hold true for other kinds of offerings, for practical reasons.[3] The priests only burn on the altar the fat portions of the animals from other kinds of offerings, which provide the fuel for them. With all burnt offerings, however, the fire burns up the entire animal. The wood for the morning burnt offering may not provide enough coals to incinerate the one in the evening. The priests need to place wood on the altar each time they offer burnt offerings in addition to those in the morning; this includes the burnt offering for the evening.

The procedure for maintaining the fire at the morning fire rite is prescribed in Lev 6:1–6 [8–13]. One of the priests[4] dons his sacred linen vest-

---

2. The only exception might be for a burnt offering of birds, because of their small size. Also, see Milgrom, who disagrees that wood needs to be added for every animal offered as a burnt offering (Milgrom, *Leviticus 1–16*, 163).

3. See Lev 2–5 for details about the grain, peace, sin, and guilt offerings. None of the regulations for these offerings indicates that wood is added to the altar. Lev 3:5 states that Aaron and his sons must burn the fat from the peace offering *on top of the burnt offering that is on the burning wood*. The priests always place the other kinds of offerings not on the wood itself, but on the burnt offerings.

4. There is normally a distinction between *the* priest, which designates the high priest or his deputy, and the regular priests. In this chapter, *the priest* simply means the one who is performing the ritual activity. The distinction between the different kinds

ments with his linen undergarments next to his body. After he removes from the altar the ashes of the previous day, he places them on its east side.[5] Then the priest takes off his sacred vestments and puts on common clothes to carry the ashes to a ritually clean location outside the camp. Finally, he adds firewood to the altar for burnt offering.[6] The relation between the ritual vesting and the removal of the ashes indicates a ritual sequence. Does the priest put on his sacred vestments again when he puts the wood on the altar? If so, then the ritual activities of the morning fire rite would require the priest to change his clothing three times in this part of the service alone.[7] That seems inefficient and impractical. Could the sequence follow another course?

The ritual arrangement for maintaining the altar fire might not entirely be spelled out in Lev 6:1–6 [8–13]. While the procedure of putting on the sacred vestments, removing the ashes from the altar, changing into common clothes, and removing the ashes from the camp presupposes a specific order, the legislation for the priest to add wood to the fire every morning may be a more general command. If so, then the addition of wood immediately follows the removal of the ashes from the altar, but before the priest changes into his common clothes and removes the ashes from the camp. The lapse of time between removing the ashes and bringing wood from outside the camp would increase the danger of the fire going out.[8] Adding wood immediately after the removal of the ashes seems most probable. The priest, therefore, most likely removes the ashes from the altar and adds the wood while wearing his sacred vestments the first time.[9]

---

of priests and their specific duties is discussed more thoroughly in the next chapter.

5. The ashes are placed on the ground next to the altar on its east side (Lev 1:16).

6. Kleinig condenses these ritual acts to three stages. First, one of the priests vests and removes the ashes from the altar to its east side. Second, he removes his vestments and carries the ashes to a ritually clean dump outside the camp. Third, he returns with wood and stokes the fire in order to burn the remaining offerings from the previous day (Kleinig, *Leviticus*, 148). Milgrom divides the removal of the ashes into two stages: first, their removal from the altar, and second, their removal outside the camp of Israel (Milgrom, *Leviticus 1–16*, 385).

7. This scenario results in the following sequence. First, the priest dons his sacred linen vestments. Second, he removes the ashes from the altar. Third, the priest changes into his common clothes. Fourth, he removes the ashes from the camp, returning with wood. Fifth, he changes into his vestments again. Finally, he adds firewood to the altar.

8. The LORD's three-fold repetition not to let the fire go out impresses upon the priests the great care they must take when removing the ashes (Milgrom, *Leviticus 1–16*, 387).

9. This assumes that someone previously brought wood to the sanctuary, a practice indicated in Neh 10:34 and 13:31. Milgrom holds that the wood for use in the service became an offering brought by the Israelites (*Leviticus 1–16*, 387–88).

The practice in the late second temple period according to *Tamid* 1–2 seems to indicate that the removal of ashes from the altar immediately precedes adding new wood.[10] The priest who is chosen to clear the ashes from the altar washes his hands and feet from the font. Then he takes a silver fire pan, clears away the glowing cinders to each side, scoops up the inmost completely burned cinders in the fire pan, and heaps them up beside the altar. The other priests then take spades and hooks to move the parts that have not been consumed to the sides of the altar. Once they have heaped up the ashes in a pile in the middle of the altar, they remove them.[11] After removing the ashes, they bring logs to put on the altar fire so that the priest who was chosen to remove the ashes can also arrange the new wood on the altar.[12] This supports the view that the priest adds wood to the altar before carrying the ashes outside the camp, and thus eliminates the need for him to change his clothes three times in the morning fire rite. Curiously, the procedure described in *Tamid* 1–2 speaks of the priest neither putting on his sacred vestments, nor removing them to carry the ashes outside the camp. It probably assumes that the priests don their sacred garments for service, based on the legislation in the Pentateuch.

In addition to the regulation in Lev 6:3–4 [10–11] about wearing the sacred vestments in the fire rite, Exod 28:42–43; 30:20–21 prescribe that the priests must wear them whenever they enter the tent of meeting or approach the altar in the courtyard. Similarly, Exod 40:31–32 describes Moses, Aaron, and his sons washing their hands and feet before they enter the tent of meeting or approach the altar. The summary, *as the LORD commanded Moses*, in Exod 40:31–32 correlates with the prescription in 30:20–21.[13] The priests probably wash their hands and feet every time they enter the tent of meeting and every time they approach the altar for burnt offering. An inseparable connection seems to exist between ritual washing and ritual vesting. Lev 6,

---

10. The *Mishnah's Yoma* 1:8–2:2 attests to this sequence (Blackman, *Moed*, 277–79).

11. Removing the ashes does not remove the coals. When the priests remove the ashes, the lit coals remain on the altar as the source of fire for the new wood that they add.

12. See Blackman, *Kodashim*, 471–76.

13. The Hebrew word, usually translated as *approach*, differs in each verse. In Exod 30:20 it is נֶגֶשׁ and in 40:32 it is קָרֵב. Cassuto sees no significant difference between the two words (Cassuto, *Exodus*, 483). The distinction between them could demonstrate the initial role of Moses as the LORD's representative to ordain the priests and inaugurate the divine service (Propp, *Exodus 19–40*, 673). Stuart claims that Exod 40:31–32 may demonstrate that Moses, Aaron, and his sons only wash their hands and feet on the occasion of the initial erection of the tabernacle; but he favors its reference to future consecutive washings (Stuart, *Exodus*, 798).

however, does not indicate whether the priest washes his hands and feet from the font before clearing the ashes.[14] Does the Pentateuch assume this?

The ordination of Aaron and his sons as priests correlates their ritual washing with their ritual vesting.[15] Exod 29:4–9 prescribes that Moses must wash the priests with water before dressing them in their vestments. The description of the ordination service in Lev 8:6–13 affirms the sequence of washing before putting on the garments to minister. In the rite of ordination, Moses washes the entire body of each priest before clothing them in their vestments, something that is not required in the daily service. From this, it may be concluded that the ordination rite establishes the sequence for any kind of ritual washing and ritual vesting for all the subsequent rites of the divine service.

Another example of the relation between washing and vesting is the ritual performance of the Day of Atonement.[16] The high priest must wash with water before donning the special vestments that he uses for some of the enactments only on that day (Lev 16:4).[17] Similarly, after performing certain rites, the high priest must go into the tent of meeting, to take off these vestments and leave them there (Lev 16:23–24). He must wash himself with water again before putting on his ornate vestments.[18] Although the Penta-

---

14. Cassuto notes the qualification (Exod 30:20–21) that the priests only wash their hands and feet before approaching the altar *to minister, to burn an offering by fire to the LORD* (Cassuto, *Exodus*, 395–96). Propp affirms that the priests must wash before making an offering, but for other activities, such as clearing the ashes from the altar, they need not wash (Propp, *Exodus 19–40*, 480). Likewise, Stuart holds that the priests wash in connection with approaching the altar to place an offering on it, implying that clearing the altar ashes requires no washing (Stuart, *Exodus*, 641).

15. See Gorman, *Ideology of Ritual*, 113–21; Klingbeil, *Comparative Study of Ritual Ordination*, 128–39; Milgrom, *Leviticus 1–16*, 501. Each discuss the sequence of washing before vesting. They address the question of whether Aaron's sons must stand almost naked while Moses dresses Aaron and anoints the tabernacle, its furniture, and Aaron in the high priest's vestments. The procedure described in Lev 8, however, may not portray the exact sequence. The prescription in Exod 29:4–9 supports the view that the vesting of Aaron immediately precedes the vesting of his sons.

16. For a full explanation about the significance of the high priest's vestments on the Day of Atonement, see Kleinig, *Leviticus*, 327–35; Levine, *Leviticus*, 101–8; Milgrom, *Leviticus 1–16*, 1009–84; Noth, *Leviticus*, 115–26; Porter, *Leviticus*, 126–31; Wenham, *Leviticus*, 230–36. Haran most thoroughly describes all the priestly vestments (Haran, *Temples and Temple Service*, 165–74).

17. The *Mishnah's Yoma* underscores that the priests wash their entire bodies before vesting, and gives its detailed description of the rites for the Day of Atonement at the temple in Jerusalem (Blackman, *Moed*, 273–312).

18. Ordinarily the priests only purify their hands and feet before performing the sacred rites; but because the high priest enters the most sacred area of the sanctuary, he must wash his entire body. Extreme holiness requires stringent preparation (Bailey,

teuch makes no such claim about priests washing their entire bodies for the daily services at the tabernacle, it, however, attests to the correlation between ritual washing and ritual vesting.

Tamid 1:4 describes two significant washings related to maintaining the fire rite at the temple in Jerusalem, one which is a complete immersion before entering the courtyard for the daily service, and the other only of hands and feet with water from the font before removing the ashes.[19] Although it never explicitly states that the priests vest, *Tamid* 1:2 provides evidence that the priests at the temple in Jerusalem wash their entire bodies prior to vesting themselves for service every day.[20] Moreover, the priests wash their hands and feet as a major part of the daily divine service at the tabernacle, and this closely coincides with them putting on their vestments. At the temple in Jerusalem, the priests probably adapt bathing their entire bodies from either the ordination rite or the Day of Atonement, or both. At the tabernacle, the priests cleanse only their hands and feet in the daily divine service, apparently *every* time they put on their sacred vestments.

When do the priests remove the burning coals for the incense rite? The Pentateuch provides little evidence to answer this question. Since the use of unauthorized fire[21] for burning incense provokes God's wrath (Lev 10:1–2), it may be assumed that the fire for the incense rite comes from the altar for burnt offering. The regulations for the Day of Atonement further strengthen this argument. In Lev 16:12 the LORD prescribes that the high priest must take a fire-pan full of burning coals from the altar and burn incense on them in the most holy place. Since the priest probably uses one pan full of coals for the altar of incense in the holy place in the daily service, the altar designated in Lev 16:12 most likely refers to the altar for burnt offering. The incense altar would not contain enough live coals for both the daily service and for burning incense in the most holy place on the Day of Atonement. Thus, it may be concluded that he takes the coals from the altar for burnt offering on the Day of Atonement. Similarly, it makes sense that the priests would take burning coals from this same altar—the one in the courtyard—for the incense rite in the daily divine service.

At exactly what point in the morning or evening service the priest removes the lit coals for burning incense remains a matter of speculation. While *Tamid* 2:5 affirms that the priest uses coals from the altar for burnt

---

Leviticus–Numbers, 193).

19. *Yoma* 3:2–4 states that no one ever enters the court to perform a ritual act unless he first immerses in water (Blackman, *Moed*, 282–84).

20. See Blackman, *Kodashim*, 471.

21. See also Exod 30:9.

offering in the incense rite, *Tamid* 5:5 indicates that at the temple in Jerusalem the retrieval of coals from the altar takes place at a later point in the service, just before entering the tent of meeting to burn incense.[22] At the tabernacle, however, the most logical time for removing the coals in the morning service is when the priest removes the ashes, since he is already at the altar. In the evening, he probably removes the coals just before adding the wood in the fire rite because the priests would need to expose the coals under the morning offering to set the new wood aflame.

Based on the preceding evidence, it may be assumed that although the sequence of ritual acts for the morning fire rite differs from that of the evening, it is essentially the same. First, the priest who performs the rite washes his hands and feet with water from the font. Second, he puts on his sacred vestments. Third, in the morning offering only, he removes the ashes from the altar and places them on its east side.[23] This exposes the live coals. In the evening, the ashes are not removed, yet the coals must be exposed and kindled for the following procedures. Fourth, the priest removes some of the burning coals for later use in the tent of meeting. Fifth, he places new wood on the exposed burning coals on the altar. In the evening offering, the fire rite ends with the new wood placed on the burning coals; but in the morning, there are two additional steps. Sixth, the priest takes off his sacred vestments and puts on his common clothes. Seventh, he carries the ashes outside the camp. The fire rite for the morning and the evening consists of the same basic activities, with the exception that every morning the priests remove the ashes from the previous day. Thus, the procedure for the morning fire rite has more steps than the one for the evening.

The ritual activities of the fire rite form the foundation of the morning and evening services. They cannot be performed at any other time in the divine service.[24] The altar fire must be maintained at all times, and that involves clearing the ashes every morning and adding new firewood in the beginning of the morning and evening services (Lev 6:1–6 [8–13]). The ritual washing and vesting ensures that the priest would safely be able to complete the tasks of the rite. Although he removes the vestments to carry the ashes outside the camp in the morning, the priest remains vested for the rites that immediately follow the fire rite in the evening. This indicates that the ministry of the fire rite is always conducted in coordination with the rites that come after it. Maintaining the fire on the altar for burnt offering is

---

22. See Blackman, *Kodashim*, 475, 489.

23. See Lev 1:16.

24. Until the ashes are removed from the altar and its fire stoked, the morning burnt offering cannot proceed (Kleinig, *Leviticus*, 148).

the first rite of the service, which prepares it for the main rites of the divine service.

The Presentation Rite

The other initial rite is the presentation[25] of materials for the offerings. It involves the presentation of a yearling male lamb, flour mixed with oil and seasoned with salt and frankincense, some wine or other fermented beverage, and bread for the high priest's offering at the entrance to the tent of meeting (Exod 29:4, 10–11; Lev 1:3; 8:1–4; 9:5).[26] The presentation rite also consists of several other activities that are necessary for performing it. There is a variation in the presentation of materials from the morning to the evening due to the difference between the morning and evening *fire* rite. The basic sequence, however, is the same. The presentation of the materials prepares them for use as an offering on the altar to the LORD in the daily service.

Although the priests most likely present all the materials together at the same time each morning and evening, it makes sense that they present these materials in a set order. The Pentateuch does not record which materials must be presented before and after the others in the daily divine service, but the order in which the text lists the materials may provide an indication of the order that the priests present them.[27] In addition, the prescriptive and

---

25. The Hebrew word הִקְרִיב, which is the *hiphil* form of קָרַב, is a term in the Pentateuch for the ritual activity of presenting something before the LORD for use as an offering on the altar (Milgrom, *Leviticus 1–16*, 145). Some modern translations, like the New International Version, New American Standard Bible, and The New Jerusalem Bible, translate both הִקְרִיב and עָשָׂה as *offer*. הִקְרִיב connotes bringing near, while עָשָׂה means to make or do something, such as in placing an offering *on the altar* (BDB 793, 897). It is a technical term that means to bring an offering, קָרְבָּן, to the LORD. The term denotes people or objects that are before the altar for burnt offering as the first ritual action in a private or public rite. Since the LORD is in the midst, קֶרֶב, of Israel (Num 11:20; 14:14), his people may approach, קָרַב, him (Exod 16:9; Lev 9:5; Num 16:40) and be near, קָרוֹב, to him (Lev 10:3). The Israelites *bring* the offerings before the LORD (Lev 3:1, 7, 12; 12:7; Num 6:16; 16:17), and the priests *present*, הִקְרִיב, the offerings to the LORD at the altar (Lev 1:15; 2:8; 6:7 [14]; Num 5:25). The various forms of קָרַב are essential to the sanctuary's ritual system (Kleinig, *Leviticus*, 44–45, 53). See Gane and Milgrom, "קָרַב," 48–135; Rattray and Milgrom, "קֶרֶב,"148–52; Fabry, "קָרְבָּן," 152–58.

26. The exact location of the *entrance to the tent of meeting* is discussed in the next chapter.

27. The various kinds of offerings are not always listed in the same order in the Pentateuch. Rainey, "Order of Sacrifices," explains that these lists of offerings fall into one of three categories: didactic order, administrative order, and procedural order. Milgrom also discusses the didactic and administrative distinction, but for a different purpose

descriptive texts for the ordination of the priests spell out a sequence for presenting its materials, and an order is seen in the inaugural service as well. The same sequence probably carries over to the daily service.

In Num 28:3-4 the LORD commands the Israelites to present two yearling male sheep without defect every morning and every evening for the daily burnt offering. This agrees with the LORD's prescription in Exod 29:38 to offer the lambs on the altar. For the lambs to become an offering, they must be presented before the LORD. The presentation rite entails a procedure for determining if the lamb is acceptable as an offering.

The Pentateuch does not explicitly prescribe that the lambs must be inspected, but it is implied.[28] The priests need to inspect the sheep to determine at least three things that qualify them as an acceptable offering to the LORD. First, the priests have to verify that the lambs are *yearlings*. Second, they must be *male*. Third, the lambs can only be *unblemished*.[29] The priests inspect the animals before they do anything else with them. The inspection probably entails an initial examination at the time the lamb is selected followed by a thorough inspection when it is presented for offering at the entrance to the tent of meeting.[30]

After it is presented, the high priest most likely places his hand on the head of the lamb.[31] Even though the Pentateuch never explicitly commands

---

(Milgrom, *Leviticus 1–16*, 382). In *every* list of offerings in the Pentateuch the grain offering always follows the burnt offering, regardless of the order for the other kinds of offerings.

28. Neh 3:31 may indicate that there was a designated place at the temple in Jerusalem for inspecting the animals brought for offering.

29. Burnt offerings from the flock must be presented without defects (Lev 1:10). For a list of defects that disqualify animals from being offered on the altar, see Lev 21:17–25.

30. The lambs at the temple are inspected the night before and on the day they are offered (*Tamid* 3:4). Just as in the case of the paschal lamb, so also the one for the daily burnt offering is inspected four days before being offered (Blackman, *Kodashim*, 478).

31. Since the high priest or his deputy singly performs the public acts for all Israel, no one else may vicariously lay his hand on the head of the lamb for the public daily burnt offering. With the individual burnt offering, the head of the family places his hand on the head of the animal to vouch that it belongs to him, and thereby vicariously secures God's approval and acceptance (Kleinig, *Leviticus*, 53). In the same way, the high priest, as the ritual head of the community of Israel, places his hand on the head of the public burnt offering to secure God's approval and acceptance for the entire community. Milgrom argues that the laying of the hand on the animal for the burnt offering neither *transfers* sin like the scapegoat, nor *identifies* the offerer with the offering to bring him closer to God, nor allows the offerer to *declare* the purpose of the offering or his innocence. Rather, the hand laying identifies ownership (Milgrom, *Leviticus 1–16*, 150–51). The high priest or his deputy puts his hand on the head of the lamb for the burnt offering because it belongs to all Israel, which he represents. Therefore, only the high priest or his deputy may place his hand on the head of the lamb for the public

the high priest to lay his hand on the head of the animal for the public burnt offering, he probably does so. Lev 1:1–17 records the legislation for the burnt offerings of individual Israelites and not the public one, but it portrays common elements about the procedure for preparing all burnt offerings. Lev 1:4 instructs individuals to place their hand on their own private burnt offering, and this may indicate that the priest should put his hand also on the head of the lamb for the public offering. Furthermore, the ordination service prescribed in Exod 29:1–37 and described in Lev 8 tells of the priests placing hands on the burnt offerings after presenting them before the LORD. The inaugural service, however, does not indicate that the priests lay hands on any of its offerings. The phrase in Lev 9:16 *he presented the burnt offering and offered it according to the ordinance* may imply, though, that the priests lay hands on the burnt offering at the inaugural service. On the one hand, this may refer to the prescription for the ordination service; but on the other hand, it most likely refers to the procedure commanded in Lev 1:3–13. Since Lev 1:4 appears to be a general command to place a hand on all kinds of burnt offerings, it probably includes laying a hand on the lambs for the public daily burnt offering.

Presenting the lambs every morning and evening involves several steps. First, a lamb is brought to the entrance of the tent of meeting so a priest can inspect it to determine that it is an unblemished yearling male. Second, he presents the lamb before the altar. Third, the high priest places his hand on its head. This sequence entails the presentation of the unblemished yearling male lamb each morning and evening. When are the other materials presented?

Various texts in the Pentateuch list the different kinds of offerings and their materials in a specific order. This could lead to the conclusion that the materials are presented in the same order that the texts arrange them. According to Exod 29:38–41; Num 28:1–8 the priests must offer a lamb together with one tenth of an ephah of fine flour mixed with one quarter of a hin of beaten olive oil as a cereal offering and one quarter of a hin[32] of wine or fermented beverage[33] as a drink offering. Moreover, Lev 2 indicates that

---

burnt offering.

32. A tenth of an ephah is a dry measure, which amounts to a little more than one quart or approximately 1.2 liters. A hin is a liquid measure that amounts to about three quarts or approximately 3.6 liters. Therefore, a quarter of a hin is approximately 1.5 pints or 0.9 liters (Propp, *Exodus 19–40*, 471).

33. The Hebrew word שֵׁכָר (Num 28:7) may refer to any kind of alcoholic beverage including wine (BDB 1016). Exod 29:40–41 specifically records that the accompanying drink offering is wine. Levine states that שֵׁכָר is only a fermented beverage made from the fruit of the vine (Levine, "*Lpny* YHWH," 219–20; *Numbers*, 374–75). This is further discussed in the next chapter.

frankincense and salt must be added to every kind of grain offering, and they are most likely presented together with the materials for the cereal offering. In Lev 1–2 the prescription for the individual burnt offering comes before the legislation for the individual grain offering. Lev 6:1–16 [8–23] arranges the statutes for the public daily burnt offering at the beginning, the public cereal offering in the middle, and the bread offering of the high priest at the end. These texts record the lambs first, the materials for the cereal offering second, the wine for the drink offering third, and the bread for the high priest's offering last. This possibly suggests that the priests *present* them in this same order.

The presentation of the materials at the ordination service follows a similar sequence. Because Exod 29:1–37 does not legislate a cereal or drink offering and Lev 8 does not record them, there is no evidence that the materials for a cereal or drink offering are presented with the animals for the burnt offering for the ordination of the priests. Both of these texts, however, state that an offering[34] of bread, cakes, and wafers from fine flour is presented together with the animals to be offered. If the bread at the ordination service is related to the bread for the daily service, then this may support the theory that the lamb is always presented first and the high priest's bread is always presented last.

The inaugural service in Lev 9 provides further evidence for a consistent sequence among its various rites; this has implications for the order of the daily service. In Lev 9:2–6 where Moses directs Aaron and the Israelites to bring[35] the materials for the service and present them before the LORD, the animals, including the ones for the burnt offering, are listed first and the cereal offering is last. Lev 9:16–17 records that Aaron presented the burnt offering before the cereal offering, just as Moses had told him. Since this passage specifies that this is the *morning burnt offering*, it may be concluded that the one in the inaugural service is the same public burnt offering that the priests offer every day. Therefore, the materials for the burnt offering are most likely always presented before the materials for the cereal offering.

In addition to the presentation of all the materials, most likely two other ritual activities are performed. These are enacted, however, in the morning presentation rite only. Since the priest who carries the ashes outside the camp removes his vestments, he must wash his hands and feet

---

34. In light of Lev 6:12–13 [19–20], the bread offering at the ordination service may be the basis for the daily bread offering of the high priest.

35. The imperative of לְקַח is used here and may be translated as *take* or *bring*. Kleinig has noted that in some contexts it may be understood as *select* (Kleinig, *Leviticus*, 209). Since the term is used for Aaron and his sons and their garments, as well as the other materials at the ordination service, it is probably best rendered as *bring*.

and then put on his sacred vestments before performing the ritual activities of the presentation rite. In the evening, he does not need to wash or vest because the ashes are not removed from the altar and taken outside the camp. His hands and feet are already washed and he is still vested from the beginning of the service. Therefore, it makes sense that in the morning the washing and vesting is enacted before any of the materials are presented.

The presentation rite consists of a sequence of enactments. First, the priest washes his hands and feet. Second, he puts on his sacred vestments. These two ritual acts are only performed in the morning. The remaining procedures for the presentation rite are identical for both the morning and evening, and are its core activities. Third, the lamb is brought to the entrance of the tent of meeting, inspected to make sure it is a yearling male without defects, presented before the LORD, and the high priest or his deputy lays his hand on it. Fourth, the materials are presented for the accompanying cereal offering. These are flour mixed with olive oil, and seasoned with salt and frankincense. Fifth, the priests present the wine or fermented beverage for the drink offering. Finally, the bread offering of the high priest is presented at the altar. This sequence of ritual activities comprises the presentation rite of the daily divine service.

The ritual activities of the presentation rite prepare the materials for use in the rites that are central to the daily service. The yearling male lambs without defect, together with the materials for the cereal offering, the wine or fermented beverage for the drink offering, and the bread offering of the high priest are brought into the presence of the LORD at the entrance to the tent of meeting. Unless these materials are presented, they cannot be offered on the altar. Although the sequence for presenting these materials is not identical in both the morning and the evening, the rite is essentially the same in each. The presentation rite necessarily comes before those that it precedes, because it prepares the materials used in the main rites of the daily service.

THE CENTRAL RITES

The Blood Rite

The blood rite is the first of three central rites performed in the daily divine service. The blood is splashed against the sides of the altar in preparation for burning incense and smoking up the offerings.[36] Part of the preparation

---

36. *Zebahim* 5:4 states that the priests at the temple in Jerusalem receive the blood of the animals for burnt offerings into more than one vessel. Then they splash the blood

entails cutting up the lamb prior to placing it on the altar. The lamb must be slain, its blood properly disposed, and the carcass sectioned before it can be smoked up. Although the preparation of the lamb comprises the bulk of the ritual activities in the blood rite, the act of splashing the blood against the altar is the most ritually significant. Because the blood rite is both a practical and ritual preparation, it necessarily precedes the enactments inside the holy place and the others that follow it at the altar for burnt offering.

The Pentateuch contains no legislation about the sequence of the blood rite for the daily divine service apart from the need to splash it on all sides of the altar (Exod 29:16; Lev 1:5, 11; 3:2, 8, 13; 8:19; 9:18). There is evidence, however, in the ordination and inaugural services as well as the requirements of the individual burnt offerings, for a consistent procedure for the blood rites of all kinds of burnt offerings, although different animals are used.[37] Two things may be concluded from this. First, there is a blood rite for the daily burnt offering.[38] Second, the sequence of acts for the blood rite of the public daily burnt offering is probably similar to the procedure for the other kinds of burnt offerings.

In Exod 29:16–17 the LORD prescribes the procedure for the blood rite in the ordination service. First, a lamb is slain.[39] It is killed in such a way

---

at the opposite corners of the altar (Blackman, *Kodashim*, 38). *Tamid* 4:1 indicates that the priest at the temple in Jerusalem stands at the northeast corner of the altar and splashes the blood on the east then north sides, with one motion. Then he moves to the opposite southwest corner of the altar and splashes the blood on the west then south sides, with one motion (Blackman, *Kodashim*, 483). Kleinig proposes that the priest splashes the blood *sideways* from a bowl against the two sides of the altar at two of its corners (Kleinig, *Leviticus*, 55). See also Milgrom, *Leviticus 1–16*, 156.

37. A lamb is used for the burnt offering in the ordination service as well as the priest's burnt offering at the inaugural service (Lev 8–9). A yearling calf and a yearling lamb are the animals offered as the burnt offerings of the Israelites at the inaugural service (Lev 9). Individual burnt offerings can be either a male from the herd, or sheep or goats from the flock, or a dove or young pigeon (Lev 1).

38. The blood from all offerings must be disposed at the altar for burnt offering at the sanctuary (Lev 17:11). This is discussed in the next chapter.

39. The term *slay*, rendering the Hebrew word שָׁחַט, does not mean *slaughter*. It refers to the ritual killing of the lamb by slaying it through the draining of its blood (BDB 1006). Slaughter means to cut the lamb into its pieces. Milgrom explains that שָׁחַט technically means slitting the throat (Milgrom, *Leviticus 1–16*, 154). He also notes that the offerer and the victim face west toward the tent of meeting when the animal is killed (Milgrom, *Leviticus 1–16*, 154–55). Likewise, *Tamid* 4:1 states that at the temple in Jerusalem the priests bind the lamb, stand it with its head to the south, and turn its face to the west. The priest is positioned on the east side of the lamb facing the west also (Blackman, *Kodashim*, 482–83). This exposes the neck of the lamb so that the priest can slash it. He then cuts the throat through the main artery so that the heart pumps all the blood out of the lamb (Kleinig, *Leviticus*, 63–64). See also Clements, "שחט," 563–66.

that all of its blood is drained from the carcass into special basins. Second, the priests take its blood to the altar for burnt offering and splash it against all of its sides.[40] Third, they cut the lamb into pieces.[41] Fourth, they wash its entrails and lower legs with water.[42] Fifth, the entrails and legs are placed with its head and other pieces. This is the procedure for the burnt offering at the ordination of Aaron and his sons.

In Lev 8:19-21 the burnt offering for the ordination of the priests appears to have a variation from its prescription in Exod 29:16-17. Lev 8 records that, the victim is killed and its blood is splashed on the altar, after which Moses cuts it into sections and burns the head, the parts, and the fat, before he washes the entrails and lower legs. The difference between the narrative account in Lev 8 and the prescriptive account in Exod 29 is that in the one case Moses burns the head, parts, and fat *before* washing the entrails and lower legs; in the other case all the parts of the animal are burned *after* the entrails and lower legs are washed. In Lev 9:12-14, the sequence for the burnt offering in the inaugural service is similar to the ordination service. Although the order slightly varies all the ritual activities of the blood rite in

---

40. One must distinguish between *splashing* and *sprinkling*. In Lev 1:11, some of the modern versions, such as the New International Version and New American Standard Bible, translate the Hebrew verb זָרַק as *sprinkle*. The Hebrew verb נָזָה in its *hiphil* form denotes *sprinkling* blood from the sin offering (Lev 4:6). זָרַק, on the other hand, means to throw, toss, or splash (BDB 284). The Pentateuch always uses the term זָרַק to describe the application of blood on the altar, from the burnt offerings. The Pentateuch only uses the term הִזָּה, sprinkle, in relation to the sin offering. Thus, *splash* represents an accurate translation for the manipulation of blood in the public daily burnt offering. Milgrom observes that there are three forms of blood manipulation from the animals of the various classifications of offerings: aspersing/sprinkling (Lev 4:6; 8:30; 16:14), daubing/smearing (Lev 4:7, 18, 25, 30, 34), and dashing/splashing (Lev 1:5, 11; 3:2, 8, 13; 8:19; 9:18) (Milgrom, *Leviticus 1-16*, 155-56).

41. The Hebrew verb נָתַח means to cut into pieces (BDB 677). Milgrom explains that the Israelites and priests dismember the lamb according to its body parts (Milgrom, *Leviticus 1-16*, 157), while Levine thinks that the term connotes cutting up by sectioning (Levine, *Leviticus*, 7). The priests do not simply hack up the lamb into random pieces. Rather, they deliberately slaughter the lamb into its sections.

42. The animal's entrails, קֶרֶב, and legs, כְּרָע, are washed with water (Lev 1:13). The New International Version translates קֶרֶב as *inner parts*. Levine understands the term as intestines (Levine, *Leviticus*, 7), while Kleinig renders it entrails (Kleinig, *Leviticus*, 52, 56). Milgrom points out that the term does not include the other internal organs that need no washing. The priests wash the organs of the digestive tract to remove feces from them (Milgrom, *Leviticus 1-16*, 159). Thus, קֶרֶב does not mean all the inward organs, but rather the digestive organs, the entrails. The legs, כְּרָע, are also washed. Milgrom understands כְּרָע as *shins*, meaning the legs below the knees (Milgrom, *Leviticus 1-16*, 159-60). Kleinig renders it as *lower legs*. He maintains that since the legs become filthy with dirt, mud, and refuse, they need washing before the priest burns them on the most holy altar (Kleinig, *Leviticus*, 52).

these services are performed according to the procedure spelled out in Exod 29. This indicates that some variations in the sequence of the rite may legitimately exist within the parameters of the ritual legislation.

The order in which the ritual acts are performed seems to be unique for the blood rite of the public daily burnt offering. There is a difference between the way the daily burnt offering and the burnt offerings in other services are enacted because of the additional activities performed in the daily divine service. The blood rite of the ordination and inaugural services as well as the individual burnt offerings do not include burning incense after the blood of the victim is splashed against the altar and prior to the burning of its pieces on the altar. Since the daily divine service includes an incense rite between the blood splashing and the smoking up of the offerings, the sequence of activities in the daily blood rite is affected. The entrails and lower legs would not be washed after the other parts of the animal are placed on the altar fire. As Exod 29:17 indicates, putting all of the parts of the animal on the fire comes after the entrails and lower legs have been washed. Furthermore, it is unlikely that any of the pieces of the daily burnt offering would be burned on the altar before the incense rite is completed. The ritual acts of the blood rite for the public daily burnt offering most likely follow a sequence different from that of any other offering.[43]

Lev 1 provides other details about the procedure for disposing the blood of every kind of burnt offering. The enactment for the blood rite of individual burnt offerings in Lev 1 is the same as that of the narrative accounts for the ordination and inaugural services in Lev 8–9. Lev 1:5, however, indicates that the blood from the burnt offering is "presented" before it is splashed against the sides of the outer altar.[44] Furthermore, Lev 1:6 adds

---

43. The family enactment of the rites for the private burnt offering should be distinguished from the public daily burnt offering. Lev 1:3–9 does not describe an unbroken chronological sequence. Rather, they prescribe two sets of acts, one performed by the lay Israelite and the other performed by the priests. While most of the ritual acts are performed sequentially, the lay person and the priests perform others simultaneously, such as the arrangement of the sectioned animal on the altar by the priest while the lay person washes the entrails and legs (Kleinig, *Leviticus*, 63). See also Gerstenberger, *Leviticus*, 26–31. Milgrom discusses whether Lev 1:3–9 portrays the proper order with the burning of some of the animal's parts preceding the washing of the entrails and legs. He supposes that the sequence stated in this pericope may refer solely to the burnt offering of individuals and not to that of the public daily burnt offering (Milgrom, *Leviticus 1–16*, 160–63).

44. Lev 7:33 speaks of presenting blood from peace offerings, and Lev 9:9 refers to the presentation of blood from sin offerings. Although the Pentateuch never mentions that the blood from guilt offerings must be presented, it may be that the blood from animal offerings is always presented before it is disposed at the altar. The word that designates the blood's *presentation*, הִקְרִיב, is the same word that is found in the presentation

that the animal must be flayed before it is cut into sections.[45] This correlates with Lev 7:8, which states that the priest who offers a burnt offering may keep the hide for himself.[46] Lev 1 gives the additional data that after the blood is drained from the animal and caught in bowls it must be presented before the LORD at the altar, and the hide must be removed from the carcass before the victim is cut into sections.

The last ritual activity of the blood rite is putting salt on the animal after it has been cut into pieces. All offerings must include salt (Lev 2:13).[47]

---

rite. Milgrom notes the ritual presentation of the blood before it is splashed on the altar, and thinks that the presentation of blood can take the form of an elevation offering (Milgrom, *Leviticus 1-16*, 155). See also Kleinig, *Leviticus*, 44-45, 55, 63-64.

45. Since Lev 1:6 does not state that he must flay/skin the *bull*, but rather the *burnt offering*, the command most likely applies to all burnt offerings. Lev 1 states the ritual procedure for the herd in greater detail as it sets the basic pattern for the burnt offerings from the flock and from the aviary (Kleinig, *Leviticus*, 58). Flay, פָּשַׁט, connotes stripping, such as the removing of clothes (Mic 3:3; 2 Chr 29:34; 35:11). Milgrom states that flaying does not include removing the skin from the head and lower legs of the victim, which would prove difficult, but refers to all the other areas of its body. He supposes that the lay Israelite skins his own burnt offering and the priests skin the public offerings, but under emergency circumstances such as in 2 Chr 35:11 the non-priestly Levites may also skin the lambs (Milgrom, *Leviticus 1-16*, 156-57). *Tamid* 4:2 states that, at the temple in Jerusalem, the priests flay the lambs for the daily burnt offering after they slay them but before they cut the lambs into pieces (Blackman, *Kodashim*, 483-84). Therefore, I consider the flaying/skinning as the first act in the slaughtering of the lamb.

46. Levine holds that Lev 1 meticulously avoids mentioning that the priests must burn the hide of the animal because they must not destroy it. Only in the case of the priestly sin offering, commanded in 4:1-21 and in similar rites of purification, shall they destroy the hide, which they burn outside the camp rather than on the altar (Levine, *Leviticus*, 41). Kleinig concurs that the hide from the burnt offering belongs to the priest who offers it (Kleinig, *Leviticus*, 168). Milgrom claims that the hide from the burnt offering of a lay Israelite becomes a prebend for the officiating priest. He holds, however, that in all cases where a priest offers an animal for himself, he must burn the entire animal, including its hide, just as in the case of a priest's cereal or bread offering (Lev 6:16 [23]). It is not clear whether Milgrom means burning the hide with the animal on the altar or outside the camp like the priests' sin offerings (Milgrom, *Leviticus 1-16*, 157). *Zebahim* 12:3-4 states that if the offering is a *most holy* offering, then the hide belongs to the priest, but if it is a *holy* offering, such as the peace offering, then the hide belongs to the lay offerer (Blackman, *Kodashim*, 78-79). The evidence seems to support the view that the officiating priest could claim the hide from the lamb for the public daily burnt offering.

47. The Hebrew word for salt is מֶלַח. *Tamid* 4:3 indicates that the salting of the lamb's members comprises the last ritual act for preparing the offering at the temple in Jerusalem (Blackman, *Kodashim*, 485-87). Levine explains that Ezra 6:9 and 7:22 requires large quantities of salt at the temple; but he doubts that the *covenant of salt* in Num 18:19 reiterates the daily use of salt in Israel's sacrificial cult (Levine, *Leviticus*, 13). Milgrom acknowledges that the offerer must add salt to all offerings. In the case of the

Ezek 43:24 and *Tamid* 4:3[48] affirm that the animals for the burnt offerings at the temple in Jerusalem are salted after they have been cut into pieces and before they are smoked up. It would make little sense for the salt to be added to the animal before it is skinned and butchered. Likewise, putting salt on the entrails and lower legs would not precede washing them with water. The most likely place within the blood rite for salting the lamb is after it is cut into pieces and its entrails and lower legs washed. There can be little doubt that is the final ritual activity within the blood rite of the daily divine service.

The blood rite of the daily divine service consists of five enactments that are carried out in a specific sequence. First, the lamb is killed by draining all of its blood into special ritual basins to present it before the LORD at the altar for burnt offering. Second, the blood is splashed against all the sides of the altar.[49] Third, after the priests flay the lamb to keep the skin from being incinerated on the altar with it, they cut the lamb into sections. Fourth, the priests wash the entrails and lower legs, before putting them with the head, fat, and its other pieces. Finally, all of the pieces of the lamb are salted. It is with a great deal of certainty that these ritual acts are performed in this order. This sequence of activities makes up the blood rite of the daily service.

The blood rite prepares for the other two central rites. Practically, it prepares the lamb to be turned into smoke on the altar. Significantly, it qualifies the agents to perform the following rites. Unless the priests perform the blood rite, none of the rites after it can be conducted. Although the blood rite prepares for the rites that it precedes, it is central to the entire daily service. Together with burning incense and smoking up the offerings, the blood rite is one of the most important parts of the daily divine service.

---

offerings of individuals, the lay Israelite must provide the salt. However, for the public offerings, including the daily burnt offering, the priests use the salt from the supplies at the sanctuary. Furthermore, he explains that all substances that are offered include salt, with the exception of wine, blood, and wood. Most likely, all offerings *burned* on the altar for burnt offering require salting (Milgrom, *Leviticus 1–16*, 191–92). Josephus describes the procedure for the individual burnt offerings (Josephus, *Jewish Antiquities*, 3:227). He states that the offerer salts the parts of the animal after cutting it into pieces. The individual who offers the animal, however, cleanses the legs and entrails after salting its other parts, but Josephus never mentions whether they salt these parts too (Whiston, *Josephus*, 131).

48. See Blackman, *Kodashim*, 487.

49. The procedure for splashing the blood against the sides of the altar is further discussed in the next chapter.

The Incense Rite

The incense rite is the most central rite performed in the daily divine service. The primary activity conducted in this rite is burning incense inside the tent of meeting on the inner altar. Tending the lamps in the morning and lighting the lamps in the evening are the other ritual acts in the holy place. To burn incense on the altar in the tent, the ashes most likely are removed and burning coals added every morning, while coals are probably also added in the evening without removing any of the ashes. The priests must also wash their hands and feet and wear specific vestments. The incense rite is composed of some of the most significant things that are done in the daily service.

It is quite certain that burning incense comes after the blood is splashed and before the offerings are put on the altar in the courtyard. The Pentateuch, however, never prescribes an order in which these must be enacted. There is the possibility that the incense offering follows the burnt offering, but most of the data indicates just the opposite.

Some evidence indicates that the incense offering and burnt offering do not follow a set sequence. Presumably, one could be performed before the other at one time but just the opposite at another time.

In 1 Chr 6:49; 2 Chr 13:11 the burnt offering is listed before the incense offering. Yet, neither of them narrates an event but only that each rite must be performed. Explanations for this alternate order may be found in Philo (*Laws* 1:171) and the *Mishnah* (*Yoma* 3:3). These sources indicate that burning incense on the inner altar in the morning comes after the blood is splashed and before the ritual materials on the outer altar are turned into smoke. In the evening, the incense is burned after the materials are placed on the outer altar. Although this may reflect the practice in a different period of Israel's history, the evidence of a *prescribed* order is lacking in these sources.[50]

At the end of the inaugural service in Lev 9:22–24 after Aaron places the offerings on the altar for burnt offering, he and Moses enter the tent of meeting. It may be assumed that they enter there to burn incense, but the text never indicates this[51] If this assumption is true then the placement of

---

50. Gane holds that in the morning the burning of incense on the inner altar precedes the smoking up of the burnt offering on the outer altar, while in the evening the incense is burned inside the tent of meeting after the burnt offering is placed on the altar in the courtyard (Gane, "Bread of Presence," 187–88).

51. Although Lev 9 does not indicate whether Moses and Aaron entered the tent of meeting to burn incense or, as Moses often did, to pray on behalf of the people, this entry establishes the precedent for the daily incense rite. In the inaugural service, the normal order is reversed to connect the final benediction with Aaron's entry into the

The Practical Order of the Daily Divine Service   43

the animals on the altar in the courtyard would precede this act. Since the inaugural service constitutes a different purpose than the daily service, however, the order of its rites is most likely different and unique. One of the most important occurrences of the inaugural service is that the divine fire *comes out* from the presence of the LORD to ignite the holy fire on the altar for burnt offering. From then on, the daily burnt offerings are smoked up on this fire at the outer altar, and this same fire is carried into the holy place to offer incense on the inner altar.[52] The unique order for the inaugural service consists of placing the materials on the outer altar before entering the tent of meeting followed by the incineration of the offerings by the holy fire. Still, the entrance precedes the smoking up of the animal on the altar by the holy fire.

The sequence of the inaugural service supports the idea that the incense rite comes first and is followed by the incineration of the materials on the altar for burnt offering. The passages from the other sources do not provide conclusive evidence to the contrary in every period of Israel's history.

Most sources in the Pentateuch indicate that the ritual activities inside the tent of meeting occur before the presented materials are burned on the altar for burnt offering. Exod 28:42–43 and 30:20 legislate that the priests must wear their sacred vestments when they *enter* the tent of meeting or *approach* the altar for burnt offering to make an offering by fire to the LORD. Exod 40:32 attests that Moses, Aaron, and his sons wash their hands and feet whenever they *enter* the tent of meeting or *approach* the altar for burnt offering. Exod 40:26–29 describes how Moses first sets up the incense altar and burns incense on it, and then afterwards sets up the altar for burnt offering to offer burnt offerings and cereal offerings. During the twelve days of the dedication of the sanctuary in Num 7:12–83, a representative from each of the twelve tribes of Israel presents incense, after which animals are presented for burnt offerings. Deut 33:10 shows the same pattern of incense being placed before the LORD prior to the burnt offerings being placed on the altar. These passages in the Pentateuch list the incense offering before the burnt offering, which most likely indicates that the incense rite is performed before the burning rite.

---

tent of meeting. Aaron enters God's presence for the first time to bring his blessing out to the assembled congregation (Kleinig, *Leviticus*, 217). Furthermore, since it is the inaugural service, the lamps would be tended on the menorah and the bread and other items set out on the table for the first time. It makes sense that at the same time, the fragrant incense would be placed on the inner altar.

52. It was established in the section on the fire rite that the coals from the outer altar are carried into the tent of meeting for use at the altar for incense.

Several texts outside the Pentateuch bear witness to burning incense before the burnt offering is offered on the altar in the daily service at the temple in Jerusalem. In 2 Chr 2:4, when he is about to build the temple, Solomon mentions burning fragrant incense earlier than he speaks of the burnt offerings smoked up every morning and evening. In 2 Chr 29:7, at the time he purifies the temple after it had become defiled, Hezekiah declares that the priests failed to burn incense and offer burnt offerings, again indicating that the incense rite comes before the burning rite.[53] Ps 141:2 implies that the incense is offered prior to the burnt offering. Sir 50:5–21 reports that the high priest emerges from the temple and then approaches the outer altar to offer burnt offerings on it. *Tamid* 5:6–7:3 provides a detailed account of the incense rite performed earlier than the burning rite at the temple in Jerusalem.[54] According to these texts, the order at the temple supports the premise that the incense rite is performed before the burnt offering is turned into smoke at the tabernacle.

Although it may be possible for the burning rite to precede the incense rite, the evidence in the Pentateuch strongly suggests that it comes after the incense rite. The analysis in the next section further strengthens this argument. Moreover, the investigation of the function and purpose of each rite in the next chapter leads to the conclusion that the incense is burned after the blood is splashed on the altar and prior to the smoking up of the daily burnt offering. I, therefore, assume that the incense rite is enacted before the burning rite in the daily divine service every morning and evening at the tabernacle.[55]

---

53. Kleinig emphasizes the integration of all the parts of the service as described in 2 Chronicles. He states that the burning up of incense correlates with the burning up of the burnt offering and that the incense is burned on the inner altar before the incineration of the offering on the outer altar (Kleinig, *Lord's Song*, 100–105).

54. See Blackman, *Kodashim*, 490–96.

55. Kleinig is one of the only contemporary scholars with interest in reconstructing the entire daily divine service at the tabernacle. He divides the service into three parts. First, there is the rite of atonement, which includes the presentation of the materials, slaughter of animals for offering, and splashing of blood against the sides of the altar. Second, the rite of burnt offering consists of the entering into the holy place to burn incense, tend the lamps, and replace the bread on the table; the approaching of the outer altar to burn the parts of the animal and the token portion of the cereal offering; then the pouring out of wine and sounding of the silver trumpets. Third, there is the sacrificial meal, in which the high priest blesses the congregation and the sacred food is eaten (Kleinig, *Leviticus*, 39). He maintains a similar order for the public daily burnt offering at the temple, based on his study of Chronicles (Kleinig, *Lord's Song*, 132). Kleinig consistently portrays the burning of incense on the inner altar prior to the incineration of the burnt offering on the outer altar. I hold that this is the correct order of the public daily burnt offering based on evidence from the Pentateuch and other sources.

Burning incense on the altar in the holy place is the primary ritual activity of the incense rite. The LORD prescribes that fragrant incense must be burned every morning and every evening on the altar in the tent of meeting (Exod 30:7–8). Offering this incense coincides with the other ritual acts that are conducted in the morning and evening services. The text adds that the incense is burned every morning when the lamps are *tended* and every evening when the lamps are *lit*. Since Exod 30:8 declares that *incense will burn regularly before the LORD*, it is the main activity inside the tent of meeting, even though other things are done at the lamps each time incense is burned.

The lamps must be tended every morning and lit every evening (Exod 30:7–8). The LORD stipulates that the lamps must be kept burning from evening until morning (Exod 27:21; Lev 24:3). Since Lev 24:4 states that the lamps must be set in order regularly, this probably refers to both tending the lamps every morning and lighting them every evening.[56] There is little doubt concerning the interrelation between the ritual activities at the lampstand and those at the incense altar. Yet, which is enacted before or after the other? The answer lies in another ritual activity.

Although the Pentateuch never records anything about removing ashes from and adding burning coals to the incense altar, these are necessary for conducting the rites in the holy place inside the tent.[57] It may be assumed that the ashes on the incense altar need to be removed at some point, and the most logical time for this is in the morning, because that is when the lamps are tended. The wicks in the lamps need to be either trimmed or replaced every morning when they are filled with oil in preparation for lighting them that evening. Thus, every morning the ashes are probably removed from the incense altar before the new burning coals are placed on it.[58] After this, the trimmings and depleted wicks are placed in the same container as the ashes from the inner altar. In the evening, the procedure is different. Since the lamps are lit in the evening, the ashes most likely are not

---

56. Milgrom holds that this could refer to setting up the lamps if the lamps can be separated from the menorah. Thus, whether they are being tended or lit, the lamps would be taken down and then set back up on the menorah (Milgrom, *Leviticus 23–27*, 2091). Exod 25:31, however, might indicate that the lamps are inseparable from the lampstand. If so, then Lev 24:4 means that the "setting of the lamps in order" refers to tending them in the morning and lighting them in the evening.

57. *Tamid* 1:4 and 3:1, 6 indicate that the ashes are cleared every morning at the Temple in Jerusalem and that burning coals are taken from the altar for burnt offering into the holy place and put on the inner altar to burn incense (Blackman, *Kodashim*, 473, 476, 479).

58. It was established in the discussion about the fire rite that the coals from the outer altar are taken into the tent of meeting for burning incense on the inner altar.

removed from the incense altar at that time. Instead, the burning coals are added on top of the altar before one of them is carried with tongs to light the lamps.[59] Putting the fire on the incense altar every morning and evening is necessary to light the lamps and burn incense inside the tent of meeting.

If my previous analysis is correct, then the incense is burned after the lamps are tended in the morning or lit in the evening. The ritual activities at the incense altar, however, coincide with those at the lamps. While both must be enacted together, burning incense is the primary ritual activity in the incense rite, and it comes at the end of it.

Is anything performed daily at the golden table upon which sits the bread of the presence? It seems unusual that nothing would be enacted there each day. According to Exod 25:30 the LORD prescribes that the bread of the presence must be on the table at all times, and Exod 40:22–23 explains that Moses put the bread on the table when he set up the tabernacle after its construction. Moreover, Lev 24:5–9 tells how it is made and replaced on the table every Sabbath. Evidently the bread of the presence sits untouched for a week, until it is replaced with new bread. There are twelve loaves placed in two piles, each containing six pieces of bread, on the gold table in the holy place.[60] Lev 24:7 records that pure frankincense is placed on each pile of bread as a memorial and an offering by fire to the LORD.[61] Thus, every

59. The Hebrew word for tongs is מֶלְקָחַיִם. Since the root form is לקח, which means *take*, it makes sense that מֶלְקָחַיִם are instruments used to take something (BDB 542, 544). In Exod 25:38, the New International Version translates the word as *wick trimmers* and the New American Standard Bible translates it as *snuffers*. The English Standard Version rightly translates it as *tongs*. In Isa 6:6 a burning coal is taken from the incense altar with tongs, מֶלְקָחַיִם. According to Exod 25:38, the tongs, as well as fire pans, are accessories to the menorah. Most likely, the fire pans are used for carrying burning coals to the incense altar every morning and evening, as well as gathering the spent wicks from the lamps and ashes from the inner altar. The tongs and the fire pans, therefore, would be used at both the menorah and the incense altar.

60. Mitchell makes a strong case that the bread of the presence on the table in the holy place is not laid out in rows, but in two piles of six each. He claims that the amount of flour described in Lev 24:5–9 would make large flat loaves that would not fit on the table that is described in Exod 25:23. He also holds that the small dishes mentioned in Exod 25:29 contain the pure frankincense that is placed on the top of each pile (Mitchell, "Leviticus 24:6," 447–48).

61. Milgrom writes that there is a difference of opinion between the rabbis and the Qumran community about where the pure frankincense from the bread of the presence is burned. The rabbis claim that it is burned on the outer altar for burnt offering, while the Qumran sectaries hold that it is burned on the incense altar in the tent of meeting. Milgrom agrees with Qumran (Milgrom, *Leviticus 23–27*, 2093–95). See also Haran, *Temples and Temple Service*, 210; Kleinig, *Leviticus*, 513, 516. The twelve golden bowls full of incense in Num 7 are most likely stored in the tent of meeting near or on the golden table. As Haran has identified, golden ritual vessels are used in the tent of meeting (Haran, *Temples and Temple Service*, 158–65). The incense that is offered in the

Sabbath the frankincense is burned and the bread is changed.[62] There are also daily ritual acts performed at the table. Exod 30:36 states that the finely ground fragrant incense must be placed before the testimony where the LORD meets with Moses. Since Moses does not enter into the most holy place to meet with the LORD, the incense must be kept somewhere in the holy place. Most likely, it is stored in containers on the table.[63] In addition, there is evidence that the oil for the lamps and the wine for the drink offering are stored on the golden table (Exod 25:29).[64] If this is so, then the ritual acts in the holy place also involve the table. The fragrant incense burned on the inner altar every morning and evening is probably taken from the golden table after the lamps are tended or lit.

The priests wash their hands and feet before entering the tent of meeting. The LORD prescribes that the priests who enter the tent of meeting must wash their hands and feet with water from the bronze font in the courtyard (Exod 30:19–20). Just as the priests wash their hands and feet at the beginning of the fire and presentation rites, so also they wash them at the beginning of the incense rite. Since the washing precedes any of the other ritual activities in the fire and presentation rites, the same holds true for burning incense. Washing is most likely the first thing enacted in the incense rite.

What about vesting in the sacred vestments? The discussion in the preceding sections on the fire and presentation rites reveals a correlation between ritual washing and ritual vesting. Furthermore, in the section on

---

daily divine service is probably taken from upon or near the golden table. The bread of the presence is never burned; rather, it is eaten by the priests. The pure frankincense that is placed on the piles represents the bread and is burned as its token portion, which explains why the bread of the presence is considered *an offering by fire to the LORD* (Lev 24:7).

62. Gane makes the case that the pure frankincense from the bread of the presence is burned only on the Sabbath at the time the priests consume the bread from the previous week. As the priests are eating the bread, the LORD is enjoying it with them in the form of pure frankincense (Gane, "Bread of Presence," 195).

63. Propp thinks that the incense burned on the incense altar in the tent of meeting is taken from the table upon which the bread of the presence sits (Propp, *Exodus 19–40*, 397).

64. Gane holds that the vessels for drink offerings at the table indicate that the daily divine service must include drink offerings both at the outer altar and in the tent of meeting (see Exod 25:29). Since Exod 30:9 prohibits pouring drink offerings on the incense altar, the vessels for the inner drink offerings are not used for *pouring out* but rather for *pouring into*. He claims that the drink offering at the table in the tent of meeting functions like the bread of the presence. It sits upon the table in the presence of the LORD, but unlike the bread, the drink offering is changed every morning and evening (Gane, "Bread of Presence," 183–89). Evidence for this interpretation appears to be lacking. See also Haran, *Temples and Temple Service*, 216–17.

the blood rite it is argued that the priests do not need to wash their hands and feet or vest again because they have already done so. In the incense rite, the priests are already vested. Most likely, the high priest is also already wearing the basic vestments similar to the other priests, because he is the one who places his hand on the lamb when it is presented. If so, he would need to don his ornate vestments before entering the holy place. Since Exod 30:19–20 requires that the priests wash their hands and feet again when they enter the tent of meeting, this is probably the place in the service where the high priest puts on his additional ornate vestments. Like the other rites, the high priest washes before donning his ornate vestments. Yet, if any of the regular priests assist him in the tent of meeting, they too wash their hands and feet before entering, even though they are already vested. There is a correlation between washing and donning the sacred ornate vestments of the high priest before entering into the holy place to perform his ministry.

All the priests are required to wear their vestments when they enter into the tent of meeting, yet the ornate vestments of the high priest hold a greater significance than the vestments of the regular priests. In Exod 28:43 the LORD stipulates that the priests must wear their vestments whenever they enter the tent of meeting. All the priests wear the basic vestments, the tunics, the sashes, and the caps. The high priest alone wears the ephod, breast piece, robe, and turban with the gold plate over the regular vestments when he enters the holy place and stands before the LORD (Exod 28:12, 29–30, 35). Exod 28 makes clear that the vestments of the high priest must be worn as a ritual activity, not merely as a preparation for burning incense.[65] Exod 28:12 records that the high priest bears on his shoulders the names of Israel engraved on memorial stones and attached to the ephod *as a memorial before the LORD*. In Exod 28:29–30 the LORD prescribes that *when he enters the holy place* the high priest bears over his heart the names of the Israelites engraved on jewels and attached to the breastpiece of judgment. Furthermore, the Urim and Thummim are placed in the breastpiece over the heart of the high priest *when he enters into the presence of the LORD*. Exod 28:33–35 legislates that golden bells and pomegranates must be attached to the hem of the high priest's robe so that the sound of the bells are heard *when he enters the holy place before the LORD*. Finally, Exod 28:36–38 requires the high priest to wear the turban with the attached gold plate, which is engraved with the words *YHWH's holiness*,[66] when he ministers in

---

65. For a full discussion about the ritual significance of the vestments of the high priest see Haran, *Temples and Temple Service*, 165–74, 210–15.

66. This inscription is discussed in chapter 3.

the presence of the LORD. While wearing the ornate vestments into the holy place the high priest performs several ritual enactments.

The incense rite is made up of a sequence of ritual acts. First, the high priest, and any priest entering the holy place with him, washes his hands and feet from the bronze font in the courtyard.[67] Second, the high priest dons and wears his ornate vestments into the tent of meeting.[68] Third, in the morning the ashes are removed and new coals are placed on the incense altar. In the evening, burning coals are placed on the inner altar on top of the ashes that remain from the morning. Fourth, in the morning the lamps are tended. After the depleted wicks are removed and put in the container with the ashes from the incense altar, the lamps are filled with oil. In the evening, a burning coal is taken with tongs from the incense altar to light the lamps. Fifth, the high priest burns fragrant incense on the inner altar. After this, he comes out of the tent of meeting. If this sequence is correct, then the high priest begins at the font, enters the holy place, goes to the incense altar, then to the lampstand, before going to the golden table, moving to the incense altar, and completing the rite by leaving the tent of meeting.

The incense rite is one of the most essential sequences of ritual acts in the daily divine service. Every part of it is equally important. While the focus of the rite is on burning incense, there is a correlation between it and the ritual activities at the font, wearing the unique vestments by the high priest, the activities at the lampstand, and those at the table. Together with the preceding blood rite and the following burning rite, the incense rite is one of the most crucial parts of the daily service.

---

67. Exod 28:43 and 30:19–20 seems to indicate that Aaron and his sons enter the tent of meeting to perform the ritual activities there. While the reference to *his sons* could be his descendants who succeed him as high priest, the context may indicate that his immediate sons also enter the tent of meeting with him. Exod 28:1 may designate both kinds of *sons,* Aaron's four sons that are mentioned by name, as well as his descendants that are the future high priests. Furthermore, Exod 28:43 refers to future priests as *descendants,* זֶרַע. Thus, the word *sons,* בְּנֵי, most likely refers to his four sons, in this context. Aaron's immediate sons probably enter into the tent of meeting to assist him there. Exod 30:7–8, however, makes it clear that the ritual activities in the tent of meeting must be performed by the high priest. If any other priests enter with him, then it is only to assist him. See Haran, *Temples and Temple Service*, 206–7.

68. Haran claims that the wearing of the vestments by the high priest constitutes three distinct ritual activities, which include the bells, the stones on the ephod and breast piece, and the diadem. Haran states that there are six ritual activities performed in the holy place, the three with the ornate vestments as well as the other three at the incense altar, the menorah, and the golden table (Haran, *Temples and Temple Service*, 216).

The Burning Rite

The burning rite is the last of the three central rites of the daily divine service. Without it the daily service could not function properly as a whole and in all of its parts. Its importance cannot be overemphasized. Together with splashing blood and burning incense, smoking up the offerings is the last of the three central and most significant rites of the daily service.

Three ritual acts are involved in placing materials on the burning coals on the altar in the burning rite.

First, the lamb is burned and so sent up in smoke on the altar for burnt offering. Two lambs are offered on the altar each day, one lamb every morning and one lamb every evening (Exod 29:38–39; Num 28:3–4).[69] New wood is placed on the burning coals before the parts of the animal are placed on the altar (Lev 1:12, 17). The burning coals are on the bottom, wood is placed on the coals, and the materials for the offerings are placed on the wood after it is ignited and reduced to new burning coals. Furthermore, Lev 3:5; 6:5 [12] suggest that the pieces of the lamb are placed on the altar and cover the entire surface of burning coals so that it becomes the foundation upon which all the other offerings are laid.[70] The lamb is the first of the ritual materials placed on the newly burning coals on the altar.

Second, the accompanying cereal offering is placed upon the pieces of the lamb on the altar. Exod 29:40–41; Num 28:5, 8 legislate that every morning and evening the cereal offering must be offered with the lamb. Unlike the lamb, however, the entire cereal offering is not smoked up on the altar.[71] Only a memorial portion of the cereal offering is actually burned (Lev 6:8 [15]). The priest takes a handful of the cereal offering, together with all of

---

69. Propp does not interpret Exod 29:38–42 as the public daily burnt offering, but rather as referring to part of the prescription for the ordination offering. He views Num 28:3–8 as the prescription for the daily burnt offering. Propp understands the burnt offering in Exod 29:38–42 as prototypical to, but not the public daily burnt offering itself, that is offered every morning and evening throughout the entire year (Propp, *Exodus 19–40*, 471). I follow the interpretation of Haran, *Temples and Temple Service*, 207; Kleinig, *Lord's Song*, 74; *Leviticus*, 4, 49; Levine, *Leviticus*, 35; Milgrom, *Leviticus 1–16*, 163, that Exod 29:38–42 prescribes the public daily burnt offering.

70. See also Exod 29:25; Lev 8:28; 9:14, 17. Placing the lamb's parts on the newly burning wood that is on the burning bed of coals would bank the fire so that the wood does not burn up as quickly as if it were placed on an open flame. Thus, the meat smolders on the burning wood and produces smoke. All other offerings on the altar, such as grain, sin, guilt, and peace offerings, are placed on top of the lamb for the public daily burnt offering to smoke up a soothing aroma to the LORD (Kleinig, *Leviticus*, 85, 91).

71. As was discussed in the section on the blood rite, the skin of the lamb is the only part of a burnt offering that is not incinerated on the altar.

the incense that had been presented on it, and puts it on the altar with the animal for the burnt offering.

Third, the bread offering of the high priest is placed upon the memorial portion of the cereal offering and the lamb on the altar fire. Lev 6:12–16 [19–23] requires this bread to be offered on the altar. The high priest offers half of it in the morning service and the other half in the evening service. Since the lamb is placed on the altar first, and the cereal offering second, the bread offering of the high priest is the last of the ritual materials placed on the altar in the daily divine service.[72]

The order in which these three ritual materials are put on the altar is reasonably certain. In both Exod 29:38–42 and Num 28:1–8 the cereal offering accompanies the lamb for the burnt offering, indicating that the lamb is placed on the altar first and the cereal offering is placed on the altar after it. In Lev 1–2, the various kinds of offerings are recorded in the following order: burnt offerings, cereal offerings, and bread offerings that could be in the form of cakes or wafers prepared either on a griddle or in a pan. Furthermore, Lev 6:1–16 [8–23] lists the regulations for the burnt offering first, the cereal offering second, and the bread offering of the high priest third. It makes the most sense that the order in which these offerings are recorded in the Pentateuch is the same order in which they are placed on the altar.[73]

There is some uncertainty about when the quarter of a hin of wine or fermented beverage[74] for the drink offering is poured out in the burning rite.[75] Based on Exod 29:40–41; Num 28:7–8 the drink offering is probably poured out every morning and evening after the lamb and cereal offering are placed on the altar.[76] Yet, is the drink offering poured out before or after

---

72. Kleinig and Milgrom claim that the daily bread offering of the high priest is the last offering of the day that is sent up in smoke on the altar (Kleinig, *Leviticus*, 154–57; Milgrom, *Leviticus 1–16*, 399). This indicates that it is also the last offering turned into smoke on the altar in the morning service, since the procedure for the morning burning rite is the same as that of the evening.

73. *Tamid* 7:3 states that the parts of the lamb are placed on the altar first, the cereal offering is placed on the altar second, and the high priest's bread offering is placed on the altar last at the temple in Jerusalem (Blackman, *Kodashim*, 486–96). This evidence supports my view, that the same order is followed in the morning and evening offerings at the tabernacle.

74. Exod 29:40 specifies that the beverage for the drink offering is wine, while Num 28:7 refers to it as a fermented beverage. This may imply that any quarter of a hin (about one liter or quart) of alcoholic beverage could be offered as a drink offering in the daily divine service.

75. Exod 25:29; 37:16; Num 4:7 indicate that the vessels used for pouring out the drink offerings may be part of those of the golden table in the tent of meeting.

76. Lev 23:13, 18, 37 prescribe that a cereal offering and a drink offering must accompany all burnt offerings, and possibly all peace offerings. See also Num 15:5, 7, 10,

52   The LORD's Service

the bread offering of the high priest is placed on it? The biblical text does not answer this question.[77] According to *Tamid* 4:3; 7:3 the drink offering is poured out at the temple in Jerusalem after all the ritual materials, including the bread offering of the high priest, are placed on the altar.[78] Since there is no evidence to the contrary, this appears to be the most logical place within the order of the service for the drink offering to be poured out.[79]

The priests wash their hands and feet as the initial ritual act in the burning rite. It was established in the sections on the fire rite and the presentation rite that according to the ritual legislation in Exod 30:20 the priests must wash their hands and feet whenever they approach the altar. Although the priests have already washed their hands and feet several times before this in the service, they must wash them once again before performing the ritual activities in the burning rite. Since the washing is a precondition for the other activities it must come first in this part of the service, just as it does in the fire, presentation, and incense rites.[80]

The only other ritual activity performed in the burning rite at both the morning and evening offerings is the high priest wearing his ornate vestments. All the priests must wear their vestments whenever they approach the altar for burnt offering to minister before the LORD (Exod 28:42–43). This is especially true for the high priest. The argument that has been made about the vestments of the high priest in the section on the incense rite also applies to the burning rite. These ornate garments serve a more ritually significant function than the regular vestments at the incense rite in the tent of meeting. The same is true about the burning rite at the outer altar, although

---

24; 28:9, 12–14, 20–21, 28–29, 31; 29:3, 4, 9–10, 14–15, 18, 21, 24, 27, 30, 33, 37. These verses indicate that the portions for the accompanying cereal and drink offerings are not always the same as those for the daily burnt offering.

77. Neither of the diagrams by Kleinig explicitly includes the bread offering of the high priest in the order of the service. He holds, however, that the drink offering comes after the placement of all the other ritual materials on the altar (Kleinig, *Lord's Song*, 132; *Leviticus*, 39).

78. See Blackman, *Kodashim*, 486–87, 495–96.

79. There is some uncertainty about where the drink offering is poured out. Is it on the other offerings that are placed on the altar? Is it beside the altar? Is it somewhere else? The question about the location of the libation is dealt with in the next chapter.

80. In the morning service, the priests wash their hands and feet at the beginning of the fire, presentation, incense, and burning rites. In the evening, they wash their hands and feet at the beginning of the fire, incense, and burning rites. The difference is because the ashes are not removed and carried outside the camp in the evening, and thus, the washing of hands and feet remains effective through the fire, presentation, and blood rites. There are, therefore, seven significant times every day that the priests wash their hands and feet from the font while they perform the duties of the daily divine service.

the functions of each rite are distinct.[81] Furthermore, just as the high priest washes before he wears the ornate vestments into the tent of meeting, so also he washes his hands and feet prior to wearing the ornate vestments in the burning rite. While the vestments of the regular priests chiefly prepare them for service, the ornate vestments of the high priest are more ritually significant. Therefore, the high priest wears his vestments in the burning rite as its second ritual act.

Based on the preceding analysis, the burning rite consists of a sequence of ritual activities. First, the priests wash their hands and feet from the font. Second, the high priest wears his vestments at the altar for burnt offering as he and the other priests perform its ritual activities. Third, the materials for the offering are placed on the altar fire. This involves three steps for both the morning and the evening. The lamb is arranged on the fire first, before the memorial portion of the cereal offering is put on the lamb, after which the bread offering of the high priest is placed on the altar. Finally, the wine or fermented beverage for the drink offering is poured out. This is the order for the burning rite of both the morning and evening offerings in the daily divine service.

The burning rite is one of the most essential parts of the daily service. Its ritual acts, together with the blood rite and the incense rite, form the core of the service. All of the rites for the morning and evening offerings coincide with the burning rite as a unified whole. Smoking up the offerings, together with the other two central rites, comprise the climax of the daily divine service.

THE CONCLUDING RITES

The Blessing Rite

The blessing rite is the first of two concluding rites in the morning and evening in the daily service. It is composed of two ritual acts, sounding the silver trumpets over the burnt offering and performing the benediction.

---

81. Haran claims that the outer vestments of the high priest are not worn in the burning rite at the outer altar. Rather, he sees them as exclusively connected to the ritual activities inside the tent of meeting (Haran, *Temples and Temple Service*, 211–12). This appears to contradict the prescription that the priests' vestments, including those of the high priest, must be worn when they enter the tent of meeting or approach the altar to minister (Exod 28:43). In Lev 16:24, the legislation for the Day of Atonement shows that the high priest wears all of his vestments at the outer altar when he places the burnt offering on the altar. Therefore, the high priest most likely wears all of his ornate garments while he performs the burning rite in the daily divine service.

The Pentateuch does not specify at what point within the service the blessing must be proclaimed. It only prescribes that it must be done.[82] In Num 6:22–27 the LORD commands Moses to tell Aaron and his sons how they are to bless the Israelites. They must say to them, "The LORD bless you and keep you; the LORD shine his face upon you and favor you; the LORD lift up his face toward you and give to you peace." By this announcement, the priests place the name of the LORD upon the Israelites for him to bless them. Since Aaron and his sons perform the benediction, it is a priestly act done in the divine service.[83] The Pentateuch, however, never legislates when it should be spoken in the service.

There are several clues within and outside the Pentateuch that help determine where the benediction occurs in the daily service.

The legislation for the daily burnt offering in Exod 29:38–43 shows a sequence of events that may shed light on the location of the blessing within the service. First, the offerings are placed on the altar, including the burnt offering and accompanying cereal offering. Second, the drink offering is poured out. Third, the LORD meets with and speaks to Moses. Finally, the LORD meets with Israel and consecrates them. In Exod 29:42 the LORD promises to regularly gather at the entrance to the tent of meeting to *speak* to Moses.[84] This verse indicates that the meeting and speaking would con-

---

82. Levine notes the etymological difficulty of the Hebrew word for bless, בֵּרֵךְ. He maintains that it is possible for it to come from בְּרָכָה, which he translates as *gift*. Therefore, to bless is to request or bestow a gift from the LORD (Levine, "*Lpny* YHWH," 227). Mitchell, however, cautions against trying to determine the meaning of ברך solely based on its etymology. Rather, a number of factors define how it must be understood, such as when, where, and by whom it is spoken. See his comprehensive analysis of the meaning of ברך in the Old Testament (Mitchell, *Meaning of brk*).

83. Since, according to Num 6:22, 27, Aaron *and* his sons are to give the blessing, and *they* will put the name of the LORD on the Israelites, it seems that all the priests announce the blessing together. *Tamid* 7:2 records that all the priests on duty at the temple in Jerusalem speak the blessing together (Blackman, *Kodashim*, 494). Sir 50:20 states that only the high priest gives the blessing. Although there is a lack of agreement, Num 6:22, 27 may support the view that all the priests announce the blessing to the congregation each morning and evening at the tabernacle. Kleinig claims that more than one priest announces the benediction (Kleinig, *Lord's Song*, 132). He, however, may have revised this view (Kleinig, *Leviticus*, 39). Mitchell, too, seems to agree that not only the high priest but all of the priests speak the benediction together (Mitchell, *Meaning of brk*, 96–98).

84. In this context, the LORD declares, *I will meet with you* (plural) *and speak to you* (singular). While Exod 29:42 refers to the LORD meeting with and speaking to Moses or the high priest, 29:43 records that the LORD will meet with the sons of Israel. Since the LORD manifests himself to the Israelites, not only through the smoke from the offerings but also through the blessing by the priests, Exod 29:43 could imply such a revelation of the LORD in the benediction too. See also Propp, *Exodus 19–40*, 355.

tinue throughout the generations of Israel. Since Moses' death would prevent him from continuing to speak to the LORD at the sanctuary, in this passage Moses most likely represents every high priest or his deputy. If so, then the LORD promises to meet with and speak to the high priest in the daily service. Exod 29:42–43 implies that after the LORD speaks to the high priest, he announces the benediction to Israel on behalf of the LORD.[85] Exod 29:38–43, therefore, indicates that the blessing comes after the placement of the offerings on the altar.

Lev 9:22–23 tells of the performance of two blessings in the inaugural service. The first blessing is announced only by Aaron, after the offerings have been placed on the altar. Following the first blessing, Moses and Aaron enter into the tent of meeting and then come out to perform the second benediction. With this second blessing, fire comes out from the presence of the LORD and consumes the offerings on the altar. Since the inaugural service is enacted for a different purpose than the daily service, its ritual activities are unique. Yet, a pattern may be determined from it. The blessings *follow* the chief rites.[86] They come after the priests have entered the tent of meeting to burn incense and have approached the altar to place the offerings on it. There is a difference, however, between the two blessings at the inaugural service. While the first blessing is apparently only an announcement of peace, due to its proximity with the peace offering, the second blessing coincides with the divine fire as an epiphany of the presence of God.[87] It makes the most sense, therefore, that in all subsequent daily services the

---

85. The blessing by the high priest is significant since he wears the gold plate, inscribed with "YHWH's holiness," on his turban. As he blesses the congregation with the three-fold name of the LORD, they see the divine name borne on his head. *Tamid* 7:2 states that at the temple in Jerusalem the high priest raises his hands to the level of the golden plate on his head while he announces the blessing to the congregation (Blackman, *Kodashim*, 494–95). Most likely, the high priest stands between the altar for burnt offering and the opening to the courtyard facing the congregation with the altar behind him (Kleinig, *Leviticus*, 218). If so, then the manifestation of the presence of the LORD in the smoke rising from the altar combines with the name of the LORD on the diadem and the words spoken to the people. The congregation sees the name, יהוה, and hears it three times in the blessing as if it is coming from the smoke rising from the altar.

86. Levine holds that the blessing spoken at the end of the inaugural service is the benediction from Num 6:24–26 (Levine, "*Lpny* YHWH," 227).

87 Kleinig claims that the first blessing coincides with the peace offering (Kleinig, *Leviticus*, 217). If the benediction from Num 6:24–26 is spoken at the first blessing in the inaugural service, then the declaration of *peace* at the end of the benediction corresponds with the peace offering, which is designated by a form of the same word, שָׁלוֹם. The purpose of the second blessing, however, is to bring the blessing of the LORD out from his presence in the tent of meeting, indicating that the LORD has emerged from it to bestow his blessing on his people. See also Levine, "*Lpny* YHWH," 243–44; Mitchell, *Meaning of brk*, 97.

blessing would coincide with the manifestation of the divine fire as the offerings are smoked up from it every morning and evening. If so, then only one blessing is announced as the epiphany of the LORD each morning and each evening *after* the offerings are placed on the altar and the smoke rises from it.[88]

Two other passages in the Pentateuch refer to the priestly blessing. Deut 10:8; 21:5 may indicate that the blessing comes after the other parts of the service. Both passages record that the LORD set apart the Levites as priests to *serve*[89] him and to *bless* in his name.[90] If their serving refers to the ritual activities in the tent of meeting and at the altar for burnt offering, then this may imply that the blessing comes after them. Thus, the two passages from Deuteronomy might confirm that the blessing is performed after the burnt offering is put on the altar.

Texts outside the Pentateuch show continuity with Deuteronomy and explain where the blessing occurs in the service each morning and evening. In 1 Chr 23:13, Aaron and his descendants are set apart to *burn incense* before the LORD, to *serve*[91] him, and to *bless* in his name. Burning incense in the tent of meeting, ministering at the altar for burnt offering, and blessing comprise the sequence of three main ritual enactments in the daily divine

---

88. Milgrom and Noth hold that the blessing comes at the conclusion of the service, based on the second blessing at the inaugural service in Lev 9 (Milgrom, *Leviticus 1–16*, 18; Noth, *Leviticus*, 58). See also Coffman, *Leviticus and Numbers*, 320; Kleinig, *Lord's Song*, 132; *Leviticus*, 217.

89. The Hebrew verb לְשָׁרְתוֹ, from שָׁרַת, in Deut 10:8; 21:5 is also used in Exod 28:35, 43; 29:30; 30:20. These contexts specify ritual acts that are performed by the high priest or regular priests in Israel's divine services. Therefore, לְשָׁרְתוֹ is best translated *to serve* or *to minister*. See also 1 Chr 23:13; Knoppers, *1 Chronicles 10–29*, 809.

90. Gray claims that all the Levites pronounce the blessing, based on Deut 10:8; 21:5 (Gray, *Numbers*, 72). See also Noth, *Leviticus*, 57–58. First Chronicles 6:48–49 distinguishes between the ritual duties of the priests and the Levites who are not priests. Furthermore, 1 Chr 23 spells out the specific duties of the Levites, who are to assist the priests. This implies that only the priests speak the benediction. See Mitchell, *Meaning of brk*, 98. The song that is sung by the Levitical choir in Chronicles, however, could be an extension of the blessing. Since the Levites no longer need to carry the tabernacle and its furnishings after entering the land, they are reassigned other duties. One of these duties, עֲבֹדָת, is to sing in the regular divine services. First Chronicles 25:1–3 refers to this work at the sanctuary as prophesying, הַנִּבָּא. By calling the singing and playing of musical instruments by the Levites *prophesying*, the Chronicler may view these duties as an extension of the blessing. For a discussion about the nature of the Levitical prophesying in 1 Chr 25:1–6, see Kleinig, *Lord's Song*, 148–57.

91. Knoppers, *1 Chronicles 10–29*, 809, holds that the verb לְשָׁרְתוֹ means to serve at the altar for burnt offering, performing ritual acts, and ministering at the sanctuary. Since the same word refers to serving at the tent of meeting in Exod 28:35, 43; 29:30; 30:20 and Deut 10:8; 21:5, it most likely designates the ministry of the daily divine service in 1 Chr 23:13.

service. This further supports the view that in Deuteronomy *serving the LORD* means to serve him by making offerings on the outer altar.[92] Since serving is distinguished from burning incense and announcing the blessing, the order in which 1 Chr 23:13 lists them probably designates the order in which they are performed. Sir 50:5–21 states that the high priest comes out of the holy place, before he puts the offerings on the outer altar, after which he pours out the drink offering. Next, he blesses the people who had prostrated themselves when the trumpets were sounded. Assuming that he comes forth from the holy place after burning incense on the inner altar, the order is similar to the one mentioned in 1 Chr 23:13. This strengthens the argument that the blessing comes after the burnt offering is placed on the altar in the morning and evening services.

The evidence from the biblical texts inside and outside the Pentateuch support the position that the benediction is announced to Israel after the offerings are placed on the altar and the drink offering is poured out at the sanctuary.

The other ritual activity in the blessing rite is sounding the silver trumpets.[93] Num 10:1–10 prescribes that two silver trumpets must be constructed and that the priests are to blow them with different sounds for different purposes. Num 10:10 states that the trumpets are sounded in the day of gladness, in the appointed times, on the first of months, and over the burnt offerings and peace offerings. At first, this does not appear to indicate that the trumpets are sounded over the burnt offerings in the daily divine service.[94] This is especially true if the *appointed times* are references to those in Lev 23,[95] which includes the Sabbath, Passover, Unleavened Bread, Firstfruits, Pentecost, Acclamation, Atonement, and Tabernacles. No mention is made of the daily burnt offering. In Num 28–29, however, which also prescribe the offerings for the *appointed times*, the public daily burnt offering is included.[96] Therefore, when Num 10:10 stipulates that the silver trumpets

---

92. See Kleinig, *Lord's Song*, 105–6.

93. Num 10:10 is the only place in the Bible that prescribes the use of the silver trumpets in the divine service (Levine, "*Lpny* YHWH," 303).

94. The reference in Number 10:8 to the sounding of the silver trumpets as a *statute forever* means that they would be a permanent feature of Israel's cult (Levine, "*Lpny* YHWH," 306).

95. Gray claims that Num 10:10 refers to the appointed times mentioned in Lev 23 (Gray, *Numbers*, 89).

96. Milgrom recognizes that the trumpets are sounded twice daily in the divine service. He attributes this to the inclusion of the daily burnt offering as an *appointed time* in Num 28:1–8; 29:39 (Milgrom, *Numbers*, 75). Budd also references Num 28–29 as the appointed times mentioned in Num 10:10, but he does not view the daily service as part of them (Budd, *Numbers*, 107–8). For a similar position, see also Noth, *Leviticus*, 75.

must be sounded over the burnt offerings at the *appointed times*, this includes the regular morning and evening offerings in the daily divine service.

Several texts outside the Pentateuch support the view that the trumpets are sounded over the burnt offerings every day. According to 1 Chr 16:6, the trumpets are blown by the priests regularly, תָּמִיד. As has been noted previously, the word תָּמִיד usually refers to the ritual activities performed in the daily divine service. In the second temple period it became the name that designated the daily service.[97] Thus, 1 Chr 16:6 gives evidence that the trumpets are played daily. It is also significant that only two men are named as the trumpet players in this verse, which seems to support that each of them sounded one of the trumpets. This verse, however, indicates that the trumpets are sounded before the ark of the testimony in Jerusalem, in the unusual era of Israel's history when the tabernacle remained at Gibeon. Yet, according to 1 Chr 16:42 two priests are responsible for blowing the trumpets at the tabernacle where the burnt offerings are offered every day (1 Chr 16:40). Evidently, trumpets are sounded at both places every morning and evening.[98] Sir 50 also speaks of the priests sounding the trumpets over the burnt offering in the daily divine service. Finally, *Tamid* 7:3 affirms that the trumpets are sounded over the burnt offering each day at the temple in Jerusalem.[99] These sources concur with the position that the priests sound forth the trumpets in the daily service, and not merely at the appointed times other than each morning and evening.

Which comes before and after the other in this part of the service, the blessing or sounding the trumpets? The Pentateuch does not answer this question. Yet, it makes the most sense that the blessing follows the sounding of the trumpets. Since the trumpets are blown after the offerings are placed on the altar, the blessing probably occurs after the trumpets are sounded.[100] As *Tamid* 7:3 shows, there are a series of times that the trumpets are played at the temple in Jerusalem. One is after the offerings are placed on the altar and the drink offering is poured out; the other is after the Levitical choir

---

97. For further discussion about the use of תָּמִיד in 1 Chr 16, see Kleinig, *Lord's Song*, 53, 136, 145; Knoppers, *1 Chronicles 10–29*, 643,

98. Kleinig and Knoppers do not hold that 1 Chr 16:42 indicates that the priests sound the trumpets at the tabernacle at Gibeon (Kleinig, *Lord's Song*, 53; Knoppers, *1 Chronicles 10–29*, 640–41). The word לְמַשְׁמִיעִים, however, which literally means *for them to cause to hear*, likely refers to the priests making sounds on them. First Chronicles 16:42 probably implies that the priests sound the trumpets both at the tabernacle at Gibeon and simultaneously before the ark in Jerusalem.

99. See Blackman, *Kodashim*, 496.

100. See Kleinig, *Leviticus*, 39.

completes each verse of their song. *Tamid* 7:2, however, indicates that the benediction takes place before the priests place the offerings on the altar.[101] While this may reflect the practice at the temple in Jerusalem in a certain period, other evidence shows a different order especially in light of the analysis of the blessing rite previously discussed. Sir 50:13–21 records that the offerings are placed on the altar before the drink offering is poured out followed by the trumpets being sounded after which the blessing is announced to the congregation. This seems to be more in line with the biblical texts previously mentioned. I assume that order. Therefore, the sounding of the trumpets likely precedes the blessing.[102]

In summary, two ritual activities are enacted in the blessing rite. First, the priests sound the silver trumpets over the burnt offering. Second, the Aaronic benediction is performed. These occur in the morning and in the evening every day in the daily divine service. The blessing rite is the first of the two concluding rites. The second concluding rite completes the service each morning and each evening.

The Meal Rite

The meal rite is the last of the concluding rites. It brings to a close the sequence of rites for the morning offering and the evening offering. The meal rite consists of two ritual acts: eating the most holy food and taking off the sacred vestments.

The Pentateuch never indicates at what point in the service that the most holy food must be eaten or when the sacred vestments must be taken off. It is most logical, however, that these acts would come at the end of the morning and the evening services.[103] Since the vestments are worn while the priests perform their ritual activities within the walls of the tabernacle and

---

101. See Blackman, *Kodashim*, 494–96.

102. This order may further be supported by 2 Chr 29:28, where the trumpets seem to be the signal for the congregation to prostrate themselves. If this is true, then the priests blow the trumpets, the people prostrate themselves, the high priest blesses them, and the Levitical choir sings its song. At the end of each verse, the trumpets are sounded and the people prostrate themselves. Evidently, this occurred repeatedly until the burnt offering was completed. See Kleinig, *Lord's Song*, 81–82, 95, 120–22.

103. Kleinig states that the flour is kept in common storage with the private cereal offerings, and from this, the priests' daily bread is made as their portion from the table of the LORD. He holds that the priests eat their bread from the cereal offerings between the morning and evening offerings as part of their midday meal in the LORD's house (Kleinig, *Leviticus*, 150). He does not state whether the priests eat meals as part of the morning and evening offerings in the daily divine service.

removed before leaving it,[104] one of the final acts that the priests perform in the divine service is taking off their vestments. Likewise, the priests can eat the most holy food from the cereal offering only after the token portion has been placed on the altar and the rest of it baked. As has been established in the discussion of the burning rite, the cereal offering is offered in the form of fine flour, not baked bread or cakes. Because it would take some time to bake the cereal offering, eating the most holy food probably comes after all the other rites have been completed. The meal rite must be the final one that the priests perform each morning and evening in the daily divine service.

The priests eat the remaining portion of the cereal offering. Since a handful of the cereal offering is burned on the altar with all of the frankincense that was presented with it (Lev 6:8–9 [15–16]), the priests eat the rest of the cereal offering as most holy food.[105] In Lev 6:9–10 [16–17], it is noted that the cereal offering, which consists of fine flour mixed with beaten olive oil, must not be baked with yeast or eaten with it.[106] Although Lev 2:4–7 indicates three ordinary ways that grain offerings may be prepared, baked in an oven, cooked on a griddle, or baked in a pan,[107] the daily cereal offering must only be baked (Lev 6:9–10 [16–17]). After the most holy food from the cereal offering is prepared, Lev 6:9 [16] specifies that the priests eat it in a holy place in the courtyard of the tabernacle.[108]

At the end of the service, the priests need to remove their sacred vestments before they leave the tabernacle precincts. The Pentateuch never

---

104. See Lev 6:4 [11], as well as the discussion about vesting and divesting in the section on the fire rite in this chapter.

105. Milgrom explains that the burnt offering, the cereal offering, the sin offering, and the guilt offering are *most holy*, while the rest, such as peace offerings, are *holy*. Furthermore, he claims that the designations *holy* and *most holy* always apply to the portions of the offerings that are eaten (Milgrom, *Leviticus 1–16*, 394–95).

106. A similar prohibition against any leavening agent in the cereal offerings is seen in Lev 2:11. Yeast and other kinds of leaven are commonly used in baking, but are excluded for practical and symbolic reasons. Practically, without leaven bread lasts longer and is less subject to mould and decay. Symbolically, the leaven is associated with corruption, sickness, and even death. Because these are ritually unclean, they are not compatible with the holiness of God and his sanctuary (Kleinig, *Leviticus*, 76–77). See also Milgrom, *Leviticus 1–16*, 188–89.

107. Kleinig identifies the prepared cereal offering as unleavened flat cakes (*Leviticus*, 151). Lev 6:9 [16] refers to the cooked portion of the cereal offering as מַצּוֹת, unleavened bread or cakes (BDB 595).

108. Because of the *most holy* status of the cereal offering, it had to be eaten in the LORD's presence at the sanctuary. The exact location is not specified in the Pentateuch, but it is probably near the altar for burnt offering on its west side (Kleinig, *Leviticus*, 150). See also Lev 10:12–13. Milgrom attests that the designation *holy place* in Lev 6:9 [16] does not mean the holy place inside the tent of meeting, but rather the tabernacle courtyard (Milgrom, *Leviticus 1–16*, 392).

states that the priests remove their vestments at the end of the service, but this may be implied in Lev 6:4 [11] in relation to the ritual vesting for maintaining the fire on the altar for burnt offering. In the section on the fire rite, it was determined that the priests could not wear the sacred vestments to carry the ashes outside the tent of meeting.[109] The sacred vestments are anointed with the holy anointing oil, and since the vestments are holy, they must only be used for holy purposes.[110] Just as it is necessary for the priest who clears the altar ashes to remove his vestments before carrying them outside the camp, so also the priests must remove their vestments before leaving the courtyard for any reason.[111]

The removal of the vestments prior to leaving the sanctuary occurs at the temple in Jerusalem too. Ezek 42:14 states that the priests must not leave the holy precincts until they have taken off their holy vestments in which they minister before the LORD.[112] They are required to put on common clothes before they go into the places that are for the people. Ezek 44:19 further explains that the reason the priests must not wear the holy vestments among the people is so that they would not transmit holiness to the people by means of them.[113] Both of these passages indicate that there are

---

109. In the fire rite, the priest who clears the ashes and adds wood to the burning coals on the altar must put on his sacred vestments before going near the altar to perform these ritual activities. He must also remove them before carrying the ashes outside the camp. This shows that the sacred vestments can never be worn anywhere except within the confines of the tabernacle courtyard.

110. See Kleinig, *Leviticus*, 147; Milgrom, *Leviticus 1–16*, 386–87, for further details about the holy nature and holy purpose of the sacred vestments.

111. In the section on the fire rite, it was noted that there is a similarity between the special vestments of the high priest and the normal vestments that he and the regular priests wear. Just as the special vestments that the high priest wears into the most holy place on the Day of Atonement must only be worn inside the tent of meeting, so also the normal vestments of the high priest and the other priests must only be worn within the courtyard and in the holy place. None of the holy garments may be worn outside the sanctuary.

112. Due to the contagious aspect of holiness, holy things must not come into contact with common things (Hummel, *Ezekiel 21–48*, 1225). The holy vestments would be desecrated by being taken out to the common area of the people. For this reason, the priests must put on common clothes to return to the common domain.

113. Hummel makes the connection between the contagious holiness of the sacred vestments and the most holy offerings. He maintains that the Pentateuch does not explicitly refer to the sacred vestments as *most holy* nor does it contain any prohibitions about the laity coming in contact with them (Hummel, *Ezekiel 21–48*, 1281). The common area of the people at the temple in Jerusalem mentioned in Ezek 42 and 44, however, is not to be confused with the entrance to the tent of meeting where the Israelites bring their offerings. Compare Block's diagram of Ezekiel's temple (Block, *Ezekiel*, 508–9) and Kleinig's diagram of the tabernacle (Kleinig, *Leviticus*, 48). The area of the people at the temple is outside the courtyard of the sanctuary, and is referred to as the

special rooms where the priests change their clothes and store their holy vestments at the temple in Jerusalem.[114] They put on their common clothes to leave the sanctuary. The practice reflected in Ezekiel further supports the idea that the priests remove their sacred vestments at the end of the service before leaving the tabernacle.

Which of the ritual acts in the meal rite comes before and after the other, eating the most holy food or divesting the sacred vestments? The Pentateuch does not explicitly answer this question. The legislation and description of the ordination service, however, may give clues to the sequence of these ritual acts. Exod 29:5–9, 29–30 prescribe the priests to wear their vestments in the ordination service. Exod 29:31–34 describes how, after this, the priests are to prepare and eat the food from the ordination offerings. Similarly, Lev 8:7–13, 30 describes the priests vesting at their ordination, and 8:31–32 reports that Moses commands the priests to cook and eat the food from their ordination offerings.[115] Since the vesting comes before the eating in each of these passages, this may indicate that the priests must wear their vestments while they eat the food from the offerings at their ordination. The precedent set at the ordination service could imply that the priests are required to wear their vestments while they eat the sacred meal every morning and evening in the daily service. Furthermore, Ezek 42:13–14 may entail the priests eating the most holy food prior to removing their sacred vestments. Verse 13 speaks of the priests eating the sacred meal in special rooms at the temple in Jerusalem, while verse 14 speaks of taking off the holy vestments before leaving the temple precincts. Since eating the most holy food is listed before the priests remove their sacred vestments, these verses may indicate the sequence of the meal rite in the daily divine service.[116] The evi-

---

outer court. Conversely, there is no courtyard of the people at the tabernacle. I see no discrepancy between the prohibitions against the priests wearing the sacred vestments outside the temple in Ezekiel and the practice at the tabernacle.

114. The area of the rooms at Ezekiel's temple where the sacred vestments must be stored is within the sacred area of the courtyard. For further explanation about the rooms in this area of Ezekiel's temple see Zimmerli, *Ezekiel*, 392–401, 459.

115. There is a relation between the initial vesting of the priests and the eating of the food at their ordination. The word for *ordination* is הַמִּלֻּאִים, the filling. At the ordination of the priests, their hands are filled with their priestly dues. See also Propp on the *filling of the hands* (Propp, *Exodus 19–40*, 452), and Milgrom's comments about the ordination service (Milgrom, *Leviticus 1–16*, 531–42). In the service, the vestments are consecrated after the priests put them on and the ceremony ends with the sacred banquet at the tabernacle in which the priests eat the remaining portion of the food that filled their hands and was offered on the altar (Kleinig, *Leviticus*, 202). See also Gorman, *Ideology of Ritual*, 103–39; Haran, *Temples and Temple Service*, 169–71; Klingbeil, *Comparative Study of Ritual Ordination*, 143–66, 177–91, 208–16.

116. Hummel implies this by connecting the place at Ezekiel's temple where the

The Practical Order of the Daily Divine Service 63

dence points to the priests eating the most holy food while they are wearing the sacred vestments.[117] They probably remove their holy garments as the last ritual act of the meal rite in the daily divine service.

The final rite for the morning offering and the evening offering is the sacred meal. Eating the most holy food from the cereal offering and divesting of the sacred clothing brings to an end all the ritual activities in the daily divine service of ancient Israel. The meal rite follows all the other rites and depends on their completion before it can be enacted. It is the last of the two concluding rites.

---

priests eat the most holy food with the place where they leave their sacred vestments. These are not two different locations, but the same place. The place where the priests eat the most holy food is where they put on and take off their sacred vestments (Hummel, *Ezekiel 21–48*, 1224–25). See also Zimmerli, *Ezekiel*, 400.

117. A comparison may be made between proper attire required for attending a banquet and the sacred vestments being required to eat the most holy food by the priests at the tabernacle. It seems unlikely that the priests would wear their common clothes while they eat the most holy food from the cereal offering. Rather, as guests at the LORD's house they must be properly clothed with the vestments that the LORD himself supplies to them while they eat the food from his holy table.

	Morning Service						
	Initial Rites		Central Rites			Concluding Rites	
	1. Fire	2. Presentation	3. Blood	4. Incense	5. Burning	6. Blessing	7. Meal
a.	Washing hands and feet with water from the font	Washing hands and feet with water from the font	Slaying lamb on north side of outer altar and presentation of blood	Washing hands and feet with water from the font	Washing hands and feet with water from the font	Sounding the silver trumpets	Baking and eating the most holy bread by the priests at the sanctuary
b.	Vesting with sacred vestments	Vesting with sacred vestments	Splashing lamb's blood against four sides of the outer altar	Putting on and wearing high priest's vestments inside the tent of meeting	Wearing high priest's vestments at the outer altar	Blessing announced by high priest in front of the outer altar	Divesting the sacred vestments
c.	Removal of ashes from outer altar and coals for use on the inner altar	Inspection, presentation, and placing a hand on first lamb	Flaying and slaughter of lamb into sections	Removal of ashes from inner altar and adding burning coals to the inner altar	Burning the lamb with its cereal and high priest's bread offerings		
d.	Adding wood to the fire on the outer altar	Presentation of flour with oil, salt, and frankincense, and wine	Washing lamb's entrails and legs, and placing them with head, fat, and pieces	Tending lamps	Pouring out of wine at the outer altar		
e.	Divesting vestments and removal of ashes outside the camp	Presentation of first half of high priest's bread offering	Salting all its sections	Burning incense on inner altar			

	Evening Service						
	Initial Rites			Central Rites		Concluding Rites	
	1. Fire	2. Presentation	3. Blood	4. Incense	5. Burning	6. Blessing	7. Meal
a.	Washing hands and feet with water from the font	(Still washed from fire rite)	Slaying lamb on north side of outer altar and presentation of blood	Washing hands and feet with water from the font	Washing hands and feet with water from the font	Sounding the silver trumpets	Baking and eating the most holy bread by the priests at the sanctuary
b.	Vesting with sacred vestments	(Still vested from fire rite)	Splashing lamb's blood against four sides of the outer altar	Putting on and wearing high priest's vestments inside the tent of meeting	Wearing high priest's vestments at the outer altar	Blessing announced by high priest in front of the outer altar	Divesting the sacred vestments
c.	Removal of coals from outer altar for inner altar and for lighting lamps	Inspection, presentation, and placing a hand on second lamb	Flaying and slaughter of lamb into sections	Adding burning coals to the inner altar	Burning the lamb with its cereal and high priest's bread offerings		
d.	Adding wood to the fire on the outer altar	Presentation of flour with oil, salt, and frankincense, and wine	Washing lamb's entrails and legs, and placing them with head, fat, and pieces	Lighting lamps	Pouring out of wine at the outer altar		
e.		Presentation of second half of high priest's bread offering	Salting all its sections	Burning incense on inner altar			

Figure 1. The sequential order of the daily divine service.

CONCLUSIONS TO CHAPTER 2

The foregoing analysis of the ritual sections in the Pentateuch leads to conclusions about the practical order of the daily divine service of ancient Israel. The daily service consists of all the ritual activities in the morning and evening throughout the entire day. The morning service and evening service are composed of three sets of enactments: the initial rites, the central rites, and the concluding rites. These follow the same order for the morning as they do for the evening, yet with some variation.

The initial rites are the fire rite and the presentation rite. Within each of these, the ritual acts are slightly different from the morning to the evening. The maintenance of the fire in the morning consists of the following sequence. The priest on duty washes his hands and feet with water from the font and puts on his sacred vestments. Then, he removes the ashes of the previous day from the outer altar, and some lit coals for later use in the tent of meeting. After this, the priest places wood on the burning coals on the outer altar. Next, he takes off his sacred vestments, puts on common clothes, and carries the ashes outside the camp. The same order occurs in the evening with the exception that the ashes are not removed from the altar, and the priest does not need to change his clothes because there are no ashes to carry outside the camp. Similarly, the presentation of materials is not identical for the morning and evening services. In the morning, after the priest washes his hands and feet from the font, he puts on his sacred vestments. The lamb is presented, inspected, and the high priest lays his hand on it, after which the cereal offering and drink offering are presented. Finally, half of the bread offering of the high priest is presented before the LORD. In the evening, the priest does not wash or vest because he has already done so in the fire rite without taking his vestments off to leave the sanctuary, such as in the morning. This is the sequence of the ritual activities for the initial rites of the daily divine service.

Three things are done in the central rites; the blood is splashed on the altar, the incense is burned in the holy place, and the offerings are smoked up on the altar. The blood rite is identical in both the morning service and in the evening service. After the lamb is slain, its blood is splashed against the sides of the altar. Then the lamb is skinned, cut into pieces, and its entrails and lower legs are washed before they are placed with its other pieces. Once the lamb has been prepared, all of its parts are seasoned with salt. There is a slight variation from the morning incense rite to the one in the evening. In the morning, after the high priest washes his hands and feet from the font, he puts on and wears his ornate vestments inside the tent of meeting. Next, the ashes are removed from the incense altar and burning coals are added to it. Then the lamps are tended, and incense is placed on the burning coals on the inner altar. In the evening, the procedure is the same except that the ashes are not removed and the lamps are not tended but lit. The final central rite is the sending up of the offerings in smoke on the altar. The morning and the evening burning rites are identical. First, the priests wash their hands and feet from the font. Then, the high priest wears his ornate vestments at the outer altar. After the lamb, cereal, and bread offering of the high priest are placed on the altar, the drink offering is poured out. Splashing the blood, burning incense, and smoking up the offerings are the central rites of the daily burnt offering of ancient Israel.

The concluding rites consist of the priests performing the Aaronic benediction and their consumption of the most holy food. The number and sequence of ritual acts are identical for both the morning and the evening offerings. In the blessing rite, the priests sound the silver trumpets before the high priest announces the Aaronic benediction. In the meal rite, the priests eat the most holy food in the courtyard before they take off their sacred vestments. The concluding rites bring the morning and evening services to a close.

The daily divine service of ancient Israel follows a set order of seven rites. The priests maintain the fire on the altar for burnt offering and then present the materials to be offered on it. They splash the blood on the sides of the altar after which they burn incense in the tent of meeting and smoke up the offerings on the outer altar. Finally, the priests perform the benediction prior to the sacred meal. These rites with all of their ritual activities are enacted every morning and evening at the tabernacle. It can be concluded, therefore, that the seven parts of daily divine service of ancient Israel are performed in the order spelled out in the preceding analysis.

3

The Ritual Function of the Daily Divine Service

WHAT, ACCORDING TO THE Pentateuch, is the ritual function and theological purpose of each rite that is divinely instituted for the daily divine service? This chapter analyses the rites of the daily service by investigating the prescriptive and descriptive texts[1] in the Pentateuch as well as relevant documents outside of it. These sources help answer three questions. First, who authorizes each rite? It is assumed that the institution of the rite establishes its ritual function and theological purpose. Second, who does what, to or with whom, with what materials, where, and when? The answer to these questions discloses how each rite functions within the divine service. Third, what is the theological purpose of each rite? This question assumes that *God* intends to accomplish something through each of the rites and it investigates his ritual objective for its performance. Thus, each of the seven rites in the daily service is examined according to three categories: its institution, its ritual function, and its theological purpose.

An investigation of the relevant texts within and outside the Pentateuch determines the function and purpose of the ritual activities that those texts depict. The *meaning* of a ritual act is not the chief thing, though. Ritual acts *do* something; they are enacted to accomplish a purpose. Since this study is a ritual analysis, its aim is not necessarily to interpret the meaning of the texts in the Pentateuch. Rather, it investigates the ritual activities that its texts portray. But since the rites of the daily service are no longer enacted

---

1. See Levine, "Descriptive Tabernacle Texts," for a more detailed explanation of the distinction between prescriptive and descriptive texts.

and cannot be observed, a ritual analysis of the divine service of ancient Israel must be based on the texts that bear witness to it. So this chapter examines the ritual texts in the Pentateuch to ascertain the ritual function and theological purpose of the seven rites in the daily divine service.

THE FIRE RITE

The fire rite is the foundation for all of the rites in daily divine service. It must be performed for the service to accomplish the goal for which it is instituted. Unless the fire rite is enacted, none of the rites function properly within the ritual system. This would also prevent the theological purpose of the divine service from being achieved. The fire rite must be performed for the others to function in coordination with it and to bring about their divinely intended outcomes within the daily service.

The Divine Institution of the Fire Rite

The answer to two key questions determines the origin of the fire rite. Who institutes it and its ritual acts? Where does the Pentateuch record who authorizes it? These questions can be answered with certainty.

The LORD institutes the fire rite by commanding the priests to keep the fire burning on the altar, so that it is never extinguished (Lev 6:1–6 [8–13]). He repeats this instruction three times to emphasize the necessity of maintaining the fire (6:2, 5–6 [9, 12–13]).[2] Why is it so necessary to prevent the fire from dying out? It is no ordinary fire! The fire that burns up the offerings on the altar at the inaugural service comes from the presence of the LORD, most likely from the most holy place in the tent of meeting (Lev

---

2. This short pericope mentions the need to maintain the fire for three different reasons: to keep it burning on the altar all night, to keep from extinguishing it when the ashes are removed, and to keep the fire burning continually, תָּמִיד. The word תָּמִיד stresses the necessity to keep the fire burning, even if the offerings are completely consumed on the altar (Milgrom, *Leviticus 1–16*, 384–89). תָּמִיד is used later in Israel's history as the name for the daily divine service at the sanctuary because it is the word by which the Hebrew Bible designates the offerings and ritual acts that must be conducted regularly/daily (Exod 25:30; 27:20; 28:29–30, 38; 29:38, 42; 30:8; Lev 5:25 [6:6]; 6:6 [13]; 24:2–4, 8; Num 28:3, 6). See Beyse, "תָּמִיד," 690–94, for an overview of תָּמִיד and its uses in the Old Testament.

9:24).³ It is divine fire, the fire of God.⁴ The disastrous event with Nadab and Abihu shows that no other fire may be used for the ritual acts at the tent of meeting without deadly consequences (Lev 10:1–2).⁵ The LORD authorizes the fire rite so that the priests can safely maintain the divine fire on the altar for burnt offering and not let it go out.⁶

The LORD also institutes the five activities performed in the fire rite. First, since the LORD commands the priests to wash their hands and feet when they approach the altar (Exod 30:17–21).⁷ They need to wash them

---

3. The presence of God that is normally hidden in a cloud is manifested at the inaugural service as the divine fire comes forth from the most holy place. In every subsequent service, the LORD meets with Israel through the fire on the altar (Kleinig, *Leviticus*, 212, 220). Milgrom discusses several possibilities of the origin of the fire. He claims that it could have come of itself, or like with the contest between Elijah and the prophets of Baal (1 Kgs 18:22–39), it could have *fallen* from heaven, or it may have originated in the most holy place, passed through the holy place where it ignited the incense on the inner altar, incinerated Nadab and Abihu, then exited to the courtyard and consumed the offerings on the outer altar. Milgrom settles on the view that the fire *comes out* from the most holy place and burns up the offerings in a flash (Milgrom, *Leviticus 1–16*, 590).

4. Levine calls the fire, the *fire of God* or *God's fire* (Levine, *Leviticus*, 58). Kleinig holds that the fire is *sacred fire* and a *theophany* of the *presence of God* (Kleinig, *Leviticus*, 146, 212). Milgrom refers to it as *divine fire* and claims that God appears as fire in his glory (Milgrom, *Leviticus 1–16*, 590–91). Each of these views seems to agree that the fire is not natural fire but the fire of God.

5. After the destruction of Nadab and Abihu, Lev 10:3 quotes the LORD, "When I am treated as holy by those who are near me, I appear in glory in the sight of all the people." This implies that when those near him, the priests, do not treat him as holy, he appears in wrath. On Mount Sinai the LORD appears to the Israelites as smoke when he descends upon the mountain in fire, which causes them to be afraid of the sight (Exod 19:16–25; 20:18–21). Exod 19:18 records that the smoke billowed up from Mount Sinai like from a furnace. Similar language describes the fire of God at the temple in Jerusalem, and Israel's fear of it. Isa 31:9 states that the LORD's fire is in Zion and his *furnace* is in Jerusalem. It is written in Isa 33:14, "In Zion sinners are in dread; trembling takes hold of the godless as they declare, 'Who of us can live with the consuming fire? Who of us can live with everlasting burning?'" Thus, on the one hand, the LORD's fire reveals his glory to those who treat him as holy, while on the other hand, it is cause for fear to those who sin against him. See also Isa 10:17; 29:6; 30:27, 33.

6. The fire rite may be compared with the other regular, תָּמִיד, parts of the service that are authorized by the LORD. Just as the burnt offering, its cereal offering, the incense, the lamps, the bread of the presence, and the high priest's vestments are regular, תָּמִיד, parts of the daily service, so too is the maintenance of the divine fire (Kleinig *Leviticus*, 143). See also Haran, *Temples and Temple Service*, 207; Levine, *Leviticus*, 36.

7. Although Lev 6:1–6 [8–13] makes no mention of the priests washing their hands and feet, Exod 30:17–21 testifies that this is done every time they conduct the prescribed activities at the altar. Cassuto, Propp, and Stuart do not hold that the priests must wash their hands before removing the ashes (Cassuto, *Exodus*, 395–96; Propp, *Exodus 19–40*, 480; Stuart, *Exodus*, 641). Ritual washing is connected with ritual vesting, however,

before they come near the altar to maintain the fire on it. Second, the LORD commands the priests to wear their sacred vestments when they approach the altar (Exod 28:43). Thus, the priest who keeps the altar fire burning must put on his sacred vestments before ministering at it (Lev 6:3 [10]).[8] Third, the removal of the ashes from the altar every morning is divinely established (Lev 6:3 [10]).[9] Fourth, the LORD commands that new wood be added to the altar fire to keep it lit (Lev 6:5 [12]).[10] Finally, the LORD orders the priests to remove their vestments and carry the ashes outside the camp at the morning service (Lev 6:4 [11]).[11] All of these texts show that the ritual acts of the fire rite are instituted by God.

The fire rite is established by the LORD. Exodus and Leviticus bear witness to his institution of each of it acts. When the priests perform the fire rite, they do not do so on behalf of themselves, or on the authority of Moses or of Israel. They enact their duties on behalf of the LORD. He commands the priests to wash their hands and feet and to vest themselves in their sacred vestments before approaching the altar for burnt offering. He requires them to remove the ashes from the altar, add new wood to the altar fire, and remove their vestments to carry the ashes outside the camp. It is the LORD, who institutes the fire rite and each of its acts in the daily divine service.

---

and Exod 30:17–21 establishes the necessity of the priests to wash their hands and feet before performing all prescribed acts at the altar for burnt offering.

8. Levine sees Exod 28:43 as a divine command for the priests to wear their sacred vestments when they minister in the tent of meeting and at the outer altar (Levine, *Leviticus*, 36). Milgrom and Propp interpret Exod 28:43 as only referring to the linen undergarments (Milgrom, *Leviticus 1–16*, 385, 502, 918; Propp, *Exodus 19–40*, 452–54). Exod 28:43, however, is most likely a reference to all of the sacred vestments mentioned in Exod 28 and not merely the priests' undergarments.

9. The analysis of the fire rite in the last chapter confirmed that the removal of ashes does not occur in the evening offering, but in the morning only. Kleinig holds that the fire rite occurs each morning as the first ritual enactment in the daily divine service at the sanctuary and, while it is not an integral part of the morning offering, it necessarily precedes it as a preparatory rite (Kleinig, *Leviticus*, 148).

10. Although Lev 6:5 [12] does not specify that wood is added in the evening, Lev 1:7, 12 may indicate this. While Milgrom holds that all of Lev 1 only prescribes the ritual activities for *private* burnt offerings (Milgrom, *Leviticus 1–16*, 163), some of the procedures indicated in it must also apply to the daily burnt offering. Lev 1:7, 12 seems to establish the need for adding wood to the altar *every* time a burnt offering is placed on it because the entire animal is burned and requires additional wood as fuel to incinerate it. An exception may be when birds are the burnt offering, since they are small.

11. The priest changes his clothes and takes the ashes outside the camp after he removes the ashes from the altar in the morning, but these are not enacted in the evening offering.

The Ritual Function of the Fire Rite

To determine the ritual function of the fire rite, five areas of inquiry must be addressed. Who is involved in it and why? What is the significance of it as a whole and each of its parts? What materials are used, and why do they matter? When is it performed, and what does this imply? Where does the rite take place, and what may be inferred by its location? The answer to these questions assists in ascertaining what the fire rite is meant to accomplish in the divine service.

Ritual Agents

The LORD is the most significant agent in the performance of the fire rite, in two ways. First, he commands Moses to implement it (Lev 6:1 [8]).[12] The priests enact the duties of the fire rite on behalf of the LORD, who authorizes it to be performed every day (Lev 6:2 [9]).[13] Second, the fire is divine fire in which the LORD reveals his glory.[14] Just as the LORD manifested himself to Moses in the burning bush and to Israel in the fire cloud and in the fire on the top of Mount Sinai (Exod 3:2; 13:21–22; 19:11–20), so also he manifests himself in the fire at the sanctuary on the altar.[15] Since the LORD reveals his glory in the fire on the altar for burnt offering, he is the primary agent in the daily divine service.

---

12. Although Moses is the ritual founder through whom the LORD institutes the fire rite, he has no distinct role thereafter in its performance in the daily divine service.

13. The high priest's authority to perform the rites of the daily service does not come from himself, but from the LORD. His word authorizes Moses to ordain Aaron and his sons and to inaugurate Israel's divine service (Kleinig, *Leviticus*, 214).

14. Budd recognizes the fire that consumes the offerings in the inaugural service as the fire of the LORD, but he does not connect this fire with the fire on the altar in the daily service (Budd, *Leviticus*, 108–10, 147–48). However, Gorman, Levine, Kleinig, and Milgrom believe that the fire on the altar is not natural fire but the same divine fire that consumes the offerings at the inaugural service (see Gorman, *Divine Presence and Community*, 45, 63; Levine, *Leviticus*, 58; Kleinig, *Leviticus*, 146, 212; Milgrom, *Leviticus 1–16*, 590–91).

15. See Kleinig, *Leviticus*, 147. Milgrom holds that the LORD's presence at the top of Mount Sinai is temporary as opposed to his permanent residence at the tabernacle. The divine fire that rested on the top of Mount Sinai is the same fire that fills the tabernacle and that incinerates the offerings on the altar for burnt offering (Milgrom, *Leviticus 1–16*, 134–38). Moses tells the priests and elders of Israel that the LORD would appear to them in the inaugural service that day (Lev 9:4) and that they would see the *glory* of the LORD (Lev 9:6). Then, the LORD's glory appeared to all Israel in the fire that issued from the tent of meeting at the conclusion of the service, fulfilling what Moses promised. Thus, the LORD established his residence among Israel at the sanctuary.

Aaron and his sons must maintain the fire on the altar (Lev 6:2 [9]). *The priest*, however, is the one who is responsible for its ritual acts (Lev 6:3, 5 [10, 12]). Since the Pentateuch normally distinguishes between Aaron, referring to the high priest, and his sons as the regular priests, the designation *the priest* probably indicates that the high priest is responsible for this task.[16] He has the authority to conduct all of the ritual acts in the daily service including the fire rite, and he is the one who deputizes the regular priests to officiate on his behalf.[17] When the high priest designates another priest to do something in his stead, it is as if the high priest does it himself.[18] Thus, the regular priests enact what is assigned to them by the high priest in the fire rite.[19] Both he and the regular priests are the main ritual agents who keep the fire from being extinguished on the altar.

The Israelites are agents probably in two ways in the fire rite, even though the Pentateuch never prescribes a ritual role for them in it. First, they are beneficiaries of the divine fire on the altar.[20] Through it the LORD dwells among them as their God.[21] Second, they most likely supply the wood for the fire. Although the Pentateuch never designates who must

---

16. Budd, Gorman, Hartley, Levine, Milgrom, and Noth do not specify that *the priest* refers to the high priest in this section but to one of the unspecified priests (Budd, *Leviticus*, 108–10; Gorman, *Divine Presence and Community*, 45–46; Hartley, *Leviticus*, 96; Levine, *Leviticus*, 35–36; Milgrom, *Leviticus 1–16*, 382–87; Noth, *Leviticus*, 53–54). Kleinig identifies *the priest* as the priest who is on duty. As the steward of the LORD's house, he is responsible for looking after his residence. Since the altar is regarded as the centre of the LORD's residence, the primary duty of the priest is to attend to the fire on its hearth (Kleinig, *Leviticus*, 146). Kleinig claims elsewhere, however, that the designation *the priest* specifically refers to the high priest or his deputy (Kleinig, *Leviticus*, 60).

17. Although Haran maintains that only the high priest performs the ritual activities inside the tent of meeting, while the regular priests are responsible for the ritual activities at the outer altar, he acknowledges that the high priest is responsible for everything that occurs at the tabernacle (Haran, *Temples and Temple Service*, 205–7). Milgrom has a similar interpretation (Milgrom, *Leviticus 1–16*, 452). See also Kleinig, *Leviticus*, 154–56.

18. This observation is important because the high priest is the only one who represents all Israel to the LORD and the LORD to all Israel. He is a unique ritual agent, without whom the ritual activities of the entire ritual system would be incomplete. The authority of the regulars priests is inseparably tied to the high priest, as the ordination service makes clear (Exod 28; Lev 8).

19. See Milgrom's insights about the different roles of the laity and the priests in both the individual offerings and the public offerings (Milgrom, *Leviticus 1–16*, 134, 382–83).

20. Israel receives the LORD's blessing both at the inaugural service and every day as the fire continues to burn within their midst (Kleinig, *Leviticus*, 214–15, 218–20).

21. Just as the initial appearance of the divine fire at the inaugural service signifies God's approval of Israel, so every subsequent offering on the altar manifests his acceptance and grace (Milgrom, *Leviticus 1–16*, 591).

bring the firewood to the tabernacle, other sources indicate that the laity supply the wood as a kind of offering to the LORD.[22] As those who supply the wood for the divine fire and as the beneficiaries of the presence of the LORD through it, the Israelites are ritual agents in this particular daily enactment.

Ritual Acts

The priest, who approaches the altar to clear the fat-drenched ashes[23] every morning and to add wood to the fire each morning and evening, washes his hands and feet from the font. He does not do this merely to remove dirt from his hands and feet, but rather for a ritual purpose.[24] The priests must wash them, *so they will not die* (Exod 30:20–21). Since they are liable to tread upon or handle impurity outside the sanctuary,[25] the priests must take care not to approach or touch the most holy altar and defile it, lest they die.[26] The washing purifies the hands of each priest to handle holy things and his feet to walk on holy ground. This daily washing is not a major ritual cleansing like washing the entire body at the ordination of the priests or before the high priest enters the most holy place on the Day of Atonement (Lev 16:4, 24).[27] Yet, it is a ritual purification necessary for approaching the holy altar and handling the holy things.

After the priest washes his hands and feet, he puts on his sacred vestments (Exod 28:43). The ritual function of the vestments is to cover the priest with God's holiness. At the ordination of the priests, they and their vestments are consecrated with both the blood from the offerings that had

---

22. The lay Israelites are responsible for bringing wood for the divine fire on the altar (Neh 10:35; 13:31). Levine claims that in late biblical times the wood for the altar fire was secured through a special collection called *the donation of wood*. Furthermore, *laying out*, עָרַךְ, wood in Lev 1:7 is the same term for laying out an offering on the altar in Exod 29:37, which suggests that the wood may be understood as an offering (Levine, *Leviticus*, 36). Milgrom details the kind of wood that is acceptable, based on rabbinic tradition (see *Tamid* 2:3–5) and notes that it is brought to the temple in Jerusalem with great ceremony (Milgrom, *Leviticus 1–16*, 158–59, 387–88).

23. Literally, it is the ashes of fat, דֶּשֶׁן. See Milgrom, *Leviticus 1–16*, 386.

24. Ritual impurity is not simply about hygiene. It has to do with something being out of its proper place. Ritually washing impurities from the hands and feet of the priests removes contaminates that have no place among the holy things of God (Douglas, *Purity and Danger*). See also Kleinig, *Leviticus*, 6–10.

25. See Propp, *Exodus 19–40*, 480, 502.

26. The priests must distinguish between the holy and the common, and between the unclean and the clean (Lev 10:10).

27. See Kleinig, *Leviticus*, 203–4, 342–43.

The Ritual Function of the Daily Divine Service 75

been put on the altar and the most holy anointing oil.[28] Since the holy vestments are never taken outside the sanctuary, they remain holy. The priests, however, risk being desecrated whenever they leave the tabernacle (Lev 21–22). When they vest, however, they are covered by the holiness of the vestments.[29] The priests may then safely approach the divine fire on the altar and perform the acts that maintain it.

The first thing that is done to maintain the divine fire is the removal of the fat-drenched ashes from the altar (Lev 6:3 [10]). These must be removed, so that the live coals may be kindled in preparation for adding new wood. If the fatty ashes are never removed from the altar then eventually they could smother the fire entirely, an occurrence that would have dire consequences.[30] The ashes are like scraps cleared from the table of the LORD so that his servants may set out his food for that day.[31] The removal of the fatty ashes from the altar prepares it for keeping the fire burning.

In the second part of the rite for the maintenance of the divine fire the priests set aside some live coals from the outer altar to use for burning incense on the inner altar. In this case, the removal of some of the coals has nothing to do with maintaining the fire on the altar for burnt offering, but for taking the divine fire inside the tent of meeting.[32] There are three reasons for using the coals from the outer altar to burn the incense inside the tent of meeting. First, the coals from the altar for burnt offering are in close prox-

---

28. Kleinig maintains that the regular priests are not consecrated like the high priest in the ordination service. He emphasizes the consecration of the vestments, and that the regular priests are holy only as long as they wear the vestments (Kleinig, *Leviticus*, 202). Lev 8:30 states, however, that Moses sprinkles the holy blood and holy oil on the regular priests, and consecrates, וַיְקַדֵּשׁ, them. The difference between the consecration of the high priest and the regular priests is that the turban, diadem, and head of Aaron are anointed when the tabernacle and its furniture are anointed, implying that these have the same ritual status. The heads of the regular priests are not anointed. Yet, they and their vestments are consecrated just as the high priest and his ornate vestments are consecrated by the blood and oil. Because the high priest is the ritual *head* of the priests and Israel, his head and its unique vestments are consecrated to signify his unique ritual status with God, the regular priests, and Israel. See also Milgrom, *Leviticus 1–16*, 494–534.

29. See Kleinig, *Leviticus*, 203.

30. If the priests allow the fire to be extinguished, God will no longer give them access to his grace (Kleinig, *Leviticus*, 147). See also 2 Chr 29:6–9 where the LORD punishes Israel because the priests failed to perform their duties at the sanctuary.

31. Milgrom and Kleinig maintain that the altar for burnt offering is a table at the LORD's house (Milgrom, *Leviticus: Ritual and Ethics*, xii; Kleinig, *Leviticus*, 204). Ezek 44:16 also refers to the altar for burnt offering as a *table*. In Num 28:2, the LORD calls the morning and evening offerings that are offered on the altar, *my food*, לַחְמִי. See also Lev 21:6, 8, 17, 21–22; 22:25; Num 28:4.

32. Haran holds that the coals for burning incense on the inner altar are taken from the altar for burnt offering (Haran, *Temples and Temple Service*, 232).

imity to the tent. It makes the most sense that the priests would remove these lit coals from the outer altar when they kindle the fire in preparation for the new wood. Second, the coals that are removed from the outer altar burn with the holy fire. Third, one of these coals burning with the divine fire will be carried with tongs from the incense altar to light the lamps in the holy place every evening. It is inconceivable that any other fire would be allowed for the ritual functions in the holy place.[33] Removing the coals for use in the tent of meeting is a practical preparation for burning incense on the inner altar.

The third way to maintain the divine fire is by placing new wood on the live coals on the altar. Since the Pentateuch gives no indication of any theological significance for the wood that is used, its sole function is to produce new live coals for the holy fire.[34]

Finally, in the morning fire rite, the priest removes his sacred vestments before carrying the ashes out of the sanctuary and outside the camp to a ritually clean place (Lev 6:4 [11]). He takes off the vestments so that they will not be desecrated, by wearing them outside the sanctuary. He leaves them in the sanctuary to preserve their holiness. Divesting also removes the holiness of the vestments from the priest, allowing him to enter into the *common* realm without indiscriminately consecrating someone by contact with them.[35] When the ashes are removed from the sanctuary and camp, they remain ritually clean but they are no longer holy. The ashes,

---

33. The coals from the outer altar are the only ones that can be used for burning incense on the inner altar. Because Nadab and Abihu offer *unauthorized/strange fire* for burning incense, failing to distinguish between holy fire and common fire, they are destroyed (Kleinig, *Leviticus*, 231). See Lev 10:1; Num 3:4; 26:61 for the references to Nadab and Abihu offering unauthorized fire and its consequences. In Lev 16:12, the LORD commands that lit coals must be taken from the outer altar into the most holy place to burn incense on the Day of Atonement. According to Num 16:46, the priest atones for the sins of Israel by the extraordinary event of burning incense on coals taken from the altar and carried in a fire pan *into the camp*. See also *Tamid* 6:1, which states that the lamps are lit from the fire taken from the altar for burnt offering (Blackman, *Kodashim*, 492). It may be concluded that the only fire acceptable for ritual purposes at the sanctuary is the divine fire on the outer altar.

34. *Tamid* 2:3 states that all kinds of wood may be used for the holy fire *except* wood from the olive tree and the grapevine (Blackman, *Kodashim*, 474). Milgrom claims that this is a sign of respect for the trees whose fruit, olives and grapes, are used for ritual purposes in the divine service. Furthermore, these kinds of wood may not burn well and produce too much smoke (Milgrom, *Leviticus 1–16*, 387–88). The Pentateuch makes no restriction to which kinds of wood may be used on the altar.

35. The sacred vestments must remain in the sanctuary, so that they will not consecrate the people (Ezek 42:14; 44:19). See Hummel, *Ezekiel 21–48*, 1225, 1281; Milgrom, *Leviticus 1–16*, 386–87.

therefore, can no longer be utilized for ritual purposes.[36] Like scraps from the table of the LORD, they are disposed in a place outside of his house. These are the final acts involved in maintaining the divine fire on the altar for burnt offering every morning.

Ritual Materials

Six ritual materials are significant for preserving the fire in the daily divine service. First, the priests wash with the water from the font (Exod 30:18–21). The water purifies their hands and feet, not merely hygienically but ritually. Since the LORD commands that this water be used for ritual purification, *he* cleanses their hands and feet when they wash.[37] Second, the linen vestments that include a tunic, a sash, and a skull-cap provide holy covering for the priest who performs the rite. The priests are also required to wear linen undergarments that cover everything from their waist to their thighs, functioning as a barrier between their private area and the sacred vestments (Exod 28:39–43).[38] Third, the ashes are a significant material. Although they are what remain from the holy offerings from the previous day, they cease to perform a ritual function and must be removed to a clean place outside the camp.[39] Fourth, the new wood provides fuel for the divine fire. The coals eventually disintegrate and wood must be added. Since it is necessary for maintaining the fire, sometimes the wood itself is viewed as an offering to

---

36. Kleinig holds that the ashes are not holy, but are ritually clean and common (Kleinig, *Leviticus*, 147). Milgrom maintains that the ashes are holy, but have no inherent powers. Their holiness is not contagious, but merely a static holiness (Milgrom, *Leviticus 1–16*, 387). Most likely the ashes are holy while they are on the altar and at the sanctuary. Once they are removed from the sanctuary and the camp of Israel, the ashes become common while remaining ritually clean.

37. Propp claims that the ritual washing with water from the font symbolizes purification from disease, death, and corruption that infects the realm outside the tabernacle. Since the hands and feet most frequently contact the unclean world, they must not bring impurity into the sanctuary or else the priests will die (Propp, *Exodus 19–40*, 501–2).

38. On the one hand, the linen undergarments create a zone between the priest's genitals and the sacred vestments, protecting him from polluting the sacred vestments by an accidental emission of semen, which could result in his death. On the other hand, they absorb, but do not transmit, holiness (Propp, *Exodus 19–40*, 452–54). See also Haran, *Temples and Temple Service*, 165–74; Kleinig, *Leviticus*, 142, 147.

39. The ashes cannot be dumped just anywhere. Thus, the ash heap outside the camp constitutes a ritually clean, yet common space designated by God (Budd, *Leviticus*, 109–10). See also Gorman, *Divine Presence and Community*, 45–46; Hartley, *Leviticus*, 94.

the LORD.⁴⁰ Fifth, the altar and its utensils are necessary equipment.⁴¹ Of all the utensils associated with the altar, the pails, the shovels, and the fire pans are especially relevant to the fire rite (Exod 27:1–8). The priest uses a shovel to remove the ashes from the altar. He carries them outside the camp in the pails. He uses fire pans to remove lit coals for later use on the inner altar. The sides of the altar practically bank the fire.⁴² Finally, the most significant material is the fire itself, in two ways (Lev 6:6 [13]). Practically, the divine fire is necessary for the entire ritual system to function as it should. Significantly, the fire manifests the glory of the LORD among his people.⁴³ These materials are essential for perpetuating the holy fire in the daily divine service.

Ritual Times

The fire rite is conducted every morning and every evening (Lev 1:7; 6:5 [12]). Although only in the morning does the priest remove the ashes from the altar and carry them outside the camp, new wood is added to the altar in both the morning and the evening before the offerings are placed on it. The morning begins at the break of day, probably once the sky brightens before the sun appears on the horizon.⁴⁴ The evening is the time after the sun goes down over the horizon and before the sky is completely dark.⁴⁵

---

40. Neh 10:35 [34] refers to the wood that is brought for the altar fire as a קָרְבָּן, the same word that designates the regular offerings, קָרְבָּן, at the sanctuary (Lev 1:2; Num 28:2). Since anything that touches the altar becomes holy (Exod 29:37), it makes sense that the Israelites view the wood for the divine fire as an offering to the LORD.

41. The altar for burnt offering is constructed of acacia wood and is overlaid with bronze. There is a horn or protrusion on each corner of the altar, and it has a bronze grating that sits inside the altar halfway between its top and bottom. The altar does not contain a closed bottom, but rather is hollow and consists of its four sides. Its height is three cubits, which is about 4 ½ feet or 1.3 meters. Its length and width are the same, five cubits, which is about 7 ½ feet or 2.3 meters. The altar is carried by two poles made of acacia wood and overlaid with bronze (Exod 27:1–8; 38:1–7). The centre of the altar is probably filled with earth and stones whenever it is set up at the tent of meeting (Kleinig, *Leviticus*, 55). For further discussion on the function and significance of the altar for burnt offering, see Milgrom, *Leviticus 1–16*, 250–51.

42. Banking a fire is any procedure that reduces the amount of oxygen to lit coals so they will burn longer, such as covering them with ashes or blocking the airflow with rocks or other objects.

43. See Kleinig, *Leviticus*, 146–47.

44. *Tamid* 3:2 indicates that daybreak is the time when the eastern sky is lit up before the sun rises. However, according to *Tamid* 1–2, the removal of the ashes and adding wood occur before dawn while it is still dark at the temple in Jerusalem (Blackman, *Kodashim*, 469–77).

45. Exod 29:39 calls this the time *between the evenings*, בֵּין הָעַרְבַּיִם, or possibly

The Ritual Function of the Daily Divine Service

It is significant that the divine fire is maintained at these times each day.[46] Renewing the fire each morning ensures that the LORD will be accessible to Israel throughout the day, while its maintenance in the evening protects them from danger throughout the night.[47] It is imperative that the priests refresh the divine fire at these times, so that the LORD can reveal his glory to his people in the offerings that the fire turns into smoke on the altar signifying that he is with them both day and night.

Ritual Locations

There are three significant locations related to the fire rite: the altar for burnt offering, the area to its east side, and a ritually clean place outside the camp of Israel (Lev 6:3–4 [10–11]).[48] While the morning fire rite involves all of these places, the one in the evening occurs only at the altar because each evening wood is added without removing the ashes. The altar functions at the tabernacle in two ways. First, it is like a hearth[49] where the fire of the LORD burns continually. Prior to modern times, the fire in private dwelling places was maintained so that a new fire would not need to be started every day. The same is true for the fire on the altar at the house of God.[50] It must

---

"between the *two* evenings," which indicates the period between sunset and dark (BDB 787–88). See also Propp, *Exodus 19–40*, 472. Haran refers to this time as *twilight* (Haran, *Temples and Temple Service*, 207).

46. The movement from night into day and from day into night can be understood as a rite of passage, the movement from one state of being to another (van Gennep, *Rites of Passage*). In the morning, the fire rite consists of the first ritual activities that transition from the previous day to the current day, as well as from nighttime to daytime. In the evening, the fire rite begins the movement from day to night.

47. In every service the LORD meets with his people through the fire on the altar, which is a daily sign of his gracious presence among them. Since God gives his grace to his people and access to himself in the fire, the priests must diligently maintain the fire each morning and evening (Kleinig, *Leviticus*, 148, 220). The LORD's protection from the dangers of the night are reminiscent of the forces of evil through Pharaoh and his army in the exodus from Egypt, when the divine fire-cloud prevented the Egyptians from harming Israel throughout the night (Exod 14:19–20). Ps 91:5 speaks of the terror of night, and Ps 104:20; 107:10; Isa 9:2; 60:2 imply the danger and evil of darkness. Ps 23:4 tells of the LORD's protection from the danger of the *shadow* of death. Since the darkness of the night can be a time of evil and danger, the maintenance of the fire in the evening may indicate the LORD's protective presence in the midst of Israel throughout the night.

48. See figures two and three.

49. In the Pentateuch, the Hebrew word for *hearth/altar-hearth* is מוֹקְדָה, and it is only found in Lev 6:2 [9]. An alternate term for *hearth* is הַרְאֵל, which is only found in Ezek 43:15.

50. The altar fire at the residence of the LORD may be compared to the fire at

remain lit at all times. Second, the altar is the LORD's table.[51] Unlike the fire at a private residence, which is the place where food is prepared, the LORD "consumes" his food through his fire on the altar. The two places at a human dwelling, one where the food is prepared and the other where it is consumed, are combined in one location at the house of the LORD, his altar.[52] The other significant place is the east side of the altar, where the ashes are placed when the priest removes them from it (Lev 1:16).[53] This is for a practical reason. Its east side is the closest to the entrance to the courtyard through which the ashes will be carried to remove them from the camp. The last significant place is the ritually clean ash heap outside the camp (Lev 6:4 [11]). The priests cannot indiscriminately dump the ashes from the offerings anywhere they want, but only where the LORD designates that depleted ritual materials must be placed.[54] The altar and the ground on its east side at the sanctuary, as well as the ash heap outside the camp, are the locations that serve a ritual function in the fire rite of the daily divine service.

---

households of the ancient world (Kleinig, *Leviticus*, 147–48).

51. Mal 1:7, 12 are the only places in the Old Testament where the altar for burnt offering is called a *table*, שֻׁלְחָן. The Pentateuch implies, however, that the altar functions as the table of the LORD at his dwelling place because both he and his guests "consume" the food from it.

52. The LORD calls the regular offerings "my food" which he does not eat with his mouth, but consumes through his fire and smells with delight on his table (Num 28:2). The offering is a sweet savor that brings pleasure to the LORD (Milgrom, *Leviticus 1–16*, 162–63). Milgrom holds that the altar is a table from which the LORD consumes his food (Milgrom, *Leviticus: Ritual and Ethics*, xii). Kleinig maintains that the LORD shares his most holy food with the priests and his holy food with the laity (Kleinig, *Leviticus*, 204, 231). Ps 50:9–13 indicates that the LORD does not need food or drink. Rather, he gives the meals from his table to his guests.

53. At the second temple, the ashes were evidently dumped at the east side of the ramp, which is on the south side of the altar (Milgrom, *Leviticus 1–16*, 171).

54. Levine claims that there are two ash piles, one near the altar on its east side and the other at a specific place outside the camp (Levine, *Leviticus*, 22, 36). He identifies the ash pile next to the altar as *the place for the ashes*, מְקוֹם הַדֶּשֶׁן (Lev 1:16), and the ash pile outside the camp as *the ash heap*, שֶׁפֶךְ הַדֶּשֶׁן (Lev 4:12).

The Ritual Function of the Daily Divine Service   81

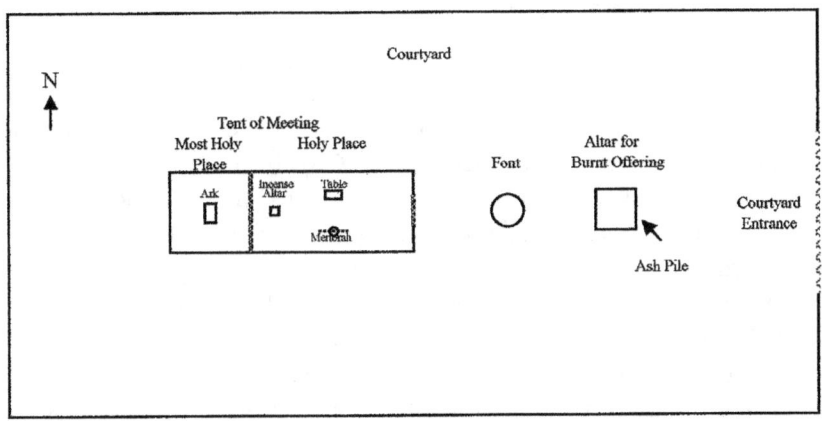

Figure 2. The tabernacle ground plan.

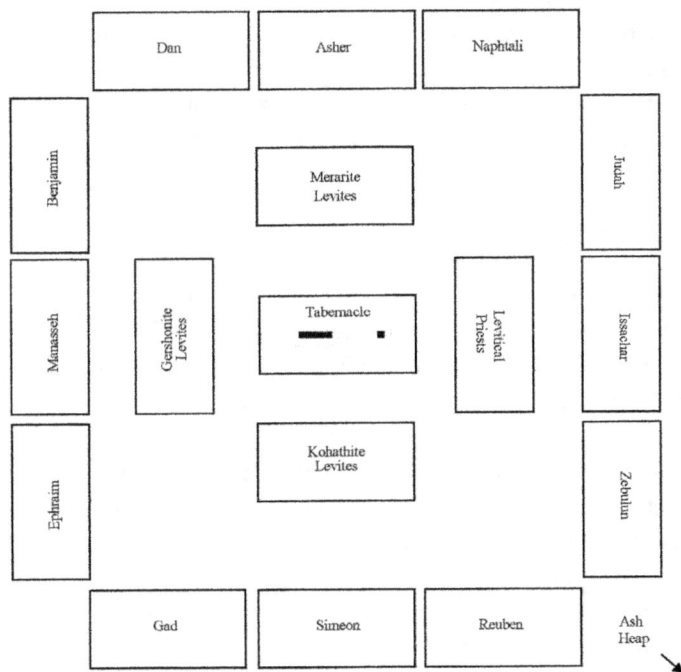

Figure 3. The camp of Israel.

Summary of the Ritual Function

The ritual function of the fire rite involves its agents, acts, materials, time, and location. The agents are the LORD, the high priest and regular priests, and the entire community of the Israelites. Each of these agents performs a specific role to keep the fire burning. The LORD institutes the fire rite, the priests enact most of its functions, and the responsibility of the laypeople is unspecified. The priest does several things. He washes his hands and feet, after which he dons his sacred vestments. He removes the fat-drenched ashes from the altar in the morning. The priest removes lit coals from the altar in both the morning and the evening to later burn incense on the inner altar, as well as for lighting the lamps each evening. Then, he adds new wood to the altar. In the morning fire rite, he divests his sacred vestments and carries the ashes outside the camp. The materials that are significant to this rite include the water, the vestments, the ashes, the new wood, the altar and its utensils, and the fire itself. These are enacted every morning while the sun is rising and every evening after the sun has gone over the horizon but before dark. There are two significant locations. One is at the altar for burnt offering and the other is at a ritually clean place outside the camp. The authorized agents perform the prescribed acts in the fire rite with its designated materials every morning and evening at its proper locations to keep the divine fire burning at all times on the altar for burnt offering.

The Theological Purpose of the Fire Rite

What is the theological purpose of the fire rite in the daily divine service? The answer to this question determines what *God* accomplishes through it. He institutes the fire rite and specifies its ritual function not merely for the priests and laity to do something, but ultimately so that he can accomplish his own purposes.

To determine the theological purpose of the fire rite, it is necessary to understand the origin of the divine fire. Although the holy fire comes out from the LORD (Lev 9), most likely from the most holy place,[55] this is not the first encounter that the Israelites have had with the holy fire. The LORD first appeared to Moses in the form of fire in the burning bush, when he called Moses to deliver the Israelites out of slavery in Egypt (Exod 3:2). The LORD first revealed himself to all the Israelites in a pillar of cloud and fire

---

55. The LORD speaks to Moses from between the two cherubim on the lid of the ark, which indicates that the LORD specifically resides in the most holy place inside the tent of meeting (Num 7:89). See also Lev 1:1–2.

through which he led them out of Egypt and into the Sinai wilderness (Exod 13:21–22). He was manifested to Israel in fire and smoke on the top of Mount Sinai (Exod 19:9–18). The cloud and the glory of the LORD, which looked like a consuming fire to the Israelites, rested on Mount Sinai where he gave instruction to Moses about constructing the sanctuary (Exod 24:15–18). After the tabernacle was constructed and its furniture set in place, the cloud covered the tent of meeting and the glory of the LORD filled the tabernacle (Exod 40:34–37). The cloud remains over the tabernacle in the daytime and the fire appears in it throughout the night (Exod 40:38). The divine fire that first appeared to Moses in the burning bush and to all Israel in the glory cloud emanates from the presence of the LORD in the tent of meeting.[56] This fire came out of the tent of meeting at the inaugural service and ignited the fire on the altar for burnt offering (Lev 9:24). Thus, the fire on the altar is the fire of God.

It is significant that the fire came out from before the LORD in the tent of meeting at the inaugural service instead of falling from heaven (Lev 9:24).[57] By igniting his holy fire on the outer altar, the LORD indicates that the place where he meets with the Israelites is at that altar, not inside the tent of meeting. This argument is further strengthened by the apparent correlation between Mount Sinai and the tabernacle.[58] The most holy place in the tent of meeting is similar to the top of Mount Sinai. Its holy place is comparable to the middle of the mountain. The altar for burnt offering in the

---

56. For further discussion about the fire in the cloud that leads Israel out of Egypt and that rests on the summit of Mount Sinai, see Kleinig, *Leviticus*, 218; Milgrom, *Leviticus 1–16*, 142–43; Propp, *Exodus 19–40*, 673, 688.

57. Fire falls from heaven and consumes the offerings on the altar at the dedication of the temple in Jerusalem (2 Chr 7:1–3). The glory of the LORD had previously moved from Mount Sinai to the tent of meeting (Exod 40:34), after which the fire consumed the offerings on the outer altar (Lev 9:24). The glory departs when the Philistines capture the ark and it probably never returns to the tabernacle after the ark is recovered (1 Sam 4:1–22). If so, then this explains why the glory cloud does not move from the tabernacle to the temple at its dedication (2 Chr 7:1–3). The fire of God and the LORD's glory would then come from heaven. The LORD does not command that the temple be constructed as he does the tabernacle. David desires to build the temple, and it is completed by Solomon (2 Sam 7:1–16; 2 Chr 6:1). The LORD, however, accepts the temple and chooses it as his dwelling place after it is built (2 Chr 7:12). See Kleinig, *Lord's Song*, 111. The LORD's command to construct the tabernacle, as well as the implementation of its inaugural service, is foundational to Israel's divine service. See Keil and Delitzsch, *Commentary on Old Testament*, 328–33, as well as Hamp's discussion of אֵשׁ (Hamp, "אֵשׁ," 424–28).

58. The tabernacle may be understood in terms of a portable Mount Sinai. It functions as a safe container for transporting God's presence from Sinai to Canaan. Like Mount Sinai, its purpose is to bridge the gap between heaven and earth (Propp, *Exodus 19–40*, 673, 687–88). See also Sarna, *Exploring Exodus*, 190–91; 203–6.

courtyard correlates with the base of the mountain. Furthermore, the glory cloud moves from the top of the mountain and enters the most holy place after the tent of meeting is constructed.[59] Moses and Aaron alone enter the holy place at the inaugural service (Lev 9:23), just as they alone are allowed to go up the mountain to meet with the LORD (Exod 19:24). The altar for burnt offering is placed outside the tent of meeting, yet within the boundary of the courtyard, similar to the altar and boundary at the base of Mount Sinai (Exod 19:12–24; 24:4). This signifies that the tabernacle takes the place of Mount Sinai as the dwelling place of God on earth.[60] Therefore, when the fire comes out from the LORD in the most holy place and ignites the fire on the altar for burnt offering, this signals that the LORD is accessible to all the Israelites through the fire at the altar.[61]

The theological purpose of the fire rite is to maintain the presence of the LORD in the fire on the altar so that the Israelites can meet with him there.[62] All of the offerings derive their holiness from that holy fire, and apart from it none of the offerings becomes holy. Through the holy fire, the LORD "consumes" his portion of the holy meal from his table. By the holy fire, the food for the priests from the altar becomes most holy and the food for the laity from the altar becomes holy. The part of the offerings that the LORD does not "consume," he gives from his table for his priests and people to eat. The fire on the altar sanctifies the food by which the Israelites partake of a communal meal with the LORD.[63] The fire rite maintains the divine fire

---

59. See Kleinig, *Leviticus*, 218.

60. Milgrom holds that there is a correlation between the distinct sections of Mount Sinai and those of the tabernacle. He asserts that the three different areas of the mountain and the tabernacle represent a division into three gradations of holiness. The summit of the mountain is like the most holy place in the tabernacle. God's voice comes from there (Exod 19:20; 25:22; Num 7:89); it is off limits to both the priests and laity; its sight is fatal (Exod 19:21, 24; Lev 16:2; Num 4:20). Moses alone is allowed to ascend to the top just as the high priest alone may enter the most holy place only once per year (Exod 19:20; Lev 16:2). The midsection of the mountain corresponds to the holy place in the tabernacle, and is partially covered with a cloud (Exod 20:21; 24:15–18). The base of the mountain, which is below the cloud, is like the outer courtyard where the altar stands (Exod 19:17; 24:4). Milgrom, therefore, concludes that there are three areas and grades of holiness at both the mountain and the tabernacle (Milgrom, *Leviticus 1–16*, 142–43).

61. In every service the LORD meets with his people through the fire on the altar as a daily sign of his gracious presence in the midst of Israel (Kleinig, *Leviticus*, 220).

62. See also Kleinig, *Leviticus*, 221.

63. The food for the priests becomes most holy through its contact with the fire on the altar. The food for the people, from peace offerings and cereal offerings, becomes holy. The most holy food for the priests communicates the LORD's holiness to them, since anything that is *most holy* has the power to make whatever it touches holy. The holy food, on the other hand, does not directly communicate God's holiness. However,

and the presence of God in it, so that the Israelites can continue to have access to him at the altar for burnt offering every morning and evening in the divine service.

Conclusion

The LORD institutes the fire rite to perpetuate his holy fire on the altar among the Israelites. The priest, who is responsible for performing it, purifies his hands and feet so that he can touch the holy altar with its utensils and walk on the holy ground near it. He is covered with the holiness of the sacred vestments, so that he can perform the ritual activities at the most holy altar. The priest removes the ashes to clear the leftovers away from the table of the LORD and to prepare for the offerings for that day. After he takes some of the live coals from the altar with which to burn incense later in the tent of meeting, the priest adds new wood to the remaining live coals so that the divine fire can be rekindled and "consume" the offerings that are placed upon it. He removes his vestments to preserve their holiness and keep from consecrating people and things outside the sanctuary when he carries the ashes away from the camp to a ritually clean place. The LORD institutes the fire rite and its ritual agents, acts, materials, time, and location to ensure that the divine fire on the altar continues to burn, so that he can remain accessible to the Israelites in the daily divine service every morning and evening at his sanctuary.

THE PRESENTATION RITE

The daily offerings are brought to the LORD in the rite of presentation after the fire is kindled on the altar. The Hebrew term for "offering" is קָרְבָּן, which means something that is brought near to God. The words that are related to the Hebrew root קרב show that an offering in the Pentateuch involves several aspects. Its noun is קָרְבָּן, which means *offering/gift*. Its *hiphil* verb form, הִקְרִיב, means *to present*, while the *qal* form, קָרַב, means *to approach/draw near*. Once an offering has been presented to the LORD, it is קָרֹב, *near*, him who dwells in Israel's midst, קֶרֶב.[64] Offerings to the LORD involve

---

through the holy food the lay Israelites have communion with God. Although the lay people do not share in God's holiness through the holy or most holy food, like the priests, yet they are sanctified by the *name* of the LORD pronounced to them in the Aaronic benediction as the smoke rises from the holy fire (Kleinig, *Leviticus*, 11–12, 231).

64. See BDB 897–99; Eberhart, "Neglected Feature of Sacrifice," 488.

all of these things, but there is more to an offering than simply bringing something near to him.[65] The things that are brought near to the LORD must also be placed on the altar for them to be an offering to him. All of the materials for the daily service must be brought near and presented before the LORD prior to being smoked up to him on the altar fire. Unless they are first presented and then placed on the altar there is no offering. Thus, the presentation rite is a necessary part of the daily divine service.

The Divine Institution of the Presentation Rite

By whose authority is the presentation rite enacted? Which sources state who institutes the presentation rite? Several relevant passages in the Pentateuch answer these questions.

The LORD commands the Israelites to *present*[66] the offerings at their appointed times (Num 28:1–2). These include the daily burnt offering with its accompanying cereal offering and drink offering, the Sabbath offering, the monthly offering, and yearly offerings at the Passover, Feast of Weeks, Day of Acclamation, Day of Atonement, and Feast of Tabernacles (Num 28–29).[67] Each of these public offerings must be presented to the LORD at the sanctuary before the priests place them on the altar for burnt offering.[68]

---

65. See Kleinig, *Leviticus*, 44.

66. The Hebrew word for present is הִקְרִיב, the *hiphil* form of קָרַב. For the other places that the Pentateuch refers to bringing near or presenting an offering to the LORD, see Exod 28:1; 29:3–4, 8, 10; 40:12, 14; Lev 1:2–3, 5, 10, 13–15; 2:1, 4, 8, 11–14; 3:1, 3, 6–7, 9, 12, 14; 4:3, 14; 5:8; 6:7 [14], 13–14 [20–21]; 7:3, 8–9, 11–14, 16, 18, 25, 29, 33, 35, 38; 8:6, 13, 18, 22, 24; 9:2, 9, 15–17; 10:1, 19; 12:7; 14:12; 16:6, 9, 11, 20; 17:4; 21:6, 8, 17, 21; 22:18, 20–22, 24–25; 23:8, 16, 18, 25, 27, 36–37; 27:9, 11; Num 3:4, 6; 5:9, 16, 25; 6:14, 16; 7:2–3, 10–12, 18–19; 8:9–10; 9:7, 13; 15:4, 7, 9–10, 13, 27, 33; 16:5, 9–10, 17, 35; 17:3–4; 18:2, 15; 26:61; 27:5; 28:3, 11, 19, 26–27; 29:8, 13, 36; 31:50. Milgrom maintains that this word is a technical term for the ritual presentation of materials to the LORD at the altar before they are incinerated on it. He states that the presentation of some materials may take the form of an elevation offering, such as in Lev 7:30. Like the elevation offering, the presentation rite transfers the ritual materials to the domain of God (Milgrom, *Leviticus 1–16*, 155, 185–86, 204, 391). Levine holds that הִקְרִיב is a technical *operative* term for the presentation of offerings before the LORD (Levine, *Numbers*, 370). For further discussion, see the section on the presentation rite in chapter 2. See also Kleinig, *Leviticus*, 44–45; Klingbeil, *Comparative Study of Ritual Ordination*, 220–22; Levine, "*Lpny* YHWH," 275, 390.

67. The public offerings in Number 28–29 may be divided into two categories: first, the legislation governing the daily, Sabbath, and monthly offerings, and second, all of the annual offerings (Levine, *Numbers*, 365–67).

68. Levine claims that the command in Num 28:3 to *present an offering by fire to the LORD* refers to all of the offerings in chapters 28–29 (Levine, *Numbers*, 371). While Num 28:3 only refers to the daily burnt offering, Num 28:2 is the LORD's command to

In the daily divine service, the LORD requires the presentation of two yearling unblemished lambs (Num 28:3).[69] The first lamb is offered in the morning and the second one is offered in the evening every day.[70] The cereal offering of fine flour mixed with olive oil, and the drink offering of a fermented beverage are also presented before the LORD (Num 28:4–8). The materials for the cereal offering and drink offering are included in the general command of the LORD to present offerings at their appointed times (Num 28:1–2; 15:2–7). Furthermore, the regular priests must present the daily cereal offering to the LORD in front of the altar (Lev 6:7 [14]).[71] Since frankincense is always part of the cereal offerings (Lev 2:1, 15; 6:8 [15]) and salt is added to all grain offerings (Lev 2:13), they are most likely placed on the fine flour mixed with olive oil before the cereal offering is presented to the LORD.[72] Thus, all of the ingredients of the cereal offering most likely are presented together. There is evidence that the drink offering is brought out of the tent of meeting when it is poured on the altar (Exod 25:29).[73] If this indicates that it is stored inside the tent, then the drink offering is probably not presented on the same day when it is poured on the altar. The wine, though, must necessarily be presented before the LORD at some time or

---

present all the public offerings at their appointed times.

69. Nowhere does the Pentateuch ever say that the lambs must be *presented*, הִקְרִיב, in the morning *and* in the evening. It is possible that both lambs, as well as both cereal offerings and both drink offerings, are presented only in the morning. Evidence for this may be found in Num 28:2–8, where the lambs and their cereal and drink offerings are *presented*, הִקְרִיב, every day (28:2–3) and are *offered*, תַּעֲשֶׂה, every morning and evening (28:4–8). However, there is other evidence that supports two presentation rites, one in the morning and the other in the evening. The bread offering of the high priest is presented, הִקְרִיב, half of it in the morning and half of it in the evening (Lev 6:13 [20]). Lev 1:2–13; 6:7–8 [14–15] coordinate the presentation of burnt offerings and the daily cereal offerings with their incineration on the altar. The daily divine service most likely consists of two presentation rites, one for the morning and the other for the evening.

70. See Exod 29:38–39.

71. There may be two different presentations with each cereal offering. The first happens when the materials are brought to the altar. The second occurs when the priest removes the token portion, before it is burned on the altar. These two presentations are similar to meat offerings, which include one presentation of the animal Lev 1:3, 10) and another of its blood (Lev 1:5) just before its application to the altar (Milgrom, *Leviticus 1–16*, 181, 391).

72. Frankincense is part of the cereal offering. It is an ordinary form of incense that is distinguished from the most holy fragrant incense burned twice daily by the priest on the altar in the tent of meeting. Salt is added to the cereal offering for two reasons. First, it is a practical preservative, which decreases the possibility of mould and decay. Second, it is symbolic of permanence, because it is a substance that lends stability to other ingredients without altering its own characteristics (Kleinig, *Leviticus*, 76).

73. This is discussed in the section on the burning rite.

other to replace what has been used. Most likely it is replenished every morning and evening in the presentation rite. The LORD commands that all of the materials for the daily divine service must be presented to him before they are offered on the altar.

The daily bread offering of the high priest must also be presented before the LORD prior to being burned on the altar (Lev 6:12–15 [19–22]).[74] This bread offering consists of fine flour mixed with oil and cooked on a griddle. Once the bread has been cooked, it must be broken into pieces, soaked in oil, and then presented before the LORD.[75] The high priest[76] is to present half of it in the morning and half of it in the evening in the daily divine service.

The LORD requires the materials for the daily service to be presented to him before they are turned into smoke on the altar. He commands the priests to present two unblemished yearling male sheep every day (Num 28:3). He directs them to bring before him the accompanying cereal offering of fine flour mixed with olive oil, with frankincense and salt added to it (Lev 6:7 [14]). The LORD prescribes the drink offering of wine or fermented beverage to be presented at the sanctuary as part of the divine service (Num 28:1–8). He instructs the high priest to bring to him a daily bread offering

---

74. The bread offering of the high priest takes place in three stages. First, the bread is prepared. Second, it is presented before the LORD by the high priest. Third, all of the bread, half of it in the morning and half of it in the evening, is burned on the altar by the high priest's successor. While every other grain offering is eaten by the priests, no one eats any portion of the bread offering of the high priest, because all of it is placed on the altar (Kleinig, *Leviticus*, 156).

75. The bread offering is not only cooked in oil but, after it is broken into pieces, it must be soaked in oil (Kleinig, *Leviticus*, 156).

76. There is some discrepancy about exactly who presents the bread offering of the high priest and when it is presented. Lev 6:13 [20] states that Aaron *and his sons*, אַהֲרֹן וּבָנָיו, must present the bread offering of the high priest. Normally, *Aaron and his sons* refer to the high priest and the regular priests, as in Lev 6:9 [16]. However, there is reason to believe that אַהֲרֹן וּבָנָיו means Aaron *and his successors* as future high priests. This especially makes sense if the bread offering is offered daily, and not merely at the occasional ordination of high priests. According to Lev 6:13 [20] the bread offering must be presented בְּיוֹם הִמָּשַׁח אֹתוֹ, which could literally be "*on the day he is anointed*." The verse states, however, that the bread offering of the high priest is a *regular/daily*, תָּמִיד, offering, and therefore, בְּיוֹם הִמָּשַׁח אֹתוֹ must be "*from the day he is anointed.*" Furthermore, since the high priest is called the "anointed priest" (Lev 4:3, 5, 16), due to being anointed on his head (Lev 8:12) in addition to the consecration like the regular priests (Lev 8:30), בְּיוֹם הִמָּשַׁח אֹתוֹ must refer to the high priest. Lev 6:13 [20] most likely prescribes that the high priest and his successors—all future high priests—must present their bread offering every morning and every evening in the daily divine service. See Kleinig, *Leviticus*, 154–57; Levine, *Leviticus*, 38–39; Milgrom, *Leviticus 1–16*, 396–97.

and present half of it in the morning and half of it in the evening (Lev 6:12–15 [19–22]). Thus, the presentation rite is instituted by the LORD.

The Ritual Function of the Presentation Rite

What is the ritual function of the presentation rite? Practically speaking, the materials for the daily divine service cannot be smoked up unless they are first brought to the tabernacle. The rite involves those who both actively and receptively are engaged in presenting the offerings before him in the correct place and at the right time. A closer analysis of the various facets pertaining to the presentation rite will help determine its ritual function.

Ritual Agents

The high priest and regular priests are the agents who perform the presentation rite. The high priest is responsible for ensuring that all of its acts are performed according to the LORD's command (Exod 28:1–2). Although he might not actually perform all of its activities, he supervises the priests when they carry them out.[77] As the ritual head of the entire community of Israel, the high priest or his deputy, places his hand on the head of the lamb for the burnt offering to designate that it belongs to all Israel and it is their offering to the LORD (Lev 1:4).[78] The high priest also presents his daily bread offering (Lev 6:13 [20]). The regular priests are the agents who perform most of the acts in the presentation rite. They present the materials for the daily burnt offering before the LORD (Lev 6:7 [14]).[79] Since the high priest and the regular priests perform most of the rite of presentation, they are its most significant agents.

---

77. In the inaugural service (Lev 9), Moses, as the founder of the ritual system, hands over the responsibility of the tent of meeting, the altar for burnt offering, and the divine service to Aaron as the high priest. Aaron exercises this authority over Moses following the death of Nadab and Abihu in Lev 10 (Kleinig, *Leviticus*, 214, 230). Milgrom holds to the superiority of Moses, the prophet, over Aaron, the priest, even after Aaron gets the better of Moses on a legal point (Milgrom, *Leviticus 1–16*, 627).

78. See Milgrom's extensive discussion about *placing the hand* on animals presented as offerings. Although the Pentateuch never states that the high priest, or any priest, should place his hand on the lamb for the public burnt offering, Milgrom concludes that all quadrupeds presented at the altar must have a hand placed on it by the one presenting it (Milgrom, *Leviticus 1–16*, 150–53). See also Budd, *Leviticus*, 47–48.

79. Milgrom asserts that the regular priests normally divide up the responsibilities so that each of them presents one of the offerings (Milgrom, *Leviticus 1–16*, 391). See also Noth, *Leviticus*, 54–57.

All of the Israelites are involved in the presentation of materials. The LORD commands the *Israelites* to present the public offerings (Num 28:1–3). Evidently, the lay people are responsible for providing the materials, such as the yearling male lamb, flour, olive oil, frankincense, salt, and wine.[80] Since the public offerings are performed on behalf of the entire community of Israel, they must provide the materials.[81] They are also beneficiaries of the presentation rite, because the priests perform its ritual acts vicariously in their stead (Exod 29:42–44). Not only does the high priest represent the LORD to Israel, he also represents Israel to the LORD (Lev 16:20–22). This is especially clear when he places his hand on the head of the yearling male lamb (Lev 1:4). Furthermore, the regular priests carry out the acts of presenting the ritual materials on behalf of Israel.[82] Since the Israelites provide the materials that are needed for the public offerings, they are ritual agents in the performance of the presentation rite in the daily divine service.

The LORD is the main ritual agent of the presentation rite in two ways. On the one hand, he is active in its performance, and on the other hand, he receives what is presented. The LORD authorizes the enactment of the presentation rite (Num 28:1–2). It is by his authority that its acts are carried out. The rite is conducted on behalf of the LORD, and he accomplishes his purpose through it.[83] Thus, he is an active ritual agent. The LORD is also a receptive ritual agent in the presentation rite. He is the one to whom the offerings are presented (Num 28:2–3). He receives the offerings as his own, when they are brought before the altar for burnt offering (Lev 6:7 [14]). Since the LORD both authorizes its ritual acts and is the recipient of the things that are presented, he is the main agent in the rite of presentation.[84]

---

80. See Milgrom's discussion about whether or not it is the high priest or the regular priests that must supply the materials for the bread offering of the high priest (Milgrom, *Leviticus 1–16*, 396–97). *Tamid* 1:3 indicates that the priests make the bread for the daily bread offering of the high priest at the temple in Jerusalem (Blackman, *Kodashim*, 471–72).

81. The Israelites are responsible for providing the materials for the offerings (Kleinig, *Leviticus*, 151).

82. The priests perform a mediating role, representing the LORD to the people and the people to the LORD (Gorman, *Divine Presence and Community*, 46–47). They, therefore, present the offering at the altar on behalf of the people (Kleinig, *Leviticus*, 149).

83. Since the LORD authorizes the offerings, he determines how, by whom, and which offerings are presented before him. The instituting word of the LORD establishes how he is active in and through the offerings. Their status, efficacy, and sanctity are established by him (Kleinig, *Leviticus*, 47).

84. See Kleinig, *Leviticus*, 75, 149.

Ritual Acts

At the beginning of the presentation rite the priests wash their hands and feet after which they put on their sacred vestments. These acts are not performed at the evening service, because only in the morning are the ashes removed from the altar and carried outside the camp. In the evening, there is no need to wash and vest since the priests have already done so in the fire rite. Yet, they must purify their hands and feet and be dressed in their sacred garments prior to performing the main acts in the presentation rite. They wash to purify their hands for handling holy things and their feet for walking on holy ground near the altar for burnt offering. They wear the sacred vestments to cover themselves with the holiness of God, which enables them to safely enact the presentation rite in the holy precincts of the courtyard. The priests must wash and vest prior to presenting the offerings before the LORD at his altar.[85]

The materials for the offerings must be brought to the tabernacle and inspected before they can be presented to the LORD.[86] The Israelites are responsible for supplying the unblemished yearling male lamb for the burnt offering,[87] the flour and olive oil mixture with frankincense and salt for the cereal offering, and the wine or fermented beverage for the drink offering (Num 28:1–8). Although the inspection of the materials for these offerings is probably not as tedious as the examination of the lamb, the priests still need to confirm that the proper ingredients in their correct amounts are presented.[88] The bread offering of the high priest is *prepared* on a griddle, *brought* well mixed, and *presented* in broken pieces (Lev 6:14 [21]). This indicates that the bread is prepared outside the sanctuary. It too needs to be

---

85. For further discussion about the ritual significance of the washing and vesting, see the section on ritual acts in the fire rite.

86. The only ritual material presented in the daily divine service that the Pentateuch requires to be *brought*, תְּבִיאֶנָּה, is the bread offering of the high priest (Lev 6:14 [21]). This may indicate that all of the offerings for the daily divine service are brought from outside the tabernacle courtyard. The Pentateuch also never states that the materials must be *inspected*. This is implied, since the LORD prescribes specific qualifications for the materials that are offered (Num 28:3–7; Lev 6:7–16 [14–23]; 22:17–25).

87. The high priest, the regular priests, and the Israelites are responsible for presenting unblemished animals for private offerings (Lev 22:18). The inspection probably starts with the Israelite who supplies the animal. Then the regular priest most likely inspects it again, after which the high priest may inspect it one last time when it is presented at the altar (Milgrom, *Leviticus 17–22*, 1870–71). A list of blemishes that disqualify animals for offering on the altar is found in Lev 22:17–25.

88. Neh 3:31 may imply that one of the gates at the temple in Jerusalem is designated for inspecting the ritual materials. *Tamid* 3:4 states that the lambs at the temple are inspected the night before and on the day they are offered (Blackman, *Kodashim*, 478).

inspected, to confirm that it is prepared with the correct ingredients in the right proportion.[89] All of the ritual materials for the offerings must be brought to the sanctuary and inspected to confirm that they are fit to be offered on the altar.

After the materials have been inspected, they are presented to the LORD at the tabernacle. The lamb for the burnt offering, the flour and oil mixture with frankincense and salt for the cereal offering, and the wine or fermented beverage for the drink offering, must be presented to the LORD before they can be offered to him on the altar (Lev 6:7–8, 12–15 [14–15, 19–22]; Num 28:1–8). The ritual presentation of the materials for the daily offerings transfers them from outside the sanctuary into the presence of the LORD at his altar, indicating their change from common use to a holy purpose.[90]

The high priest, or his deputy, places his hand on the head of the lamb to designate that it belongs to Israel.[91] Since the accompanying cereal offer-

---

89. The flour mixed with oil is baked on a griddle as flat bread. First Chronicles 9:31 identifies a specific Levite family, who also served as gatekeepers at the temple in Jerusalem, as the ones who prepared the bread offering in the postexilic period (1 Chr 23:29). The bread is then brought to the sanctuary broken in pieces and soaked in oil. It is presented by the high priest to the LORD before being burned on the altar (Kleinig, *Leviticus*, 156).

90. Num 28:2 emphasizes that the offerings of the LORD must be *presented at the appointed time*, לְהַקְרִיב לִי בְּמוֹעֲדוֹ (Levine, *Numbers*, 370). However, מוֹעֵד not only means *appointed time*, it can mean *appointed place* (BDB 417–18). When the ritual materials are presented before the LORD at the entrance to the tent of meeting, פֶּתַח אֹהֶל־מוֹעֵד לִפְנֵי יְהוָה (Exod 29:42), their function changes according to the change of location. The LORD's presence creates a ritual topography with decreasing impurity and increasing holiness the closer a person or object comes to him (Kleinig, *Leviticus*, 8–9). Since the priests bring the ritual materials from the common realm and present them before the LORD in the holy realm, the ritual status of the materials changes from common to holy. Similarly, the materials that are placed on the most holy altar change from being holy to most holy. Both the appointed time every morning and evening, and appointed location at the tent of meeting, determine the purpose for which the materials are used.

91. There is no text in the Pentateuch that requires the priest to place a hand on the lamb for the daily burnt offering. Lev 1:4 implies, however, that placing a hand on the animal's head is a key part of the presentation rite of the daily burnt offering, not merely when individuals present their burnt offerings before the LORD. Milgrom holds that *laying/placing a hand*, יָד שִׂים, must be distinguished from *hand leaning*, סָמַךְ יָד. When the hand is placed on the head of a person, such as in Gen 48:18, the expression refers to an act of blessing. Hand leaning implies that pressure is placed on the object (Amos 5:19; Judg 16:29; 2 Kgs 18:21), and in the case of animals presented for offering on the altar, hand leaning designates ownership (Milgrom, *Leviticus 1–16*, 150–52). While I agree with Milgrom's reason for "leaning" the hand on the head of the offering, *putting/placing/laying the hand* is, nonetheless, an accurate way to describe what happens when someone carries out this ritual act. Thus, *placing or laying a hand* is used throughout this book as the translation for סָמַךְ יָדוֹ.

ing and drink offering, as well as the bread offering of the high priest, are presented in the hands of the priests, there is no need to lay hands on them again.[92] The Israelites are instructed to place a hand on several kinds of individual offerings, and the priests place their hands on animals in the ordination service (Lev 3:1–2, 7–8, 12–13; 4:3–5, 14–16, 22–25, 28–30, 32–34; 8:14–15, 18–19, 22–23).[93] In each of these cases, placing a hand designates ownership of a quadruped presented as an offering.[94] Furthermore, the offerer presents and lays a hand on the head of the animal so that the LORD will accept and atone for the person when it is offered on the altar (Lev 1:3–4).[95] As the ritual representative of the entire community of Israel (Exod 29; Lev 8–9), the high priest places his hand on the head of the lamb for the public daily burnt offering to designate that the lamb belongs to the entire community of Israel (Num 28:2–3). In this ritual act, the lamb is designated to secure the LORD's atonement vicariously for Israel through splashing its

92. Laying a hand on an offering is not required when it can be carried by hand. The animal for the guilt offering does not require placing a hand on it because the money, which can be brought by hand, could be offered in the place of the animal (Lev 5:14–19; 7:1–7). Likewise, the cereal and bread offerings (Lev 2:1–16; 5:11–13; 6:7–16 [14–23]), as well as offerings of birds (Lev 1:14–17; 5:7–10), are carried to the sanctuary in a person's hands. Thus, there would be no question about ownership, such as with a quadruped, which would probably be dragged into the courtyard by a rope (Milgrom, *Leviticus 1–16*, 151–52).

93. Each of these passages tells of a specific procedure. Bringing or presenting the animal is always first; next is placing the hand on it; then it is slain, followed by the disposal of blood. The presentation of the animal in these private and special offerings is coupled with the hand placing, implying consistency with the presentation and hand placing in the presentation rite for the daily divine service. For other examples of ritual hand placing on a quadruped in the Pentateuch, see Exod 29:10, 15, 19; Lev 16:21; 24:14; Num 8:10, 12; 27:18, 23; Deut 34:9.

94. See Milgrom, *Leviticus 1–16*, 152.

95. There are three basic interpretations for placing a hand on the animal. First, it transfers or confers something from the person to the animal, whether that is sin (Lev 16:21), pollution (Lev 24:14), authority (Num 27:23), or a particular spirit (Deut 34:9). In such cases, both of the person's hands are placed on the recipient and he declares what is imparted. This does not seem to match the daily burnt offering, especially since only one hand is placed on it and there is no evidence that any words are spoken. The second view identifies the offerer with the animal so that it becomes a vicarious substitute through its *death*. This is unlikely, because the death of the animal is ritually insignificant. In the third view, the hand placing indicates ownership, so that it could be used vicariously on the person's behalf, to receive God's approval and acceptance. This last view is probably the best interpretation (Kleinig, *Leviticus*, 53). Milgrom recognizes these same three views, but adds a fourth, which views the hand placing as a declaration, to enable the offerer to declare the purpose of the offering or to declare his innocence. Milgrom does not hold, however, that there is any evidence for this perspective, and he believes that the hand placing shows ownership (Milgrom, *Leviticus 1–16*, 150–53). See also Levine (Levine, *Leviticus*, 6–7).

blood against the altar and to gain his acceptance of the Israelites as it is smoked up on the altar.[96] When the high priest, or his deputy, places his hand on the head of the lamb, he is claiming that the entire community of Israel owns it and that they will benefit from its flesh and blood being offered on the altar in the following ritual enactments.[97]

Ritual Materials

There are six ritual materials used in the presentation rite. The first is the water that the priests use to wash their hands and feet; the second involves their sacred vestments.[98] The third and main materials for the presentation rite are the two unblemished yearling male lambs (Exod 29:38–41; Num 28:3–4). The Pentateuch does not specify why this particular kind of animal is offered, but the lamb most likely represents Israel.[99] The lambs are yearlings and, therefore, not taken from the breeding stock. Furthermore, since they are males, they are more economically expendable than females, which supply milk and offspring. As males, however, they may represent headship.[100] It is significant that the lambs are physically unblemished,[101] which

---

96. The animal secures God's approval and acceptance of the offerer in two ways. First, God atones for him as the animal's blood is splashed against the altar. Second, God gives the offerer access to himself when the animal is smoked up on the altar for burnt offering. God accepts the burnt offering and the person who presents it to him at the sanctuary (Kleinig, *Leviticus*, 53, 63–66).

97. See Kleinig, *Leviticus*, 53.

98. For further discussion about the significance of the water and the vestments, see the section on ritual materials in the fire rite.

99. Isa 5:17; Hos 4:16 seem to compare Israel with lambs, כְּבָשִׂים. This is a similar idea to Jer 23:1–4; Ezek 34:1–31, where Israel's leaders are shepherds and Israel is a flock, צֹאן. The only reference to a lamb mentioned in the Pentateuch prior to the ones for the daily burnt offering in Exod 29:38, is in Exod 12:5, the animal for the Passover in Egypt. However, as that text makes clear, the Passover animal could be taken either from the sheep or from the goats, מִן־הַכְּבָשִׂים וּמִן־הָעִזִּים תִּקָּחוּ. Therefore, the lamb for the daily burnt offering is probably not significantly related to the Passover, but most likely it represents Israel, since through the lamb for the burnt offering Israel is accepted by God (Lev 1:4).

100. See Milgrom, *Leviticus 1–16*, 147. There are at least two possible reasons why the animals for private burnt offerings must be males. First, since the males are less valuable than female breeding stock, males are usually eaten. Furthermore, it takes fewer males to breed a herd or a flock. Second, the male represents the entire herd or flock, as its head. In addition, male animals represent the male head of the family that presents the offering (Kleinig, *Leviticus*, 61). The same reasons probably apply to the public burnt offering. When the high priest, the ritual head of the community, lays his hand on the head of the lamb, he designates it to represent all of Israel.

101. The two yearling male lambs, כְּבָשִׂים בְּנֵי־שָׁנָה שְׁנַיִם, must be unblemished,

The Ritual Function of the Daily Divine Service 95

most likely symbolizes ritual perfection.[102] The fourth ritual material is the cereal offering. Its ingredients are one tenth of an ephah of choice flour[103] mingled with one fourth of a hin of beaten olive oil (Num 28:5).[104] It is presented with an unspecified amount of frankincense (Lev 6:8 [15]) and salt (Lev 2:13). Yet, the amount of frankincense is small enough for all of it to be removed with the handful of the cereal offering that is burned on the altar (Lev 2:2, 16; 6:8 [15]).[105] This offering is presented before the LORD, so that it becomes the most holy bread that the priests eat from the LORD's table.[106] Fifth is the drink offering (Exod 29:40–41; Num 28:7–10), which is one fourth of a hin of *wine* (Exod 29:40)[107] or *fermented beverage* (Num 28:7).[108]

תְּמִימִם (Lev 22:17–25). Levine notes that the blemishes that disqualify animals from being offered at the sanctuary are almost identical to the blemishes that disqualify priests from serving at the sanctuary (Levine, *Leviticus*, 140–41). See also Kleinig, *Leviticus*, 447; Milgrom, *Leviticus 17–22*, 1836–40. Although the list of blemishes in Lev 22:17–25 specifically refers to private offerings brought by individuals, they most likely also apply to determining the soundness of the animals for the public offerings. See Levine, *Numbers*, 371.

102. See Kleinig, *Leviticus*, 477–78.

103. Milgrom holds that the choice flour, סֹלֶת, is wheat grits or semolina, not ordinary flour, קֶמַח (1 Kgs 4:22) (Milgrom, *Leviticus 1–16*, 179). Kleinig is less certain about its exact identity, but he agrees that סֹלֶת is produced from wheat and not from barley. He believes it is the highest quality material, since it is listed with luxury items such as honey and oil (Ezek 16:13, 19). It probably consisted of husked grits of wheat with the bran removed, or it could have been finely sifted white wheat flour (Kleinig, *Leviticus*, 70). Propp suggests that one tenth of an ephah is equal to about 1.2 liters, or a little more than one quart. He notes that the same volume of grain is an omer (Propp, *Exodus 19–40*, 471). Milgrom points out, however, that an ephah is estimated to be approximately 22.8 liters, which means that one tenth of an ephah is about 2.3 liters or almost two and a half quarts (Milgrom, *Leviticus 1–16*, 398).

104. A hin is about 3.6 liters, or approximately three quarts (Propp, *Exodus 19–40*, 471). Therefore, one fourth of a hin of beaten olive oil, בְּשֶׁמֶן כָּתִית רֶבַע הַהִין, amounts to about 0.9 liter or three fourths of a quart. The oil is *clear beaten olive oil* and is produced by pounding olives in a mortar rather than squeezing them in a press (Cassuto, *Exodus*, 369–70). This results in the finest grade of olive oil (Propp, *Exodus 19–40*, 427).

105. See Milgrom, *Leviticus 1–16*, 181.

106. See Kleinig, *Leviticus*, 150–51.

107. The drink offering of one fourth of a hin of wine, וְנֶסֶךְ רְבִיעִת הַהִין יָיִן, accompanies each lamb (Exod 29:40). The ritual use of wine is unusual, because fermented substances, such as leavened bread or date honey, are usually associated with impurity (Propp, *Exodus 19–40*, 472). One fourth of a hin is about a liter or a quart of liquid measure (Stuart, *Exodus*, 630).

108. The Hebrew word is שֵׁכָר. The *Hebrew and English Lexicon* translates it as *intoxicating drink, strong drink* (BDB 1016). Kleing identifies it as beer or a similar fermented beverage distinguished from wine (Kleing, *Leviticus*, 225). Levine's insightful discussion of שֵׁכָר determines that it cannot refer to *beer*. He argues beer is made from fermented grain, a substance that is forbidden on the altar. According to Num 15,

It probably signifies that the daily offerings are a kind of banquet in the presence of the LORD, the best parts of which he reserves for himself.[109] The last material is the bread offering of the high priest (Lev 6:12–16 [19–23]). It is made with the same substance and quantity as each daily cereal offering, one tenth of an ephah of choice flour (Lev 6:13 [20]).[110] It is prepared with oil and cooked on a griddle[111] to produce flat bread. Then, it is presented broken into pieces and soaked in oil (Lev 6:14 [21]).[112] The bread offering of the high priest is half the amount of the daily cereal offering. It is divided in two, so that half of it may be presented in the morning and the other half presented in the evening (Lev 6:13 [20]). Since the entire bread offering of the high priest is incinerated on the altar (Lev 6:15–16 [22–23]), it likely signifies his total dedication to serving the LORD.[113] These six materials are brought into the presence of the LORD and are designated for ritual use in the daily service.

Ritual Times

The presentation rite is conducted regularly every day (Lev 6:13 [20]; Num 28:3).[114] The priests are required to present the daily offerings every

---

all drink offerings must be from wine. The שֵׁכָר in Num 28:7 probably refers to a liquid made from grapes or another fruit of the vine, possibly new wine or grappa (Levine, "Lpny YHWH," 219–20; *Numbers*, 374–75). The fermented beverage most likely refers to forms of alcoholic liquid from grapes that are stronger than wine. See also Oeming, "שֵׁכָר," 1–5.

109. In societies where people rarely eat meat, wine, like oil and fat, is associated with the best foodstuff. Often, the best parts of the meal are reserved for those who are honored. Therefore, the wine is reserved for the LORD, who is honored above all. Interestingly, Isa 25:6–8 prophesies that a time would come when the LORD would not reserve the best for himself, but that he would prepare a feast to share the best of meats and the finest of wines with the guests at his banquet. A foretaste of this feast may be indicated in Exod 24:11; 1 Chr 29:22 (Kleinig, *Leviticus*, 89, 94–95).

110. The text does not specify an amount of oil that must be used to prepare the bread. See the footnote above about the substance and the amount of the choice flour.

111. עַל־מַחֲבַת means *on a griddle*. The *Hebrew and English Lexicon* defines מַחֲבַת as a flat plate, pan, or griddle for baking (BDB 290). They note that only ritual texts in the Scriptures use this word to describe a cooking utensil (Lev 2:5; 6:7 [14]; 7:9; 1 Chr 23:29), but in Ezek 4:3 it describes an iron plate that signifies a wall of iron.

112. The procedure for preparing the daily bread offering of the high priest resembles that of daily life in ancient Israel. They would prepare this kind of bread, break it into pieces, and soak it in oil just before eating it (Kleinig, *Leviticus*, 156).

113. See Kleinig, *Leviticus*, 156–57.

114. In both Num 28:3 and Lev 6:13 [20], the offerings must be presented before the LORD regularly, תָּמִיד. Although Lev 6:13 [20] does not specify it, Num 28:3 adds

morning when the sun rises and in the evening at twilight.[115] Although the acts are slightly different in the morning than they are in the evening, the rite of presentation has the same purpose at both,[116] to present the food of the LORD in the times appointed by him (Num 28:2).[117] Thus, the materials for the daily divine service are presented every morning and every evening, to supply his table with food at dawn and at dusk every day.[118]

Ritual Locations

Two locations are significant in the presentation rite. The first is somewhere outside the courtyard of the tabernacle. This is the place where the Israelites select and initially inspect the lambs for the burnt offering. It is most likely also outside the courtyard that the choice flour is mixed with the olive oil, and the frankincense and salt are added to it. The drink offering of wine or another fermented beverage from the vine is selected before it is brought to the tabernacle. The bread for the offering of the high priest is prepared on a griddle somewhere outside the sanctuary area. After these materials are prepared, they are brought to the tabernacle.[119] The second significant location is the *entrance to the tent of meeting*.[120] This is the space from the doorway of the courtyard to the doorway of the tent, where the altar for burnt offering and the font are placed (Exod 29:42; 38:8; Lev 1:5; 4:7, 18; 17:4–6).[121] While

---

that the offering is presented each day, לְיוֹם. Thus, the offerings must be presented every day, without exception.

115. For further details about the exact time of the morning and evening, see the section on ritual time in the fire rite.

116. See the section on ritual acts.

117. לַחְמִי . . . בְּמוֹעֲדוֹ.

118. The offerings are presented not exactly at dawn and not exactly at sundown. Before clocks were invented, it was likely impossible to find a more precise way of determining time than the sun's rhythms (Stuart, *Exodus*, 629). Thus, the LORD provides his food both in the beginning of the day and as night is falling.

119. See the section above on ritual acts, especially the discussion of the bread offering of the high priest in Lev 6:12–16 [19–23].

120. Hebrew פֶּתַח אֹהֶל־מוֹעֵד. The *Hebrew and English Lexicon* renders פֶּתַח as *opening, doorway, entrance* (BDB 835). Haran holds that פֶּתַח אֹהֶל־מוֹעֵד is deliberately vague and undefined, yet insists that this cannot be outside the courtyard (Haran, *Temples and Temple Service*, 184–85). Milgrom claims that פֶּתַח can refer to the area in front of doorways, and not merely the threshold itself (Milgrom, *Leviticus 1–16*, 147). See Bartelmus, "פֶּתַח", 173–91.

121. This area includes the entire space from the door of the tent to the door of the courtyard. Since Lev 1:5 states that the altar for burnt offering is located in the entrance to the tent of meeting, the altar does not mark its boundary but encompasses the altar in its entirety. Furthermore, Lev 1:11 shows that the lay offerer slaughters his

the priests have access to any part of the courtyard, most likely the lay Israelites are limited to the east and north sides of the altar.[122] This leads to the conclusion that when offerings are brought before the LORD at the entrance to the tent of meeting, their ritual presentation takes place on the east side of the altar.[123] The selection, preparation, and initial inspection takes place outside the walls of the courtyard, but the presentation of the offerings occurs between the altar for burnt offering and the entryway of the courtyard.[124] The movement from the common area outside the tabernacle and into the holy area in front of the altar signals a change of status and purpose for the materials that are presented to the LORD. Both areas are ritually significant to the presentation rite in the daily divine service.

---

offering at the north side of the altar, giving the laity access to an area beyond the front of the altar. Furthermore, the two curtains at the door of the tent and the door of the courtyard consist of identical material and craftsmanship (Exod 26:36; 27:16), indicating that the entire courtyard comprises the same degree of holiness (Milgrom, *Leviticus 1–16*, 147–49).

122. While Lev 1:11 gives lay offerers access to the north side, in addition to the east side, of the altar, 1:13 may indicate that they have access to the west side between the altar and the tent, because the font may supply the water necessary for washing the entrails and legs of the slaughtered animals. The Pentateuch never states, however, that the water for washing the parts of the animal comes from the font.

123. The phrase *before the LORD*, לִפְנֵי יְהוָה (Exod 29:42) probably designates the area to the east side of the altar. While פֶּתַח אֹהֶל־מוֹעֵד may spell out the entire area from the tent doorway to the courtyard opening, the entrance to the tent of meeting before the LORD, פֶּתַח אֹהֶל־מוֹעֵד לִפְנֵי יְהוָה, could mark out the space from the altar to the opening of the courtyard. See Milgrom, *Leviticus 1–16*, 155.

124. The entrance, פֶּתַח, to the tent of meeting, אֹהֶל־מוֹעֵד, is the tabernacle's eastern courtyard. It extends from the altar to the courtyard entrance, and is the zone where the Israelites come to interact with the LORD by approaching him and presenting their offerings. Although the altar itself is completely out of bounds for the laity, they may access the east and north sides of the altar (Kleinig, *Leviticus*, 53). Lev 2:8 seems to confirm that the laity cannot access the altar itself. Milgrom, however, suggests the possibility that a layperson may even touch the altar because he distinguishes between "touching" it and "encroaching" it to minister at it (Milgrom, *Leviticus 1–16*, 148). His view appears to agree with the directives in Num 1:51; 3:10, 38; 17:13; 18:3–7 where the Levites and the laity are forbidden from *approaching* the altar to perform the divine service. However, neither the laity nor the Levites are permitted to touch the altar because it is most holy (Exod 29:37; 30:22–29) and they have not been anointed to enact its rites. Furthermore, the altar is both covered and carried by poles that are inserted into it, as is the case with all of the most holy furniture (Exod 25:13–15, 27–28; 27:6–7; 30:4–5; 35:12–13, 15–16; 37:4–5, 14–15, 27–28; 38:5–7; 39:35, 39; 40:20; Num 4:6, 8, 11, 14), so that even the Levites do not touch the altar when it is moved.

The Ritual Function of the Daily Divine Service

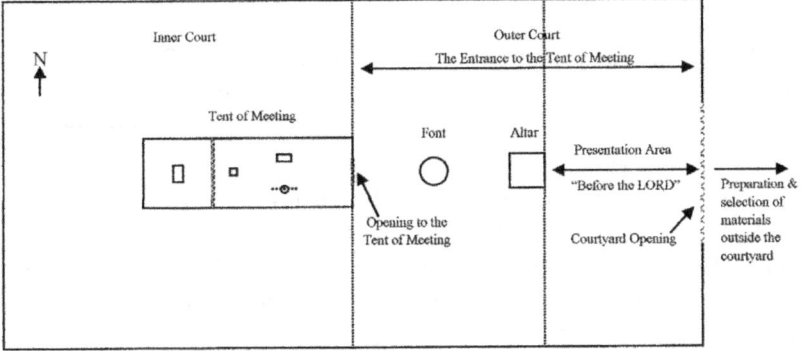

Figure 4. The tent of meeting and the courtyard.

Summary of the Ritual Function

The ritual function of the divine service depends on the interaction between its various components. The agents are the priests, the Israelites, and the LORD. The priests conduct the presentation rite at the sanctuary. The Israelites are responsible for supplying the materials that the priests present as offerings, as well as their initial inspection and preparation. The LORD receives the offerings that are presented to him, which he authorizes for the daily divine service. The acts involve the following. The priests wash and vest before they inspect and present the lamb for the burnt offering. Next, the high priest places a hand on the head of the lamb, after which the priests present the cereal offering and drink offering. Then, the high priest presents his bread offering. Four categories of materials are brought to the tabernacle for the priests to present before the LORD. The first is the unblemished yearling male lamb. The second is one tenth of an ephah of choice flour mixed with one quarter of a hin of beaten olive oil, with frankincense and salt. The third is one quarter of a hin of wine or fermented beverage. Finally, the bread offering of the high priest is made from one tenth of an ephah of choice flour cooked with oil on a griddle. Half of it is presented in the morning and half of it is presented in the evening. All of these offerings are presented before the LORD every morning at dawn and every evening at twilight. The Israelites bring the materials for the offerings to the tabernacle, and the priests present them at the entrance to the tent of meeting between the altar for burnt offering and the opening to the courtyard. The presentation rite ensures that the materials are presented to the LORD for the daily divine service at the tabernacle.

The Theological Purpose of the Presentation Rite

What is the theological purpose of the presentation rite? This question assumes that God achieves an intended purpose through its enactment. Furthermore, the LORD accomplishes two ritually significant things through the presentation rite.

First, he favorably accepts both the offerings and the agents who present them at the entrance to the tent of meeting (Lev 1:3–4).[125] The presentation of the materials in the hands of the priests and placing a hand on the head of the lamb by the high priest, designate the materials as belonging to all Israel[126] so that the LORD accepts them and their offerings.[127] When the high priest presents his daily bread offering, the LORD favorably accepts it and confirms him as the ritual head of Israel and as the representative of the LORD to them.[128] Through the presentation of the materials for the daily divine service the LORD accepts both the materials and the entire community of Israel, including its priests.

---

125. The Hebrew word רָצוֹן means *goodwill, favor, acceptance, will, desire, pleasure* (BDB 953). Variations of the form לְרָצוֹן, *for acceptance*, always occur in ritual contexts (Exod 28:38; Lev 1:3; 19:5; 22:19–21, 29; 23:11; Ps 19:15; Isa 56:7) to express divine favor of someone, or in the case of Jer 6:20 divine disfavor. In Lev 1:3, the third person masculine singular pronominal suffix on לִרְצֹנוֹ can refer to either the offering or the person who brings the offering or both (Kleinig, *Leviticus*, 53). Levine claims that since the antecedent of לְרָצוֹן in Lev 1:3 is the one who presents the offering, the offering is accredited to the person (Levine, *Leviticus*, 6). לְרָצוֹן functions as a ritual term to identify offerings that benefit the offerer, as long as the materials and procedures are correct (Hartley, *Leviticus*, 19). Milgrom points out two significant aspects of לְרָצוֹן. First, for the person presenting the offering to be acceptable to the LORD, the offering must be unblemished. In Lev 22:17–30, which specifies blemishes that disqualify animals from being offered, there are seven references to forms of the word רָצוֹן. This indicates the necessity of presenting unblemished offerings, for the offerer to be accepted by God. Second, רָצוֹן is only associated with burnt offerings (Lev 22:19–20; Jer 6:20) and peace offerings (Lev 19:5; 22:21, 29), never with sin offerings or guilt offerings. This suggests that the sin and guilt offerings strictly serve expiatory functions, while the burnt and peace offerings secure God's favor and acceptance of the one who presents the offering (Milgrom, *Leviticus 1–16*, 149–50). See also Propp, *Exodus 19–40*, 450.

126. The *acceptance*, לְרָצוֹן, of the offerer in Lev 1:4 involves both placing his hand on the head of the animal and bringing the animal before the LORD (Milgrom, *Leviticus 1–16*, 153).

127. The high priest bears the responsibility for all of the offerings presented by the Israelites (Exod 28:38; Num 3:10). The regular priests only perform their duties under the direction and supervision of the high priest.

128. Although the bread offering of the high priest must be presented in the daily divine service, it probably has no immediate effect for Israel or the other priests. It is only for the high priest. Lev 6:15 [22] supports this view, since the high priest's successor places the bread offering on the altar. See Kleinig, *Leviticus*, 154, 156–57.

Second, the LORD supplies the offerings for the altar. He receives the public offerings to be presented before him as his *food* (Num 28:2). When the priests and Israelites present the daily offerings in obedience to the LORD's command, he is providing the food for his own table. The LORD shares his food with his priests, and provides their daily bread from his table while they are on duty at the sanctuary.[129] Through the presentation rite, the LORD accomplishes the practical purpose of replenishing the food that both he and the priests "consume" from his table, the altar for burnt offering.

The LORD accomplishes his purposes through the presentation rite. As the priests present the materials for the offerings before him and designate them for use in the divine service, the LORD favorably accepts his people by accepting their offerings. Since the LORD himself establishes the offerings that are presented at his sanctuary, he provides the food to replenish his table. Through the rite of presentation in the daily divine service, the LORD accepts his people and provides for the holy food that his priests eat from his altar at the sanctuary.

Conclusion

The LORD institutes the presentation rite in order to accept the priests and Israelites through the daily offerings that they present to him every morning and evening. As the agents perform its ritual acts with its prescribed materials at its specified time and location, the presentation rite changes the status and use of the materials presented at the tabernacle. The priests ritually purify their hands to handle holy things and their feet to walk on holy ground near the altar for burnt offering. They put on their sacred vestments, covering themselves with the holiness of the LORD, to perform the ritual enactments within the holy precincts at the entrance to the tent of meeting. The priests inspect and present a yearling male lamb each morning and evening, and the high priest or his deputy places his hand on its head.

---

129. Levine maintains that there is a difference between presenting an offering to the LORD and presenting an offering to other deities in the ancient Near East. For the latter, the pervasive mode of offering is *presentation*, even though there is some evidence for offerings by fire. The offerings of pagan gods are placed before them on a platform or table and the deity receives the offerings by *viewing* them, not by consuming them. Priests or other attendants eat the food offerings of the deity. If an altar is used, it is not for burning any part of the offering. It functions merely as a table. Thus, the deities receive the offerings by "sight" and not in any other way. The LORD, however, receives his offerings not by sight, but as they ascend to him in smoke from the holy fire on the altar (Levine, *Numbers*, 400–402).

The priests present the accompanying cereal and drink offerings before the LORD, and the high priest presents his bread offering to him, half of it in the morning and half of it in the evening as part of the ritual enactments each day. The LORD institutes the presentation rite to supply the offerings for his altar, and to accept his priests and his people through them in the daily divine service.

THE BLOOD RITE

The ritual use of animal blood in the daily divine service may seem foreign or even repulsive to people in the modern world, but in animistic societies blood is a significant and powerful substance. To them blood is the supernatural life-force that enlivens and empowers animals and humans. It is both living and life giving; it exists in both the material and the spiritual realms. The pagan neighbors of ancient Israel drank blood or ate meat with the blood in it to gain the vitality, virility, fertility, and energy of the animal for themselves. They also used blood to feed the spirits of the dead or the gods of the underworld as well as to appease the evil spirits to protect themselves from bad fortune. Sometimes blood was used to invoke the powers of the underworld for divination. The LORD forbids all of these uses of blood for the Israelites. Instead, he requires that blood can only be used ritually at the altar for burnt offering at the tabernacle for Israel's atonement, not because the blood in itself atones but because the LORD institutes the blood rite and the use of the blood from his offerings for this purpose.[130]

The Divine Institution of the Blood Rite

The LORD institutes the blood rite by authorizing the performance of its ritual acts.[131] There are two categories of enactments that are performed in the blood rite. The first are those acts that relate to the manipulation of the blood. The second are the ones that prepare the carcass for its incineration. This section examines these two classifications of activities to ascertain the institution of the blood rite in the daily divine service.

The LORD authorizes the ritual disposal of blood from the lamb for the daily burnt offering. He requires the priests to present the blood and splash it against the sides of the altar in the courtyard (Lev 1:5). The blood

---

130. See Kleinig, *Leviticus*, 365–68.
131. The ritual acts and their significant terms, such as slaying, presenting, splashing, flaying, and slaughtering, are discussed in the section on the blood rite in the previous chapter.

rite is enacted for all burnt offerings of quadrupeds (Lev 1:10–11). It is also prescribed for the burnt offering at the ordination service (Exod 29:15–16; see Lev 8:19) and is enacted for the burnt offering of the people at the inaugural service (Lev 9:12, 16). Since all burnt offerings involve the ritual disposal of blood, it may be concluded that presenting and splashing the blood from the daily burnt offering are divinely instituted.

The LORD commands the Israelites to put the blood of animal offerings on the altar (Lev 17:1–11).[132] Since the blood from their offerings cannot be disposed in any other place for any other purpose than the blood rite on the altar, this applies foremost to the blood from the lambs for the daily burnt offering.[133] The LORD decrees that he himself gives the blood on the altar to make atonement for all of the Israelites.[134] Through his command and promise, God founds the blood rite as a necessary part of the daily divine service; his word empowers the perpetual enactment of the blood rite on the altar at the sanctuary.[135] The LORD's command to apply the blood of offerings on the altar divinely institutes the blood rite for the daily divine service.[136]

---

132. The LORD gives the blood to atone, לְכַפֵּר, for the Israelites' lives (Lev 17:11). לְכַפֵּר is a technical ritual term that refers to the application of blood by the priests to the altar for burnt offering (Kleinig, "Blood for Sprinkling," 129). The LORD's assignment of blood "for you upon the altar" institutes the application of blood to the altar for the benefit of the Israelites as his gift to them (Gilders, *Blood Ritual*, 169). See also Lang, "כִּפֶּר," 288–303; Levine, *In the Presence*, 63–77.

133. Milgrom holds that the command to put the blood on the altar in Lev 17:11 applies only to the peace offering (Milgrom, *Leviticus 17–22*, 1473–78). However, as Kiuchi and Kleing point out, Lev 17:8 mentions the burnt offering and the peace offering together (Kiuchi, *Leviticus*, 319; Kleing, *Leviticus*, 357). Since Lev 17:11 does not refer to a specific offering, it most likely refers to the blood from all animal offerings.

134. The phrase וַאֲנִי נְתַתִּיו לָכֶם is a formula of divine assignment that is similar to other formulas that grant a portion of the offerings to the priests (Lev 7:34; 10:17; Num 18:8, 11–12, 19) or to the Levites (Num 18:21, 24, 26) as what is due to them for their service at the sanctuary. In Lev 17:11, the divine assignment grants the blood to the Israelites for the exclusive use on the altar in the blood rite (Kleinig, *Leviticus*, 357).

135. Lev 17:11 founds the blood rite as one of the most important parts of the ritual system. Here, the LORD constitutes the blood rite and he establishes the practice of ritual atonement (Kleinig, *Leviticus*, 367). Lev 17:11 does not merely announce what the LORD would accomplish for Israel through the blood rite, but that it actually empowers the rite to atone for his people through the faithful performance of it (Kleinig, "Blood for Sprinkling," 126).

136. When Deut 12:1–28 anticipates the Israelites' settlement into their land, it stipulates that they must bring all of their offerings to the sanctuary. Deut 12:27 states that the blood from the Israelites' offerings must be put on the altar for burnt offering. This supports the position that the blood rite established in Lev 17:11 is intended to be carried out regularly at the sanctuary after the LORD's people settle in their own land.

In addition to the ritual disposal of blood, the LORD authorizes the priests to prepare the carcass for its placement on the altar.[137] He commands that the burnt offering must be killed and flayed to remove the skin before it is cut into pieces (Lev 1:5–6).[138] In both the inaugural service and the ordination service, the priests slaughter the burnt offering and then hand the animal to Aaron in pieces (Exod 29:17; Lev 8:20, 21; 9:14, 30). Furthermore, the entrails and lower legs are washed before the burnt offering is put on the altar (Lev 1:9, 13).[139] The LORD also requires every offering to be dashed with salt (Lev 2:13), including the sectioned pieces of the animal for the daily burnt offering.[140] These acts must be performed in the blood rite of the daily divine service to prepare the lamb for being smoked up on the altar.

The blood rite is instituted by God. He commands the Israelites to ritually dispose the blood of their domestic animals, especially that from the daily burnt offering and all offerings, at the tabernacle. He authorizes the priests to perform the ritual acts involved with the manipulation of blood in the daily divine service. Furthermore, he institutes the ritual activities of the blood rite that prepare the carcass to be burned on the altar fire. The LORD establishes the blood rite by prescribing the disposal of blood on the altar at the tabernacle and by authorizing the priests to perform its acts in the daily divine service.

The Ritual Function of the Blood Rite

What is the ritual function of the blood rite? Splashing blood against the sides of the altar for burnt offering seems like a strange ritual act. Why not just pour out the blood on the ground or use it for some other practical

---

137. See the analysis of the blood rite in chapter 2 for further information about the rationale to include the ritual acts that prepare the carcass in the blood rite.

138. Although Lev 1:12 does not specify that the animal must be flayed before it is cut into pieces, this must be assumed on the basis of Lev 1:6. Furthermore, Lev 7:8 gives evidence that the skin is never burned on the altar but is kept by the priest who offers it.

139. Occasionally, instead of repeatedly mentioning them, the Pentateuch assumes that ritual activities are performed, such as those related to preparing the carcass (Milgrom, *Leviticus 1–16*, 157, 159, 163, 166).

140. While Hartley and Kleinig identify the salt in Lev 2:13 with cereal offerings, neither of them make mention of salt being put on the pieces of the lamb for the burnt offering (Hartley, *Leviticus*, 32–33; Kleinig, *Leviticus*, 74, 76, 79–80). Levine and Milgrom on the other hand, hold that salt is placed on all offerings, including the lambs for the daily burnt offering (Levine, *Leviticus*, 13; Milgrom, *Leviticus 1–16*, 191–92). *Tamid* 4:3 indicates that the priests salt all of the pieces of the lamb for the daily burnt offering at the temple in Jerusalem (Blackman, *Kodashim*, 487). Num 18:19 may also imply that salt must be added to animal offerings.

purpose in the daily life of the ancient Israelites? It has already been determined that God establishes the blood rite according to his word. The following examination delves further into the practical reasons for its institution.

Ritual Agents

The high priest and the regular priests are the agents who perform this rite. Since the high priest represents the entire community of Israel, only he or his deputy can perform its primary task, splashing the blood on the altar.[141] In the inaugural service, Aaron performs the main part of the blood rite for each kind of offering, as his sons assist him by catching the blood in bowls and handing it to him. This indicates that the regular priests perform a secondary role in the corporate blood rites, even though they are the chief agents who perform the activities for the offerings of individuals (Lev 1:5, 11). Since the inaugural service is a public event, its blood rite is performed by the high priest, as the representative of the entire community. Just as Aaron alone splashes the blood in the inaugural service in Lev 9:12, so also Moses alone performs the blood rite in the ordination service in Lev 8:19 as the founder of the divine service. Both instances imply that the chief representative of the LORD must perform the public blood rite for the entire community. Furthermore, on the Day of Atonement, only the high priest disposes the blood of all of the public offerings. It may be concluded, therefore, that the high priest or his deputy, as the head of the community of Israel, must enact the corporate blood rites including the one for the public daily burnt offering.[142]

The people of the entire community of Israel are ritual agents in a general sense in the performance of the daily blood rite.[143] Since the foundational command in Lev 17:11 to put the blood of offerings on the altar is in the broader context of the entire chapter, the agents listed there must also be agents in the blood rite of the daily divine service.[144] Lev 17:2 addresses the whole community and therefore, all of the Israelites, whether native born or alien, whether priest or laity, are agents in the public rite of disposing the blood.[145] Furthermore, because the high priest, as the chief agent, carries out the blood rite, the rest of the people of Israel are its beneficiaries.

---

141. See Exod 28:30, 38, which states that Aaron, the high priest, bears the judgment for all of the offerings of the Israelites in the divine service.

142. Lev 17:5, 6 seem to imply that "the priest," הַכֹּהֵן, which, with the definite article, ה, usually means the high priest, performs the blood rite also for peace offerings.

143. See Lev 17:1–2, 10, 13, 15.

144. See the section above on the divine institution of the blood rite.

145. The audience in Lev 17:2 is the same audience in Lev 22:18, which is in the

106   The LORD's Service

The instituting agent is the LORD since he commands who must splash the blood against the altar (Lev 17:11). He accomplishes his purposes through the priests who dispose of the blood on his behalf (Lev 1:5–6, 9, 11–13). Through them, the LORD pardons and releases his people from their sins and cleanses them from their impurity. In the blood rite, the priests represent the LORD who acts through them for the benefit of the Israelites.[146]

Ritual Acts

The first ritual act involves slaying the lamb.[147] The lamb is taken to the north side of the altar (Lev 1:11) where its throat is cut through the artery and all of its blood is drained out as the priests catch it in bowls.[148] This procedure accomplishes two functions. On the one hand, the lamb is slain to collect its blood in bowls so that it can be presented before the LORD.[149] On the other hand, the lamb must be killed before its carcass can be cut into

section that lists the qualifications for the individual offerings of the Israelites. These are the only two places in Leviticus where Aaron, his sons, and the Israelites—the high priest, regular priests, and lay people—are addressed. Thus, the entire community is responsible. In both chapters, the individual offerings must be distinguished from the public offerings. Yet, both kinds of offerings are part of the entire ritual system conducted at the sanctuary and are not entirely exclusive to each other (Kleinig, *Leviticus*, 355, 362–63, 476). Lev 17:2 is within an address to the whole community, and therefore all of the Israelites, whether native born or alien, whether priest or laity, are ritual agents in the blood rite at the sanctuary.

146. Everything centers on the presence of the LORD at the tent of meeting and his altar. All the offerings are brought to him and performed for him on his behalf. He institutes the blood rite and warns the Israelites against the misuse of blood from their offerings. The LORD is the main agent in the blood rite (Kleinig, *Leviticus*, 363).

147. See the section on the blood rite in chapter 2 for an analysis of the order and procedure of its ritual acts, as well as further discussion about the word שָׁחַט, which is translated here as *slay*.

148. For a discussion about differing interpretations about the Hebrew word שָׁחַט, see Hartley, *Leviticus*, 269–71; Levine, *Leviticus*, 112–13. In ritual contexts, this term refers to ritually slitting the main neck artery to drain the blood from the animal so that it may be applied to the altar in the blood rite (Kleinig, *Leviticus*, 55). The word שָׁחַט is also found in the Pentateuch in Gen 22:10; 37:31; Exod 12:6, 21; 29:11, 16, 20; 34:25; Lev 1:5, 11; 3:2, 8, 13; 4:4, 15, 24, 29, 33; 6:11 [18]; 7:2; 8:15, 19, 23; 9:8, 12, 15, 18; 14:5–6, 13, 19, 25, 50–51; 16:11, 15; 17:3; 22:28; Num 11:22; 14:16; 19:3.

149. The lamb is not offered by being ritually slain, even though the slaying happens before the LORD (Lev 1:5, 11). Furthermore, the animal's death by itself does not hold any special ritual significance (Kleinig, *Leviticus*, 53, 63). The purpose for killing the animal by cutting its main neck artery is to collect its blood so that it may be splashed on the altar.

pieces to burn it on the altar. Slaying the lamb at the daily service prepares for the ritual activities that follow it.

The second ritual act is the disposal of its blood, which involves a twofold procedure: presenting the blood before the LORD and splashing it on the altar for burnt offering.[150] Similar to the presentation of the materials in the presentation rite, the blood is presented before the LORD at the altar to effect a change of ritual status and function (Lev 1:5). After that, it is no longer profane blood with a common function; it is now holy blood to be used for a holy purpose.[151] Splashing the blood against the sides of the altar is the most significant activity of the blood rite since it accomplishes a theological purpose. Once the blood has been drained from the animal, caught in bowls, and presented before the LORD, it must be tossed against the sides of the altar to accomplish its ritual function by its proper disposal.[152] On the one hand, the presentation of the blood is ritually significant since it effects a change in its status from common to holy. On the other hand, its presentation does not accomplish the purpose of the blood rite but prepares for it. Splashing the blood against the four sides of the altar ritually disposes of the blood to accomplish the LORD's intended purpose (Lev 17:11).[153] Thus, the blood is presented and splashed as the two main ritual acts in the blood rite.

---

150. For a more detailed discussion about the Hebrew words for present, הִקְרִיב, and splash, זָרַק, see the sections on the presentation rite and the blood rite in chapter 2. See also the section on the presentation rite in this chapter for further information about the ritual function of the presentation of materials.

151. Presenting the blood could be enacted as an elevation offering. See Lev 7:30–33; Milgrom, *Leviticus 1–16*, 155. While the Pentateuch does not command the priests to elevate the blood in the presence of the LORD, this would be an appropriate ritual act to effect the change of the blood's status from common to holy.

152. See Lev 17:11. Since all the blood is dispersed on the altar, it is entirely excluded from human use, including for both sacred and secular purposes (Kleinig, *Leviticus*, 64, 368).

153. The application of the offering's blood on the altar is a rite of atonement because the blood that is reserved *for* the altar is also given to atone for Israel *from* the altar. Thus, God grants his people to use the blood only for their atonement. This ritual disposal of the lamb's blood exclusively qualifies the Israelites to participate in God's holiness through the daily divine service (Kleinig, *Leviticus*, 65, 357, 368).

Its third ritual activity is slaughtering the lamb.¹⁵⁴ Before it is cut into parts, it must be flayed.¹⁵⁵ This involves removing all of the skin with the exception of that from the head and lower legs, which would be practically impossible to dislodge from them. Once the lamb has been flayed, the priests may then section it into its pieces that will be burned on the altar. Since the skin is not burned, it is left intact and given for the personal use of the priest who presents the lamb.¹⁵⁶ The animal is cut into pieces by dividing both its inner and outer members. Not only are its outer parts dismembered from each other, the entrails of the lamb are also separated from its other inner organs and fat. The head, fat, and other pieces are placed together, while the lower legs and entrails are kept apart from them for later use. The lamb is flayed and slaughtered to prepare it for its incineration on the altar.

The fourth ritual activity in the blood rite has to do with the priests washing the entrails and lower legs. Since the entrails are filled with fecal matter, which is not authorized for placement on the altar, they must be swilled with water to wash out the impurity. Likewise, the lower legs, which are dirty with refuse and other contaminants from the ground where the lamb walked, need to be washed so as to keep pollutants from contacting the altar. Once the entrails and lower legs have been cleansed with water, they are placed together with the head, fat and other pieces. Washing the entrails and lower legs prepares them to be placed on the altar fire. The washing cleanses them to prevent ritual impurities such as feces, urine, and refuse from contaminating the other pieces of the animal and from defiling the altar with unclean substances.¹⁵⁷

---

154. The Hebrew word נָתַח means slaughter, to cut up the lamb into its sections. While some scholars (Kleinig, *Leviticus*, 55; Levine, *Leviticus*, 7; Milgrom, *Leviticus 1–16*, 154) use the word *slaughter* to designate the ritual killing of the animal, it is helpful, however, to distinguish between the slaying and the cutting up of the lamb. Slaying the lamb is the ritual cutting of the main neck artery to drain its blood, while slaughtering the lamb refers to cutting it into its pieces after its blood has been drained. See also the New American Standard Bible on Lev 1:5–6 for a similar distinction between slaying and slaughtering. This term is discussed further in the section on the blood rite in chapter 2.

155. See the section on the blood rite in chapter 2 for more information regarding the flaying, פָּשַׁט, of the skin from the lamb.

156. The hide is a prebend for the officiating priest (Milgrom, *Leviticus 1–16*, 156–57, 411). The hide of the daily burnt offering seems to be devoid of any ritual significance. Therefore, it could be removed from the sacred realm at the sanctuary and used for common purposes by the priest who receives it. See also Kiuchi, *Leviticus*, 129–30; Kleinig, *Leviticus*, 168; Levine, *Leviticus*, 7, 41.

157. Dirt and excrement defile the altar, and therefore, the lower legs and the entrails must be washed out to remove filth, bodily fluids, and undigested food (see Hartley, *Leviticus*, 22; Kleinig, *Leviticus*, 56). While it may be argued that dirt of itself

The Ritual Function of the Daily Divine Service 109

The final ritual activity in the blood rite is salting all of the parts of the animal. The Pentateuch provides little evidence for the ritual function of salting and only states that salt must be added to every offering.[158] It could function as a preservative due to its stabilizing character, just as it does for the cereal offering.[159] When applied to the sectioned parts of the lamb, however, the salt most likely draws out the residual blood from the meat before it is placed on the altar.[160] If so, then putting salt on the pieces of the lamb completes the necessary removal of blood so that none of it is burned with the offerings.[161]

Ritual Materials

Three ritual materials are used in the daily blood rite. The first and most significant is the blood that is drained from the lamb.[162] Since the blood is

---

does not defile the altar since the altar sits on the ground, it is evident that dirt and excrement are not acceptable ritual substances that may be offered *on* the altar.

158. See Lev 2:13.

159. Hartley claims that salt acts as a preservative and a seasoning for the cereal offering (Hartley, *Leviticus*, 33). Since the priests eat the remaining portion of the cereal offering, it makes sense that the salt functions as a means of adding flavor. However, none of the meat from the burnt offering is eaten by the priests. Therefore, it is unlikely that salt functions as its seasoning. Kleinig and Milgrom maintain that the salt functions practically as a preservative (Kleinig, *Leviticus*, 76; Milgrom, *Leviticus 1–16*, 191).

160. Levine claims that it is not expected that cereal offerings would be salted, and that this likely reflects the tendency toward ritual uniformity. He does not recognize a ritual function for salting cereal offerings, such as for seasoning or as a preservative. Levine, however, stresses the importance of salting the parts of the slaughtered animal, which functions to remove whatever blood remains in the sectioned carcass (Levine, *Leviticus*, 13).

161. Kiuchi holds that the command in Lev 2:13 to apply salt to offerings is the final prescription for various loyalty offerings (Kiuchi, *Leviticus*, 72–73). He does not make it clear if he thinks salting is the final ritual act of preparation before the offerings are burned on the altar. Ezek 43:24 seems to indicate that salting is the final ritual act prior to the incineration of burnt offerings on the altar. Milgrom, however, questions whether the injunction to add salt applies to all offerings. He suggests that only the parts of the offering that are burned on the altar require salting. This implies that Ezek 43:24 may be a general command to salt only those parts of the animal that are burned on the altar (Milgrom, *Leviticus 1–16*, 192). Practically speaking, salting the pieces of the lamb is the last thing that happens before the offerings are burned on the altar.

162. Bronze bowls are used for splashing the blood. According to Exod 27:3; 38:3; Num 4:14, bronze bowls, הַמִּזְרָקֹת, are utensils used at the altar for burnt offering. The Pentateuch does not state how these bowls function at the altar, yet it is most logical to assume that they are utilized in the blood rite. The bronze bowls must be distinguished from the silver bowls mentioned in Num 7:13, 19, 25, 31, 37, 43, 49, 55, 61, 67, 73, 79, 84, 85, which contain cereal offerings of fine flour mixed with oil. Therefore, the bronze

splashed against the four sides of the altar to bring about atonement for Israel, the blood is the primary ritual substance in this rite. The second ritual material is the water for cleaning the entrails and lower legs of the lamb.[163] It cleanses these parts of the lamb so that the contaminants on them will not defile the altar and other parts of the daily burnt offering. The third ritual material is the salt.[164] After the blood is splashed on the altar and all of the parts of the lamb are sectioned and ready to be smoked up, salt is put on them to preserve them from corruption and to draw out the remaining blood from them.

Ritual Times

The blood rite occurs at the break of day and just before nightfall (Exod 29:38–39; Num 28:3–4).[165] Since the blood of every Israelite offering must be applied to the altar (Lev 17:11), it may be concluded that this happens every morning and every evening after the lamb is slain and its blood drained from its artery into the bowls.[166] All of the ritual acts of the blood rite, such

---

bowls are most likely used in the blood rite to catch the blood as it drains from the lamb and to splash it against the sides of the altar. None of the texts in the Pentateuch that speak of blood rites state that bowls are used (Exod 29:12, 16, 20; Lev 1:5, 11; 3:2, 8, 13; 4:5–7, 16–18, 25, 30, 34; 5:9; 6:23 [30]; 7:2, 14; 8:15, 19, 24; 9:9, 12, 18; 16:14–15, 18; 17:6, 11; Num 18:17; 19:4; Deut 12:27). The use of bronze bowls in the blood rite is implied, since they are accessories to the bronze altar.

163. Where does this water come from? The Pentateuch does not answer this question. Wenham claims that the water probably comes from the font that stands between the altar for burnt offering and the tent of meeting (Wenham, *Leviticus*, 54). Second Chronicles 4:6 states, however, that the ten additional basins at the temple in Jerusalem were used for washing the things of the burnt offering, while the font was used exclusively by the priests for their own ritual cleansing. Milgrom supposes that the "things" washed in the basins are the entrails and lower legs of the daily burnt offering, and not merely the utensils used in the blood rite (Milgrom, *Leviticus 1–16*, 160). As *Tamid* 4:2 indicates, the washing is most likely enacted on the north side of the altar (Blackman, *Kodashim*, 484). Since the water is holy, having contacted the most holy font (Exod 30:28–29), it seems unlikely that it would be used for such a menial purpose. The water for washing the entrails and lower legs in the daily blood rite most likely comes from a source other than the most holy font.

164. Milgrom claims that supplies of salt are kept at the sanctuary for use with the public offerings, while private offerings would be salted from the individual's personal supply (Milgrom, *Leviticus 1–16*, 191). Levine notes that, according to Ezra 6:9; 7:22, large quantities of salt were delivered to the temple in Jerusalem for use in the divine services (Levine, *Leviticus*, 13). See also Ezek 43:24.

165. For details about the exact time, see the sections on the fire rite and the presentation rite in this chapter.

166. See the blood rite in chapter 2 about the method of splashing the blood against

as flaying and slaughtering the lamb, washing its entrails and legs, and salting all of its parts, are performed twice each day. There is an additional temporal element in that splashing the blood on the altar must happen prior to burning incense and smoking up the offerings, because the blood rite prepares for the ritual acts that follow it. The blood rite is enacted as the sun is rising and setting every day to prepare the priests and people for what occurs in the rest of the divine service.

Ritual Locations

The blood rite is enacted in two significant locations. Both places are within the courtyard of the sanctuary. First, the north side of the altar for burnt offering is the place where the lamb is slain (Lev 1:11),[167] but the Pentateuch provides no rationale for this location. This is also the site where the lamb is flayed, cut into pieces, and its entrails and lower legs washed. The north side of the altar functions as the most practical area for preparing the lamb, since the font sits to the west, the entryway to the courtyard is east of the altar, and its south side is most likely a location for other ritual functions.[168] The second and most significant ritual location is the altar for burnt offering.[169] The blood is splashed on all sides of the altar (Lev 1:5, 11)[170] to make atonement on it (Lev 17:11).[171] Since the altar for burnt offering is where atonement

---

the sides of the altar for burnt offering.

167. Only flock animals offered as burnt offerings, sin offerings, and guilt offerings are slain on the north side of the altar. Flock animals offered as peace offerings are slain at the entrance to the tent of meeting, on the east side of the altar, where all bovine offerings are slain (Milgrom, *Leviticus 1–16*, 164–65). The daily burnt offering is always killed and slaughtered on the altar's north side.

168. The north side of the altar is the most practical place for the slaughter of the lamb, since the west side is the place of the font, the east side is the place of the ash heap and entrance, and the south side at the temple in Jerusalem is the place where the priests ascend to the top of the altar. See Hartley, *Leviticus*, 23; Milgrom, *Leviticus 1–16*, 164. See also Ezek 40:39–42. The priests probably eat the most holy food either on the south or on the southwest side of the altar, because it is the opposite location from the muddy refuse covered area on its north side. Thus, the designation of the north side of the altar as the place for preparing the lamb serves the practical purpose of preserving the other locations around the altar from becoming soiled.

169. See the section on the ritual materials for the fire rite in this chapter for a detailed description of the altar for burnt offering.

170. עַל־הַמִּזְבֵּחַ סָבִיב is literally rendered *around/in a circuit on the altar* (BDB 686–87). This indicates that all four sides of the altar must have blood splashed against them. The method of splashing is discussed in the section on the blood rite in the previous chapter.

171. Practically speaking, the altar for burnt offering is the most important piece of

occurs, it is the most ritually significant location in the blood rite.[172] The north side of the altar in the courtyard and the four sides of the altar itself are its two significant ritual locations.

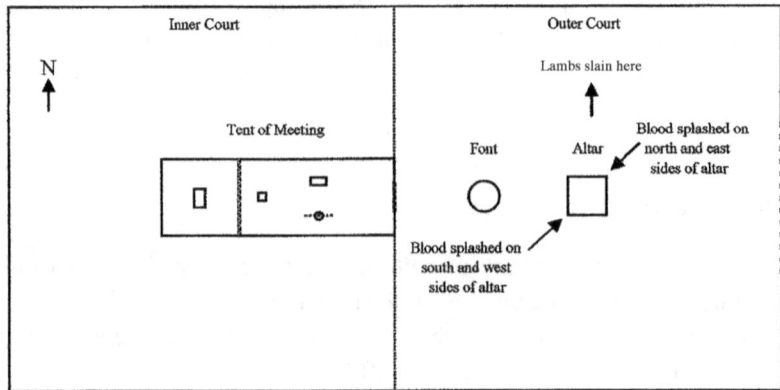

Figure 5. The altar and its north side.

Summary of the Ritual Function

The blood rite involves its agents who perform its acts with certain materials at the proper times in the correct locations. Although the entire community of Israel and the regular priests are agents in a general sense, the LORD and the high priest are its main agents. The LORD institutes the ritual disposal of blood and commands the high priest to perform its corresponding acts on his behalf. The regular priests assist him as he kills the lamb by cutting the neck artery. They catch its blood in bowls and hand it to the high priest, who presents it before the LORD. The high priest then splashes the blood against the sides of the altar as the regular priests skin the lamb, cut it into pieces, wash its entrails and legs, and salt its sections in preparation to turn it into smoke on the altar. The blood rite is enacted with the ritual materials necessary for completing its function. The blood is ritually disposed only

---

furniture at the sanctuary, since it is the location for the LORD's theophany where he meets with Israel every morning and evening in the divine service, and it is the place of atonement (Kleinig, *Leviticus*, 55).

172. There is only one legitimate location where the blood of Israel's offerings must be placed: at the authorized altar for burnt offering at the sanctuary (Milgrom, *Leviticus 1–16*, 251). The LORD issues two commands about the ritual location of the blood rite. First, the Israelites must bring all their offerings to the central sanctuary and present them at the altar because anyone who offers them anywhere else is treated as a murderer and is excommunicated (Lev 17:1–9; Deut 12:20–27). Second, all the blood from their offerings must be applied to the altar (Lev 17:6, 11; Deut 12:27). Under no circumstances can the blood be used anywhere else (Kleinig, "Blood for Sprinkling," 126).

on the altar. The water cleanses the entrails and lower legs to prevent contamination of the altar and other parts of the offering. The salt preserves the pieces of the lamb and extracts the remaining blood from the meat. The bowls catch the blood so that it can be tossed on the altar. The lamb is prepared at the north side of the altar and the blood is splashed on its four sides. The blood rite properly disposes of the blood from the victim in the daily service each morning and evening.

The Theological Purpose of the Blood Rite

Lev 17:11 establishes the theological purpose of all blood rites at the altar, including the one for the daily burnt offering.[173] The LORD gives the blood on the altar to make atonement for the lives of the Israelites, because it atones by means of the life in it.[174] When the high priest splashes the blood on the altar, the LORD himself grants atonement for his people.[175] The problem is

---

173. Milgrom holds that Lev 17:11 only refers to the blood from the peace offerings and not from any other kind of offering (Milgrom, *Leviticus 17–22*, 1473–79). However, Milgrom's view is probably incorrect because 17:10 mentions *all* blood and 17:8 speaks of the burnt offering together with the peace offering (Kleinig, *Leviticus*, 357). I hold that Lev 17:11 refers to the blood of all animal offerings.

174. According to Milgrom, the atoning power lies in the *altar*, not in the blood (Milgrom, *Leviticus 17–22*, 1472). Kleinig holds that there are three basic taboos associated with the ritual use of blood in ancient Israel. First, the life of a person or animal is in its blood (Deut 12:23; Lev 17:11, 14) and, therefore, the blood may not be consumed. Second, the exclusive use of blood for ritual purposes on the altar prevents its misuse in other non-Israelite ritual acts. Third, and most importantly, the taboos forbidding the use of blood as food or as a ritual material for pagan religions are the result of the LORD's institution of the blood rite as part of the daily rites at the sanctuary (Kleinig, "Blood for Sprinkling," 125–26). Kleinig points out that since the blood must be applied to the altar in order for atonement to occur, the blood *on* the altar makes atonement *from* the altar. Furthermore, he states that לְכַפֵּר means to make atonement or to perform the rite of atonement, which he understands as the application of blood to the altar. Finally, he discusses the three main ways that בַּנֶּפֶשׁ has been construed and notes the difficulty in translating the בְּ. The first interpretation views it as a *bet essentiae* which understands that the blood *is* life or that the blood is the essence of life. The second view, the *bet pretii*, supposes that the blood is at the cost of the life of the animal or that the blood is in exchange for the life of the person. The third view is the *bet instrumenti*, which understands that the blood is an instrument or means by which atonement is made. The third view is preferred and may be understood as the blood that makes atonement by means of the life (Kleinig, *Leviticus*, 357). See also Hartley, *Leviticus*, 274–76. While elements of all three views may be implied, the *bet instrumenti* is most likely the primary aspect.

175. The Hebrew words for atonement are כִּפֶּר and כֹּפֶר. As Kleinig notes, there is no small amount of discussion among scholars about the etymology and meaning of these terms (Kleinig, "Blood for Sprinkling," 129). He renders כִּפֶּר as *purify* or *cleanse*

that the text does not explain what atonement is or what it accomplishes in the daily divine service. A closer examination of Lev 17:11 will help determine how the blood rite atones at the daily service.

Atonement occurs in three simultaneous ways (Lev 17:11). First, the blood is placed on the altar to make atonement.[176] This ritual act may also be understood as *performing the rite of atonement*, because the blood must be put on the altar for atonement to happen.[177] Second, the placement of blood from the offering on the altar propitiates God.[178] When the high priest

---

from ritual impurity and explains that when it is used together with עַל נֶפֶשׁ it functions as a denominative of כֹּפֶר and means *ransom for a life* (Kleinig, *Leviticus*, 357). Schwartz summarizes the debate about the meaning of כִּפֶּר. He claims that there is no etymological or semantic relation between the words כִּפֶּר and כֹּפֶר, stating that the former word is usually rendered as *wipe away, purge, cleanse, expiate* and the latter word means *ransom* or *payment*. Sometimes the word כִּפֶּר is a denominative verb that is derived from the noun כֹּפֶר and in such cases it too should be translated as *ransom*. He points out that the long-held view that כִּפֶּר and כֹּפֶר mean *cover*, is completely erroneous. Finally, he holds that in Lev 17:11, כֹּפֶר is used in a unique sense and is the only place in the Bible where *ransom* is connected with the blood rite (Schwartz, "Prohibitions Concerning Eating Blood," 51–56). Levine sees a connection between כִּפֶּר and כֹּפֶר. He makes the case that כִּפֶּר does not so much involve the restoration of a broken relationship with God, but it is the means by which to combat the evil forces of impurity to protect the holiness of the LORD (Levine, *In the Presence*, 55–91). Milgrom believes that כִּפֶּר in Lev 17:11 is a ransom from the crime of murdering the animal for the offering (Milgrom, *Leviticus 17–22*, 1472–79). Gorman cautions that כִּפֶּר does not only mean *ransom* but that it carries a broad range of meanings and each must be identified according to the specific function within a specific ritual activity (Gorman, *Ideology of Ritual*, 189). Kiuchi makes the case for understanding כִּפֶּר and its related terms as both a purifying and guilt bearing ritual act (Kiuchi, *Purification Offering*, 87–109). Rodriguez argues for substitution as the main understanding of atonement in Lev 17:11. The blood of the offering is substituted for the Israelites and transfers their sins to the sanctuary where God removes them from people in order to restore their covenant relationship with him (Rodriguez, *Substitution in Hebrew Cultus*, 233–60). Brichto sees atonement as a ritual decontamination and purification of the sanctuary, but his main thrust is that atonement is a legal *composition* that involves the offering/making of and accepting of an agreement in order to reconcile the LORD with his people (Brichto, "Slaughter and Sacrifice," 19–36). Gilders understands כִּפֶּר and its related terms as a *removal* of sin and impurity which *effects ransom* for the LORD's people (Gilders, *Blood Ritual*, 22, 28–29, 72–78, 164–78). The blood rite most likely includes all of these elements of atonement at the same time. See figure six. See also Eberhart, "Neglected Feature of Sacrifice," 486–87; Lang, "כִּפֶּר," 288–303.

176. The phrase עַל־הַמִּזְבֵּחַ, upon the altar, specifies the physical location where atonement occurs in the blood rite.

177. Atonement is most often a technical term that refers to placing blood on the altar for burnt offering (Kleinig, *Leviticus*, 357; "Blood for Sprinkling," 129–30). See also Levine, *In the Presence*, 64–65, 73.

178. The term *propitiate* is the aspect of atonement that is directed toward or does something to God in order to placate his wrath towards his people because of their

tosses the blood on the sides of the altar, the wrath[179] of God is appeased and the sins of Israel are paid for by this ritual act.[180] Third, the LORD declares that the blood by means of its life is what makes atonement for the lives of his people.[181] Atonement expiates the community of Israel at the same time that God is propitiated by the blood on the altar.[182] Since God's wrath is averted through the blood rite, the LORD releases the Israelites from their sins.[183] The payment of blood to God on the altar ransoms the community

---

sins and ritual impurities. The blood on the altar appeases God because it cleanses the Israelites from impurity and releases them from their sins.

179. God's wrath, קֶצֶף, and being angry, קָצַף, is the result of his people's disobedience and ritual impurity, which desecrates his holiness. Any unclean person who comes into his presence at the sanctuary incurs God's wrath and the danger of destruction both for the person and for the entire community of Israel. Thus, one of the purposes of atonement is to daily appease God's wrath so that he will release his people from their sins and ritual impurities. For references in the Pentateuch to God's wrath at his people, see Lev 10:6; Num 1:53; 16:22; 17:11; 18:5; Deut 1:34; 9:7-8, 19, 22; 29:27.

180. While Milgrom recognizes the reconciliatory aspect of atonement, being "at one" with God, he denies that blood rites constitute any effect upon God. The restoration of a relationship with God is only the result of removing impurity and sin from the offerers, which allows them to come into his presence (Milgrom, *Leviticus 1–16*, 1079-84). Gilders holds that atonement involves the restoration of peace with God. Atonement obtains security from a serious threat to life and well being, and therefore, it may be viewed as an *appeasement payment* to restore a right relationship with God (Gilders, *Blood Ritual*, 171).

181. The blood on the altar makes atonement עַל־נַפְשֹׁתֵיכֶם, for your lives, the lives of his people. Kleinig maintains that the blood atones for the lives of God's people by means of, or on the basis of, the life power in it. This is the view of the *bet instrumenti* discussed above. The power of the blood in the rite of atonement, however, does not come from the life in the blood but from the LORD who institutes its use for the purpose of atonement on the altar for burnt offering (Kleinig, *Leviticus*, 358, 366).

182. The term *expiation* is the facet of atonement that is directed toward the people, and is the theological result of propitiation. Just as the blood rite propitiates God by appeasing his wrath, so it also expiates the Israelites, ransoms them, and releases them from sin.

183. To be forgiven, נִסְלַח, is closely associated with atonement in the Pentateuch, especially in relation to the sin offering and the guilt offering that individuals must offer as a remedy for specific sins (Lev 4:20, 26, 31, 35; 5:10, 13, 16, 18, 26; 19:22; Num 15:25-26, 28). The forgiveness that results from the blood rite of the daily divine service is for the general sins of the entire community. The basic sense of the *niphal* verb נִסְלַח has to do with the *release* of a person from the burden and penalty of sin, and in the Pentateuch its subject is always God as the one doing the releasing (Exod 34:9; Lev 4:20, 26, 31, 35; 5:10, 13, 16, 18, 26; 19:22; Num 14:19-20; 15:25-26, 28; 30:6, 9, 13; Deut 29:19). In the Pentateuch, נִסְלַח is a ritual term that is always connected to the blood rite, whereby the Israelites are released from their sins. Through the blood rite God removes their impurity and guilt caused by their sin, freeing them from its penalties, and thereby allowing them to participate in the divine service at the sanctuary without desecrating and defiling it (Kleinig, *Leviticus*, 104-5) See also Hausmann, "סָלַח," 258-65; Levine, *In the Presence*, 64-65.

116   The LORD's Service

of Israel from their bondage in sin and the evil powers of ritual impurity.[184] Furthermore, the blood of the offering substitutes the life of the animal for the lives of the people;[185] and the impurity of Israel is exchanged for purity.[186] As the blood is splashed on the altar, the rite of atonement propitiates, appeases, and makes payment to God for him to expiate, release, ransom, substitute the life of the offering for the lives of the Israelites, and to ritually purify them from their sins and uncleanness.[187] In the blood rite, atonement involves the altar, the LORD, and the Israelites at the same time.

---

184. The blood ransoms the Israelites from death because the blood of the animal compensates for their lives. Through the placement of blood on the altar, the LORD frees the Israelites from their defilement by sin (Kleinig, "Blood for Sprinkling," 129–30).

185. There is a relationship between the animal's life and human lives in the blood rite; the action and effect of atonement has something to do with this relationship (Gilders, *Blood Ritual*, 170). Rodriguez holds that the relationship between the life of the animal and the lives of the offerers is substitution. The sins of the people are transferred to the animal so that its life-blood may be given on the altar in exchange for the life-blood of the offerers. By placing the sin-loaded blood of the animal on the altar, God removes it from his people (Rodriguez, *Substitution in Hebrew Cultus*, 244, 254–55). There is no evidence in the Pentateuch, however, that the sins of the people are transferred to the animal except in the case of the scapegoat on the Day of Atonement. The lambs for the daily burnt offering most likely do not bear the iniquities of the Israelites, since this is the stated function of the priests (Exod 28:38; Lev 10:17; Num 18:1).

186. The societal and religious categories of purity and impurity do not have so much to do with hygiene as they do with order and disorder. Since disorder and impurity are chaotic, they threaten order and purity. Thus, purity and impurity are ritual states of being and ritual powers in contrast and in conflict with each other (Douglas, *Purity and Danger*). Most cultures classify people and things as clean or unclean from their own perspective and judgment. Through the ritual legislation in the Pentateuch, God redefines all natural systems of purity and impurity and subordinates them to his own holiness. The LORD becomes the point of reference and determines what is ritually clean and ritually unclean (Kleinig, *Leviticus*, 7).

187. These aspects of atonement are throughout the Pentateuch: appeasement (Gen 32:21; Exod 32:30; Num 17:11–12), ransom (Exod 30:12–16; Num 35:31–33), substitution (Lev 1:4; 17:11), forgiveness for sins (Lev 4:20, 26, 31, 35; 19:22; Num 15:25, 28), and forgiveness for guilt (Lev 5:6, 10, 13, 16, 18; 5:26 [6:7]; 10:17; Num 5:8). Most often in the Pentateuch, atonement is identified as a ritual purification from uncleanness (Exod 29:33, 36–37; 12:7–8; 14:18–21, 29, 31, 53; 15:15, 30; 16:16–18, 20, 27, 30; Num 6:11; 8:12, 21; Deut 21:8).

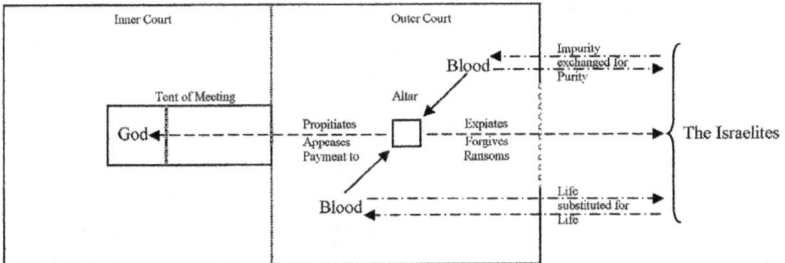

Figure 6. The rite of atonement.

Since Lev 17:11 is tied thematically to the atonement of offerings in other services, these services provide clues for determining what the LORD achieves through the blood rite in the daily divine service. The prescription for the ordination service declares that atonement purifies the altar for burnt offering (Exod 29:36). Due to the correlation between the seven-day atonement for both the altar and the priests (Exod 29:33, 35–37), the application of blood from the ordination offering to the right ear lobes, right thumbs, and right big toes of the priests implies that their atonement is also a ritual purification.[188] The descriptive account of the ordination service further attests to the blood purifying the altar and the priests (Lev 8:15, 34).[189] Rites of atonement precede the theophany of the LORD at the inaugural service (Lev 9). The offerings of the priests and the people make atonement for them (Lev 9:7) through the blood of their offerings (Lev 9:8–9, 12, 15–16). Since the blood rites occur before the theophany in the inaugural service, they are ritual purifications that cleanse the priests and people so that the theophany of the LORD will be a blessing and source of joy for them rather than a manifestation of his wrath if they defile his sanctuary (Lev 9:15).[190] Lev 17:11 is most closely connected with the ritual legislation for the manipulation of blood on the Day of Atonement that is prescribed in

---

188. The blood rite for the priests at their seven-day ordination resembles the blood rite and the seven-day period of ritual purification for Israelites who have been cured from an infectious skin disease (Lev 14:14–17). The entire process of ordination, including the blood daubing on their right ears, thumbs, and big toes, is an act of ritual purification (Kleinig, *Leviticus*, 192–93, 199, 201, 203–4).

189. The relationship between the altar and the priests is established by the blood rites in the ordination service. The exclusive control of the blood by the priests permits them exclusive access to the altar and other locations within the sanctuary where blood is applied (Gilders, *Blood Ritual*, 188–89).

190. The blood rite in Lev 9:15 is a *rite of purification* that cleanses Aaron and the Israelites from all their ritual impurities as a preparation for the LORD's theophany (Kleinig, *Leviticus*, 208, 218–19).

Lev 16.[191] The blood from the sin offerings of the priests and the laity on the Day of Atonement ritually cleanse the most holy place, the tent of meeting, and the altar for burnt offering from the ritual impurities of the Israelites (Lev 16:15–19). The burnt offering for the priests and the burnt offering for the people make atonement (Lev 16:24, 34) and purify the priests and the laity (Lev 16:30).[192] Since the atonement through the blood rites in these services are chiefly ritual purifications, it may be concluded that one of the main purposes for the disposal of blood in the daily divine service is for the LORD to cleanse the Israelites from their ritual impurities.

---

191. The chiastic arrangement of Lev 16:29–17:11 emphasizes the institution of atonement in 17:11 and its connection with the performance of atonement on the Day of Atonement.

> A *Atonement* and denial of *selves* (16:29–31)
>   B *Perpetual ritual statute* (16:31)
>   C The role of the *priest* in performing the rite of atonement (16:32)
>   D Atonement for the *tent of meeting* (16:33)
>   E Atonement for the *children of Israel* (16:34a)
>   F Fulfillment of the *LORD's* command to *Moses* (16:34b)
>   F The *LORD's* speech to *Moses* (17:1)
>   E Speaking to the *children of Israel* (17:2)
>   D Offerings at the *tent of meeting* (17:4)
>   C Offerings to the *priest* (17:5)
>   B *Perpetual ritual statute* (17:7)
> A *Atonement* for your *selves/lives* (17:11)

Since Lev 16 is linked to Lev 17, atonement most likely has a similar purpose in each chapter (Kleinig, *Leviticus*, 358–59).

192. Milgrom claims that the purgation rites on the Day of Atonement exclusively purify the sanctuary, and only indirectly do they purify the people. For him, the "purity" of the people comes mainly through their obedient acts of ceasing from labor and their self-denial on this day, not from the ritual acts that the high priest performs at the sanctuary (Milgrom, *Leviticus 1–16*, 1049, 1056–57). Kleinig holds that the blood rites on the Day of Atonement purify both the sanctuary and the people (Kleinig, *Leviticus*, 333–34, 342–47). Levine points out that the blood is physically put on the sanctuary, the tent, and the altar to purify them. Since no blood is placed directly on the people, they are simply beneficiaries of the blood rites (Levine, *In the Presence*, 65). Brichto makes the case that the *kipper* acts on the Day of Atonement purge the sanctuary as the direct object of the blood rites and it purges the Israelites as indirect objects (Brichto, "Slaughter and Sacrifice," 33–34). I have discovered an apparent distinction between the purposes of the blood rites of the sin offerings and the blood rites of the burnt offerings on the Day of Atonement. While both kinds of offerings are said to make atonement for the priests and people (Lev 16:5–6, 11, 17, 24), the sin offerings only make atonement for the sanctuary (Lev 16:16, 18) and the burnt offerings do not make atonement for the sanctuary (Lev 16:24). Since the burnt offerings make atonement only for the priests and people on the Day of Atonement, this implies the same purpose for the blood rite in the daily divine service.

The Ritual Function of the Daily Divine Service 119

The purification that results from the blood rite prepares the Israelites for the rites that follow it. Purification is not an end in itself, but rather qualifies the Israelites to come into the presence of their holy God at the tabernacle.[193] Since the LORD commands Aaron to distinguish between the holy and the common, and between the unclean and the clean (Lev 10:10),[194] the Israelites must be separated from the things that make them ritually unclean, so that the LORD will not kill them for defiling his sanctuary (Lev 15:31).[195] The holy and the common as well as the unclean and the clean are powers that influence the ritual status of the Israelites.[196] If they approach the LORD in a state of impurity, then his holiness destroys them.[197] Since impurity and holiness are entirely incompatible, the Israelites must be purified to prepare them for encountering their holy LORD at his dwelling place in the divine service.[198]

193. Some scholars assume that putting blood on the altar sanctifies. They claim that the blood of an offered animal is inherently holy or most holy, and they suppose that it must sanctify the altar and the people by its placement on the altar (Gorman, *Ideology of Ritual*, 186–87; *Divine Presence and Community*, 103; Wenham, *Leviticus*, 245). Blood, however, is not holy or most holy. The only occasions where blood consecrates are when it is taken from a most holy area of the sanctuary and placed upon something or someone else, such as in unique parts of the service on the Day of Atonement (Lev 16:15–19) and at the ordination of the priests (Exod 29:21; Lev 8:30). Since the blood is not taken from the altar and applied to something or someone in the daily divine service, the blood rite does not sanctify. It purifies Israel and prepares them for their sanctification later in the service.

194. See also Ezek 44:23. Milgrom claims that two of the four states of being can exist simultaneously, either sacred or common and either pure or impure. He explains the possible combinations of categories the following way: Sacred/Pure, Common/Pure, Common/Impure. He acknowledges that the sacred and the impure are exclusive to each other and that the pure may be either sacred or common while the common may be either pure or impure (Milgrom, *Leviticus 1–16*, 616).

195. The blood rite addresses the problem of the LORD's desire to meet with his sinful, unclean people without desecrating and defiling his holiness by their impurity, which would result in their death and destruction. The LORD solves this dilemma by establishing the blood rite to ritually purify his people (Kleinig, *Leviticus*, 368).

196. As figure seven illustrates, the categories of the holy and the common and the unclean and the clean create three interlocking spheres. These represent states of being as well as ritual powers that influence each other. See Kleinig for a similar diagram and his discussion on this topic (Kleinig, *Leviticus*, 6–10). Douglas believes that purity and impurity as well as the sacred and the profane are contagious. They are powers that transition persons and objects from one ritual status or condition to another (Douglas, *Purity and Danger*, 3–5, 7–29, 110, 130, 160–80).

197. Since the Israelites live in the common created realm, they are caught between the holy presence of God and the ritual impurity of Sheol. If the Israelites become defiled and bring their uncleanness into the holy realm of God, then they defile the sanctuary—the worst form of sacrilege—and the result is death (Kleinig, *Leviticus*, 322).

198. Through the blood rite the Israelites are ritually purified and, therefore,

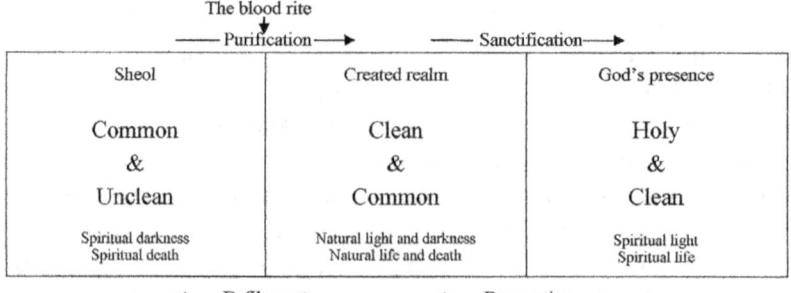

Figure 7. The relation of the blood rite to the three ritual spheres.

The theological purpose of splashing blood on the altar in the daily divine service is to make atonement. Atonement propitiates God, expiates the Israelites, and ritually purifies and prepares them to encounter God and his holiness at his tabernacle. Since the Israelites are constantly influenced by the evil powers of ritual impurity, they need to be continually purified so that they are not destroyed by the power of God's holiness. The LORD establishes the blood rite to cleanse his people of their sins and uncleanness, so that they will not desecrate and defile his holy dwelling within their midst. Through their purification, the LORD prepares his priests and people to receive his blessing and share in his holiness. As the priests splash the blood on the altar, the LORD qualifies the Israelites to participate in the rites that sanctify them and to prepare the priests to perform all of the remaining rites in the service. The LORD makes atonement for his people so that they may safely come into his presence and receive his blessing.

Conclusion

The LORD institutes the blood rite to perform a ritual function in the daily divine service for a theological purpose. He establishes the ritual disposal of blood, and gives specific instructions about the preparation of the carcass. The functioning agents in the blood rite, the high priest and regular priests, slay the lamb, manipulate its blood, cut it into pieces, wash its entrails and

---

qualified to participate in God's holiness (Kleinig, *Leviticus*, 368). Furthermore, the blood rite is part of the preparatory section in Israel's daily divine service, which clears the way for the priests to enter into the LORD's presence as well as for the Israelites to meet with him at the altar in the daily divine service. When the priests splash the blood on the altar, the LORD accepts and qualifies the Israelites for access to his gracious presence (Kleinig, "Blood for Sprinkling," 127, 131).

lower legs, and put salt on all of its parts. The LORD designates the blood, water, and salt as the main ritual materials that the priests use in the blood rite. He requires that the lamb must be slain on the north side of the altar, after which its blood is presented before him, and then splashed on the altar for burnt offerig every morning and every evening. Through the blood rite, the LORD atones for Israel, ritually purifies them from their uncleanness, and prepares them to safely meet him at the tabernacle.

THE INCENSE RITE

The incense rite is not what a person in the ancient world would expect.[199] In the temples of pagan cultures, their idols would be placed in the area corresponding to the most holy place in the tabernacle. The lay people had access to the idol and could bring it gifts of food, drink, and other materials to gain favor with their gods. At Israel's sanctuary, however, only the high priest performs the ritual acts inside the tent of meeting and, with the exception of one day of the year, even he does not have access to the Ark of the Covenant and its atonement seat in the most holy place. Furthermore, no one, possibly not even the high priest, ever sees the ark. The food and drink[200] that is set out on the table in the holy place is not food for God as it is in the pagan temples, and, other than the short time that the high priest performs his ritual acts inside the tent in the evening, the light from the lamps burns where no one can see it. The incense burned inside the tent of meeting hardly penetrates the veil that separates the most holy place from the holy place. All of this seems to turn common conceptions in the ancient religious world upside down.

The Divine Institution of the Incense Rite

The Pentateuch bears witness that the LORD institutes the incense rite when he authorizes the priest to burn incense on the altar in the tent of meeting as well as the ritual acts that coincide with it. There are several coordinated components that the LORD establishes for the incense rite.

He institutes incense to be burned daily on the golden altar in the tent of meeting.[201] The LORD prescribes that incense must be burned on this

---

199. See Kleinig, "Blood for Sprinkling," 124–25; *Glory and Service*, 5–15.

200. There is evidence in the Pentateuch that the daily drink offering is stored on the table in the holy place (Exod 25:29). See the section on the burning rite in this chapter for further discussion about this

201. The incense is burned daily, תָּמִיד, (Exod 30:8) in the tent of meeting as one of

altar as an essential part of the daily divine service (Exod 30:7–8);[202] and there is evidence that initially Moses carried out the LORD's command (Exod 40:26–27).[203] The Pentateuch bears witness in several places that the LORD authorizes incense to be burned on the incense altar (Exod 30:1, 9, 35–37; 31:11; 35:15; 37:25–29; 39:38; Deut 33:10).[204] There is additional evidence that incense was burned in the holy place at the first and second temples in accord with the LORD's prescription (1 Sam 2:28; 1 Chr 6:49; 23:13; 2 Chr 2:4; 13:11; 26:18; 29:7; 1 Macc 4:49–50; *Tamid* 6:1–3).[205] It may be safely concluded that burning incense on the altar in the holy place is divinely instituted.[206]

The LORD authorizes the daily maintenance of the lamps inside the tent of meeting.[207] The priest must regularly keep the lamps burning from evening until morning, as a perpetual statute (Exod 27:20–21). The lamps are trimmed every morning and lit every evening (Exod 30:7–8).[208] They

---

the main ritual activities every morning and evening within the ritual system.

202. Many scholars acknowledge that incense must be burned on the incense altar inside the tent of meeting every day in the divine service. See Cassuto, *Exodus*, 391, 400, 482; Hamilton, *Exodus*, 508, 518; Haran, *Temples and Temple Service*, 244; Houtman, "Function of Holy Incense," 462; Propp, *Exodus 19–40*, 474–75; Sarna, *Exodus*, 199; Stuart, *Exodus*, 634.

203. Sarna and Stuart hold that the LORD's prescription in Exod 30:1–9 about burning incense in the holy place is first implemented by Moses, according to Exod 40:26–27 (Sarna, *Exodus*, 236; Stuart, *Exodus*, 789).

204. Haran, Milgrom, and Stuart hold that Deut 33:10 is not about burning incense on the inner altar but rather to burning incense on portable censers (Haran, *Temples and Temple Service*, 238–39; Milgrom, *Leviticus 1–16*, 597; Stuart, *Exodus*, 633). Deut 33:8 indicates, however, that verse 10 refers to the high priest burning incense. Because the main task of the high priest is to burn incense on the golden altar every day, the incense in Deut 33:10 most likely refers to that which is on the altar in the holy place.

205. Haran and Milgrom do not hold that 1 Sam 2:28 has to do with the incense burned in the tent of meeting every day, assuming that the priests occasionally offer incense in censers in the courtyard (Haran, *Temples and Temple Service*, 238; Milgrom, *Leviticus 1–16*, 597). The LORD, however, never commands the priests to regularly offer incense in censers, except for the high priest on the Day of Atonement. 1 Sam 2:28 probably refers to burning incense in the holy place on the altar.

206. In other periods of Israel's history incense is offered as part of the daily divine service because it is divinely authorized by the LORD (Kleinig, *Lord's Song*, 29–30, 89, 104, 106).

207. The daily maintenance of the lamps is seen in the signature word תָּמִיד (Exod 27:20; Lev 24:2–4), which denotes all the ritual acts in the daily divine service.

208. Whereas Exod 27:21 states that the lamps are kept in order from evening until morning, Exod 30:7–8 adds that they are tended in the morning and lit in the evening. Hamilton claims that there is a chiastic structure between the evening and morning in Exod 27:21 and the mention of morning and evening in Exod 30:7–8 (Hamilton, *Exodus*, 507). The two passages are closely related and the latter one provides further

were lit when the tabernacle was first set up, *as the LORD commanded Moses* (Exod 40:25; Num 8:2–3).[209] The lamps are regularly kept in order as a perpetual statute (Lev 24:2–4);[210] and they must burn in the tent of meeting as part of the ritual system (Exod 25:37; 35:14; 39:37). Sources outside the Pentateuch declare that the lamps burn in the sanctuary as prescribed according to the law (2 Chr 4:20);[211] and they are tended and lit in the holy place in the divine services at the temple in Jerusalem (1 Sam 3:3; 2 Chr 13:11; 29:27; Sir 26:17; 1 Macc 4:50; 2 Macc 1:8; 10:3; *Tamid* 6:1). In addition, the LORD commands the Israelites to provide clear olive oil so that the lamps may burn regularly in the holy place (Exod 25:26; 27:20–21; 35:8, 14, 28; 39:37; Lev 24:2; Num 4:9, 16).[212] He instituted the lamps to be daily tended and lit on the golden menorah as part of the incense rite.[213]

The bread of the presence must be set before the LORD regularly.[214] He prescribes that this bread shall be put on the golden table in the tent of meeting and sit there every day (Exod 25:30).[215] Even though the bread is replaced once per week on the Sabbath (Lev 24:8), it is considered *daily/ continual bread* upon the table of the LORD inside his tabernacle (Num 4:7).[216] Pure frankincense is placed on each of the two piles of bread and

---

details about the ritual activities associated with the menorah.

209. The formula *as the LORD commanded Moses* stresses two related ideas that are basic to the priestly ideology. First, all the details of the ritual law are directly communicated by God to Moses. Second, the ritual law is promptly carried out by Moses and the Israelites (Levine, "*Lpny* YHWH," 272). See also Cassuto, *Exodus*, 482.

210. Lev 24:2–3 is an almost verbatim repetition of Exod 27:20–21 (Kleinig, *Leviticus*, 512) that fulfils its command (Haran, *Temples and Temple Service*, 209; Milgrom, *Leviticus 23–27*, 2084).

211. For further discussion about 1–2 Chronicles' use of the Law of Moses as foundational for Israel's ritual acts at the divine service, see Kleinig, *Lord's Song*, 29–30,

212. The command in Exod 27:20 to bring clear olive oil for burning in the lamps is a prescription that mandates an ongoing obligation, as opposed to the one-time directive to bring olive oil for the construction of the tabernacle in Exod 25:6 (Sarna *Exodus*, 175). God himself commands the Israelites to bring the oil for burning in the lamps, implying that this command is essential to the institution of the ritual acts associated with the menorah in the incense rite (Kleinig, *Leviticus*, 516).

213. See Haran, *Temples and Temple Service*, 208–9.

214. The Hebrew word תָּמִיד designates the regular ritual act of changing the bread of the presence every Sabbath. Although the bread is not changed daily, it remains before the LORD continually and serves a different ritual function by the "act" of sitting before the LORD. It is worth noting that the first use of the word תָּמִיד is in connection with the bread of the presence (Exod 25:30; see Lev 24:8; Num 4:7).

215. The bread of the presence is further mentioned in texts both within and outside the Pentateuch (Exod 35:13; 39:36; 40:23; 1 Sam 21:6; 1 Kgs 7:48; 1 Chr 9:32; 23:29; 28:16; 2 Chr 2:3; 4:19; 29:18; Neh 10:33; 1 Macc 1:22; 4:51; 2 Macc 1:8; 10:3).

216. לֶחֶם הַתָּמִיד (Num 4:7) may be understood as "regular bread" in the sense that it

burned as its token portion so that the bread is considered a fire offering to the LORD (Lev 24:6–7).[217] His command to place the pure frankincense on each pile of the bread constitutes an inseparable part of the incense rite.[218] The bread of the presence is set before the LORD in the holy place regularly, and it must remain before him daily.

The LORD authorizes the high priest to wear the ornate vestments in the daily incense rite. There are five divinely instituted acts that occur as the high priest wears these vestments before the LORD.[219] First, he bears the names of the twelve tribes of Israel on the two stones fastened to the shoulder pieces of the ephod (Exod 28:6–12). Second, he daily bears the names of the Israelites over his heart on the twelve stones in the breastpiece of judgment (Exod 28:13–29). Third, the high priest regularly carries the Urim and Thummim over his heart inside the breastpiece (Exod 28:30). Fourth, the bells attached to the hem of the robe jingle when the high priest enters and exits the holy place (Exod 28:31–35). Finally, the high priest daily wears the golden diadem with the engraved words "YHWH's holiness" that is attached to the turban on his head (Exod 28:36–38).[220] The LORD institutes these

---

is changed regularly on the Sabbath (Haran, *Temples and Temple Service*, 210). See also Gane, "Bread of Presence," 198–203. The phrase לֶחֶם פָּנִים לְפָנַי תָּמִיד (Exod 25:30) refers, however, to the presence of the bread before the LORD at all times/continually (Stuart, *Exodus*, 575). The bread of the presence may be viewed both ways at the same time. It is both, regular bread changed regularly every Sabbath, and daily bread which remains daily/continually before the LORD.

217. What is meant by the *pure frankincense* is discussed below in the section on the ritual materials. The finely ground spiced incense (Exod 30:36; see Lev 16:12) is most likely taken from the golden bowls at the table for the bread of the presence and daily burned on the incense altar, showing the close association between the incense and the bread (Exod 25:29; 37:16; Num 4:7; 7:14, 20, 26, 32, 38, 44, 50, 56, 62, 68, 74, 80, 84, 86).

218. Kleinig and Gane hold that the frankincense is an essential part of the bread (Kleinig, *Leviticus*, 513–14, 516; Gane, "Bread of Presence," 196–97). Gane claims, however, that the pure frankincense is placed directly on the piles of bread, while Kleinig maintains that it is placed in containers on top of the bread. It seems that for the pure frankincense to be offered as a token portion for the bread, it must come into direct contact with it, similar to the token portion of the cereal offering (Lev 2:1–2).

219. The ornate vestments of the high priest are not merely worn as a preparation for doing his ritual duties inside the tent of meeting. Rather, these vestments are ritual appurtenances in and of themselves just like the incense altar, the menorah, and the table. Several ritual acts are accomplished when the high priest wears his ornate vestments in the daily service (Haran, *Temples and Temple Service*, 212). For further details concerning the prescriptions for the high priest's vestments, see Cassuto, *Exodus*, 372–85; Hamilton, *Exodus*, 484–92; Propp, *Exodus 19-40*, 431–50; Sarna, *Exodus*, 177–85; Stuart, *Exodus*, 605–17.

220. The Hebrew is קֹדֶשׁ לַיהוָה. There is some disagreement in the rabbinic tradition about what words appear on the golden plate. One view holds that both words are inscribed there, while the other view is that only the Tetragrammaton, יהוה, is on it

five ritual acts, which are accomplished as the high priest wears his ornate vestments before him in the daily divine service.[221]

The LORD establishes the incense rite with each of its parts in the daily service. He authorizes the high priest to burn incense on the golden altar, to tend and light the lamps on the menorah, to maintain the bread of the presence on the table, and to wear his ornate vestments. Five distinct ritual acts occur when the high priest wears his ornate vestments in addition to the activities performed at the table, menorah, and incense altar.

The Ritual Function of the Incense Rite

The incense rite is composed of all the ritual acts that are performed in relation to burning incense in the daily divine service in the holy place. It is the most complex of all the rites in the daily service. Since it is the central rite, its acts are some of the most essential parts of the service.

Ritual Agents

The only ritual agent who performs the incense rite is the high priest. All of its ritual acts are conducted by him.[222] Only he burns incense on the inner altar (Exod 30:7–8), tends and lights the lamps on the menorah (Exod 27:20–21; 30:7–8; Lev 24:3–4; Num 8:2–3), and maintains the bread of the

---

(Haran, *Temples and Temple Service*, 169; Sarna, *Exodus*, 184). The Pentateuch, however, states that both words are inscribed on the plate (Exod 28:36). Kleinig translates קֹדֶשׁ לַיהוָה as *YHWH's holiness*, accentuating that the LORD is holy *through* his high priest when he wears the holy name on his forehead (Kleinig, *Leviticus*, 190, 198). Cassuto renders it "Holy to the LORD," emphasizing that the high priest is holy to the LORD when he wears the holy crown (Cassuto, *Exodus*, 384). קֹדֶשׁ לַיהוָה is best translated "YHWH's holiness." קֹדֶשׁ is a noun and must be rendered *holiness*. לַיהוָה is probably best understood as a possessive; holiness belongs to YHWH. Therefore, קֹדֶשׁ לַיהוָה is *YHWH's holiness*. See also Kornfeld, "קדשׁ," 521–26, 527–30, 543–44; Ringgren, "קדשׁ," 527, 530–43, 544–45; Hamilton, *Exodus*, 492; Propp, *Exodus 19–40*, 447–48.

221. Haran maintains that the ornate vestments of the high priest involve three ritual activities, based on the three references to them as regular/daily, תָּמִיד, vestments (Exod 28:29, 30, 38). He concludes that there are six regular ritual acts inside the tent of meeting, three by wearing the vestments and three at the menorah, table, and altar (Haran, *Temples and Temple Service*, 213–16). There are, however, only the five ritual acts mentioned above that are associated with wearing the ornate vestments that the text describes as *before the LORD*, לִפְנֵי יְהוָה (Exod 28:12, 29, 30, 35, 38).

222. The ritual acts performed inside the tent of meeting are considered the sole prerogative of the high priest. While the regular priests are never forbidden to go into the holy place inside the tent, they are assigned no ritual function there (Haran, *Temples and Temple Service*, 205–7).

presence on the golden table (Lev 24:8).[223] Only he wears the ornate vestments as he carries out the ritual acts of the incense rite (Exod 28:2–38).[224] The high priest is the sole agent who enacts the incense rite and all of its ritual activities inside the tent of meeting in the daily divine service.

There are other agents involved with the incense rite. These include the high priest's deputy selected from the regular priests, the Israelite community, and the LORD. Since it is practically impossible for the high priest to perform the ritual acts in the incense rite *every* day, his deputy must act in his place on occasion.[225] The deputy functions in the stead of the high priest and conducts all of the ritual activities in the incense rite inside the tent of meeting, including wearing the ornate vestments. The high priest's deputy probably assists him regularly in the performance of this rite, enabling him to be familiar with the ritual activities inside the tent of meeting.[226] The entire community of Israel is responsible for supplying the incense for burning on the inner altar, the oil for the lamps, and the bread for the table (Exod 25:2, 6; Lev 24:2–8). Furthermore, they are beneficiaries of the ritual acts performed in the incense rite.[227] Finally, the LORD is a ritual agent, who institutes the incense rite and accomplishes his own purposes as the high

---

223. Although Moses is the archetypal priest as the founder of the divine service, after the inaugural activities Aaron, the first high priest, takes over. The high priest alone, or his deputy, burns incense, attends the lamps, and maintains the bread of the presence (Kleinig, *Leviticus*, 515).

224. The occupants of the sacred offices must be distinguished from the laity, and so their vestments, as the insignia of their offices, are ordained by God. Furthermore, there is a difference between the offices and vestments of the regular priests and the office and vestments of the high priest (Sarna, *Exodus*, 176–77).

225. There is little evidence in the Pentateuch about the high priest's deputy, but a clue may be in Lev 6:15 [22]. The priest who burns the daily bread offering of the high priest on the outer altar is the successor to the high priest. Most likely the priest who will become the next high priest is his usual deputy, and this would normally be his oldest son (see Exod 28:1; Lev 10:1–16; Num 3:2–4; 20:25–28; Deut 10:6). See Kleinig, *Leviticus*, 154–55. Since the high priest could become temporarily disqualified to serve due to ritual uncleanness, he must have a deputy to serve on his behalf on such occasions (Lev 13–15). The high priest could also become permanently disqualified to perform ritual acts (Lev 21). See Kleinig, *Leviticus*, 456–60.

226. At those times when the deputy functions as the high priest, one of the other regular priests most likely assists the deputy as he performs the incense rite. In the second temple period, several of the regular priests served as "deputies" of the high priest at the incense rite (*Tamid* 3:1, 9; 5:2, 4; 6:1–3). See Blackman, *Kodashim*, 476, 481–82, 488–89, 491–93. Practically speaking, it makes sense that the high priest or his deputy would need an assistant when he performs the incense rite.

227. The incense rite is performed for the benefit of the Israelites. They also supply the oil for the lamps, incense for the altar, and flour for the bread. Although the Israelites themselves do not enter into the tent of meeting to perform the incense rite, all that the high priest does in the incense rite is done for them (Kleinig, *Leviticus*, 515–18).

priest executes its ritual activities.²²⁸ Although the high priest solely enacts it, his deputy from the regular priests, the whole Israelite community, and the LORD are ritual agents in the daily incense rite.

Ritual Acts

The main ritual act that the high priest performs in the tent of meeting every day is burning incense on the golden altar (Exod 30:7–8). He places incense on the live coals on the golden altar to smoke up the fragrant offering.²²⁹ Since the burning coals are taken from the outer altar and put on the inner altar, the holy fire burns the incense on it.²³⁰ The activities at the incense altar guarantee that the fragrant incense is regularly burned before the LORD to accomplish his purposes.²³¹ The smoking up of incense on the inner altar is the primary ritual activity in the incense rite.²³²

There are two additional ritual acts that are performed every day at the golden menorah. In the morning the wicks of the lamps are trimmed and oil is added to them, and in the evening the lamps are lit (Exod 27:21; 30:7–8; Lev 24:1–4). While tending the lamps prepares them, lighting the lamps serves their main function, to illumine the residence of the LORD.²³³ There may not be a practical need for the lamps to burn in the holy place in the

228. Haran holds that the LORD is a ritual agent who both benefits from the service of the high priest and in response acts as Israel's benefactor. He claims that the ritual acts at the inner altar, menorah, and table provide for the "physical" needs of the LORD within his residence, while the ritual acts accomplished by the ornate vestments of the high priest stimulate the LORD's "senses" and draw his gracious attention to the Israelites (Haran, *Temples and Temple Service* 203–21). See also Gane, "Bread of Presence," who claims that the LORD is Israel's creator in residence among them.

229. Smoking up fragrant incense in the holy place may be viewed as symbolically providing for the need of the LORD's "sense of smell" within his dwelling place (Haran, *Temples and Temple Service*, 216, 218–19). See also Hamilton, *Exodus*, 519.

230. The divine fire connects the outer altar with the inner altar. The holy fire that smokes up the incense on the incense altar is the same holy fire that smokes up the offerings on the altar for burnt offering coordinately in the divine service each morning and evening.

231. The sense of smell plays a more prominent role in the ancient world than in western cultures. The incense at the sanctuary cleanses the air of the stench from ritual impurities caused by death and decay (Houtman, "Function of Holy Incense," 458–64).

232. Burning incense on the inner altar can only be explained in relation to all the other ritual acts performed every day inside the tent of meeting at the menorah and table as well as the high priest wearing the ornate vestments (Haran, "Uses of Incense," 128).

233. The lamps provide for the LORD's "sense of sight" in his residence (Haran, *Temples and Temple Service*, 208–9, 218–19).

morning. Although it is uncertain whether the rising sun shines through the opening of the tent into the holy place, it is conceivable that some light could pass through the screen at the entryway of the tent or at least along its sides.[234] If so, then at the evening offering the high priest would need the light of the lamps to conduct the incense rite in the dark holy place since the sun is already below the horizon on the opposite side of the tent farthest from its entrance.[235] It may be, however, that the live coals carried into the tent for the incense altar give enough light for the high priest to enter there and perform his duties in both the morning and the evening.[236] Tending the lamps on the golden menorah in the morning guarantees that they will give light inside the tent of meeting when they are lit in the evening.[237]

There are three ritual activities that the high priest performs regularly at the golden table. First, the bread of the presence is removed then eaten by the priests and new bread is set out on the table each Sabbath (Lev 24:5–9). The pure frankincense that sits on the piles of bread is removed to be burned, while a new amount of it is placed on each fresh pile (Lev 24:5–7).[238] Most importantly, since the bread must remain on the golden table in the holy place every day, its presence there in the incense rite may be considered a ritual "act" (Exod 25:30).[239] Second, every morning and evening the high

---

234. See figure five, which illustrates the doorway of the tent facing to the east. See also Exod 26:35–36; 40:22–28; Num 3:38.

235. Sarna holds that the primary function of the lamps is to illuminate the area in front of it at night time, especially the table on the opposite of the room (see Kleinig, *Leviticus*, 513). In addition, he claims that the menorah contains a symbolic significance due to its shape and the terminology that Exod 25:31–37 ascribes to it (*Exodus*, 164–66). For detailed examinations about the symbolism of the menorah, see Meyers, *Tabernacle Menorah*; Yarden, *Tree of Light*. Their views are discussed in more detail below.

236. See the discussion in the section on the fire rite in this chapter about the live coals that are carried from the altar for burnt offering into the tent for use in the incense rite.

237. The lamps provide light for the high priest at the evening incense rite but they do not serve any practical purpose throughout the rest of the night. The lamps ultimately serve a theological purpose, which is discussed below (Kleinig, *Leviticus*, 517). See also Milgrom, *Leviticus 23–27*, 2084–91.

238. Although changing the bread with its pure frankincense is not a ritual act that is performed every day, it is still necessary for maintaining the daily presence of the bread and pure frankincense. The bread with its pure frankincense is changed as part of the daily incense rite on the Sabbath, and is, therefore, part of *that* day's divine service.

239. See the section about the divine institution of the bread of the presence. The bread gains its significance from the LORD's presence in the holy place. Unlike the food offered to pagan gods, the bread of the presence does not feed the LORD. Rather, the LORD feeds his priests with this most holy bread every Sabbath. Most significantly, since the Israelites must provide the flour for the loaves, the twelve loaves represent the

priest takes some of the finely ground fragrant incense from its container that is upon the golden table to burn upon the incense altar (Exod 30:34–36).[240] Third, there is evidence that the daily drink offering is stored and prepared upon the golden table so that it may be poured out at the altar for burnt offering in the courtyard.[241] The ritual acts associated with the golden table connect the bread with its pure frankincense, the fragrant incense for smoking up on the incense altar, and the wine for the drink offering at the outer altar.

The high priest wears his ornate vestments as part of the incense rite (Exod 28:43).[242] On the one hand, donning the vestments prepares the high priest to enact the incense rite in the tent of meeting. On the other hand, when he wears the ornate vestments, certain parts of them accomplish different ritual purposes.[243] Donning and wearing the ornate garments at the incense rite ensures that the high priest is prepared to perform the activities at the inner altar, menorah, and table as well as the ritual acts that are accomplished by wearing them inside the tent of meeting.

The high priest performs one other act that prepares for the incense rite. He washes his hands and feet from the font before he puts on his vestments prior to entering the tent of meeting (Exod 30:18–21; 40:30–32).[244] Washing his hands prepares him to handle the holy vestments and all the materials associated with the inner altar, menorah, and table. Washing his feet prepares him to walk on holy ground inside the tent of meeting. The ritual washing is an essential preparation for the incense rite.

---

twelve tribes before the LORD continually inside the tent of meeting (Kleinig, *Leviticus*, 518).

240. Exod 25:29 makes clear that golden containers are part of the table's appurtenances. Because the Israelite leaders on the day of dedication present incense in twelve golden containers, they are most likely used for storing the incense on or near the golden table in the tent of meeting (Num 7:14, 20, 26, 32, 38, 44, 50, 56, 62, 68, 74, 80, 84, 86). According to Exod 37:16, the accessories are עַל־הַשֻּׁלְחָן, on the table. Just as the twelve loaves sit upon the table, so also the twelve containers sit upon the table representing the twelve tribes of Israel in the presence of the LORD.

241. The two kinds of libation vessels, קְשׂוֹתָיו וּמְנַקִּיֹּתָיו, are part of the accessories for the golden table (Exod 25:29, 37:16; Num 4:7). These are not mentioned in connection with any of the other pieces of the tabernacle furniture. The wine for the drink offering at the outer altar is most likely stored and prepared upon the golden table in the holy place.

242. See the section on the divine institution of the ornate vestments of the high priest above.

243. See Haran, *Temples and Temple Service*, 212. The Pentateuch spells out the purposes for which each of the five significant parts of the vestments is worn in the holy place (Exod 28:12, 29–30, 35, 38).

244. See the section on the fire rite for further details about this ritual act.

Ritual Materials

The first significant material for the incense rite is the fragrant incense.[245] The fragrant incense is a compound of four ingredients: stacte, onycha, galbanum, and pure frankincense (Exod 30:34–36).[246] Stacte, onycha, and galbanum are spices mixed together probably in equal parts. One part of the three-spice mixture is most likely combined with one part of the pure frankincense, resulting in the compound of fragrant incense.[247] There is evidence that the fragrant incense is salted after it is prepared, but it is not clear if the salt is considered another ingredient or if it serves a practical purpose (Exod 30:35).[248] The fragrant incense is ground into a fine powder and placed inside the tent of meeting.[249] This mixture of spices is the only kind of incense that is smoked up before the LORD in the holy place (Exod 30:7–9).[250]

The second "material," which is the most important one, is the holy fire. It is brought from the outer altar and placed on the incense altar. The

---

245. The Hebrew is קְטֹרֶת הַסַּמִּים, which can be understood as "spiced incense," emphasizing that the spices make the unique fragrance of the incense smoked up in the holy place. For references to the spiced incense in the Pentateuch, see Exod 25:6; 30:7; 31:11; 35:8, 15, 28; 37:29; 39:38; 40:27; Lev 4:7; 16:12; Num 4:16. See also 2 Chr 2:3; 13:11.

246. The first three spices according to their Hebrew names are נָטָף וּשְׁחֵלֶת וְחֶלְבְּנָה. The pure frankincense in the Hebrew is לְבֹנָה זַכָּה. It is worth noting that incense, קְטֹרֶת, is a compound of ingredients and should not be confused with frankincense, לְבֹנָה, which is a single ingredient. For an analysis of the ingredients for the spiced incense, see Feliks, "Incense of the Tabernacle," 125–49.

247. See Haran, *Temples and Temple Service*, 241–45.

248. Cassuto holds that the Hebrew word מְמֻלָּח, means "mixed" and is related to מֶלַח, to salt/season (Cassuto, *Exodus*, 400). Propp discusses the difficulty of Cassuto's interpretation and prefers to render מְמֻלָּח as "salted" (Propp, *Exodus 19–40*, 485–86). The incense is probably salted after the other ingredients have been mixed together.

249. It is unclear if the unground portion of the fragrant incense is ever used in any way outside the tent of meeting. Lev 10:1 suggests that Nadab and Abihu may have put this incense on the strange fire in their fire pans and offered it before the LORD. Their transgression was not the use of the incense but the use of unauthorized fire, fire that is not from the altar for burnt offering and, therefore, not holy fire. Similarly, in the case of Korah's rebellion, incense is offered in fire pans at the outer altar (Num 16:6–35). The remedy to quell the LORD's anger against Israel for their rebellion is for Aaron to burn incense in his fire pan in the camp (Num 16:46–50). See Haran for more analysis of the uses of incense outside the tent of meeting (Haran, *Temples and Temple Service*, 231–41).

250. The pure frankincense on the bread of the presence may also be burned on the incense altar each Sabbath but the text does not specify whether it is burned on the incense altar or at the altar for burnt offering (Kleinig, *Leviticus*, 514).

mixture of finely ground spices and pure frankincense is put on the live coals to smoke up the spiced incense in this rite.²⁵¹

The third ritual material used in the incense rite is the beaten olive oil for the lamps (Exod 27:20; Lev 24:2).²⁵² Beating olives produces the purest form of olive oil, which is required for the lamps that burn throughout the night in the holy place. Oil from beaten, rather than pressed, olives produces the least amount of smoke, and thus prevents the ornate curtains from being soiled with soot inside the tent of meeting.²⁵³ This oil is of the highest quality and signifies that only the best olive oil is utilized inside the holy place before the LORD.²⁵⁴

The fourth ritually significant materials in the incense rite are the bread and the wine on the table.²⁵⁵ Twelve flat loaves, each containing two-tenths of an ephah of fine flour, are baked. These loaves are placed in two piles, six loaves in each pile, on the table.²⁵⁶ A portion of pure frankincense is put on the top of each pile of bread to be burned as its token portion on the Sabbath (Lev 24:5–9).²⁵⁷ The wine on the table could be either regular grape wine or any alcoholic beverage made from the vine (Exod 29:40; Num 28:7).²⁵⁸ This beverage is never drunk by the priests, but sits on the table

---

251. See the section on the fire rite for further analysis of the holy fire.

252. The Hebrew שֶׁמֶן זַיִת זָךְ כָּתִית is literally "beaten pure olive oil." For other references to the oil for the lamps, see Exod 25:6; 35:8, 14, 28; 39:37.

253. For the difference between beaten olive oil and olive oil produced from a press, see Kleinig, *Leviticus*, 512, 516; Levine, *Leviticus*, 164; Propp, *Exodus 19–40*, 427–28; Sarna, *Exodus*, 175–76.

254. Haran and Milgrom claim that ritual substances employed inside the tent of meeting are always of the highest quality, something not always required of the materials in the courtyard (Haran, *Temples and Temple Service*, 164; Milgrom, *Leviticus 17–22*, 2086–87).

255. The daily drink offering that is poured out at the altar for burnt offering in the courtyard is most likely stored on and taken from the table in the tent of meeting. The only vessel mentioned for the drink offering is one of the appurtenances related to the golden table in the tent of meeting (Exod 25:29; 37:16; Num 4:7).

256. Mitchell argues that the bread is placed in two piles of six loaves each instead of two rows (Mitchell, "Leviticus 24:6," 447–48).

257. The pure frankincense, לְבֹנָה זַכָּה, must be distinguished from the fragrant incense, קְטֹרֶת סַמִּים, and from the regular frankincense, לְבֹנָה. The token portion of the pure frankincense is probably burned on the outer altar each Sabbath. Exod 30:7–9 seems to limit what is offered on the inner altar to the fragrant incense. Furthermore, Lev 24:7 refers to the pure frankincense on the bread of the presence as its token portion, אַזְכָּרָה, the same term used for the token portion of the cereal offering (Lev 2:2, 9, 16). Since the bread of the presence may be understood as a bread offering (מִנְחָה) with its token portion, the pure frankincense is most likely forbidden from being burned on the inner altar according to the prohibition in Exod 30:9.

258. See the section above on the presentation rite for further discussion about the

until it is poured out as a drink offering at the outer altar (Lev 10:9). The bread and the wine are as ritually important as the incense and the oil for the incense rite.[259]

The fifth set of things that are used in the incense rite are the ornate vestments of the high priest.[260] The basic vestments include six items: a turban, a breastpiece, an ephod, a robe, a sash, and a tunic (Exod 28:4).[261] These have additional ornaments, which perform ritual functions when the high priest wears them inside the tent of meeting.[262] First, a plate of pure gold[263] with the words "YHWH's holiness" engraved on it fastens to the turban. The turban[264] is made of finely twisted linen and the plate fastens to its front with a blue cord (Exod 28:36–38). Second, twelve gems[265] are mounted on the breastpiece. The breastpiece[266] is fabricated from the same material as the ephod, with gold, blue, purple and scarlet yarn, and finely twisted linen. It is square, a span long and a span wide, folded double,[267] forming a pouch into

---

materials for the daily drink offering.

259. Most likely all four of the ritual substances, the bread, wine, incense, and oil, are placed on the table as indicated by the four different accessories to the table (Exod 25:29). The four substances are equal in ritual importance.

260. The garments of the high priest are בִגְדֵי־קֹדֶשׁ, holy vestments לְכָבוֹד וּלְתִפְאָרֶת, for glory and splendor (Exod 28:2). The same may also be said of the vestments of the regular priests (Exod 28:40). See Cassuto, *Exodus*, 386; Propp, *Exodus 19–40*, 451. Since the sanctuary is differentiated from the profane realm, the priests' clothing at the sanctuary must be distinguished from common clothing. Although the vestments of the regular priests adorn them with glory and splendor at the sanctuary, the ornate vestments of the high priest distinguish him from the other priests and adorn him with more glory and splendor than them (Sarna, *Exodus*, 176–77).

261. If the linen undergarments are considered to be part of the high priest's vestments then there are seven of them. Haran claims that there are eight vestments that the high priest wears, an ephod, a breastpiece, a robe, a diadem, a tunic, a girdle, a turban, and breeches (Haran, *Temples and Temple Service*, 166–70). Since the two stones on the shoulder pieces of the ephod and the twelve gems on the breastpiece are not separate vestments, the pure gold plate/diadem is considered part of the high priest's turban. Although they are required, the linen underpants are probably not considered *holy* vestments but function as a barrier between the private body parts of the high priest and the holy vestments. Propp points out that if the priest emitted semen while wearing the holy vestments then they would be defiled and the high priest would die (Propp, *Exodus 19–40*, 453–54).

262. See Exod 28:12, 15, 29–30, 35, 38.

263. צִיץ זָהָב טָהוֹר.

264. הַמִּצְנֶפֶת.

265. הָאֲבָנִים.

266. הַחֹשֶׁן.

267. A span, זֶרֶת, is half a cubit, which is approximately nine inches or twenty-three centimeters (Propp, *Exodus 19–40*, 439).

The Ritual Function of the Daily Divine Service 133

which the Urim and Thummim[268] are placed. The twelve gems mount on the breastpiece in gold filigree settings that are placed in four rows, three gems in each row. The gems in the first row are ruby, topaz, and beryl; in the second row are turquoise, sapphire, and emerald; in the third row are jacinth, agate, and amethyst; in the fourth row are chrysolite, onyx, and jasper.[269] Each gem is engraved with one of the names of the tribes of Israel (Exod 28:15–30). Third, two onyx stones[270] are fastened to the shoulder pieces of the ephod. The ephod[271] is made with gold, blue, purple, and scarlet yarn, as well as finely twisted linen. Its woven waistband is one piece with the ephod and made with the same materials. The names of the twelve tribes of Israel are engraved on the onyx stones, six names on each stone, in the order of their birth. The stones are mounted in gold filigree settings and attached to the shoulder pieces of the ephod. Two braided chains of pure gold, like a rope, are fastened to the settings (Exod 28:6–14). Fourth, golden bells[272] and pomegranates made from blue, purple, and scarlet yarn attach to the hem of the robe. The robe[273] is made entirely of blue cloth, with an opening for the head in its centre. There is a woven edge around this opening, like a collar, to keep it from tearing. The bells and pomegranates alternate all the way around the hem of the robe (Exod 28:31–35; 39:22–26). Fifth, the sash[274] is embroidered with finely twisted linen and blue, purple, and scarlet yarn. Sixth, the tunic[275] is made of fine linen (Exod 28:39; 39:27, 29). The high ornate vestments of the high priest are necessary for the high priest to perform the incense rite.[276]

The incense is burned on the incense altar inside the tent of meeting.[277] The incense altar is constructed from acacia wood (Exod 30:1). Its dimen-

---

268. הָאוּרִים וְאֶת־הַתֻּמִּים

269. The first row is אֹדֶם פִּטְדָה וּבָרֶקֶת, the second is נֹפֶךְ סַפִּיר וְיָהֲלֹם, the third is לֶשֶׁם שְׁבוֹ וְאַחְלָמָה, and the fourth is תַּרְשִׁישׁ וְשֹׁהַם וְיָשְׁפֵה.

270. אַבְנֵי הַשֹּׁהַם

271. הָאֵפֹד

272. פַּעֲמֹנֵי זָהָב and רִמֹּנֵי

273. מְעִיל

274. אַבְנֵט

275. הַכֻּתֹּנֶת

276. For an analysis of the materials and significance of the vestments, see Haran, *Temples and Temple Service*, 165–74.

277. The inner altar is מִזְבֵּחַ מִקְטַר קְטֹרֶת, a place for smoking up incense. For examinations about the relation of מִזְבֵּחַ to זָבַח, see Cassuto, *Exodus*, 389–92; Propp, *Exodus 19–40*, 420, 473–74, who hold that since Exod 30:9 forbids any other kind of offering except incense on the inner altar, burning the fragrant incense must be considered an offering that is smoked up before the LORD like the ones at the outer altar.

sions are one cubit long, one cubit wide, and two cubits high. The horns on each corner of the altar comprise one piece with the altar (Exod 30:2). The top, sides, and horns are overlaid with pure gold;[278] and a gold molding encircles the altar (Exod 30:3). Two poles of acacia wood overlaid with gold insert into two gold rings on each side of the altar when it is carried (Exod 30:4-5). The altar is designed so that the incense may be smoked up from the square flat area between the four horns on the corners of its top.[279]

The bread with its pure frankincense, the wine, the fragrant incense, and the oil for the lamps sit on the pure table.[280] The table is constructed from acacia wood and its dimensions are two cubits long, one cubit wide, and one and one half cubits high (Exod 25:23). It is overlaid with pure gold[281] and it has a gold molding and a rim around the table with another gold molding around the rim (Exod 25:24-25). Four golden rings attach to its sides into which poles of acacia wood overlaid with gold are inserted to carry it (Exod 25:26-28). There are four accessories with the table, all of them made of pure gold. First, the dishes most likely hold the piles of bread.[282] Second, the bowls contain the fragrant incense.[283] Third, the pitchers are used for the wine of the drink offering.[284] Finally, the jugs probably store the oil for the lamps and are used for filling them.[285] The golden table with its

278. Pure gold, זָהָב טָהוֹר, is the finest quality produced from additional procedures to remove impurities in the refining process (Sarna, *Exodus*, 159).

279. For further details about the design and construction of the incense altar, see Propp, *Exodus 19-40*, 473-74. For an illustration of a possible design of the incense altar, see Haran, *Temples and Temple Service*, 236.

280. The table is called the pure table, הַשֻּׁלְחָן הַטָּהֹר, in Lev 24:6, which is probably a reference to the pure gold that overlays the table according to Exod 25:24 (Milgrom, *Leviticus 23-27*, 2097).

281. See footnote 277 about *pure gold* for the incense altar.

282. The Hebrew word for dish is קְעָרָה. This may be a mould in which the bread is placed after it is baked in order to retain its shape (Sarna, *Exodus*, 163). The bread remains in these dishes/moulds throughout the week.

283. Most likely כַּפֹּתָיו are *bowls*. See the section on ritual acts for further analysis of these containers.

284. There are two containers on the table for pouring out liquids that have been the topic of speculation, its pitchers and jugs, וּקְשׂוֹתָיו וּמְנַקִּיֹּתָיו. See Cassuto, *Exodus*, 339; Haran, *Temples and Temple Service*, 216-17; Noth, *Leviticus*, 206; Propp, *Exodus 19-40*, 395-97; Sarna, *Exodus*, 163. Much of this speculation has occurred because it is assumed that the verb יָסַךְ, *to pour out*, only means to pour out a נֶסֶךְ, *drink offering*, since the two words are derived from the same root. This is not necessarily the case, however, since any liquid can be poured out for reasons other than a drink offering (BDB 650). Num 4:7 specifies that only one kind of the table's vessels is for pouring out a drink offering, the drink offering pitchers, קְשׂוֹת הַנָּסֶךְ.

285. The jugs, הַמְנַקִּיֹּת, on the table are most likely the containers that store and are used to pour the clear olive oil for the lamps (Propp, *Exodus 19-40*, 396-97). The

dishes, bowls, pitchers, and jugs is a necessary piece of furniture for the daily incense rite.

The oil burns in the seven lamps on the menorah, the seven-branched lampstand.[286] The menorah is constructed of pure gold.[287] It is hammered into a base and shaft with flower-like cups, buds, and blossoms (Exod 25:31). Six branches extend from each side of the shaft with three cups shaped like almond flowers with buds and blossoms on each branch (Exod 25:32–33). The central shaft of the menorah contains four cups shaped like almond flowers with buds and blossoms at the top of the shaft and under each pair of branches.[288] The entire menorah is made of one piece of hammered gold (Exod 25:34–36). Three additional kinds of accessories accompany the menorah, all of them made of pure gold (Exod 25:37–38). First, there are seven lamps that rest on each of the seven branches of the menorah. The second are tongs, and the third are fire pans. The menorah, its tongs, its fire pans, and its lamps are constructed from an entire talent of pure gold (Exod 25:39).[289]

Ritual Times

The incense rite is enacted in the morning and in the evening every day of the week. Each morning when the sun is rising and each evening after the sun has gone below the horizon but before dark, the high priest smokes up the finely ground fragrant incense on the inner altar (Exod 30:7–8). In the morning the seven lamps on the menorah are replenished with fresh wicks

---

only accessories for the menorah are the lamps, fire pans, and tongs (Exod 25:37–38), but the vessels for the lamps' oil are not listed with it. Since the bowls for the fragrant incense sit on the table, the jugs for the oil most likely sit on the table as well. The jugs on the table are probably used for pouring the clear olive oil into the lamps. The jugs, however, may store the holy anointing oil on the table, since there is a close connection between the anointing oil and the fragrant incense (Exod 30:22–38; 37:29).

286. The menorah, הַמְּנוֹרָה, derives its name from נֵר, lamp. Thus, the menorah is the holder of the lamps (Levine, *Leviticus*, 165).

287. See footnote 277 about *pure gold* for the incense altar.

288. The description of the menorah evokes the imagery of an almond tree. Meyers and Kleinig claim that the tree symbolism of the menorah correlates with the tree of life in the Garden of Eden, and Kleinig further compares the burning lamps with the natural luminaries (Meyers, *Tabernacle Menorah*, 133–81; Kleinig, *Leviticus*, 517–18). Yarden also makes the connection between the menorah and the burning bush/tree on Mt. Sinai (Yarden, *Tree of Light*, 35–53). Hachlili rejects the concept of the menorah as a symbolic "tree" because she believes that it has a unique function only as a lampstand in the tabernacle (Hachlili, *Menorah*, 38–39).

289. See Hachlili, *Menorah*; Yarden, *Tree of Light*, for their investigations into the menorah's characteristics, as well as illustrations and pictures of artifacts.

and oil, while the lamps are lit at the evening (Exod 27:20–21; 30:7–8; Lev 24:1–4). Although neither the bread on the table nor its pure frankincense are handled in the morning or evening except on the Sabbath, the bread and its pure frankincense are constantly present on the table in the holy place (Exod 25:30; Lev 24:5–9).[290] Furthermore, there is a connection between the bread of the presence and burning incense, tending/lighting the lamps, and the drink offering, because the finely ground fragrant incense, the oil, and the wine are kept with the bread on the table (Exod 25:29; 37:16).[291] The close proximity of all these ritual materials indicates that everything on the table, including the bread, is necessary for the correct enactment of the incense rite every morning and evening. In addition, the ornate vestments of the high priest must be worn in the tent of meeting every morning and evening as he conducts all of the acts of the incense rite (Exod 28:43). The ritual time of the incense rite is each morning and each evening every day of the week.[292]

Ritual Locations

There are five ritual locations related to burning the fragrant incense. First, the altar in the holy place is its most significant location. This altar sits in the middle of the tent, centrally located between the Ark of the Covenant, the table, and the menorah (Exod 40:20–28).[293] This location shows that the there is a correlation between the altar and the other three pieces of furniture.[294] Most importantly, the incense altar is the closest ritual location to the ark and its atonement seat in the most holy place, which indicates that the daily ritual acts performed at the incense altar form the heart of the entire rite (Exod 30:6, 36; 40:26).[295] Second, the menorah is located on the

---

290. If the bread of the presence and its frankincense are not on the table each morning and evening, then the incense rite is not complete.

291. The function of the table appurtenances is discussed in the section on ritual materials.

292. For further analysis of the ritual time, see the sections on the ritual time for each preceding rite. See also Kleinig, *Leviticus*, 516.

293. See Propp, *Exodus 19–40*, 420, 474; Levine, "*Lpny* YHWH," 272.

294. The high priest always performs all of the ritual acts at the altar, menorah, and table. Each location inside the tent of meeting, including the ark and atonement seat in the most holy place, correlates to all the others (Haran, *Temples and Temple Service*, 217, 220).

295. Exod 30:6 indicates that *the* place where the LORD meets with the high priest is at the incense altar. Although the LORD is present above the testimony, the high priest may not proceed past the incense altar but meets with the LORD at that location. The altar is closely associated with the LORD's presence in the most holy place. See also

south side of the holy place, probably halfway between the doorway and the veil that separates the most holy place from the holy place inside the tent (Exod 40:24). Third, directly on the opposite side of the holy place from the menorah is the table on the north side (Exod 40:22).[296] The fourth significant location for the incense rite is the font that stands between the doorway of the tent and the altar for burnt offering in the courtyard (Exod 30:18; 40:30).[297] These ritual locations are where the incense rite is conducted.

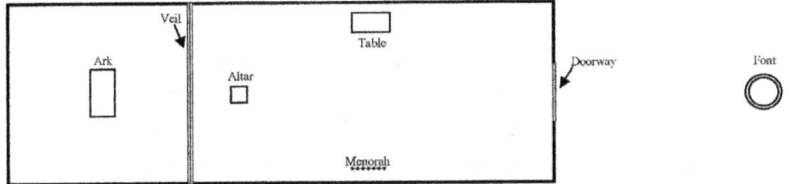

Figure 8. The ritual locations of the incense rite.

Summary of the Ritual Function

The incense rite performs several complementary functions. The high priest enacts the incense rite on behalf of the Israelites as the LORD commands him. Wearing his ornate vestments qualifies him for service in the holy place. He burns fragrant incense on the inner altar so that the sweet aroma will rise up before the LORD. The high priest tends the lamps on the menorah in the morning and lights them in the evening to illumine the holy place throughout the night. He replenishes the bread of the presence and other materials on the table so that all of the ritual activities which correlate with it may be enacted.

The Theological Purpose of the Incense Rite

The theological purpose of the incense rite is not explicitly stated in the Pentateuch. Trying to determine its purpose is further complicated because it is

---

Sarna, *Exodus*, 193.

296. The area from the menorah to the table probably marks the innermost boundary that the regular priests may not pass when they enter the tent of meeting to assist the high priest while he performs the incense rite. Similarly, the incense altar is the border beyond which the high priest is not allowed to advance except on the Day of Atonement. These boundaries denote forbidden thresholds that may only be crossed by those who are authorized to do so.

297. See Sarna, *Exodus*, 197.

the most complex of all the rites in the daily divine service. From a human perspective it also does not make sense. Why do lamps burn throughout the night in a room where no one is present? Why does bread sit untouched there for an entire week? Why is incense smoked up in a place where no one can smell it? How can wearing garments have any effect on someone not wearing them? On the surface these appear to be useless ritual acts with no divine or human purpose. However, further investigation reveals that the incense rite is one of the most theologically significant enactments of the daily divine service.

The fire is the most important element of the incense rite. The fire that first appeared in the burning bush and on the top of Mount Sinai and which led the Israelites in the pillar of smoke is the same fire that moved into the most holy place in the tent of meeting and then came out to light the fire on the altar for burnt offering (Lev 9:24). This holy fire is taken from the altar for burnt offering into the tent of meeting and put on the incense altar.[298] The holy fire of God burns in the lamps on the lampstand like on a golden tree with branches. Just as the burning bush/tree burned on Mount Sinai (Exod 3:2), so also the "tree" of the lampstand burns in the holy place;[299] and just as the glory cloud gives light throughout the night among the Israelites (Exod 13:21–22), so also the lamps give light throughout the night in the holy place.[300] The light is divine light because it burns with the fire of the LORD. In addition, God meets with his high priest there through the most holy fire on the incense altar where he produces the most holy smoke from the most holy incense. The LORD's fire does not smoke up the incense for his sake, but rather, for Israel (Exod 30:36). Without the divine fire the incense rite cannot accomplish the purposes for which the LORD institutes it.

The LORD accomplishes two purposes through the fragrant incense that is smoked up by the holy fire on the inner altar. First, the smoke reveals

---

298. The sections on the fire rite in chapter 2 and this chapter further analyze the nature and significance of the holy fire.

299. For further analysis of the menorah in relation to the burning bush/tree and the tree of life, see Kleinig, *Leviticus*, 516–18; Meyers, *Tabernacle Menorah*, 95–156; Yarden, *Tree of Light*, 35–53.

300. Kleinig holds that the lamps perform two symbolic functions. First, the lamps are luminaries (Lev 24:2) like the sun and moon that give light in the world (Gen 1:14–16). The light of the lamps burns with the fire of God and is, therefore, supernatural light that enlightens the Israelites with his holy presence (Ps 90:8). Second, the lamps reside in front of the Ark of the Covenant in which are the two tablets of stone with the Decalogue inscribed on them (Lev 24:3). Due to its proximity to the ten words on the tablets, the lampstand is associated with the word of the LORD that enlightens his people (Ps 19:8). Furthermore, in Num 7:89—8:4 God's speaking in the tent of meeting coincides with the maintenance of the lamps by the high priest (Kleinig, *Leviticus*, 517).

the presence of the LORD to the Israelites. As the high priest emerges from the tent of meeting, the incense that fills the holy place and envelops him there accompanies him out to the courtyard. The assembled congregation smells the most holy smoke of the incense that is produced by the fire of God. Like the pillar of cloud that both reveals and conceals the presence of God, so the incense conceals and reveals the divine presence from which it comes.[301] When the Israelites smell the sweet incense they smell the sweetness of God as a revelation of his presence with them and his grace and favor toward them. As they smell his approval and acceptance of them, they realize that the LORD is pleased with them. The aroma of the fragrant incense reveals to the Israelites that the LORD dwells among them with his mercy and blessing for them.[302] Second, the LORD sanctifies the Israelites with the most holy incense. On the one hand, the most holy smoke in the holy place sanctifies and keeps the high priest and his vestments holy, both of which represent the entire community of Israel.[303] On the other hand, the incense sanctifies the assembled congregation and the entire camp of Israel as the smoke spreads among them and enshrouds them. Since the smoke is most holy, it sanctifies every ritually clean person and thing that it contacts.[304] The LORD reveals himself to the Israelites as they smell the fragrant incense emerging from before him in the holy place, and he sanctifies his people as the most holy incense permeates the sanctuary and the camp of Israel.

The ornate vestments of the high priest serve intercessory purposes in the incense rite. The golden plate on the front of the turban accomplishes

---

301. There is evidence that the people see the smoke of the incense coming from the shrine as the high priest emerges from it (Sir 50:6–10). The fragrant incense produces a thick cloud of smoke that fills the holy place and engulfs the high priest (see Isa 6:4). Thus, when he comes out of the tent of meeting, the smoke accompanies him into the courtyard and is smelled by the people.

302. Sir 50:5–11 describes the pleasing smell of the fragrant incense when the high priest comes out of the holy place, which indicates that the odor spread among the assembled congregants and probably further. Since the fragrance that comes from the presence of the LORD is not a stench but a pleasant aroma, this signifies that the LORD is pleased with his people.

303. The high priest acts on behalf of Israel when he offers their gifts before the LORD as he wears the golden plate on his forehead (Exod 28:38). The names of the twelve tribes on the shoulder pieces and breastpiece of his vestments represent Israel (Exod 28:9–12, 21, 29), as do the twelve loaves that he sets on the table in the holy place (Exod 25:30; Lev 24:5–9).

304. Most holy things have the power to convey holiness and make holy whatever they contact (Exod 29:37; 30:29). The phrase קֹדֶשׁ קָדָשִׁים תִּהְיֶה לָכֶם, it will be most holy *for you* (plural), indicates that the fragrant incense sanctifies the people (Exod 30:36). For a more comprehensive analysis of contagious holiness related to the tabernacle furniture and offerings, see Kleinig, *Leviticus*, 145; Milgrom, *Leviticus 1–16*, 443–56,.

two things (Exod 28:36–38). On the one hand, the high priest bears the guilt of the holy gifts of the Israelites. On the other hand, the Israelites and their gifts are accepted by the LORD. As Israel's intercessor, the high priest presents them as favorable to God because he bears their guilt on their behalf. Since the LORD covers the high priest with his holiness, he does not account Israel's guilt against him.[305] Furthermore, when he wears the names of the twelve tribes on his shoulders, the high priest bears the Israelites on his shoulders into the presence of the LORD for a memorial to him (Exod 28:7–12).[306] In addition, the breastpiece of judgment accomplishes two things (Exod 28:15–30). On the one hand, the high priest carries the Urim and Thummim inside the breastpiece to bear the judgment of Israel over his heart;[307] and, on the other hand, he bears the names of the twelve tribes of Israel over his heart on the outside of the breastpiece for remembrance before the LORD.[308] By bearing the judgment and the names of the Israelites over his heart when he enters into the holy place, the LORD signals that the Israelites are dear to his heart and that he judges them graciously rather than in wrath. Finally, the golden bells on the hem of the robe jingle when the high priest enters and exits the holy place before the LORD so that he will not die (Exod 28:35). The sound of the bells evoke the favor of the LORD upon the high priest and the Israelites whom he bears into his presence on his shoulders and over his heart so that he will sanctify them by the most holy incense.[309] While the Israelites constantly remain with the LORD

---

305. The high priest personally and in reality bears the guilt of the Israelites. At his death even those who are unintentionally guilty of shedding innocent blood are free from the threat of the avenger of blood and may return from the cities of refuge to their own homes (Num 35:25, 28). See also Propp, *Exodus 19–40*, 449–50.

306. See the footnote below and also Haran, *Temples and Temple Service*, 213, 216.

307. There is much speculation about the nature and function of the Urim and Thummim, whether they are used for making decisions like casting lots or rolling dice, or whether they play a more general role. Their function is described as מִשְׁפָּט, judgment (Exod 28:30), which may be either a favorable or unfavorable judgment. The breastpiece itself is called the "breastpiece of judgment" (Exod 28:15) and probably derives its name from the function of the Urim and Thummim, which are placed inside of it. Since they are borne over the heart of the high priest, the judgment of the LORD is favorable toward him and Israel whom he bears into the presence of the LORD. See Haran, *Temples and Temple Service*, 213–14; Propp, *Exodus 19–40*, 442–43; Sarna, *Exodus*, 181–82.

308. The word זִכָּרוֹן, memorial, denotes something written down and taken to heart. In the case of the breastpiece, the names are written and fastened over the heart of the high priest, signifying that the זִכָּרוֹן is a taking to heart by the LORD, whom he represents. The term also refers to the names on the shoulder pieces, which are also "over his heart" in a sense (Propp, *Exodus 19–40*, 437–38, 443). See also Eising, "זָכַר," 77–79; Haran, *Temples and Temple Service*, 213–14; Kleinig, *Leviticus*, 491.

309. See Haran, *Temples and Temple Service*, 214.

symbolically through the twelve loaves of the bread of the presence on the table (Lev 24:5–9), the high priest also bears the Israelites out as the bells jingle to indicate that they journey together with the LORD wherever they go.[310] When the high priest wears these vestments, he represents Israel to the LORD and the LORD to Israel.[311]

Through the ritual activities of the incense rite the LORD accomplishes some of the most significant purposes of the daily divine service. The fire on the altar and in the lamps discloses the gracious and illuminating presence of God inside the holy place. By the smoke of the incense, the LORD reveals his favorable presence to Israel and sanctifies them as it wafts among the assembled congregation and throughout the camp. Since the high priest wears his ornate vestments, the LORD accepts Israel and sanctifies them; yet through the bread of the presence on the table the LORD keeps them in his presence. The theological purposes of the incense rite are for the LORD to reveal his favorable presence with Israel, to sanctify them, and to accept them in his presence at his sanctuary.

Conclusion

The LORD institutes the incense rite so that it may accomplish his main purpose for it and the whole service. He establishes the fragrant incense to be burned on the holy fire upon the incense altar, the lamps to be tended and lit on the menorah, the bread of the presence to be maintained on the table, and the ornate vestments to be worn by the high priest in the holy place. The LORD determines the ritual function of each of these as part of the incense rite in the holy place. The high priest performs all the ritual activities of

---

310. While the stones on the shoulder pieces and the breastpiece with the names of the twelve tribes consist of a ritual function when the high priest *enters* the holy place (Exod 28:12, 29–30), only the golden bells serve a ritual purpose when the high priest both enters *and* exits from it (Exod 28:35). The protection by the bells from death is intercessory since it involves the entrance to and exit from the LORD's presence in the holy place.

311. Before the LORD, the ornate vestments may function like a military armor that protects the high priest and Israel, whom he represents, from the power of impurity. The gold plate would function as a helmet, the ephod like a coat of mail (Exod 39:23), the ephod and breastpiece like outer armor, and the bells may represent protection for the feet and legs. Haran hints at this function of the vestments (Haran, *Temples and Temple Service*, 219). Before Israel, his vestments may function as the royal garments of the LORD, the king whom he represents to them. The gold plate on his head would be like a crown, the robe like a royal gown, the inscribed names on the ephod and breastpiece like a royal signet, and the bells announce the arrival of the king. This interpretation presupposes that the ornate garments of the high priest serve a mediating function. See Propp, *Exodus 19–40*, 446.

the incense rite every morning and evening inside the tent of meeting with the fragrant incense for the altar, the oil for the lamps, the bread and other materials on the table, and as he wears his vestments. Through the incense rite the LORD reveals himself to Israel and sanctifies them so that he may remain with them, and for the Israelites to interact with him in his holy presence in the daily divine service.

THE BURNING RITE

The burning rite of Israel is peculiar among other religions in the ancient world. Normally, an idol of a deity would be housed inside a shrine where the people could bring their offerings. When foodstuff was offered to the deity, it was placed before the idol inside the shrine. The offerings of Israel are unique in more than one way. The lay people cannot enter the shrine of the LORD inside the tent of meeting to bring him their offerings. Only the priests enter the enclosed tent, while the people bring their offerings only up to the altar in the courtyard. The offerings are seldom taken into the tent. The God of Israel gains no benefit from the offerings of the Israelites but benefits them through their offerings.

The Divine Institution of the Burning Rite

The LORD authorizes Israel to turn the carcass for the public burnt offering into smoke and to offer with it the cereal offering, the drink offering, and the bread offering of the high priest. Each of these offerings is prescribed by the LORD in the Pentateuch.[312]

The public daily burnt offering is divinely instituted.[313] Two yearling male lambs must be burned regularly every day on the altar for burnt offering. One lamb is smoked up in the morning and the other at twilight (Exod 29:38–39, 41; see Num 28:3–8). Since the burnt offering must be performed *regularly*,[314] it is offered throughout the generations of the Israelites. It is also

---

312. The priests must also wash their hands and feet (Exod 30:18–21) and wear their sacred vestments (Exod 28:43) in the burning rite just as they do for the other rites. See the section in this chapter on the fire rite for additional details about these ritual acts.

313. עֹלַת תָּמִיד, a regular burnt offering (Exod 29:42), is distinguished from עֹלָה, a burnt offering (Lev 1:3). The former designates the daily burnt offering whereas the latter refers to any other kind of burnt offering, such as that of an individual.

314. The Hebrew word for regular in this context is תָּמִיד. In post-exilic times the regular burnt offering and the daily service were simply known as the *Tamid*. See Dan 8:11–13; 11:31; 12:11. Although the regular burnt offering was first enacted at the

offered *every day*.³¹⁵ In addition, the daily burnt offering must be offered regularly at the entrance to the tent of meeting before the LORD (Exod 29:42). Because it is only offered at the sanctuary, it is the public offering for the entire community of Israel within whose midst the LORD dwells in that place (Exod 29:43, 45). Since this burnt offering and its accompanying offerings are divinely instituted, they must be offered on the altar regularly every morning and evening at the tabernacle.

The public daily cereal offering³¹⁶ is also divinely instituted. This offering, which consists of one-tenth of an ephah of fine flour mixed with one-fourth of a hin of beaten olive oil, must be offered with each lamb (Exod 29:40–41; Num 28:5, 8). Unlike the lamb for the burnt offering, however, the entire cereal offering is not turned into smoke on the altar.³¹⁷ Although the remaining part of it is used in one of the following rites (Lev 6:9 [16]),³¹⁸ the entire amount of frankincense together with one handful of the flour mixture must be smoked up as its token portion on the altar (Lev 2:1–2; 6:8 [15]).

The LORD prescribes the accompanying drink offering in the burning rite.³¹⁹ It consists of one-fourth of a hin of wine or fermented beverage and is offered with each lamb (Exod 29:40–41; Num 28:7–8). While it is not entirely clear whether this offering is poured on the fire on the altar for burnt offering or whether it is poured elsewhere,³²⁰ the drink offering is essential to the daily burning rite.

---

installation of the priests (Exod 29), it was thereafter to be regularly performed (Sarna, *Exodus*, 192). See also Propp, *Exodus 19–40*, 471.

315. לַיּוֹם may be rendered *for the day*, meaning each/every day, which indicates that the regular burnt offering is established as the *daily* burnt offering (Exod 29:38).

316. הַמִּנְחָה is any kind of offering made from flour. In this context it is the cereal offering that accompanies the daily burnt offering. This daily מִנְחָה is distinguished from others and is called a *cereal offering* rather than a grain offering (see NIV), because it is not an offering of whole grains. It is some processed form of grain, such as flour or more likely, grits. See Fabry, "מִנְחָה," 407–17, 420–21; Kleinig, *Leviticus*, 70; Milgrom, *Leviticus 1–16*, 179; Weinfeld, "מִנְחָה," 417–20.

317. The legislation for the daily cereal offering (Exod 29:40–41; Num 28:5, 8) does not specify its ritual procedure and could lead to the assumption that the entire cereal offering is burned on the altar. Only a handful of it, however, is smoked up (Lev 6:7–11 [14–18]). Furthermore, the prescription for the cereal offering (Lev 6:7–11 [14–18]) must be distinguished from the legislation for the private cereal offerings (Lev 2:1–16). See Kleinig, *Leviticus*, 143, 149–53, but also Milgrom, *Leviticus 1–16*, 389–91, for an alternate view.

318. See the meal rite below.

319. נֶסֶךְ, drink offering (Exod 29:40), is related to the verb נָסַךְ, to pour out, and therefore, a drink offering is an offering that is poured out to the LORD (BDB 650).

320. This is analyzed in greater detail below. See Kleinig, *Leviticus*, 225, 231; Propp,

The LORD requires that the bread offering of the high priest[321] must be burned on the altar for burnt offering. One-tenth of an ephah of fine flour prepared on a griddle as a flat bread must be smoked up on the altar regularly each day (Lev 6:13–14 [20–21]). Half of it is offered in the morning and the other half in the evening. Unlike the public cereal offering where only a token portion is burned, all of the bread offering of the high priest must be smoked up on the altar (Lev 6:15–16 [22–23]).[322] It is placed on it, not as a half-loaf, but crumbled into pieces and well mixed with oil (Lev 6:14 [21]). The bread offering of the high priest is not technically part of the daily burnt offering like the accompanying cereal and drink offerings are. Rather, it is an offering burned every morning and evening in the daily divine service.[323] Since the high priest is the chief Israelite, his bread offering is the foundation upon which all of the individual offerings of the people are placed.[324]

Since the burning rite is instituted by the LORD, he establishes its primary ritual acts. The burnt offering and token portion of its accompanying cereal offering are turned into smoke, the drink offering is poured out, and the bread offering of the high priest is burned in the daily divine service.

Exodus 19–40, 472; Stuart, *Exodus*, 630.

321. מִנְחָה תָּמִיד, regular bread offering, is that which the high priest offers daily (Lev 6:13 [20]). Like the accompanying cereal offering, the bread offering of the high priest is a מִנְחָה because it is made from grain. It is prepared and offered to the LORD in the form of pita-like flat bread. Only the high priest's מִנְחָה is called תָּמִיד. Since the daily cereal offering as well as the daily drink offering are inseparable parts of the daily burnt offering, עֹלַת תָּמִיד, they too are considered תָּמִיד even though the Pentateuch never explicitly refers to them by this term. See Exod 29:42; Levine, "*Lpny* YHWH," 169–70.

322. The Hebrew term כָּלִיל refers to burning the entire bread offering of the high priest on the altar. In some contexts it is used as a synonym for the burnt offering as well since it is burned completely (Deut 33:10; see Deut 13:16). In other contexts (1 Sam 7:9; Ps 51:19) it occurs together with the noun for the burnt offering, עוֹלָה (Kleinig, *Leviticus*, 155). See Kapelrud, "כָּלִיל," 182–85.

323. Levine does not think that the high priest offers a bread offering every day, but only on the occasion of his ordination (Levine, *Leviticus*, 38–39). Milgrom, however, makes the case that Num 4:16 and Neh 10:33 refer to the bread offering of the high priest that is offered every day in the divine service (Milgrom, *Leviticus 1–16*, 398–99). See also Hartley, *Leviticus*, 97–98.

324. For a discussion about whether all the priests must enact this kind of offering see Milgrom, *Leviticus 1–16*, 396–97. In practice, the high priest's successor offers his daily bread offering on his behalf (Lev 6:15 [22]), indicating that it is an individual offering upon which other individual offerings are placed. See also Kleinig, *Leviticus*, 154–55.

The Ritual Function of the Burning Rite

The burning rite is the climax of the morning and evening services. The entire daily divine service centers in this rite, builds up to it, and gains its significance from it.[325] Thus, a careful analysis of the ritual function of the burning rite is critical for understanding the entire service.

Ritual Agents

The ritual agents ordained to perform the burning rite are the high priest, the priest who will succeed the high priest, and the regular priests (Exod 29:44; Lev 6:2, 7, 13, 15 [9, 14, 20, 22]).[326] Unlike the ritual activities for the incense rite,[327] the Pentateuch does not explicitly specify who must perform the burning rite except for the bread offering of the high priest, which is enacted by his son who will become the next high priest (Lev 6:15 [22]).[328] The Pentateuch does not tell which priest must put the burnt offering and its cereal offering on the altar or pour out the drink offering.[329] It may be

---

325. Sarna identifies the daily burnt offering as the core of the entire ritual system (Sarna, *Exodus*, 192).

326. אַהֲרֹן וּבָנָיו, Aaron and his sons, in the Pentateuch generally refers to the high priest and the regular priests. It can specifically mean the high priest and his descendants who will succeed him throughout the generations. The phrase seems to be ambiguous and may refer to all of them: the high priest, his successor(s), and the regular priests, as it is probably intended in this context. See Milgrom, *Leviticus 1–16*, 396–97.

327. In the section on the incense rite, it was determined that only the high priest or his deputy burns incense (Exod 30:7), lights the lamps (Lev 24:3), wears the ornate vestments in the holy place (Exod 28), and performs the main ritual acts inside the tent of meeting.

328. There is disagreement about what ritual function the high priest's successor performs. The New International Version indicates that the future high priest merely prepares the bread offering, implying that the high priest himself burns it on the altar. The New Jerusalem Bible and the English Standard Version imply that the high priests only offer this offering at their ordination. Although Levine acknowledges that there is a daily bread offering of the high priest, he does not hold that the high priest's successor offers it (Levine, *Leviticus*, 38–39). See also Hartley, *Leviticus*, 97–98. While the high priest himself *presents* his bread offering every day, the anointed priest who will succeed him most likely burns it on the altar, וְהַכֹּהֵן הַמָּשִׁיחַ תַּחְתָּיו מִבָּנָיו יַעֲשֶׂה (Lev 6:8 [15]), every day (Kleinig, *Leviticus*, 154–55).

329. Other than the specific agent who burns the bread offering of the high priest, the text does not explicitly dictate which agent must perform the other acts in the burning rite. It simply states that the priest, הַכֹּהֵן, must put the burnt offering on the fire (Lev 6:5 [12]). Since the designation הַכֹּהֵן, the priest, can specifically refer to the high priest, this might mean that he normally performs the burning rite. Furthermore, in Lev 6:7–8 [14–15], the third person masculine singular pronoun *he* may specifically refer to Aaron as the one who burns the token portion of the cereal offering on the altar,

concluded that any of the priests may conduct any activities of the burning rite except for the bread offering of the high priest, but most likely they do so only at the direction of the high priest who is responsible for supervising the entire divine service.[330] Certainly he can enact the burning rite, except for his own bread offering, if he chooses to do so,[331] yet all the priests on duty enact the burning rite.

The LORD and the people of Israel are also involved. The LORD institutes its ritual acts and is the one on whose behalf the priests conduct it. He acts through the priests to accomplish his purposes for the sake of Israel.[332] They benefit from the ritual acts that the LORD accomplishes for them through his priests. Although they serve a different function than the priests, the LORD and the people of Israel are also part of the burning rite in the daily divine service.

Ritual Acts

The yearling male lamb, the token portion of the cereal offering, and the bread offering of the high priest are smoked up on the altar for burnt offering as the most significant parts of the burning rite in the daily divine service. All of the pieces of the lamb's carcass are placed on the burning coals on the altar. The fatty meat and pieces of the lamb produce smoke from the altar.[333] Then, a handful of the cereal offering, which includes all of

---

which indicates that this is the duty of the high priest. It is not entirely clear, though, who performs this act. See Milgrom, *Leviticus 1–16*, 396–97.

330. Since Aaron, the first high priest, is mentioned by name in the legislation for the burning rite (Exod 29:44; Lev 6:2, 7, 13 [9, 14, 20]), the high priest is always responsible for its enactment. This is true for all of the offerings at the tabernacle (Exod 28:38).

331. See *Tamid* 7:3 for evidence of the high priest performing the burning rite in a different period of Israel's history (Blackman, *Kodashim*, 495–96).

332. See Kleinig, *Leviticus*, 149–50, 155.

333. The Hebrew word הִקְטִיר technically does not mean *to burn* but *to make smoke* or *to turn an offering into smoke*. The offerings on the altar coals do not flame up so much as they smolder and produce a large quantity of sweet-smelling smoke. The same word is also used for the smoking up of incense (Exod 30:7–8; 40:27; Num 16:40), which shows a relation between burning incense on the inner altar and burning offerings on the outer altar (Kleinig, *Leviticus*, 56). The purpose of putting an offering on the altar is not to incinerate it but for it to become smoke. According to Milgrom, some ancient religions believe that turning an offering into smoke is the only way to reach celestial beings. Since הִקְטִיר is distinguished from שָׂרַף (Lev 4:12, 21; 10:16; 16:27–28; Num 19:5–6, 8), which means to incinerate something apart from the altar, the offering is not destroyed but rather is transformed, sublimated, or etherealized into smoke so that it may ascend to the dwelling of God in heaven (Milgrom, *Leviticus 1–16*, 160–61). Eberhart also notes the difference between הִקְטִיר and שָׂרַף, claiming that the burning rite

the frankincense with it, is put on the altar.³³⁴ Since the token portion of the cereal offering is composed of a high volume of olive oil and frankincense, it ignites quickly and produces an intense cloud of aromatic smoke.³³⁵ Finally, the crumbled oil-soaked pieces of the bread offering of the high priest are burned on the altar. Similar to the daily cereal offering, this offering too begins to burn as soon as it touches the fire and produces a strong cloud of smoke.³³⁶ The production of smoke from burning these offerings on the altar is the central purpose of the daily divine service.

In another ritual act in the burning rite the drink offering is poured out. Its ritual function, however, is not explicitly stated in the Pentateuch. Unlike the offerings that are prepared in the courtyard, the drink offering is brought out from the holy place inside the tent of meeting. The only vessel that the Pentateuch designates for pouring the drink offering is a golden pitcher,³³⁷ which is one of the accessories with the golden table inside the tent of meeting (Exod 25:29; 37:16; Num 4:7; see 1 Chr 28:17). The wine is most likely kept in these golden pitchers inside the tent of meeting and brought out for the drink offering at the outer altar in the daily service.³³⁸ The drink offering is not burned on the altar fire to produce smoke. Yet, for a ritual material to be an *offering* it must be placed somewhere on the altar.

---

is the climax of the offering. He holds that the smoking up of a ritual substance on the altar is what qualifies a ritual act as an *offering for God* (Eberhart, "Neglected Feature of Sacrifice," 485–93). He fails to address, however, whether or not the drink offering is smoked up on the altar. See also Clements, "שָׁחַט," 9–16.

334. The handful of the cereal offering with its frankincense is called אַזְכָּרָה, but the meaning of this term is uncertain. It may be understood as the *memorial portion* of the cereal offering, but most likely refers to its *token portion* that functions as a substitute for the entire cereal offering. See Eising, "זָכַר," 79–80; Kleinig, *Leviticus*, 70–71; Milgrom, *Leviticus 1–16*, 181–82.

335. Propp refers to an experiment that recreated the cereal offering. The mixture became the consistency of peanut butter that ignited quickly when placed on a fire and burned with a bright flame for nearly ten minutes (Propp, *Exodus 19–40*, 471–72).

336. Since the Pentateuch never states that frankincense is offered with either the bread offering of the high priest or the bread offerings of individuals, it may be assumed that frankincense is omitted from all kinds of cooked grain offerings (Milgrom, *Leviticus 1–16*, 183–84).

337. קַשְׂוָה

338. See the section on the ritual materials of the incense rite in this chapter for further information about the vessels on the golden table. Haran claims that the golden pitchers inside the tent of meeting cannot be used for pouring out drink offerings at the outer altar. He supposes that the outer altar must have its own vessels (Haran, *Temples and Temple Service*, 216–17). There is no evidence to support his view. Cassuto holds that the golden pitchers are taken from the table in the tent of meeting for use at the outer altar. He does not believe that wine is kept in the pitchers in the holy place, but that it is stored in the courtyard (Cassuto, *Exodus*, 339–40).

Thus, the drink offering is most likely poured out on the side of it.[339] The exact location where this takes place is examined later in this chapter.

The priests wash their hands and feet at the beginning of the burning rite as a specialized ritual function. Unlike when they wash for purification before entering the tent of meeting, the priests wash their hands and feet after they come out of the holy place for a completely different purpose.[340] A clue for determining this purpose may be seen in a similar ritual washing on the Day of Atonement. On that day the high priest washes his entire body after he has completed his ministry in the most holy place (Lev 16:24). The purpose of this washing can hardly be a ritual cleansing from impurity.[341] Rather, it removes the contagion of the super holiness with which he is engulfed in the presence of God in the most holy place. The high priest washes his body so that he will not be the means of sanctification for the area, objects, and people that he touches.[342] Similarly, every day after the high priest

---

339. If it is true that the wine for the drink offering is kept in the holy place, on the golden table, then it is most holy and consecrates whatever it touches. This ritual function provides evidence that the drink offering is not poured on top of the altar on the fire. While it may be possible for some kinds of drink offerings to be poured on the fire (Num 15:10?), the prohibition of burning כָּל־שְׂאֹר וְכָל־דְּבַשׁ, any leaven or any honey, on the altar may include wine (Lev 2:11). There is some question about what דְּבַשׁ, "honey," is. This is probably not only bee honey, but fruit honey or nectar. Because the wine for the drink offering is fermented, which could be considered leavened, and is a liquid from fruit it must not be burned on the altar. Rather, it is poured out somewhere other than on the altar fire (Milgrom, *Leviticus 1–16*, 188–90). For further analysis of דְּבַשׁ, see Caquot, "דְּבַשׁ," 128–31.

340. See the sections in this chapter on the ritual acts for the fire rite, presentation rite, and incense rite for discussions about the priests washing their hands and feet as a ritual purification.

341. Since everything in the holy place is most holy, it is impossible for the hands and feet of the high priest to become ritually impure in his performance of the incense rite inside the tent of meeting.

342. It is unlikely that the high priest washes his entire body on the Day of Atonement to remove impurity with which he might be contaminated by the scapegoat. Since he is immune from the impurities that are removed from the tabernacle, the washing most likely removes the super holiness that he contracts by entering the most holy place (Milgrom, *Leviticus 1–16*, 1048–49). This view is further supported in that the high priest removes and stores inside the tent the special vestments that he only wears on the Day of Atonement (Lev 16:4, 24). The high priest removes these unique vestments and takes a unique ritual bath to protect himself, his fellow priests, and the congregation from sacrilegious contact with the super holiness of the LORD (Kleinig, *Leviticus*, 344). The super holiness that the high priest contracts in the most holy place is primarily from two things, the incense and the soil upon which he walks inside the most holy place. The super holiness must be washed off before resuming his regular duties. Similarly, in the daily divine service the most holy incense and ground that the high priest touches with his hands and feet in the holy place must be washed off. God alone is an agent of contagious holiness. The high priest, regular priests, and the Israelite people

emerges from the holy place, he must wash the most holy fragrant incense and soil from his hands and feet so that *he* does not consecrate the place where he walks and the things or people that he touches outside the sanctuary. This is true for anyone who goes in and comes out of the tent of meeting. This washing in the burning rite performs a ritual function that is distinct from the other washings in the daily divine service.

The ornate vestments of the high priest manifest God and his gracious appearance to his people in the burning rite. Just as his vestments have a ritual function in the incense rite, so they do in the burning rite but in a different way. Whereas the high priest represents Israel to the LORD as he wears his ornate vestments into the holy place for the incense rite, conversely in the burning rite he represents the LORD to Israel, manifesting his gracious presence to them.[343] Just as the high priest bears Israel on his shoulders and over his heart by the names of the twelve tribes as well as the judgment of Israel by the Urim and Thummim in the incense rite, so also he does at the burning rite (Exod 28:9–13; 29–30). Yet, two parts of the vestments function most significantly in both the incense rite and the burning rite. The one involves the golden bells and pomegranates on the hem of his robe which make sounds when he enters and comes out of the tent (Exod 28:31–35). Upon entering the holy place, the LORD hears the sound of the bells; when he comes out of the tent to the altar, the Israelites hear the sound. The other is the inscription "YHWH's holiness" on the golden plate on the head of the high priest.[344] This is the only vestment that the Israelites see when the high priest emerges from the tent to approach the altar.[345] Both the bells and the inscription function in two different ways depending on whether the high priest approaches God or the people. When he goes into the holy place, the bells are heard by God as an act of intercession, but when he comes out of the tent, the people hear the bells as a proclamation of God's acceptance

---

can never be the means of conveying holiness but they are sanctified by means of most holy things (Kleinig, *Leviticus*, 1–13).

343. For further analysis of the character and function of the vestments at the burning rite, see Propp, *Exodus 19–40*, 445–46, 522–27.

344. The golden plate on the forehead of the high priest when he approaches the altar from the tent of meeting functions as a sign to the Israelites of the favor of the LORD. Since the high priest bears the guilt of Israel by wearing the golden plate on the front of his turban when he offers the holy offerings on their behalf (Exod 28:38), the Israelites behold the LORD's graciousness toward them when they look upon the golden plate while the high priest offers their offerings at the burning rite.

345. The altar for burnt offering is three cubits high, which is approximately 1.3 meters, or 4.5 feet, tall (Exod 27:1). Therefore, the altar hides from Israel's view all of the ornate vestments of the high priest except the plate on his turban when he comes out of the tent and approaches the altar.

of them. Likewise, when he goes into the tent, the inscription is seen by God as an act of intercession on behalf of the Israelites, but when he comes out, the people see the inscription as a theophany, a gracious manifestation of their heavenly king.[346]

Ritual Materials

There are three categories of ritual materials for the burning rite. The first and most important is the holy fire on the altar for burnt offering. The fire turns all of the offerings placed on it into smoke. The burning rite as well as the whole divine service and the entire ritual system cannot function properly without the holy fire on the outer altar. The second are the things that are burned on the altar and smoked up by the holy fire. These are the two yearling male lambs, the cereal offering of flour, oil, and frankincense, and the bread offering of the high priest, each seasoned with salt. The third ritual material is the wine or fermented beverage that is not burned on the altar fire but is poured on the side of it.

Ritual Times

The offerings are smoked up every morning and every evening. The morning offering functions as a rite of passage from night to day and the evening offering is the transition from day to night. The entire period from the morning of one day to the morning of the next day marks the extent of the entire daily service with its two significant times in the morning and in the evening (Exod 29:39; Lev 6:2, 5 [9, 12]; Num 28:3–4). Thus, there are not two services each day, but half of the daily divine service is enacted in the morning and its other half is enacted in the evening.[347]

---

346. The golden plate is originally called a ציץ, a shiny thing (BDB 847) in the legislation for making the sacred vestments (Exod 28:36). Other texts (Exod 29:6; 39:30; Lev 8:9) further describe the golden plate as a holy crown, נזר (BDB 634). This may indicate that the golden plate on the front of the turban is a kingly headdress. If so, then the high priest may be viewed as a royal figure, representing the LORD as the king of Israel. See also Cassuto, *Exodus*, 383–84; Kleinig, *Leviticus*, 189–90.

347. See the analysis in the section on the fire rite in this chapter for further details about the significance of the morning and evening offerings.

The Ritual Function of the Daily Divine Service 151

Ritual Locations

There are three significant ritual locations associated with the burning rite. The first is the altar for burnt offering and the second is the font, both of which are in the courtyard at the entrance to the tent of meeting. The priest washes his hands and feet with water from the font, and the altar is where the offerings are smoked up.[348] The third location is not certain. Exactly where is the drink offering poured out? Most likely it is not poured on the altar fire even though it is always part of the daily burnt offering.[349] The Pentateuch only states that the drink offering must be poured out *in the holy place* (Num 28:7),[350] which leaves its precise location undesignated. There are three clues, however, that help narrow the place where the drink offering is poured. First, the *holy place* where the bread from the daily cereal offering must be eaten is beside the altar in the courtyard (Lev 10:12–13).[351]

---

348. These locations are discussed more thoroughly in previous sections of this chapter.

349. Num 15:3–10 could give the impression that drink offerings are poured on top of the burnt offering on the altar, depending on how it is translated. Stuart and Propp hold this view (Stuart, *Exodus*, 630; Propp, *Exodus 19–40*, 472). The drink offering that is offered עַל־הָעֹלָה, which could be translated *on the burnt offering* (Num 15:5), is best rendered as *in addition to* or possibly *together with* the burnt offering (Levine, "*Lpny* YHWH," 386, 392). The preposition עַל may also mean *near, next to, beside,* or *by* (BDB 752). It is impractical that the wine would be poured out on the altar fire since the liquid could begin to extinguish it. There would be the danger of completely extinguishing the holy fire in the pilgrim festivals when there are an abundance of drink offerings. It is highly improbable that any drink offerings are poured on top of the burnt offerings on the altar.

350. The drink offering is poured out בַּקֹּדֶשׁ, which may be rendered *at/in the sanctuary* or *at/in the holy place*. The term does not exclusively refer to any one area of the tabernacle. In addition to designating the most holy place inside the veil in the tent of meeting by its longer name קֹדֶשׁ הַקֳּדָשִׁים (Exod 26:33, 34), this area can also simply be called the holy place, הַקֹּדֶשׁ (Lev 16:2–3, 16–17, 20, 23, 27, 33). The holy place, הַקֹּדֶשׁ, is also the first room in the tent of meeting where the incense altar, menorah, and table reside (Exod 26:33; 28:29, 35; 29:30; 31:11; Lev 4:6; 6:16, 23 [23, 30]; 10:18; Num 4:12, 15). Most often the various forms of קֹדֶשׁ in the Pentateuch designate the entire area within the walls of the courtyard as the *holy place*, which is probably best to translate as *sanctuary* so that it may be distinguished from the two holy locations inside the tent of meeting (Exod 28:43; 30:24; 35:19; 36:1, 3–4, 6; 38:24–27; 39:1, 41; Lev 5:15; 6:20 [27]; 7:6; 10:4, 17–18; 14:13; 20:3; 21:23; 24:9; 27:3, 25; Num 3:28, 31–32, 47, 50; 4:16; 7:13, 19, 25, 31, 37, 43, 49, 55, 61, 67, 73, 79, 85–86; 8:19; 18:3, 5, 16; 28:7; 31:6). The New Jerusalem Bible and English Standard Version wrongly indicate that the drink offering is poured in the holy place inside the tent of meeting (see Num 28:7).

351. The phrase אֵצֶל הַמִּזְבֵּחַ, beside/near/at the location of the altar, specifies where the most holy food must be consumed by the priests. Since this area beside the altar is בְּמָקוֹם קָדֹשׁ, at a holy place, this narrows the area at the sanctuary, בַּקֹּדֶשׁ, where the drink offering must be poured out (Num 28:7). So, the drink offering is poured out at

Second, and most importantly, Exod 28:43 calls the altar for burnt offering *the holy place*, which is most likely also the meaning of *the holy place* in Num 28:7. Third, the prohibition against pouring drink offerings on the altar for incense in the tent of meeting (Exod 30:9) hints that this is precisely what must be done at the altar for burnt offering.[352] Since the burnt offering and the cereal offering are offered on top of the altar, the accompanying drink offering is poured out somewhere on the altar as well. Furthermore, the prescription for the daily burnt offering with its cereal and drink offerings states that these shall be offered *on the altar* for burnt offering (Exod 29:38–40).[353] Other evidence suggests that the drink offering is poured out at the base of the altar where the blood from the sin offering is also poured.[354] In addition, fermented drink offerings are probably restricted from being burned on the altar fire because anything that is either leavened or fruit nectar is forbidden from being smoked up on it (Lev 2:11). Since alcoholic beverages from vine fruits may be understood as both leavened and containing fruit nectar, the drink offerings are not burned on the altar fire.[355] Therefore, it may be concluded that the drink offering is poured on the side of the altar and runs down onto the ground upon which it rests at the sanctuary.[356] So the three significant ritual locations at the burning rite include the font, on the top of the altar where the holy fire is located, and the side of the altar at its base.

---

the altar.

352. In addition to the warning against offering strange incense on the inner altar, the LORD commands that burnt offerings, grain offerings, and drink offerings must not be offered there either (Exod 30:9).

353. The LORD commands that the daily burnt offering be offered עַל־הַמִּזְבֵּחַ, on the altar (Exod 29:38). But עַל does not only mean *on top of* but it can be *on the side of*. When referring to the burnt offering and the cereal offering, עַל־הַמִּזְבֵּחַ is on top of the altar, but for the drink offering it means on the side of the altar.

354. Sir 50:15 states that the base of the altar is the place where the drink offering is poured out. Furthermore, the Greek version of this passage renders the wine as αἵματος σταφυλῆς, blood of grapes, which may draw a correlation between the wine and the blood that is put on the outside of the altar in the blood rite. See also Propp, *Exodus 19–40*, 472.

355. Milgrom holds that the wine is not burned on the altar hearth but poured out at the base of the altar so as not to violate the prohibition against smoking up any fermented substance on the altar (Milgrom, *Leviticus 1–16*, 189). See also Kleinig, *Leviticus*, 72–73.

356. Although the Pentateuch does not state on which side of the altar the drink offering is poured, it is probably on the side closest to the tent of meeting. Since the ashes are placed on the east side of the altar (Lev 1:16), the animals are slain and slaughtered on its north side (Lev 1:11), and a ramp to the top of the altar is probably on its south side (Exod 20:26), the drink offering is most likely poured out at the altar's west side.

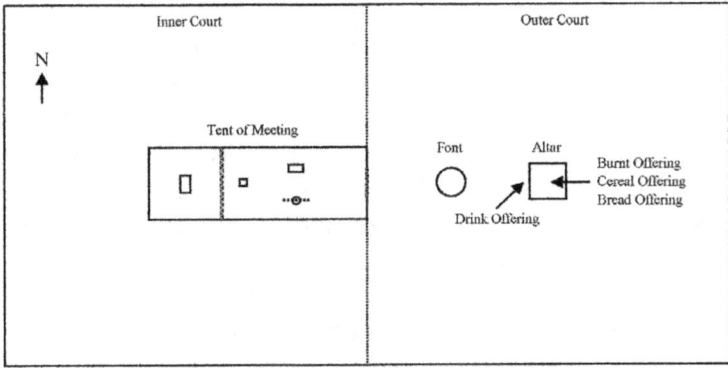

Figure 9. The burning rite at the altar.

Summary of the Ritual Function

Every morning and evening the high priest comes out of the tent of meeting to perform the burning rite with the other priests on behalf of the LORD. As he wears the holy crown on the front of his turban, the assembled congregation sees the reflected glory of the LORD their king who comes out of his dwelling to serve them at his altar. They hear the message of the LORD's favor toward them in the sounding bells on the hem of the high priest's robe as he approaches the altar. The high priest or another priest designated by him places the burnt offering and its accompanying cereal offering on the altar fire. The son who will become the next high priest places the bread offering of his father on the fire. One of the priests pours out the drink offering on the outside of the altar at its base. The offerings placed on the altar fire produce a pungent cloud of smoke that ascends from the altar in the courtyard. So then, the main ritual function of the burning rite is so that smoke can be produced from the altar for burnt offering.

The Theological Purpose of the Burning Rite

What does God accomplish through the burning rite? From a human perspective, the answer to this could be that it is not the work of God but that of man. It is not obvious that God does anything. The priests perform the acts; they place the offerings on the altar; they pour out the drink offering. The smoke and the aroma from the offerings rise to God in the heavenly realm. If he is the recipient of the offerings, how could he accomplish anything through them? In other cultures, the priests and people give offerings to their gods to make the deities favorable to them or to provide the deities with what they need to survive.[357] The God of Israel, however, has no need for food (Ps 50:8–13) and he cannot be bribed (Deut 10:17). Rather, through the burning rite the LORD serves Israel in three distinct ways, by meeting with them, sanctifying them, and dwelling among them.

The LORD meets with Israel every morning and evening in the burning rite to reveal himself to them (Exod 29:43).[358] His theophany occurs in three ways. First, the LORD manifests himself to the Israelites through sight. When the high priest approaches the altar for burnt offering, the assembled congregation beholds the golden crown on the front of his turban with the words "YHWH's holiness" (Exod 28:36–38).[359] This is the only place at the sanctuary where the divine name, יהוה, is actually seen. By wearing the LORD's crown, the high priest represents him to Israel as a personal royal king.[360] Although the high priest is not God, he functions as an icon or image of God to the people when he conducts the divine service.[361] The Israelites cannot see the holy fire on the altar, but instead, the smoke from the offerings reveals God's presence there.[362] Like the pillar of fire and cloud that manifests God's presence in the exodus (Exod 13:20–22), so this column of smoke is a theophany to the Israelites every morning and evening at the altar for burnt offering.[363] Second, the Israelites hear the sounding bells on the hem of the high priest's robe as he approaches and ministers at the altar

---

357. See Kleinig, *Leviticus*, 40–43.

358. See Kleinig, *Leviticus*, 64–65.

359. For further discussion about *YHWH's holiness*, see the section on the incense rite in this chapter.

360. Anointing the head of the high priest is prototypical to that of the kings of Israel and may indicate, moreover, that the high priest functions in a royal capacity (Lev 8:12).

361. The high priest wears the golden crown with the divine name inscribed on it not merely as an adornment but to carry the LORD's holiness personally as he places the offerings on the altar. "YHWH's holiness" removes the guilt of the Israelites from their offerings at the sanctuary (Milgrom, *Leviticus 1–16*, 511–12). By wearing the LORD's holiness the high priest makes the offerings of the Israelites acceptable to the LORD (Haran, *Temples and Temple Service*, 215) and the Israelites themselves are accepted by the LORD (Exod 28:38). See also Propp, *Exodus 19–40*, 446–48, 534–27.

362. The only time that the lay Israelites see the holy fire at the tabernacle is at the inaugural service when it comes out of the tent of meeting, consumes the offerings, and ignites the fire on the altar for burnt offering (Lev 9:23–24). After that, the fire is hidden from them and only manifested by the smoke from the offerings. For examples of sight taboos at the tabernacle, see Haran, *Temples and Temple Service*, 175–81.

363. See Kleinig, *Leviticus*, 217–20; Milgrom, *Leviticus 1–16*, 588–91.

(Exod 28:33–35).³⁶⁴ The sound announces that the LORD, through his personal representative, is at his altar to serve his people there like a gracious king who provides his guests with a feast at his table.³⁶⁵ Third, the LORD manifests himself in the aroma of the offerings. When the high priest emerges from the tent of meeting and approaches the altar, the fragrant incense that engulfs him in the holy place comes out to the outer altar with him (Sir 50:1–11).³⁶⁶ This powerful incense intermingles with the smoke from the altar and disperses among the congregants and throughout the camp of Israel (Exod 29:41; Num 28:2, 6, 8). The soothing scent of the offerings reveals the favorable presence of the LORD to the Israelites.³⁶⁷ Through the burning rite in the daily divine service, the LORD meets with his people and reveals his gracious presence among them by the unique things that they see, hear, and smell.

The LORD sanctifies the Israelites, the tabernacle, and his priests through the burning rite (Exod 29:43–44). Israel is consecrated by the glory of the LORD (Exod 29:43), the theophanic pillar of smoke that is produced by the holy fire on the altar.³⁶⁸ The divine fire turns the offerings on the altar into most holy smoke, which permeates throughout the assembled congregation and the entire camp of Israel to sanctify them every morning and evening.³⁶⁹ The smoke from the offerings also sanctifies the tent of meeting

364. The Pentateuch does not specify who hears the sound of the bells and the ambiguous passive וְנִשְׁמַע, he will be heard, may imply that the high priest is heard *by God* when he enters the tent of meeting and *by the people* when he comes out. For further analysis of the purpose of the bells, see Propp, *Exodus 19–40*, 445–46.

365. Haran holds that there is no ritual function that the ornate vestments of the high priest fulfill apart from the holy place inside the tent. He asserts that they are only worn for ritual purposes inside of it (Haran, *Temples and Temple Service*, 214). Yet, the Pentateuch expressly states that the bells will be heard both when the high priest enters the holy place before the LORD *and when he comes out* (Exod 28:35). Since the high priest comes out of the tent of meeting to perform the burning rite at the outer altar, the bells serve a ritual purpose there just as they do inside the tent of meeting.

366. See Propp, *Exodus 19–40*, 514.

367. See Kleinig, *Leviticus*, 66.

368. The glory is the pillar of fire and cloud that leads the Israelites out of Egypt, rests on the top of Mount Sinai, and moves into the most holy place over the ark of the testimony. This same glory comes out of the tent of meeting and ignites the fire on the altar for burnt offering at the inaugural service. God appears in the form of fire (Deut 9:3), and his glory is seen in his holy fire (Exod 24:17). From an anthropological perspective, fire is like a doorway to the spiritual realm. On the one hand, burnt offerings are transmitted to God through fire. On the other hand, God manifests himself to the earthly realm through fire (Milgrom, *Leviticus 1–16*, 590). See also Propp, *Exodus 19–40*, 514.

369. The Hebrew of Exod 29:43 is וְנֹעַדְתִּי שָׁמָּה לִבְנֵי יִשְׂרָאֵל וְנִקְדַּשׁ בִּכְבֹדִי. This may be translated two ways. It could be, "I will meet there with the sons of Israel and *it* will be

and the altar for burnt offering at the tabernacle (Exod 29:44). Everything that the most holy smoke touches is consecrated and becomes holy (Exod 30:36). Since the tent of meeting and the altar are most holy, the smoke functions to reconsecrate them each morning and evening.[370] Furthermore, the altar for burnt offering and the ground at the tabernacle are sanctified by the most holy drink offering. Since the wine for this offering is brought out from the table inside the tent of meeting, it is most holy and sanctifies whatever it touches.[371] When the priest pours out the drink offering on the side of the altar at its base, it flows onto the ground and the most holy wine consecrates the altar and the ground at the tabernacle. Finally, the priests are sanctified at the burning rite. Since all of the tabernacle furnishings, including the pitcher for the drink offering, the font, and the altar for burnt offering are most holy, they impart holiness to the priests when they touch them (Exod 30:22–29). The primary way the priests are sanctified in this rite is through the most holy smoke from the altar for burnt offering (Exod 29:44).[372] The main theological purpose of the burning rite is to sanctify and reconsecrate the Israelites, the tent and altar, and the priests every day at the divine service.

---

consecrated by my glory." It also may be translated, "I will meet there with the sons of Israel and *he* will be consecrated by my glory." The first translation is ambiguous and may interpret the third masculine singular form, *it*, as a reference either to the tabernacle (Cassuto, *Exodus*, 388; Sarna, *Exodus*, 192) or to Israel. The second translation understands the third masculine singular as a reference to Israel. Since the next verse (Exod 29:44) speaks of the consecration of the tent, the altar, Aaron, and his sons, the current passage probably means that Israel is consecrated by the glory of the LORD. For additional interpretations, see Dozeman, *Exodus*, 659; Propp, *Exodus 19–40*, 472–73.

370. Their daily reconsecration is probably necessary due to the desecrating power of the common realm within which the tabernacle moves and rests. See Kleinig's discussion about how the holy and the common influence each other (Kleinig, *Leviticus*, 6–13).

371. Although the Pentateuch never states that the wine from the drink offering is most holy, three clues help draw the conclusion that it is. First, the daily burnt offering with its accompanying cereal offering and drink offering sanctifies the Israelites, the priests, the tent, and the *altar* (Exod 29:38–44). Second, only the incense that is kept and used inside the tent of meeting is most holy (Exod 30:36), indicating that all materials there are most holy. Third, the blood from a sin offering that is taken into the tent of meeting has a different status than the blood of a sin offering that is not taken into the tent of meeting (Lev 6:23 [30]). On the Day of Atonement the blood of the sin offerings that is taken into the tent of meeting not only functions as it normally does for purification, it also sanctifies the altar (Lev 16:19). See Kleinig, *Leviticus*, 343–47. Based on these three observations, it may be assumed that whatever materials are inside the tent of meeting are most holy. See also Haran's analysis of the grades of sanctity at the tabernacle (Haran, *Temples and Temple Service*, 175–88).

372. Although the Pentateuch does not call the smoke from the burnt offering most holy, it has sanctifying power (Exod 29:38–44).

The LORD dwells among the Israelites and this is the most profound purpose of the burning rite (Exod 29:45–46). God's residence at the tabernacle within the midst of Israel indicates that he accomplishes two things through this rite at the altar. First, the LORD accepts the Israelites through their offerings (Exod 28:38). In the daily divine service, the priests offer the public offerings on behalf of the entire community and the LORD accepts them by the three main stages of the daily burnt offering. The first stage is the presentation of their offerings before his altar.[373] The second stage occurs when the priests splash the blood of the lamb against the four sides of the altar for their atonement.[374] The third stage, the burning rite, completes God's acceptance of Israel every day at the divine service. The sweet aroma from the altar bears witness that the LORD accepts his people and that he is sweet toward the Israelites as he dwells with them as their gracious God.[375] Second, the LORD dwells among the Israelites not to be served by them but for him to serve them.[376] In this part of the service, the LORD shares his Sabbath-like rest with his people, not merely on one day of the week but every morning and evening.[377] The smoke from the altar is an aroma that sets both God and Israel at rest (Exod 29:41). On the one hand, God is set at rest by the aroma and is favorable toward the Israelites. On the other hand, the people of Israel are set at rest by the aroma of the favorable presence of God among them.[378] The LORD dwells in the midst of his people at the tabernacle that he may accept them and share his rest with them.

---

373. The offerings are presented at the entrance to the tent of meeting before the LORD. He accepts the offerings as well as those for whom they are presented (Lev 1:3), favoring them and treating them graciously (Kleinig, *Leviticus*, 65).

374. Just as with the private burnt offerings (Lev 1:4), so also through the rite of atonement with the public burnt offering the LORD accepts his people and cleanses them from their sins (Kleinig, *Leviticus*, 65–66).

375. The pleasing aroma operates both physically and spiritually at the same time. Physically, the aroma is pleasing on account of its sweet scent. Spiritually, the sweet aroma reveals the LORD's pleasure with his people. By smelling the sweet aroma the LORD's people experience his pleasure and acceptance of them (Kleinig, *Leviticus*, 66).

376. See Stuart, *Exodus*, 630–31.

377. There are two different Hebrew words that are normally associated with the LORD's rest, the noun שַׁבָּת and the verb נוּחַ. The former term primarily means to have rest as a result of ceasing from labor, while the latter one has to do with resting by settling down, having calm quietness as opposed to turmoil, or sitting (BDB 628, 992). The two words are used together in Exod 20:11, 23:12, and Deut 5:15, indicating that they are closely related. The Sabbath-like rest of ceasing from work correlates with the calming rest that the LORD shares with his people through the divine service.

378. The phrase לְרֵיחַ נִיחֹחַ אִשֶּׁה לַיהוָה (Exod 29:41) has been the subject of much discussion among scholars. For an overview of the main points, see Milgrom, *Leviticus 1–16*, 161–63, 252–53. The phrase and similar ones are a formula for God's approval

The theological purpose of the burning rite at the daily service of ancient Israel turns pagan assumptions and perspectives upside down.[379] Burning the daily offerings might be perceived as a human act of worship toward God, but the LORD accomplishes his own purposes in smoking up the offerings. Instead of the Israelites initiating the meeting with the LORD at the tabernacle, he comes to meet them so that he might manifest his presence with them through the sights, sounds, and scents at the altar. Rather than offering gifts to the LORD in order to gain his favor, he sanctifies the Israelites, the tent and altar at the tabernacle, and his priests by the daily offerings. God does not dwell among the Israelites so that they may serve him with food or drink, but for him to invite and serve them at his table and give them rest with him in his residence.

Conclusion

The LORD institutes the ritual enactment of the burnt offering for him to meet with his people. The high priest personally represents the LORD as he wears the royal vestments at the altar. Through him the LORD meets with the Israelites to reveal himself and serve them from his table at his residence. The aroma from the offerings makes and keeps his sanctuary and his people holy, so that he will continue to accept them and share his daily Sabbath-like rest with them as he dwells in their midst. The LORD institutes the burning rite and authorizes its ritual function, not to be served by the Israelites, but for him to meet with them, share his holiness with them, and dwell with them as their gracious benefactor every day through the divine service.

THE BLESSING RITE

The blessing rite is different from the other rites in the daily divine service. Whereas the other rites involve no prescribed spoken words, the blessing rite does. The performance of these prescribed words sets the blessing rite

---

of offerings and his acceptance of the Israelites through them (Lev 1:13, 17; 2:2, 9, 12; 3:5, 16; 4:31; 6:1, 7 [8, 14]; 8:21, 28; 17:6; 23:13, 18; Num 15:3, 7, 10, 13–14, 24; 18:17; 28:6, 8, 13, 24, 27; 29:2, 6, 8, 13, 36). It may be translated *as a pleasing aroma a gift to the LORD* or *an aroma a gift that pleases the LORD* (Kleinig, *Leviticus*, 57–58). The element of *rest* should not necessarily be excluded, and the phrase may be rendered *as a soothing/quieting/restful aroma a gift of/for the LORD*. The LORD's dwelling in the midst of Israel is pleasurable rest for both God and his people through the daily offerings.

379. See Kleinig, *Leviticus*, 42.

in a unique category of ritual acts. It is the only spoken ritual enactment. Yet, like every other part of the daily divine service, it does not just express an idea but it accomplishes something. The benediction does not merely inform the people about God's attitude toward them and his desire to bless them. It actually grants his blessing.[380] When the priest speaks the words of the benediction, the LORD accomplishes what the blessing says. On the one hand, the blessing rite is similar to the other rites because it functions within the divine service to accomplish God's purpose. On the other hand, it is unparalleled because it is the only part of the daily service in which the LORD has given specific words that must be spoken by the priests in the divine service.

The Divine Institution of the Blessing Rite

The LORD establishes the blessing rite by instituting its two chief ritual acts. In Num 6:24–27 he authorizes its words, "The LORD bless[381] you and guard you; the LORD shine his face upon you and be favorable to you; the LORD lift up his face toward you and give you peace."[382] These words of blessing

---

380. The blessing is not effective because the words have magical power but because the benediction is a performative utterance commanded by God. The words must be spoken in the proper situation by an authorized person in the correct form, and if any of these elements are missing then the speech act is invalid. All the words of the benediction must be announced only by the authorized priest as God's mediator at the tabernacle in order for God to bestow his blessing on his people (Mitchell, *Meaning of brk*, 63, 167–69, 171–76). Austin distinguishes between three types of speech acts: locutionary, illocutionary, and perlocutionary. The first is speaking a certain sentence with a certain sense or reference, which aims at the *meaning* of what is spoken. The second intends a certain *force*, such as informing, ordering, or warning. This kind of act attempts to bring about a specific outcome. The third achieves an outcome by speaking, such as convincing, persuading, deterring, or even surprising or misleading. These three types of speech do not necessarily need to be separated since a single spoken sentence may have a locutionary meaning which has an illocutionary force that achieves a perlocutionary effect. Austin also emphasizes that for a speech act to be valid, it must be spoken according to an accepted procedure, which includes the utterance of certain words by certain persons in certain circumstances (Austin, *Words*, 6, 14–15, 23–24, 26, 34–36, 52, 94–95, 98–103, 108, 115–19, 120). Speaking the benediction by the priest at the sanctuary does not merely convey the meaning of the words spoken. Rather, the benediction accomplishes what the LORD intends when the priests speak those words. See also Kleinig, *Leviticus*, 24.

381. Mitchell notes that יְבָרֶכְךָ is a *piel*. It is, therefore, a general term for God's bestowal of benefits upon the Israelites. The LORD's blessing conveys his *attitude* of goodwill rather than him giving protection and peace (Mitchell, *Meaning of brk*, 96).

382. יְבָרֶכְךָ יְהוָה וְיִשְׁמְרֶךָ
יָאֵר יְהוָה פָּנָיו אֵלֶיךָ וִיחֻנֶּךָּ

are spoken at the inaugural service (Lev 9:22–23).[383] Thus, his name must be placed upon the Israelites for their blessing through the priestly benediction at the daily service (Num 6:27).[384] The LORD also commands Moses to construct two silver trumpets that the priests are to sound over the offerings on the altar every time the divine service is conducted.[385] The LORD institutes the words of the benediction and sounding the silver trumpets so that the priests can deliver his blessings to his people in the daily divine service.[386]

The Ritual Function of the Blessing Rite

The LORD institutes the blessing rite to fulfill a practical purpose in the daily service. As unique as the blessing rite is within the service, still it and its ritual activities are parts of an organic ritual system. It is sometimes the case that unusual things play important roles within their own context and that is also the case with the ritual function of the blessing rite in the daily divine service.

Ritual Agents

The ritual agents participate in the blessing rite in distinct ways. The Pentateuch states that *Aaron and his sons* are to bless the Israelites (Num 6:23). There are two ways this could be understood. On the one hand, this could limit the agent who blesses to the high priest in each generation.[387] On the

---

יִשָּׂא יְהוָה פָּנָיו אֵלֶיךָ וְיָשֵׂם לְךָ שָׁלוֹם

383. See Kleinig, *Leviticus*, 217; Levine, *Leviticus*, 57; "Lpny YHWH," 215–16, 243–44; Milgrom, *Leviticus 1–16*, 586–87.

384. Since the LORD authorizes the priests to pronounce the blessing in his name, it is not they but the LORD who initiates the blessing (Milgrom, *Numbers*, 50–51). See also Ashley, *Numbers*, 149.

385. Some scholars maintain that the trumpets are not sounded at the daily service but only on special feast days (Ashley, *Numbers*, 188–89; Cole, *Numbers*, 162–63; Harrison, *Numbers*, 169; Levine, "Lpny YHWH," 306). Others hold that the silver trumpets are sounded each day in the divine service (Kleinig, *Lord's Song*, 79–82; Douglas, *In the Wilderness*, 121). For a discussion of the uses of the silver trumpets, see Milgrom, *Numbers*, 72–75; Kleinig, *Lord's Song*, 34–39, 78–82, 90.

386. Further evidence in Num 10:10; 28:2, which list the daily burnt offering together with the weekly, monthly, and yearly offerings, shows that the trumpets are sounded in the daily service by the use of the term מוֹעֵד, *appointed times*.

387. This is the practice described in Sir 50:19–23. It may be argued that since Aaron is the only priest who gives the benedictions at the inaugural service (Lev 9:22, 24) then the benediction is spoken only by the high priest in the daily service (see 1 Chr 23:13). See also Ashley, *Numbers*, 148–50; Harrison, *Numbers*, 132–34; Kleinig, *Leviticus*, 217.

other hand, all of the priests on duty might, together with the high priest, bless the congregation.[388] Most likely, however, the high priest or his deputy normally speaks the blessing at the tabernacle.[389] The agents who sound the trumpets are easily identified. They are *the sons of Aaron*, the regular priests (Num 10:8). Thus, the high priest does not sound them.[390] The LORD is also a ritual agent in the blessing rite because he authorizes the priests to perform its ritual functions on his behalf. The assembled worshipers are the main beneficiaries of the blessing rite, even though there is some evidence that the congregants make shouts of acclamation as they prostrate themselves (Lev 9:24).[391] Thus, the high priest and the regular priests are the chief agents who perform the blessing rite in the daily service.

Ritual Acts

There are two main ritual acts that are performed in the blessing rite. In the first place, the high priest speaks the words of the benediction to the congregation of Israel. As the personal representative of the LORD, the high priest faces the congregation and raises his hands toward them to announce the benediction.[392] The blessing is the only prescribed time in the service that the divine name, יהוה, is spoken. In the second place, the regular priests blow the two silver trumpets over the burnt offering. The priests sound the trumpets over the burnt offering to draw attention to it and to signal that the benediction is about to be proclaimed.[393] The announcement of the blessing

388. *Tamid* 7:2 indicates that all the priests either stand together with the high priest as he announces the benediction or they pronounce it together with the high priest (Blackman, *Kodashim*, 494–95). See also Deut 10:8; 21:5; Milgrom, *Numbers*, 50, 52; Levine, "*Lpny* YHWH," 227–28.

389. This view is further strengthened by the understanding that in the early days of the tabernacle there were only three priests, Aaron and his two remaining sons. Since the two priests would be responsible for sounding the two trumpets, Aaron the high priest speaks the benediction.

390. Just as the regular priests play an assisting role with the burnt offerings (Lev 1:5, 8, 11) they also enact the secondary ritual act of sounding the trumpets at the blessing rite. The high priest does not sound the trumpets because his primary act in the blessing rite is to announce the benediction.

391. See *Tamid* 7:3 (Blackman, *Kodashim*, 496); Sir 50:16–21.

392. Since this is the posture of the high priest at the inaugural service (Lev 9:22) it is probably the usual way that the benediction is given to the congregation (Kleinig, *Leviticus*, 212). Both the shiny plate on the forehead of the high priest and his face turned toward the people may relate to the phrase in the blessing, *the LORD shine his face upon you* (Num 6:25).

393. The entire pericope dealing with the silver trumpets (Num 10:1–10) is surrounded on both sides by descriptions about the glory cloud (Num 9:15–23; 10:11–36).

and sounding the trumpets are the two most audible ritual acts that the priests conduct in the daily divine service.

Ritual Materials

The ritual materials in the blessing rite consist of the trumpets and the high priest's vestments. The two trumpets are constructed of hammered silver (Num 10:2).[394] They are the only musical instruments that the LORD ordains for use in the divine service.[395] Although the Pentateuch gives no further details about the trumpets, other sources suggest that these are probably less than a cubit long, straight, and slender with a flared opening.[396] Trumpets were used in the ancient world to herald the presence of a king or his representative and to signal a royal announcement. The holy attire on the high priest, especially the golden crown, shows the Israelites that the ambassador of their heavenly king is declaring the blessing of the LORD on his behalf.[397] The two silver trumpets and the vestments of the high priest in the blessing rite lead the Israelites to conclude that their royal LORD is present to bestow his benefits upon them in the daily service.

Ritual Times

The blessing rite is performed every morning and evening in the daily divine service. The LORD blesses the Israelites at the beginning of the day so that his blessing will be with them as they set about their daily tasks, and he blesses them at the ending of each day so that his blessing will rest upon them throughout the night.[398]

In the section on the burning rite, it was determined that the smoke from the altar correlates with the cloud and the presence of the LORD. Similarly, the trumpets relate thematically to the LORD's presence (Kleinig *Lord's Song*, 34). Although the priests sound the trumpets in the blessing rite, this ritual act is not disconnected from the burning rite. All of the rites and their ritual activities are organically connected within the daily ritual system.

394. שְׁתֵּי חֲצוֹצְרֹת כֶּסֶף מִקְשָׁה

395. See Kleinig, *Lord's Song*, 79.

396. See Milgrom, *Numbers*, 72–73. For more information about the construction and function of the trumpets and other instruments described in the biblical witness see Friedrich, "salpigx, salpizw, salpisthj," 71–88; Sendrey and Norton, *David's Harp*, 113–31; Sendrey, *Music in Ancient Israel*, 331–43; Stainer, *Music of the Bible*, 153–65.

397. For further details about the ornate vestments of the high priest, see the sections on the ritual materials in the incense rite and the burning rite.

398. See the other sections on ritual time in this chapter.

Ritual Locations

Where do the priests sound the trumpets and the high priest announce the benediction? The priests sound the trumpets at the altar for burnt offering because they are required to sound them *over* it (Num 10:10). The priests blow the trumpets over the burnt offering facing the altar. This ritual act is probably performed in one of three places: on one or both sides of the altar to the north and/or south, on the east side facing the tabernacle, or on the west side of the altar facing the congregation. The last view is most likely the correct one because the trumpets sound as a memorial *for the Israelites* before the LORD (Num 10:10). The priests probably blow the trumpets in such a way as to sound them over the burnt offering and toward the people, which can only be from the west side between the altar and the tent of meeting.[399] The most logical place where the high priest announces the benediction is on the east side of the altar facing the congregation.[400] This indicates that the high priest is standing in a mediating position to enact a mediating function. Thus, the priests sound the trumpets from behind the altar and the high priest blesses the congregation from the front of the altar in the courtyard.

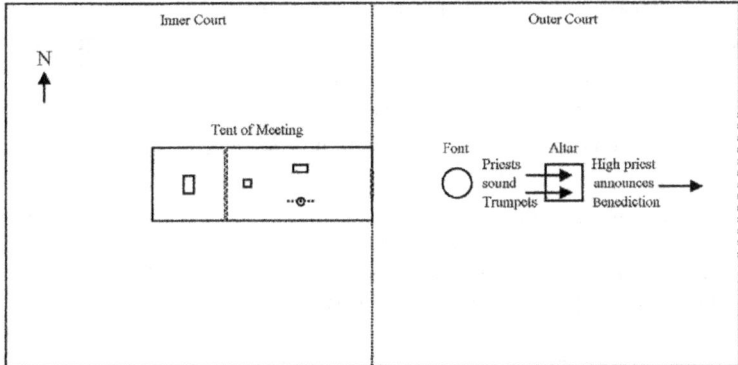

Figure 10. The ritual locations of the blessing rite.

    399. Kleinig makes the case that at the temple in Jerusalem the priests sounded the trumpets from the east side of the altar facing the congregation and Levitical musicians (Kleinig, *Lord's Song*, 80–81). This is a logical conclusion if the command to sound the trumpets *over* the burnt offering is not taken literally (Num 10:10). It should be taken into consideration that there may be different practices at different periods of Israel's history.

    400. If he stood behind the altar, then both the altar and the smoke would conceal him and his ornate vestments. In front of the altar the people see him unhindered in his full regalia. At the inaugural service the priest announces the first and abnormal benediction from upon the altar. The normal location for the daily service, however, is in front of the altar (Kleinig, *Leviticus*, 218–19).

Summary of the Ritual Function

The blessing rite announces the blessing and favor of God among his people. It declares that the LORD blesses his people through the ministry of the priests in the divine service. Like the trumpets that herald the arrival of an earthly king, so the sound of the trumpets proclaims that the royal LORD of Israel is coming to meet them. Through the person of his emissary, the high priest, the LORD comes to bless his people by granting them everything that the benediction announces to them. This meeting does not happen merely on random occasions; the LORD comes to bless his people every morning and evening in the blessing rite at his dwelling place among them.

The Theological Purpose of the Blessing Rite

The LORD accomplishes two central purposes through the blessing rite each morning and evening in the divine service.

First, he blesses the Israelites by placing his name upon them (Num 6:27).[401] Just as the LORD places his name at his sanctuary (Deut 12:3, 5, 11, 21; 14:23, 24; 26:2), so also his people must come to that place in the service for the LORD to place his name on them and bless them through the benediction (Exod 20:24).[402] The Aaronic benediction invokes the name of the LORD, יהוה, three times.[403] The threefold pronouncement of the name of YHWH signals its superlative use,[404] which only occurs in the divine service

---

401. Milgrom thinks that the name of the LORD is *figuratively* put upon or called down upon the Israelites through the medium of the benediction. The result is that the LORD declares his ownership of Israel (Milgrom, *Numbers*, 52). While the Israelites are the LORD's own people, the benediction holds a deeper purpose than simply claiming ownership of them.

402. Deut 12:2–5 distinguishes the LORD's chosen place, הַמָּקוֹם אֲשֶׁר־יִבְחַר יְהוָה, where he puts his name to dwell, לָשׂוּם אֶת־שְׁמוֹ שָׁם לְשִׁכְנוֹ, from the place where pagan idols and their names are put. Since the LORD's name dwells at his chosen place, he puts his name on the Israelites through the Aaronic benediction at that place to bestow his favor and blessing on them. See Tigay, *Deuteronomy*, 118–20; Craigie, *Deuteronomy*, 216–18.

403. Levine holds that the use of the *name* is relevant but not central to the priestly blessing. The purpose of pronouncing the divine name is for the priests to "open the door" for the LORD to bless his people. God must be invoked by his personal name for him to come with his blessings (Levine, "*Lpny* YHWH," 228). Num 6:27, however, coincides the LORD's grace with the placement of his name on Israel through the benediction. The name is not merely "relevant"; it is necessary for Israel's blessing. See Mitchell, *Meaning of brk*, 97.

404. Scholars note that the threefold structure of the benediction in Hebrew is a rising crescendo of 3, 5, and 7 words with increasing numbers of syllables and consonants.

at the sanctuary. With each declaration of the divine name, the LORD imparts two benefits. The LORD blesses and guards the Israelites (Num 6:24).[405] The LORD shines his face upon them and shows his gracious favor to them (Num 6:25).[406] The LORD lifts his face toward his people and gives them peace (Num 6:26).[407] These are not mere wishes for their future prosperity,[408] but rather the LORD bestows the very things that the words say when the high priest speaks them in the divine service.[409] Most importantly, the

---

The first phrase of each verse may invoke the movement of the LORD toward his people, while the second calls for his activity on their behalf. What are identified as six actions, bless *and* guard, shine *and* be gracious, bestow *and* give peace, may express three consequential actions. The LORD's blessing may result in his guarding; his shining face may result in his grace; his bestowal of favor may result in his peace. The first and last phrases of the benediction summarize its substance, "The LORD bless you ... and give you peace." See Levine, "*Lpny* YHWH," 236–44; Milgrom, *Numbers*, 51; Mitchell, *Meaning of brk*, 96–97, 182–83.

405. יְבָרֶכְךָ יְהוָה וְיִשְׁמְרֶךָ To bless is to grant substantial gifts and material blessings (see Gen 24:1; 17:16; 27:10; Exod 23:25; Deut 7:13; 14:24; 16:15; Job 1:10; 42:12). To guard or watch over has to do with the LORD's safety and security such as on journeys or missions (Exod 23:20; Josh 24:17) as well as protection from defeat (1 Sam 30:23) by enemies (Levine, "*Lpny* YHWH," 227).

406. יָאֵר יְהוָה פָּנָיו אֵלֶיךָ וִיחֻנֶּךָּ By his shining face, the LORD shows his favor and generosity toward his people. When someone's face "lights up" he shows that he is well disposed rather than portraying an angry countenance toward others. The face of God effects either wrath or blessing. His shining face brings blessings, but when he is angry the light of his face departs and danger follows. The LORD's gracious favor, like his blessing, consists of him granting material well being to his people (Levine, "*Lpny* YHWH," 227–28). The shining as well as the lifting up of the face of the deity are themes found in other ancient religions (Levine, "*Lpny* YHWH," 236–37). Israel's experience with the shining, יָאֵר, face of God is unique, however, since they see the light from the glory cloud and, more significantly, the shining/radiant skin on the face of Moses, קָרַן עוֹר פָּנָיו, (Exod 34:29–35). Moses is the only human in the Old Testament who shines with the divine light and manifests God's presence in that unique manner (Aalen, "אוֹר," 164–65). The *face* of God is equivalent to his presence in which he reveals his "face" in various and concealed ways. For a thorough analysis of what is meant by God's face, פָּנִים, and the ways that he reveals himself see Simian-Yofre, "פָּנִים," 589–615.

407. יִשָּׂא יְהוָה פָּנָיו אֵלֶיךָ וְיָשֵׂם לְךָ שָׁלוֹם The lifting up of the LORD's face toward his people indicates that he is favorable to them. In the benediction, the LORD pays attention to his people, encounters them, and kindly looks them in the face. Granting peace to Israel has to do with providing for their physical well being, not merely for their inner tranquility and state of mind (Levine, "*Lpny* YHWH," 228).

408. See Harrison, *Numbers*, 132; Levine, "*Lpny* YHWH," 244.

409. There is a distinction between blessings in different contexts. There are many examples of blessings throughout the Pentateuch (see Levine, "*Lpny* YHWH," 237–38; Mitchell, *Meaning of brk*, 29–161). Each of these comprises specific significance and effect depending on who is blessing whom, how, when, and where. In the divine service, the LORD blesses the Israelites by a performative utterance of the Aaronic benediction (Kleinig, *Leviticus*, 24).

LORD places his name on them to sanctify them and keep them holy. The name of the LORD is so holy that it is protected by the second commandment (Exod 20:7) and he warns against desecrating the "name of his holiness" (Lev 20:3; 22:2, 32). For this reason, the divine name is his sanctuary name, the only name by which he is called at the sanctuary alone.[410] Even though it is not referred to as "most holy," nonetheless it has the power to sanctify the people when it is placed on them through the announcement of the Aaronic benediction.[411] The LORD places his name on his people to bless and sanctify them.[412]

Second, the blessing rite is theophanic and reveals the gracious presence of the LORD with his people at the tabernacle. In the inaugural service, the theophany of the LORD in the divine fire occurs coincidentally with the benediction (Lev 9:23–24).[413] This event interprets the theological purpose of the benediction in each subsequent service. The LORD reveals his gracious presence in the daily divine service both visibly and audibly. At the same time that the visible revelation of God's presence is beheld in the smoke from the altar, the congregation hears the words of the benediction revealing the favorable presence of the LORD among them. The benediction announces that the LORD is present with his people for blessing rather than disapproval. Since the divine fire no longer appears to the Israelites at the tabernacle in the daily service but is evidenced in a hidden way by the smoke, the LORD most clearly "appears" by revealing his face and manifesting his gracious presence to them through the Aaronic benediction.[414] Furthermore, sounding the silver trumpets over the burnt offering announces the presence of the LORD at the altar. Just as trumpets signal the arrival of an earthly king, so the trumpets at the tabernacle proclaim to Israel the advent of their royal LORD. The LORD also reveals his presence visibly at the blessing rite through his personal representative, the high priest in his ornate vestments. The assembled congregation beholds the high priest standing before them in his glorious attire with the divine name inscribed on his

---

410. Later in Israel's history the divine name was only spoken at the sanctuary while its supplement "Lord" was spoken in synagogues and elsewhere among God's people (*Tamid* 7:2).

411. See Kleinig, *Leviticus*, 11–12, 451.

412. Placing (שִׂים) the name of the LORD upon the Israelites echoes God placing his holy name in the sanctuary (Deut 12:5, 21; 1 Kgs 9:3; 11:36; 14:21; 2 Kgs 21:4, 7; 2 Chr 6:20; 12:13; 33:7). Their bodies may thereby become shrines of the LORD.

413. At the inaugural service, the theophany that follows the benediction shows God's approval and blessing to his people (Mitchell, *Meaning of brk*, 97).

414. The LORD reveals his *face*, as is indicated by the Hebrew word פָּנָיו, face/front, which is used twice in the Aaronic benediction (Num 6:25, 26). See Kleinig, *Leviticus*, 218–20.

holy crown.⁴¹⁵ Since the high priest represents the LORD, the inscribed name reveals the LORD's presence. The combination of the visible elements, the sound of the trumpets, and the name of the LORD in the benediction become a powerful theophany for the people of Israel.⁴¹⁶

Through the blessing rite, the LORD places his name on the Israelites to bestow his gifts and blessings on them, and he manifests his favorable presence among them through the things they hear and see at the tabernacle in this rite.

Conclusion

The blessing rite in the daily divine service is unique because the other rites do not require any spoken words. The LORD institutes the blessing rite to announce his favor and blessing through the Aaronic benediction. Whereas in the Ten Commandments the LORD forbids the misuse of his name (Exod 20:7; Deut 5:11), he authorizes the correct use of his name in the daily divine service by instituting the blessing rite. The promise that the LORD comes with blessing wherever he causes his name to be remembered (Exod 20:24) is fulfilled by the benediction in the blessing rite at the tabernacle. The high priest places the divine name three times upon the Israelites so that God will reveal his protecting, gracious, peaceful presence to them. By sounding the trumpets and declaring the benediction an audible manifestation of the

---

415. The personal representation of the LORD extends in a significant way beyond the high priest as he speaks the benediction. The references to the illuminating and lifted up face of the LORD brings to mind the visibly shining face of Moses. Aaron, the first high priest, is as a prophet who speaks on behalf of Moses and he is as God to Aaron, (וְדִבֶּר־הוּא לְךָ אֶל־הָעָם וְהָיָה הוּא יִהְיֶה־לְּךָ לְפֶה וְאַתָּה תִּהְיֶה־לּוֹ לֵאלֹהִים) (Exod 4:16). See also Exod 7:1. When the high priest announces that the LORD shines and lifts up his face in blessing, the people recall that Moses spoke the word of the LORD with a radiant face and called them who had run away in fear back to himself. It is significant that Moses with his shining face ordains, washes, and clothes Aaron in his ornate vestments. Since the benediction is the only time in the divine service that the congregation sees the high priest facing them in his full regalia, at that moment he represents and reveals to them that their royal LORD is a personal being who favorably shines and lifts up his countenance upon them and speaks gracious words to them. See Cassuto, *Exodus*, 448–510; Haran, "Shining of Moses' Face," 159–730; Propp, *Exodus 19–40*, 618–23; Sarna, *Exodus*, 220–21.

416. Since the priest stands in front of the altar, between it and the assembled congregation, the people see him as if he is superimposed over the smoke rising from the altar. They see the smoke, the priest, the ornate vestments, and the shiny plate with the divine name all at the same time. When he announces the benediction, the words they hear come from the midst of the smoke by him who is clothed in royal garments and crowned with the name of the LORD.

presence of the LORD occurs through the blessing rite in the daily divine service.

THE MEAL RITE

The meal rite concludes the daily divine service. Once all of the preceding ritual activities are completed, the priests eat the most holy food as a sacred meal in the presence of the LORD at the tabernacle. After they perform their assigned tasks on behalf of the LORD, he then feeds them. Even though the meal is their share for conducting the LORD's ministry, it is more significant than mere bodily nourishment. The LORD establishes the meal rite as the final rite of the service, so that he may provide for his priests what they need for their continued ministry in his presence at his dwelling place.

The Divine Institution of the Meal Rite

In Lev 6:7–11 [14–18] the LORD institutes the meal rite for the morning and evening offerings of the daily divine service. He authorizes the priests to eat the remaining portion of the daily cereal offering from which the token portion is put on the altar fire in the burning rite (Lev 6:7–11 [14–18]).[417] Although the food from most of the other kinds of offerings is eaten at the meal rite in the morning, only the daily cereal offering is eaten at the meal rite in both the morning and the evening in the daily service.[418] The ritual meal occurs at the inaugural service (Lev 10:12–13), confirming that the LORD institutes the meal rite as part of the daily service.[419] While the fire "eats up" the offerings on the altar at the inaugural service (Lev 9:24), the priests eat the cereal offering at the tabernacle (Lev 10:12–13). So it is at the daily service. As the offerings are burned on the altar each morning and evening the priests eat the cereal offering.[420]

---

417. See Kleinig, *Leviticus*, 149–52.

418. In addition to the public cereal offering, the morning meal rite includes food for the priests from the other kinds of grain offerings (Lev 2:10), from the guilt offerings (Lev 5:13; 6:10 [17]; 7:6), and from the sin offerings (Lev 6:19–23 [26–30]; 10:18). The bread of the presence is also eaten in the morning meal rite on the Sabbath (Lev 24:9).

419. There is a correlation between the divine fire and the sacred status of the offerings at the inaugural service and each successive service. All the offerings derive their holiness from the holy fire on the altar, and none of them are holy apart from the divine fire on the altar (Kleinig, *Leviticus*, 231).

420. Milgrom holds that the cereal offering in Lev 6:7–11 [14–18] is not the accompanying offering that is part of the daily burnt offering, but rather one of the independent and private cereal offerings mentioned in Lev 2 (*Leviticus 1–16*, 389–91).

The Ritual Function of the Daily Divine Service   169

The divine institution of the daily meal rite is found in two additional details of its legislation. The LORD gives to the priests the remaining part of the cereal offering as their *portion* (Lev 6:10 [17]).[421] Since they are not assigned a piece of ground once they enter into the land of Israel, the priests depend on the offerings of the Israelites for their livelihood. The LORD provides the priests their portion of the daily cereal offering, just as he provides the Israelites their portion of the land for their livelihood. The share of the daily cereal offering for the priests is their *perpetual due* (Lev 6:11 [18]).[422] Like a generous king with his courtiers, the LORD gives food from his altar to the priests as their daily stipend for their ministry in his presence.[423] The LORD establishes the meal rite to provide for the priests their portion of the food from the fire offerings[424] as their perpetual due from him.

---

421. The noun חֵלֶק, portion/share, is etymologically related to the verb חָלַק, which means to divide/apportion/share (BDB 323–24). It usually refers to the allotment of land assigned by the LORD to the Israelites. Since the priests, like their Levitical relatives, receive no portion of the land, their allotment is the food that the LORD gives them from the offerings (Kleinig, *Leviticus*, 143–44). For other references to the words חֵלֶק and חָלַק, see Num 18:20; 26:53, 55–56; 31:36; Deut 4:19; 10:9; 12:12; 14:27, 29; 18:1, 8; 29:26; 32:9.

422. The Hebrew חָק־עוֹלָם, perpetual due, is distinguished from חֻקַּת עוֹלָם, perpetual statute, in the Pentateuch. While the two phrases are related linguistically from the same verbal root, חָק־עוֹלָם normally designates the divinely instituted part of the offerings that the priests receive as their perquisite of food for their service at the sanctuary. The only time that חָק־עוֹלָם refers to an offering from which the priests do not receive a portion is the bread offering of the high priest. It is חָק־עוֹלָם לַיהוָה, the perpetual due to/for/belonging to the LORD (Lev 6:15 [22]). The חָק־עוֹלָם that is not לַיהוָה? belongs to the priests or to the priests and their families (Exod 29:28; Lev 6:11 [18]; 7:34; 10:13–15; 24:9; Num 18:8, 11, 19). See Levine, *Leviticus*, 37; Milgrom, *Leviticus 1–16*, 214–15, 395, 400, 433, 435–36, 618–19; Kleinig, *Leviticus*, 144, 155.

423. See Kleinig, *Leviticus*, 80.

424. The Hebrew word אִשֶּׁה (Lev 6:10–11 [17–18]) may be translated as *gift* (Kleinig, *Leviticus*, 52, 57), *food gift* (Milgrom, *Leviticus 1–16*, 161–62), or *offering made by fire* (Levine, *Leviticus*, 201; "*Lpny YHWH*," 389; *Numbers*, 371). אִשֶּׁה is probably best translated as *fire offering*, due to the apparent etymological connection with אֵשׁ, fire. It usually refers to the remaining part of an offering that is eaten by the priests after its token portion has been burned on the altar. This might not apply, however, to its use in Lev 24:7, 9; Num 15:10. Other references to אִשֶּׁה in the Pentateuch are Exod 29:18, 25, 41; 30:20; Lev 1:9, 13, 17; 2:2–3, 9–11, 16; 3:3, 5, 9, 11, 14, 16; 4:35; 5:12; 7:5, 25, 30, 35; 8:21, 28; 10:12–13, 15; 21:6, 21; 22:22, 27; 23:13, 18, 25, 27, 36–37; Num 15:3, 13–14, 25; 18:17; 28:2–3, 6, 8, 13, 19, 24; 29:6, 13, 36; Deut 18:1. See also Eberhart, "Neglected Feature of Sacrifice," 489; Hamp, "אֵשׁ," 423–28.

The Ritual Function of the Meal Rite

The meal rite involves the consumption of the most holy food from the public cereal offering (Lev 6:7–11 [14–18]). Whereas the cereal offering was presented before the LORD in the presentation rite and its token portion burned on the altar in the burning rite, its remaining part is cooked and consumed in the meal rite. The most holy food must be prepared in a certain way, eaten by specific people, at its proper time, and in a designated location for the meal rite to function as the LORD intends it within the daily divine service.

Ritual Agents

The ritual agents at the meal rite are the host and the guests.[425] The host is the LORD. He gives the most holy cereal offering to the priests as their regular portion from his table, the altar for burnt offering (Lev 6:10–11 [17–18]).[426] Just as the priests serve the LORD's people in the other rites at the daily service, so the LORD serves the priests as their host with his most holy food in the meal rite.[427] The LORD's guests are the high priest and any priest on duty who has been involved in the service. Even a male descendant of Aaron who is not qualified to officiate in the tent or at the altar because he has a physical deformity may still eat the most holy food (Lev 21:16–23),[428] but any priest who is ritually unclean may neither minister at the sanctuary nor eat the most holy food (Lev 21:1–22:16).[429] Every priest who serves in any capacity is the LORD's guest at the divine service that day, and he is entitled to receive the holy provisions from the table of his gracious host.

---

425. See Kleinig, *Leviticus*, 149–52.

426. Through the daily cereal offering God provides for the priests and feeds them as his guests from his table. The presentation of the cereal offering culminates in the holy meal that the priests eat in the presence of God (Kleinig, *Leviticus*, 151).

427. See Kleinig, *Leviticus*, 149–50.

428. The descendants of Aaron who are physically unsound may not offer offerings in the tent or on the altar before the LORD at the sanctuary but they are not deprived of eating the most holy food, since they are not to blame for their bodily defects. The legislation in Lev 21:16–23 implies that priests with physical defects are permitted to perform any tasks other than entering into the holy place or contact with the outer altar, such as preparing the public offerings, disposing of leftovers, and assisting the laity with their offerings. See also Lev 7:6; Levine, *Leviticus*, 145; Milgrom, *Leviticus 1–16*, 407; Kleinig, *Leviticus*, 165, 166.

429. See Kleinig, *Leviticus*, 444–60; Levine, *Leviticus*, 140–47.

Ritual Acts

Two ritual acts occur in the meal rite. Most importantly, the portion of the cereal offering for the priests is eaten. It must be made into unleavened loaves and baked in an oven (Lev 6:9–10 [16–17]) before it is eaten. Although the Pentateuch does not specify whether the entire cereal offering must be eaten at once or if it can be left over for consumption at a later time (see Exod 12:10; Lev 7:15–18), most likely all of it is eaten at each service because it must be consumed near the altar (Lev 10:12).[430] After the meal, the priests take off their sacred vestments. This "ritual act" is more of a consequence of the culmination of the service than part of it. The priests most likely wear the sacred vestments while they are eating the most holy food.[431] Since they are in a holy place eating holy food from the holy altar served by their holy LORD, it is fitting that they would wear the holy vestments for this special ritual occasion. After the holy banquet is completed, they divest the sacred garments and put on common clothes before leaving the sanctuary.[432]

Ritual Materials

The ritual material of the meal rite is the bread made from the cereal offering of fine flour and olive oil.[433] The cereal offering is baked without leaven (Lev 6:10 [17]);[434] and it is made into unleavened bread (Lev 6:9 [16]).[435] Three different vessels may be used for preparing any grain offering: in a pan,[436] on

---

430. Unlike the *holy* food from the peace offering or the Passover, the *most holy* food from the cereal, sin, and guilt offerings cannot be taken outside of the holy grounds of the tabernacle. This is true regardless of whether or not all of the food is consumed in the meal rite. The volume of food on the Sabbath, such as from the bread of the presence, or on other days when there is additional food from sin and guilt offerings may prevent the priests from eating all of it at once. See also Milgrom, *Leviticus 23–27*, 2098–99.

431. The Pentateuch does not state whether the priests leave their sacred vestments on while they eat the most holy food or if they divest before eating. The ordination of the priests in Lev 8 indicates that the priests are vested while they eat the food from the offerings in the courtyard of the tabernacle. See the section on the meal rite in chapter 2, which spells out the reasons for wearing the vestments in the meal.

432. Concerning the sacred vestments, see Ezek 42:14; Milgrom, *Leviticus 1–16*, 446–53.

433. See the section on the ritual materials in the presentation rite.

434. לֹא תֵאָפֶה חָמֵץ

435. מַצּוֹת

436. מַרְחֶשֶׁת

a griddle,[437] or in an oven/fire pot[438] (Lev 2:4–7). Since grain offerings that are baked in an oven are distinguished from those that are made in a pan or on a griddle (Lev 7:9),[439] it may be concluded that because the daily cereal offering is "baked" it must be prepared in an oven. Grain offerings baked in an oven are of two kinds, unleavened bread or unleavened thin bread depending on whether the flour is mixed with oil before it is made into dough or whether the flat slabs of dough are daubed with oil after they have been prepared (Lev 2:4).[440] Since the legislation for the daily cereal offering does not specify into which of these two kinds of bread it must be baked (Lev 6:9–10 [16–17]), most likely it may be either one of them.

Ritual Times

The meal rite occurs at the end of the divine service every morning and evening. Although the Pentateuch does not state when the most holy bread must be eaten, there is evidence that it is eaten as a holy meal at the end of the morning and evening services. Based on the ordination service, the bread is probably eaten on the day it is offered and, if any is left over, then it must be burned (Exod 29:34; Lev 8:31–32). The legislation for the daily cereal offering is part of the broader prescription for the daily burnt offering (Lev 6:1–11 [8–18]). Since the daily burnt offering and its accompanying cereal offering are smoked up every morning and evening (Exod 29:38–42), and because the priests must eat the remaining portion of the cereal offering as their daily stipend (Lev 6:9–11 [16–18]), it may be concluded that the ritual time for the meal rite is toward the end of the divine service each morning and each evening.[441]

---

437. מַחֲבַת

438. תַּנּוּר

439. וְכָל־מִנְחָה אֲשֶׁר תֵּאָפֶה בַּתַּנּוּר וְכָל־נַעֲשָׂה בַמַּרְחֶשֶׁת וְעַל־מַחֲבַת

440. מַצּוֹת ... וּרְקִיקֵי מַצּוֹת חַלּוֹת. For more details about the two kinds of bread, see BDB 319, 956.

441. In the holy meal, the priests mainly eat the most holy bread from the daily cereal offering. There is uncertainty about when the priests eat the most holy food from the other kinds of offerings. Most likely the daily burnt offering is the first offering placed on the altar at the beginning of the day and the last offering at the end of the day. If so, then the other offerings are burned on the altar at some time between the two daily offerings and their most holy food eaten as a midday meal. Kleinig holds that the daily cereal offering may be eaten in the middle of the day (Kleinig, *Leviticus*, 150).

Ritual Locations

The food is eaten in a sacred meal at its designated location. The bread from the daily cereal offering is eaten in a holy place in the courtyard of the tent of meeting beside the altar (Lev 6:9 [16]; 10:12–13).[442] Both the entrance to the tent of meeting (Exod 29:31–32; Lev 8:31) and the entire courtyard (Lev 6:9, 19 [16, 26]) are holy areas.[443] The area near the altar is also designated as a holy place (Lev 10:12–13).[444] Since the bread from the daily cereal offering must be eaten in a holy place, it probably may be eaten anywhere in the courtyard of the tabernacle.[445] Does the phrase "beside the altar" (Lev 10:12) indicate a more specific location, however? The same terms describe where the offal of bird offerings and the ashes are placed on the east side of the altar (Lev 1:16; 5:22 [6:3]). Although it is not forbidden, this seems to be an unlikely practical location to eat the most holy food.[446] The phrase "beside the altar" implies close proximity to it and is most likely somewhere in the eastern half of the courtyard because the altar rests in its centre.[447] Since the north side of the altar is where the burnt offerings are slain and slaughtered (Lev 1:10–13), it is unlikely that the priests eat the meal there. They probably eat the most holy food somewhere near the south-west side of the altar, but certainly within the courtyard of the tabernacle (Lev 6:9 [16]; 10:12).[448]

---

442. The food from the occasional and the individual offerings is eaten in this same location (Lev 6:19 [26]; 7:6; 10:17–18; 24:9).

443. See Milgrom, *Leviticus 1–16*, 392–93.

444. בְּמָקוֹם קָדֹשׁ . . . אֵצֶל הַמִּזְבֵּחַ

445. See Milgrom, *Leviticus 1–16*, 392, 393, 618; Kleinig, *Leviticus*, 143.

446. See Milgrom, *Leviticus 1–16*, 618; Gerstenberger, *Leviticus*, 127.

447. Levine holds that the priests eat the cereal offering in the eastern courtyard in front of the altar (Levine, *Leviticus*, 37, 61–62). See Lev 8:31. Kleinig claims that the priests probably eat their meals in the western half of the courtyard, the location indicated in Ezek 42:1–14; 46:19–20 (Kleinig, *Leviticus*, 143). Milgrom makes the case that, although the most holy food may be eaten anywhere in the courtyard, the priests probably eat it in the inner court on its western side. He claims that there may be a bipartite division of the courtyard, however, which marks off its inner/western court as the area from the *altar* to the west wall of the courtyard. If this is true, then it is not the opening to the tent but the outer altar that defines the boundary between the inner and outer courtyard. There is reason to think that in practice the priests eat the most holy food between the porch and the altar (see Joel 2:17), which has a higher degree of sanctity than the forecourt to the east of the altar (Milgrom, *Leviticus 1–16*, 392–94, 451–56). Milgrom's theory of a bipartite courtyard that is divided at the altar explains how the priests could eat the most holy food both in the inner court and beside the altar. See figure eleven.

448. See Kleinig, *Leviticus*, 150, 233.

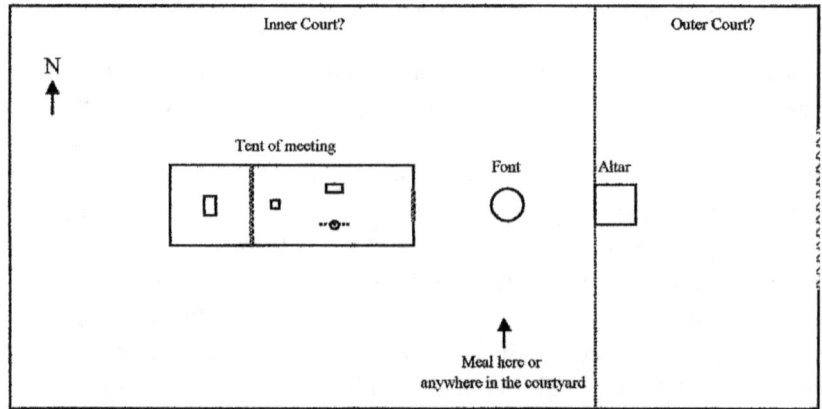

Figure 11. The location of the meal rite.

Summary of the Ritual Function

The final rite at the daily service involves the LORD serving his priests. He gives them their perpetual due from his table, the altar for burnt offering, so that they receive its nourishment. Strengthened by their share of food from the LORD, they perform the divine service each morning and evening. The strength that they receive from the LORD's food is not only physical. It is divine strength. The LORD hosts the priests as his guests at his table to empower them for their continued ministry in his presence.

The Theological Purpose of the Meal Rite

The LORD sanctifies his priests through the meal rite in the daily divine service. Since the cereal offering and the food from the sin and guilt offerings are most holy, they sanctify (Lev 6:10–11 [17–18]; see Exod 30:29).[449]

---

449. Levine claims that the most holy things do not sanctify the things or people that contact them. While he acknowledges that impurity is physically contagious and transmitted by direct contact, he maintains that holiness is not communicable at all. Rather, anyone or anything that comes into contact with the most holy things must already be in a ritual state of holiness, such as the priests who are consecrated to touch the most holy things (Levine, *Leviticus*, 37–38). See also Hartley, *Leviticus*, 97. Milgrom holds that Levine's view must be categorically rejected. He maintains that the most holy things impart holiness to other things, but not to people (Milgrom, *Leviticus 1–16*, 443–56). See also Kiuchi, *Leviticus*, 124–25. Haran is correct in his explanation that both qualified things and qualified people are sanctified by touching most holy things

Although the priests, like the Israelites, are sanctified by the most holy smoke from the incense, the burnt offering, and the benediction,[450] they receive a fuller participation in the holiness of the LORD to strengthen them for their ministry before him.[451] This additional reception of sanctification empowers them to continue to serve in the presence of their super holy God.[452] The LORD's promise to consecrate his priests (Exod 29:44) extends beyond the seven days of their ordination (Exod 29; Lev 8). In the daily divine service he consecrates and keeps his priests holy as they eat the most holy food of the LORD from his most holy table in the meal rite.

The theological purpose of the meal rite of Israel is unique in the ancient world. Unlike the pagan gods, the LORD does not eat food nor is he nourished by it. The "food of God,"[453] rather, is his provision of the most holy food for his priests so that *they* are its beneficiaries, not him.[454] Among the pagans, the food offerings are placed on an altar so that the deity may eat it in a spiritual fashion, after which the priests eat it for their nourishment and consume it representatively for the deity.[455] Whereas in pagan cultures the priests serve

---

(Haran, "Priestly Image of Tabernacle," 216–26). See also Wenham, *Leviticus*, 121. Kleinig holds that the key to understanding contagious holiness is found in the formula, כֹּל אֲשֶׁר־יִגַּע בָּהֶם יִקְדָּשׁ, "everyone/everything that touches them will be consecrated" (Lev 6:11 [18]) because the *qal* form of קָדַשׁ always means "become holy" (see Milgrom, *Leviticus 1–16*, 443–46). This formula, which is found elsewhere only in Exod 29:37; 30:29; Lev 6:20 [27], is connected with the most holy things that communicate the LORD's holiness by physically contacting them. Since the bread from the daily cereal offering is most holy, the LORD conveys his holiness to the priests and sanctifies them as they eat it (Kleinig, *Leviticus*, 144–45, 151–52).

450. See the sections on the theological purpose of the incense rite, the burning rite, and the blessing rite in this chapter.

451. See Kleinig, *Leviticus*, 79–80, 151–52.

452. There are three grades of holiness: super holy, most holy, and holy. That which is super holy is protected not only by taboos of touch but of sight (Milgrom, *Leviticus 1–16*, 454). God alone is super holy, as is seen in his threefold designation, קָדוֹשׁ קָדוֹשׁ קָדוֹשׁ, Holy Holy Holy (Isa 6:3; cf. Rev 4:8). The super holy God makes things most holy, קֹדֶשׁ קָדָשִׁים (Lev 6:10 [17]), so that he can impart his holiness safely to other things as well as to ritually clean people. Anything qualified to touch the most holy things is consecrated, יִקְדָּשׁ, by them (Lev 6:11 [18]); it becomes a holy thing, קֹדֶשׁ (Lev 21:22).

453. In the Pentateuch, the אֱלֹהִים לֶחֶם, bread of God (Lev 21:6, 8, 17, 21–22; 22:25; Num 28:2, 24), includes everything that is both offered as an אִשֶּׁה, a gift of food to the LORD (Lev 3:11, 16; 21:6, 21; Num 28:2, 24), and the food that the priests receive as their portion from the LORD's offerings on his altar (Kleinig, *Leviticus*, 446). See also the references to the bread of the priests in Lev 3:11; 22:7, 11, 13.

454. See Kleinig, *Leviticus*, 79.

455. See Gerstenberger, *Leviticus*, 87; Milgrom, *Leviticus 23–27*, 2092.

their deities to provide for their "needs," among the Israelites the LORD provides food and serves his priests to nourish and to sanctify them.[456]

Conclusion

The LORD institutes the meal rite to nourish his priests and to sanctify them for their continual ministry at his dwelling place. Every morning and evening after the priests complete their service to Israel on behalf of the LORD, he then invites the priests to sit at his table while he serves them his divine food. Once their ministry is fulfilled and they have eaten the sacred meal in the presence of the LORD, the priests who are leaving the sanctuary take off their holy vestments and leave them there in anticipation of the next time they will serve before the LORD. The ministry of the priests in the daily divine service regularly ends with the LORD providing for their nourishment and sanctification so that they may continue to conduct the ritual activities of the daily divine service before the LORD at his tabernacle.

CONCLUSIONS TO CHAPTER 3

The LORD institutes the rites of the daily divine service and determines their ritual function so that he can accomplish his purposes through them. The fire rite maintains the holy fire at the tabernacle so that the LORD may continue to reside among the Israelites. The presentation rite provides the materials for the daily service. The blood rite prepares the lambs to be placed on the altar and more importantly atones for the sins and ritual impurities of the people. The incense rite maintains the bread of the presence and the lamps inside the tent of meeting. More significantly, the most holy incense manifests the presence of the LORD to the Israelites and sanctifies them at the tabernacle and throughout the camp. Through the burning rite the LORD meets with his people, sanctifies them, and reveals his gracious presence to them in the smoke from the altar. In both the incense rite and burning rite the high priest wearing his sacred vestments serves as a mediator by bringing Israel into the presence of the LORD inside the tent of meeting and by bringing the LORD out to the people at the altar in the courtyard. The blessing rite announces the presence of God at the altar for burnt offering and places his divine name upon the assembled congregation to bless them with his protection, favor, and peace. In the meal rite the LORD provides the priests with their daily bread for nourishment and serves them his most

---

456. See Kleinig, *Leviticus*, 152.

holy food from his table to sanctify them for their continued ministry in his holy presence. The LORD authorizes these rites and their ritual activities. He determines who does what, to or with whom, with what materials, at what time, and in what location. The LORD does all this to bestow gifts and blessings upon his people through the daily divine service.

4

The Theological Purpose of the Daily Divine Service

THE LORD FOUNDS THE daily divine service so that he may dwell among the Israelites (Exod 29:45–46). The holy LORD, however, cannot dwell among a sinful and unclean people because he would destroy them for desecrating his holiness. To alleviate this danger, God establishes the daily divine service as a ritual system, which is comprised of its subsystems of agents, acts, materials, times, and locations that operate in coordination with each other to achieve the LORD's purpose of purifying and sanctifying the Israelites, so that he may dwell among them for their benefit.[1] Each subsystem within the divine service defines how the Israelites may safely access the presence of God, and these involve guarding taboos of proximity, touch, and sight.[2] The limitations that God places upon the Israelites not only protect them from destruction, they guard the LORD and his sanctuary from desecration and defilement that would result in him abandoning his residence among them.

THE SYSTEM OF RITUAL AGENTS

The LORD establishes his agents in his ritual system and spells out what he does through or for each of them (Exod 29; Lev 8; Num 18). His agents

---

1. See Kleinig, *Leviticus*, 3–4, 7–8.

2. See Haran, *Temples and Temple Service*, 175–87; Milgrom, *Studies in Levitical Terminology*, 10–12.

serve as mediators.³ Although the LORD originally intended for the lay Israelites to bring their offerings into the courtyard of the tabernacle and perform some of the preparatory acts involved with them (Lev 1:2–6, 9–14; 2:1–2; 3:1–2, 6–8, 12–15; 4:27–35), following the rebellion instigated by Korah (Num 16:1–34) as well as the Israelites' grumbling against Moses and Aaron (Num 16:41–50), the LORD further restricts who may access the courtyard.⁴ No longer are the Israelites allowed to approach the tent of meeting without being accompanied by the Levites, who perform the ritual acts in their stead (Num 18:22–23). The Levites mediate between the Israelites and the priests. On the one hand, the Levites serve on behalf of the Israelites (Num 3:7–8, 41, 44, 11–12; 8:10–11, 14–19; 18:6).⁵ On the other hand, they serve as assistants to the priests (Num 3:6–7, 9; 8:22; 18:2–4, 6). Since the Levites are not consecrated and ordained, they may neither encroach upon any area of the tabernacle that is limited to the priests, nor touch any of the most holy furniture, nor eat the most holy food, nor perform any of the ritual acts that are the exclusive duties of the priests (Num 18:1–7).⁶ The Levites ensure that the Israelites will not bear their own guilt by encroaching upon the sanctuary. Instead, they bear the guilt of the Israelites before the LORD (Num 18:22–23) as agents of atonement for them

3. See Birkholz, "Matter of Life and Death," 49, 51–59.

4. Levine seems to interpret Num 18:22–23 as barring lay Israelites from ever entering into the courtyard after the rebellion in Num 16 and 17 (Levine, "*Lpny* YHWH," 451). This may be the ritual basis for the construction of a second courtyard outside the entrance to the sanctuary in Jerusalem, which may be alluded to in 1 Kgs 8:64; 2 Chr 4:9; 6:14; 7:7; 20:5; 29:16 (see 29:25); Jer 19:14; 26:2; 36:10 and is described in Ezek 10:5; 40:17, 20, 31, 34, 37; 42:1, 3, 7–9, 14; 44:19; 46:20–22. While Haran acknowledges the tendency of the Pentateuch to restrict the courtyard to the exclusive domain of the priests, he holds that the Levites and Israel's laity have limited access to the courtyard on specific occasions (Haran, *Temples and Temple Service*, 181–87). Milgrom thinks that the lay Israelites continue to access the courtyard, but only with the accompaniment of the Levites, who assist them in preparing their offerings (Milgrom, *Studies in Levitical Terminology*, 10–11).

5. The Levites' work/service, עֲבֹדָה, along with doing guard duty is one of their two main tasks at the tabernacle. While guard duty is the life-long responsibility of the Levites and of every Israelite priest and layman in one manner or another (Birkholz, "Matter of Life and Death," 51–53), the Levites' work at the tabernacle lasts only from age twenty-five to age fifty (Num 8:24–26). The nature of their work is never to officiate over rites, which is the job of the priests, but to do the hard physical labor of dismantling, transporting, and reassembling the tabernacle as well as performing some of the preparatory activities for the offerings (see 2 Chr 29:34; 30:17). See Milgrom, *Studies in Levitical Terminology*, 60–87.

6. The Levites are not ordained or consecrated like the priests (Exod 29; Lev 8); rather they are purified for their work of assisting the priests (Num 8:5–21). Thus, their work is not holy but menial.

(Num 8:19).[7] Furthermore, the Levites do guard duty in two ways.[8] First, they guard against unauthorized encroachment by performing the preparatory ritual acts on behalf of the Israelites when they present their offerings (Num 18:23), and second, by their encampment between the tabernacle and the Israelites (Num 1:53; 3:23, 29, 35, 38).[9]

The regular priests mediate between the Levites and the high priest. Since their normal place of service is at the outer altar, the regular priests guard against the encroachment of the Levites and bear their own guilt at the altar and in the sanctuary area (Num 18:1–5). The regular priests also serve the high priest and perform their duties at his discretion, thus serving in an intermediary capacity between the Levites and the high priest (Num 3:10, 38; 18:5, 7).[10] The high priest is responsible for all of the service at the tabernacle including the supervision of the regular priests and the Levites.[11] He is the last line of defense against encroachment by unauthorized priests and Levites.[12] He alone bears the guilt of all Israel before the LORD, including that of the priests, Levites, and laity (Exod 28:38). The high priest stands between Israel and the LORD, which makes him uniquely qualified to represent the LORD to Israel.[13] If an unauthorized person breaks in to encroach upon the LORD, then he breaks out in wrath toward Israel (Num 1:51; 3:10,

---

7. The Levites are not agents who perform rites of atonement, which is the exclusive duty of the priests, but most likely they atone for the Israelites by drawing God's wrath upon themselves for an unauthorized encroachment instead of upon the entire community of Israel (Milgrom, *Studies in Levitical Terminology*, 28–33). See Birkholz, "Matter of Life and Death," 51–52.

8. The Hebrew מִשְׁמֶרֶת שָׁמַר is a technical term that means *do guard duty* (Milgrom et al., "מִשְׁמֶרֶת," 72–78). For further analysis of this phrase, see Birkholz, "Matter of Life and Death," 37–40; Milgrom, *Studies in Levitical Terminology*, 8–16; Haran, *Temples and Temple Service*, 181–84; Kleinig, *Leviticus*, 194, 204, 381; Levine, "Lpny YHWH," 141–42. Milgrom holds that the guard duty of the Levites involves weapons with which they kill unauthorized people that encroach the sanctuary. Since an encroacher is an enemy who intends to murder all of Israel by defiling the sacred precincts and inciting God's wrath, he must be killed out of self-defense (Milgrom, *Studies in Levitical Terminology*, 21, 27).

9. See Birkholz, "Matter of Life and Death," 34–40, 51–59; Haran, *Temples and Temple Service*, 181–87; Milgrom, *Studies in Levitical Terminology*, 5–59.

10. It should be noted that even priests could be disqualified from officiating in the sanctuary (Lev 21:1–22:16). The same penalty against unauthorized encroachment of a Levite or Israelite applies also to unauthorized priests (Milgrom, *Studies in Levitical Terminology*, 38–43).

11. See Olyan, *Rites and Rank*, 33.

12. See Birkholz, "Matter of Life and Death," 32–36; Milgrom, *Studies in Levitical Terminology*, 22–27.

13. This is thoroughly discussed in chapter 3 on the incense rite, the burning rite, and the blessing rite. See also Knohl, *Sanctuary of Silence*, 154–55.

The Theological Purpose of the Daily Divine Service 181

38; 18:7), but through the authorized agency of the high priest the LORD blesses Israel (Lev 9:23–24; Num 6:22–27) as he had promised to do in Exod 20:24. Thus, Israel's clergy do guard duty against unauthorized encroachment of the LORD. The Levites intervene between Israel and the regular priests; the regular priests mediate between the Levites and the high priest; the high priest stands between all of the Israelites and the LORD.[14] Through this system of ritual agents the LORD ensures his continual dwelling among the Israelites as the personnel at the sanctuary guards against breaking the taboos of approaching the sacred locations in the tabernacle, touching its most holy furniture, and seeing the areas inside the tent of meeting.[15]

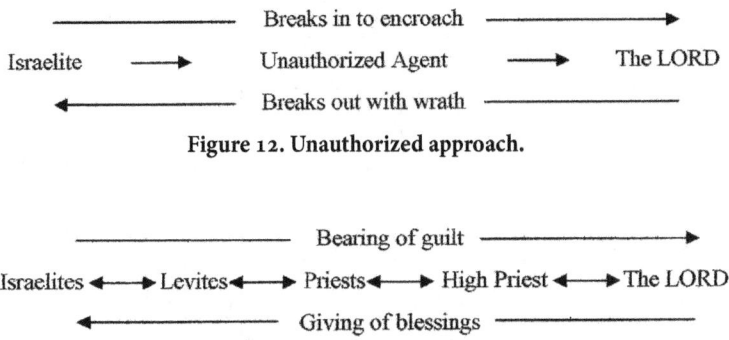

Figure 12. Unauthorized approach.

Figure 13. Authorized mediation.

---

14. See Kleinig, *Leviticus*, 235–36, 338–39; Kiuchi, *Purification Offering*, 77–85; *Leviticus*, 293; Milgrom, *Studies in Levitical Terminology*, 8–10; Olyan, *Rites and Rank*, 27–36.

15. See Haran, "Priestly Image of Tabernacle," 216–26.

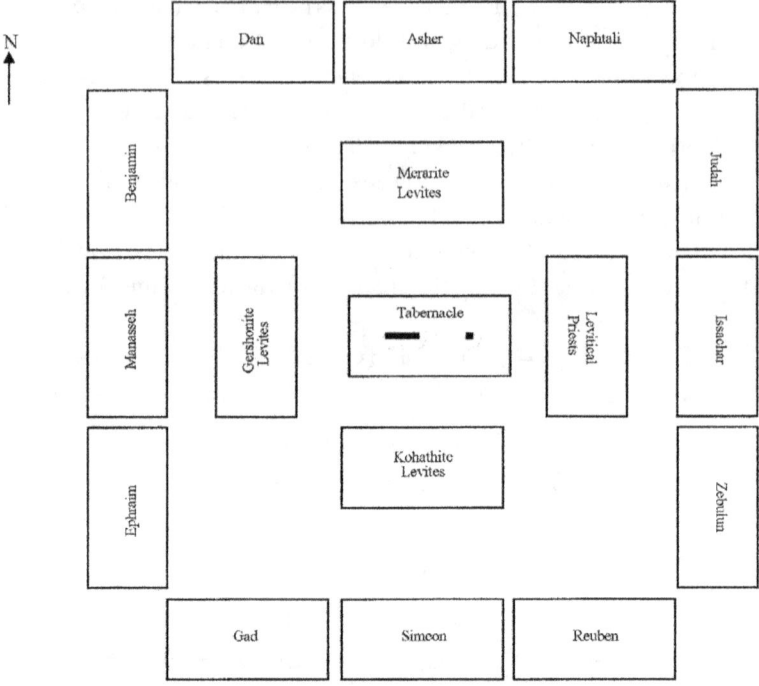

Figure 14. The Levitical barrier between the Israelites and the tabernacle.

THE SYSTEM OF RITUAL ACTS

Through the system of ritual acts in the daily service, the LORD maintains his presence at the tabernacle. Every day in the divine service, the LORD accomplishes four chief things that result in his continued dwelling among his people. First, since the LORD chooses to be present in the fire at the outer altar, he establishes the fire rite to perpetuate his holy presence there.[16] If the fire is extinguished then the LORD will no longer be accessible at the altar and none of the rites can be enacted effectively, which would result in the LORD's departure from Israel.[17] The holy fire must be maintained for him to dwell with them.

---

16. Since the fire on the altar first came from the glory cloud in the most holy place at the inaugural service, it is the fire of God (Lev 9:23–24). Thus, the priests must maintain the fire by not letting it be extinguished for the LORD to continue to dwell at his tabernacle among the Israelites (Lev 6:2, 5–6 [9, 12–13]).

17. The divine fire is necessary for the operation of the entire ritual system. No

Second, the LORD purifies the whole community of Israel from defilement through the rite of atonement. Since God's holiness is entirely incompatible with ritual impurity, he cannot dwell among sinful and unclean people or else he will destroy them. The rite of atonement is the way that the LORD cleanses his people to remove the threat of their destruction. Atonement occurs when the blood from the daily burnt offering is splashed on the sides of the outer altar (Lev 17:11). The blood substitutes the life of the lamb for the lives of the Israelites and through it the LORD exchanges Israel's impurity for purity.[18] While the application of blood to the altar remains the chief means of purification, atonement probably results secondarily from the high priest daily bearing the Israelites' guilt into the holy place where their impurity is destroyed by its contact with the most holy incense.[19] The rite of atonement moves the Israelites from a status of ritual impurity to ritual purity, which enables the LORD to dwell with them at his tabernacle without destroying them.

Third, the LORD sanctifies the Israelites so that he may dwell among them and share his holiness with them (Exod 25:8; 29:43–46). The corporate impurities of the Israelites are *brought in* before the LORD through the agency of the high priest in the incense rite and God takes away these impurities so that the high priest can *bring out* the LORD's holiness to them. The LORD's holiness is imparted to the Israelites through the sweet smell of the incense that mingles with the smoke from the burnt offering and through his most holy name that they behold on the crown and spoken in the benediction. The LORD exchanges Israel's impurities for his holiness and he daily sanctifies them so that he may continue to dwell with them and keep

---

other fire is authorized for use at the outer altar or inside the tent of meeting for burning incense and lighting the lamps. Without the holy fire and the LORD's presence in it, the tabernacle would no longer function as the LORD's residence among the Israelites (Kleinig, *Leviticus*, 146–47). See also Olyan, *Rites and Rank*, 16.

18. See the section on the blood rite in chapter 3.

19. According to Exod 28:38 when the high priest wears the holy crown into the tent of meeting he bears the guilt of the Israelites concerning their holy offerings so that the LORD will accept them. Since the high priest's crown is inscribed with the name of the LORD, that name protects him from destruction as he bears the Israelites' guilt there. The incense most likely atones for the Israelites' guilt by destroying it (Num 16:46–47; see 1 Chr 6:49) because ritual uncleanness cannot coexist with that which is most holy (Lev 7:19–21; 19:8; 22:3, 9; Num 18:32; 19:13, 20). See Kleinig, *Leviticus*, 6–8; Olyan, *Rites and Rank*, 15–17. Houtman discusses the destructive effect of the incense upon defilement (Houtman, "Function of Holy Incense," 458–65). See also Kiuchi, *Purification Offering*, 87–109; Rodriguez, *Substitution in Hebrew Cultus*, 233–60; Gilders, *Blood Ritual*, 22, 28–29, 72–78, 164–78.

sharing his holiness with them (Exod 31:13; Lev 20:8; 21:8, 15, 23; 22:9, 16, 32; see Ezek 20:12; 37:28).[20]

Finally, the LORD daily reveals that he is present among the Israelites and continues to dwell with them. As the high priest emerges from the tent enwrapped in the most holy incense the congregation beholds the divine name on his holy crown. After he places the burnt offering on the divine fire, the smoke reveals to the people that the LORD is favorably present with his mercy, grace, and compassion as he had declared in Exod 34:6–7. When the priests sound the trumpets and the high priest moves in front of the altar to announce the LORD's benediction to the people, his theophany occurs for them.[21] By the aromas they smell, the sights they see, and the sounds they hear at the tabernacle these theophanic enactments show that the LORD is their God who dwells among them for their benefit and blessing. Through

---

20. Although Rodriguez introduces the term *exchange*, he does not speak of the exchange of Israel's guilt for the LORD's holiness (Rodriguez, *Substitution in Hebrew Cultus*, 250–56). Kiuchi deals with the priests bearing Israel's guilt before the LORD, but he does not relate it to any kind of exchange (Kiuchi, *Purification Offering*, 98). Although Kleinig mentions the inward and outward movements of the high priest in relation to the most holy place on the Day of Atonement, he is careful to not use the word *exchange* to describe any of its ritual functions (Kleinig, *Leviticus*, 338–47). The rites for the Day of Atonement imply the function and purpose for the high priest bearing Israel's guilt into the tent of meeting. In addition to the rites on the Day of Atonement that remove the impurities of the Israelites (Lev 16:6, 11, 15, 24, 30, 33–34), the tent of meeting, the altar for incense, and the altar for burnt offering must also be purified from Israel's sins to be re-sanctified (Exod 30:10; Lev 16:16, 18–20). This indicates that the guilt and sins of the Israelites are absorbed by the sanctuary and its furniture. But how? The LORD most likely receives the guilt of the Israelites that are borne into his presence by the high priest (Exod 28:38). Every day the altar for burnt offering, the incense altar, and the tent of meeting take in the people's guilt. The most holy incense protects the high priest and removes Israel's unintentional corporate sins from him each day but all of their sins are destroyed by the super holiness of the LORD himself on the Day of Atonement. The LORD takes to himself the guilt of the high priest and the entire community through the blood of their sin offerings that is placed on the atonement seat by the high priest in the most holy place. He does not, however, keep their guilt in himself but through the agency of the high priest the LORD places them on the scapegoat through which they are removed from the sanctuary and sent to the most unclean realm in the wilderness. Thus, an exchange takes place. Israel's impurities are exchanged for God's holiness. The rites for the Day of Atonement not only purify Israel and the sanctuary, they reconsecrate the tent of meeting, the incense altar, and the altar for burnt offering through the blood from the sin offerings, which has the power to sanctify because of its contact with the super holiness of the LORD at the ark in the most holy place. A similar exchange of Israel's impurity for the LORD's holiness takes place in the daily divine service as the high priest brings in the community's guilt before the LORD and brings out his holiness to them through his most holy incense, the smoke from the offerings, and the name of the LORD seen on his crown and spoken in the benediction.

21. See the sections on the incense rite, the burning rite, and the blessing rite in chapter 3.

this system of ritual acts the LORD maintains his presence at the sanctuary in his holy fire; he cleanses the Israelites from defilement; he sanctifies them; and, he manifests his gracious presence as he dwells among them.[22]

Part 1

The LORD's presence maintained in the Holy Fire

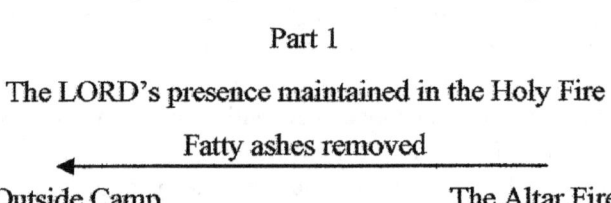

Parts 2 and 3

Israel's purification and sanctification

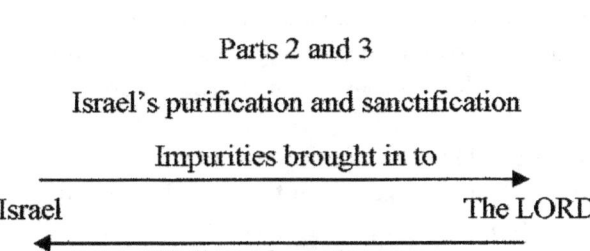

Part 4

The Theophany of the LORD

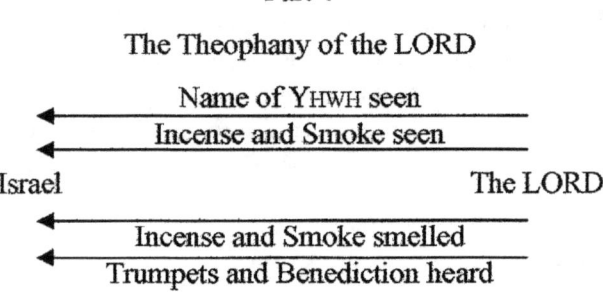

Figure 15. The theological purpose of the main parts of the system of ritual acts.

THE SYSTEM OF RITUAL MATERIALS

The LORD works through the system of ritual materials in the daily divine service to purify and sanctify the Israelites, so that he may dwell among

22. See figure fifteen.

them and manifest himself as their God. He uses the materials in the daily service as his means to accomplish two things that are necessary for him to continue to reside among them. The first involves an anthropological system that distinguishes that which is unclean[23] from that which is clean[24] (Lev 7:19; 10:10; 11:32, 36, 47; 13:59; 14:57; 15:8; 17:15; 20:25; 22:4; Num 19:19; Deut 12:15, 22; 15:22; see Job 14:4; Eccl 9:2; Ezek 22:26; 44:23).[25] Since clean things and people are defiled by contact with other ritually unclean people or things, the LORD institutes the instruments through which he purifies them.[26] In the daily divine service the usual means of purification are the blood of the lamb on the altar and the water from the font. Since the font and the altar are most holy, they sanctify the water and the blood that touches them. The holy water cleanses the hands and feet of the priests by contact and the holy blood purifies the Israelites vicariously through atonement.[27]

The second has to do with a theological system that distinguishes that which is holy[28] from that which is common[29] (Lev 10:10; 20:3; 21:6; 22:2, 15, 32; see Ezek 20:39; 22:26; 42:20; 44:23; Amos 2:7).[30] Since holy things and people are desecrated by contact with unclean people or things, the LORD establishes the means through which they may be sanctified and become holy again. The most holy things, such as the tabernacle and its furniture, the incense, the smoke and most holy food from the offerings, the vestments of the priests, and the benediction sanctify whatever and whomever they touch (Exod 30:26–29). The purification occurs through the *holy* things in the daily service, and this shows that the anthropological system is combined with and subordinated to the theological system.[31] While the LORD institutes the holy things to purify the Israelites, he establishes the most holy things to sanctify them so that his holiness can be protected from desecration and his people safeguarded from destruction by contact with him.[32]

---

23. הַטָּמֵא

24. הַטָּהוֹר

25. See Kleinig, *Leviticus*, 6; Olyan, *Rites and Rank*, 38–62.

26. Just as there are grades of holiness so there are also grades of impurity. The pagan deities are absolutely unclean, the things and people that he contacts are most unclean, and things and people that contact those that are most unclean become unclean (Olyan, *Rites and Rank*, 38–39, 50–51).

27. See the section on the blood rite in chapter 3.

28. הַקֹּדֶשׁ

29. הַחֹל

30. See Kleinig, *Leviticus*, 6–11; Olyan, *Rites and Rank*, 15–37.

31. See Kleinig, *Leviticus*, 7; Milgrom, *Leviticus 1–16*, 615–17, 731–33.

32. A distinction should be made between the corporate and the individual means of purification. The holy blood of the lamb purifies Israel corporately because it is part

The Theological Purpose of the Daily Divine Service 187

Furthermore, just as the LORD's super holiness consecrates the most holy furniture at the tabernacle by means of the holy anointing oil (Exod 30:22–29), so also the LORD sanctifies the most holy offerings through contact with his holy fire.[33] Similarly, in the daily service the priests and the people do not contract the LORD's holiness by touching him, but he cleanses them by means of the holy things and shares his holiness with them by means of most holy things.[34] The LORD accomplishes the purification and sanctification of the Israelites among whom he dwells by means of the super holy, most holy, and holy things so that he may continue to reside among them as their God (Exod 25:8; 29:45–46).[35]

---

of a public offering (Lev 17:11). The holy water purifies the priests' hands and feet as individuals (Exod 30:17–21), but because they perform the public daily burnt offering on behalf of Israel the purification of their hands and feet is connected with the Israelites' offering. While it is clear that some rites of purification for individuals are effective through the means of a holy substance, such as the blood which is applied to the altar from individual burnt, peace, sin, and guilt offerings (Lev 1:5; 3:2; 4:30; 7:2), it is unclear if the ashes of the red heifer are considered *holy* or simply *pure* (Num 19). Sprinkling the heifer's blood toward the front of the tent of meeting, however, seems to imply that its ashes are holy (Num 19:4). Milgrom holds that only the dynamic forces of the holy and the unclean exercise power over the static categories of the clean and the common (Milgrom, *Leviticus 1–16*, 732). If this is true, then the ashes of the heifer are not merely pure but holy. See also Levine, "*Lpny* YHWH," 462. There are purification rites for individuals, however, that do not involve holy substances (Lev 14:1–9; 15:1–27) but these must be understood together with the broader context of Israel's purification rites (see Lev 14:10–32; 15:28–33). There are three kinds of purification and sanctification rites: individual, which deal with one person, corporate, which have to do with the entire community, and comprehensive, which affects the entire community as well as the tabernacle and its furniture such as on the Day of Atonement. Although the individual, corporate, and comprehensive rites of purification and sanctification form an organic whole, I focus on the corporate rites of purification and sanctification that occur in the daily divine service.

33. The most important ritual thing in the daily service is the holy fire. It is the powerful medium of the LORD's presence that produces either his wrath against unauthorized encroachment or his grace for the use of right materials by authorized agents. The most holy incense, the burnt offering with its cereal offering, and all of the offerings that are burned on the holy fire derive their holiness from that fire. None of them are holy or most holy apart from the holy fire (Kleinig, *Leviticus*, 231–32).

34. The distinction between the holy and the common and between the unclean and the clean is not merely a theoretical system. They are practical criteria under which the daily divine service is enacted. Since the holy and most holy things are always connected with the LORD's presence at the sanctuary, the priests must safeguard God's holiness and protect the people from the deadly consequences of desecration by unclean things and people (Kleinig, *Leviticus*, 236–37).

35. Olyan employs the term *superior holiness* to describe God's preeminent sanctity as it relates to a hierarchical or graded holiness together with the most holy and the holy things, which derive their power from him (Olyan, *Rites and Rank*, 33–34). See also Haran, *Temples and Temple Service*, 175–88.

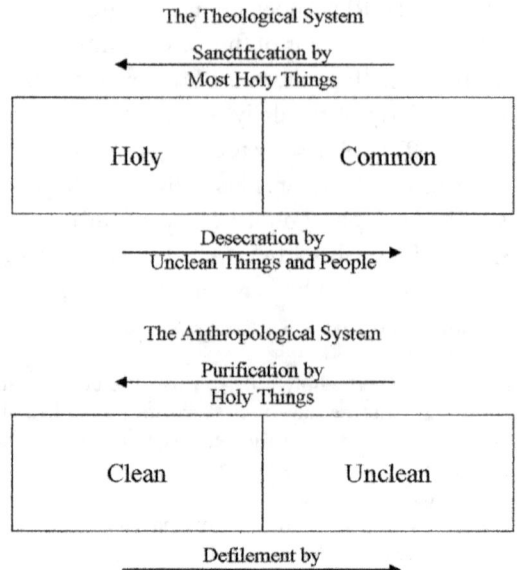
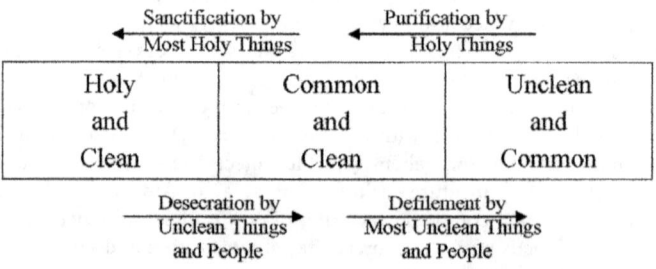

Figure 16. The theological and anthropological systems.

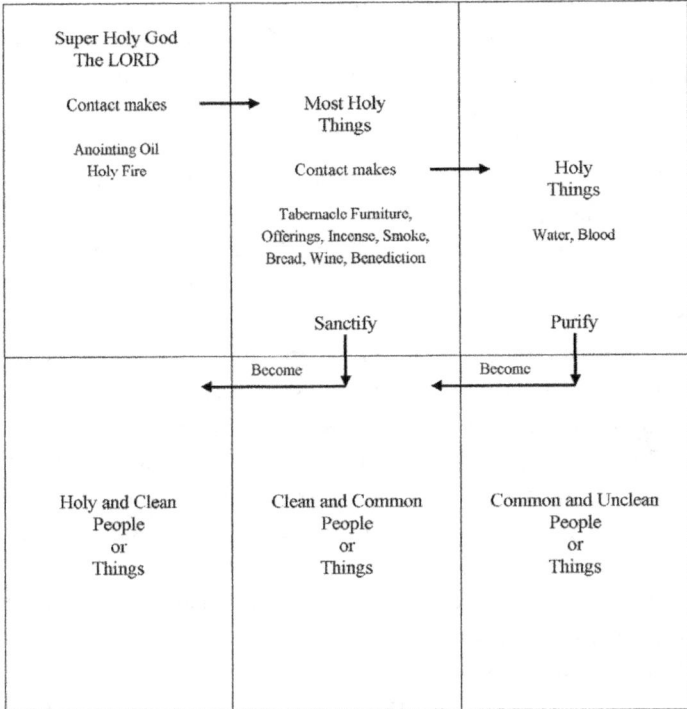

Figure 17. The LORD's means of purification and sanctification through the system of ritual materials.

THE SYSTEM OF RITUAL TIMES

The LORD maintains his presence among the Israelites at the tabernacle through the ritual calendar that he established for them.[36] The daily service must be enacted every morning and every evening for the LORD to continue to dwell with his people at his residence in the camp (Exod 29:38–39).[37]

---

36. The system of ritual times is composed of the ritual calendar (Lev 23; Num 28–29). The Hebrew word for such a time is מוֹעֵד, which means an *appointed time* or *appointed place* (see BDB 417–18). Several ritually significant matters are related to this word, such as the tent of *meeting* where the LORD *meets* with his priests (Exod 25:22; 30:6, 36; Num 17:4) and *meets* with the Israelites (Exod 29:42–43) at the *appointed times for meeting* with them there (Lev 23:4, 37, 44). Thus, the Israelites become the *congregation* that meets with the LORD in the appointed place at the *appointed time* (Kleinig, *Leviticus*, 487).

37. For a philosophical discussion about sacred time in Israel and other ancient cultures, see Eliade, *Sacred and Profane*, 68–113.

He establishes the morning and evening offerings to perpetuate his presence in the holy fire at the altar, to purify the Israelites from their uncleanness, to sanctify them, and to manifest his divine presence to them.[38] Although the system of ritual times involves yearly, monthly, and weekly rites of passage that ensure the LORD's continued residence with his people, the daily passage of time from night into day and day into night is foundational to the entire ritual calendar (Lev 23; Num 28–29).[39] The service in the morning reveals that God is graciously present with the Israelites throughout the day, and the service in the evening assures his presence with them during the night.[40]

The morning and evening services are built around a complex rite of passage, which consists of two specific rites of passage.[41] The first is based on the anthropological system that distinguishes between the unclean and the clean.[42] This rite brings about the community's purification from the ritual pollution that they have contracted between the time of the previous service and the next one. While Israel's purification occurs specifically when the blood is splashed on the sides of the altar (Lev 17:11), this rite of passage involves all of the ritual acts including the maintenance of the fire, the presentation of the materials, and the presentation of the lamb's blood followed by putting the blood on the altar.[43]

The second is based on the theological system which distinguishes between the holy and the common.[44] This rite of passage moves the community from a common to a holy state. Since the Israelites may be desecrated by the forces of impurity through their contact with unclean things and people, they constantly need to be sanctified.[45] Their sanctification is brought about through the series of ritual acts that occur after the high priest emerges from the tent of meeting, including their contact with the most holy incense and smoke from the altar, seeing the name of the LORD

---

38. See the discussion above.

39. For a thorough analysis of the ritual calendar's appointed feast days, see Kleinig, *Leviticus*, 487–97, 501–7. See also Gorman, *Ideology of Ritual*, 33–34, who discusses the systemic nature of ritual time.

40. This is discussed in the sections on ritual time in chapter 3.

41. See van Gennep, *Rites of Passage*; Turner, *Ritual Process*; Milgrom, *Leviticus 1–16*, 566–69.

42. See Kleinig, *Leviticus*, 6–7; Olyan, *Rites and Rank*, 38–62.

43. These may be considered *preparatory* ritual acts because they are not an end in themselves. See the order of the daily burnt offering in figure one. The passage from impurity to purity in the divine service prepares Israel for their sanctification.

44. See Kleinig, *Leviticus*, 6–7; Olyan, *Rites and Rank*, 15–37.

45. See figures 16 and 17.

The Theological Purpose of the Daily Divine Service 191

on his holy crown, and hearing the divine name spoken in the benediction. In addition, the priests are sanctified by eating the most holy food at the conclusion of the service.[46] Furthermore, the ritual acts that sanctify the community also manifest the LORD's presence to them. Through the combination of the anthropological and the theological systems, the service each morning and evening places these two rites of passage together. Hence the incense rite is the intermediate or *liminal* stage of the service that reflects the *liminal* status of Israel.[47] This is the most dangerous and uncertain part of the divine service, for if the high priest fails to rightly perform or complete the ritual activities inside the tent of meeting then the community will not be sanctified and the LORD will abandon his tabernacle among them.[48] By the enactment of these rites of passage in the divine service, the LORD is perpetuating his gracious presence among his people through the system of ritual times so as to order their lives according to the pattern of purification and sanctification, day to day, week to week, month to month, and year to year.[49]

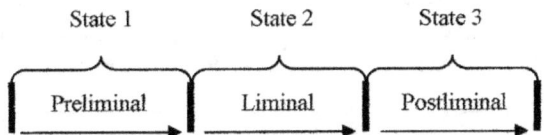

Figure 18. The states of the rites of passage.

46. See the sections on the incense rite, the burning rite, the blessing rite, and the meal rite in chapter 3.

47. Van Gennep explains that rites of passage are divided into three subcategories: separation, transition, and incorporation. He calls rites of separation *preliminal*, rites of transition *liminal*, and rites of incorporation *postliminal*. Certain ceremonies may be so complex that rites of separation, transition, and incorporation may be included in a larger framework of rites (van Gennep, *Rites of Passage*, 13, 20–21, 82). Van Gennep also views the three subcategories as states of being in some ritual contexts and this idea is further developed in Turner, *Ritual Process*, 94–167. I believe that rites of passage can involve states of being as well as stages in the ritual process. Based on this assumption, the morning and evening offerings may be understood as complex rites of passage at the crucial turning points from night to day and from day to night.

48. See Turner, *Ritual Process*, 92–113, 166–67; Douglas, *Purity and Danger*, 119–20.

49. See Kleinig, "Witting or Unwitting Ritualists," 16–17.

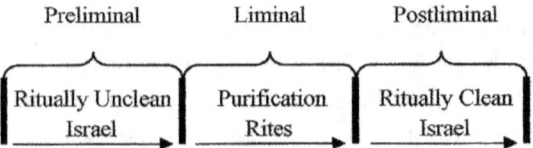

Figure 19. The purification rites of passage.

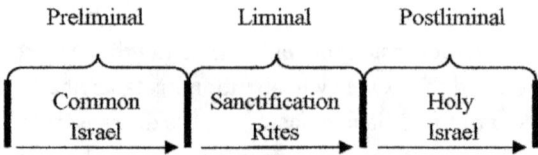

Figure 20. The sanctification rites of passage.

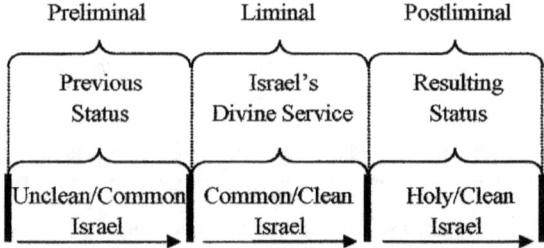

Figure 21. The states of the divine service's complex rite of passage every morning and evening.

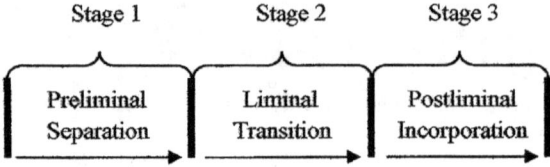

Figure 22. The stages of rites of passage

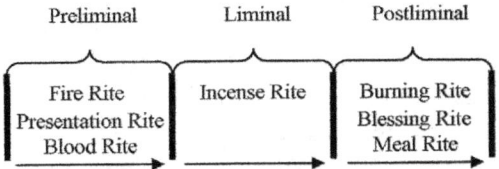

Figure 23. The stages of the daily service's complex rite
of passage every morning and evening

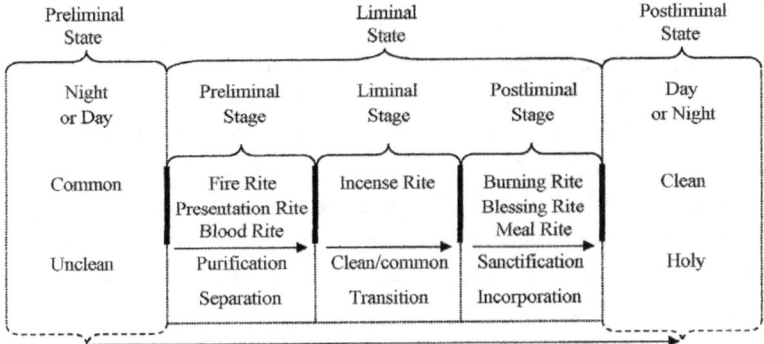

Figure 24. Israel's status in relation to the stages of the divine service according to
the complex rite of passage every morning and evening.

THE SYSTEM OF RITUAL LOCATIONS

The LORD fixes boundaries through the system of ritual locations to designate the areas where Israel's priests and laity may safely access his presence for their benefit in the daily divine service. Since the LORD dwells among the Israelites at the tabernacle in the middle of the camp, he establishes barriers to safeguard his holiness from desecration and to protect his people from destruction by unauthorized encroachment.[50] At the tabernacle are four ritual locations that are designated by the phrase *before the LORD*.[51] First, the most holy place[52] is the location of the ark of the testimony[53] with

---

50. See the discussion above concerning the system of ritual agents.
51. לִפְנֵי יְהוָה.
52. קֹדֶשׁ הַקֳּדָשִׁים.
53. אֲרוֹן הָעֵדוּת.

its atonement seat.⁵⁴ This is the inner-most room inside the tent of meeting that functions as the throne room of God.⁵⁵ The sanctity of this ritual space is so extreme that the high priest alone is permitted to enter there only one day of the entire year (Exod 16:33; Lev 16:13; Num 17:7).

Second, the outer room inside the tent is the holy place.⁵⁶ The high priest enters there every morning and every evening in the daily divine service to tend or light the lamps and to burn incense on the golden altar. The LORD meets in this place with his closest associates, the priests and especially the high priest, to conduct his business on Israel's behalf and for their benefit each day (Exod 27:21; 28:12, 29–30, 35, 38; 30:8; 40:23, 25; Lev 4:6–7, 17–18; 24:3–4, 6, 8; Num 27:5, 21).

Third, the area in the courtyard⁵⁷ that is between its entrance and the tent is also designated as a location "before the LORD." This is the place that is often referred to as the *entrance to the tent of meeting*.⁵⁸ There the LORD conducts his public business; there the offerings are presented to him, burned on the altar, and eaten by the priests every day.⁵⁹ This is also the location where the LORD meets with the Israelites to manifest his presence to them (Lev 1:5, 11; 3:1, 7, 12; 4:4, 15, 24; 5:26 [6:7]; 6:18 [25]; 7:30; 8:26–27, 29; 9:2, 4, 21; 10:1–2, 15, 17, 19; 12:7; 14:11, 12, 16, 18, 23–24, 27, 29, 31; 15:14–15, 30; 16:1, 7, 10, 18, 30; 19:22; 23:11, 20, 28, 40; Num 3:4; 5:16, 18, 25, 30; 6:16, 20; 8:10–11, 21; 10:9–10; 15:15, 25, 28; 16:7, 16–17, 38, 40; 18:19; 26:61; 31:50, 54; Deut 10:8; 18:7; 26:5, 10, 13; 27:7).

Finally, the ritual location where the entire community assembles on rare occasions is outside the entrance to the courtyard.⁶⁰ Since the designation *before the LORD* refers to his presence, this can also indicate the area just outside the courtyard that is in close proximity to the tabernacle and the

---

54. הַכַּפֹּרֶת

55. See Kleinig, *Leviticus*, 47.

56. הַקֹּדֶשׁ

57. חָצֵר

58. This is discussed in the section on the ritual location of the presentation rite in chapter 3. The area that is most often called the entrance to the tent of meeting, פֶּתַח אֹהֶל מוֹעֵד, is between the altar and the threshold into the courtyard. It may, however, refer to the entire area from the opening to the courtyard to the threshold of the tent.

59. Since the entrance to the tent of meeting in the courtyard is the point of contact between the LORD and his people, this location is the ritual bridge between heaven and earth (Kleinig, *Leviticus*, 62–63).

60. The area between the altar and the entrance to the courtyard is not large enough to accommodate the entire community. On occasions when the whole community is summoned *before the LORD*, the territory of the camp to the east of the sanctuary probably functions as an extension of the LORD's presence at the entrance to the tent of meeting. See also Milgrom, *Leviticus 1–16*, 147–49.

ark of the testimony (Lev 9:5; Num 7:3; 14:37; 20:3; 32:20–22, 27, 29, 32; Deut 1:45; 4:10; 6:25; 12:7, 12, 18; 14:23, 26; 15:20; 16:11; 19:17; 23:14; 24:4, 13; 29:10, 14). Although this is the place where the entire community assembles on rare occasions, the Pentateuch never refers to the area outside the courtyard as *holy*. It is common, yet ritually clean.[61]

These four locations are separated by three boundaries. The first boundary is the courtyard wall with its entryway[62] on the east side of the altar (Exod 27:9–18; 38:9–18). The second is the exterior of the tent of meeting and its opening[63] on the west side of the altar (Exod 26:1–30, 36–37; 36:8–34, 37–38). The third is the veil[64] that separates the holy place from the most holy place inside the tent (Exod 26:31–33; 36:35–36; Lev 16:2). As each threshold is passed from outside the courtyard into the tent of meeting, the locations increase in holiness.[65] Furthermore, this graduation in sanctity from one place to the next brings with it taboos regarding sight, touch, and approach.[66]

---

61. The ritual status of the entire camp of Israel is ambiguous. Num 5:1–4 implies that the camp must be kept ritually clean because of the tabernacle in its midst. See also Lev 15:31. The *persons*, however, are called to be "people of holiness" in Exod 22:31. So there must be a distinction between the ritual status of the camp and that of the people. The camp is clean and common, while the people are clean and holy. The proximity of the camp to the sanctuary, though, may indicate that the entire camp is a transitional location, which functions as a barrier between the holy realm and the common realm. See figure 26.

62. The entryway to the tent, פֶּתַח, is distinguished from the entryway to the courtyard, שַׁעַר. While the former word indicates a doorway to a simple enclosed structure, the latter term is usually associated with a gate to a walled open area (BDB 1044).

63. פֶּתַח

64. פָּרֹכֶת

65. The most holy place is the most sacred location, the holy place is less holy, and the courtyard is least holy (Deut 23:14). All other places are not holy but common. See Haran, *Temples and Temple Service*, 175–88; Gorman, *Ideology of Ritual*, 32, 55–57, 72, 111–12; Jenson, *Graded Holiness*, 89–93; Olyan, *Rites and Rank*, 22–25; Kleinig, *Leviticus*, 5–6.

66. Haran was the first to develop the notion of the three taboos of sight, touch, and approach (Haran, *Temples and Temple Service*, 175–87). He, however, limits the taboos of sight only to the area and furniture inside the tent. All of the three main areas of the tabernacle, the courtyard, the holy place, and the most holy place, however, are guarded by the taboos of sight, touch, and approach but in gradations. Furthermore, the taboos are marked off by the three thresholds of the tabernacle: the gate of the courtyard, the doorway of the tent, and the veil separating the holy place from the most holy place. Although the high priest on the Day of Atonement approaches the ark and its atonement seat, he does not see or touch it (Lev 16:12–15). Every other day of the year he must not approach the most holy place and its ark. He is only allowed to see, touch, and approach the holy place and its furniture as well as everything in the courtyard. The regular priests evidently do not have free access to the holy place but may only

Like the three areas that are holy, there are four significant *common* locations: the ritually clean camp of Israel (Lev 10:14), the ritually clean place immediately outside the camp (Lev 4:12; 6:4 [11]; Num 19:9), the unclean non-Israelite habitation (Lev 14:40, 41, 45), and the most unclean place in the wilderness where the scapegoat carries Israel's sins once a year (Lev 16:10, 21–22, 26).[67] The most unclean wilderness is the extreme opposite location from the most holy place where the LORD dwells.[68] These seven geographic areas comprise the system of ritual locations that mark the boundaries where the Israelites may, on the one hand, avoid ritual impurity and, on the other hand, access the LORD's gracious presence for their purification and sanctification in the daily service.[69]

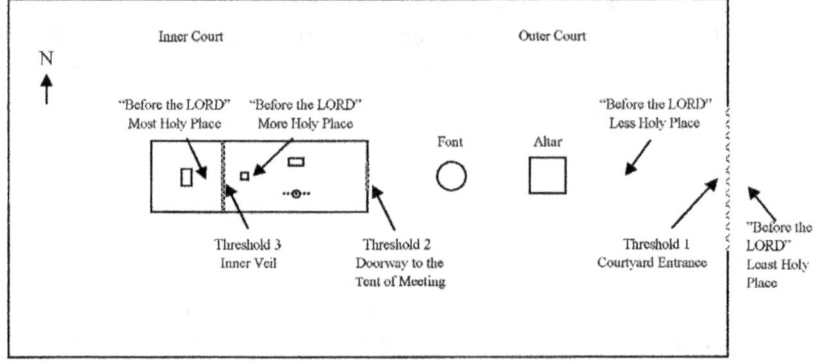

Figure 25. Grades of holiness "before the LORD."

---

accompany the high priest there to see and approach its furnishings, though they probably do not touch them. The regular priests primarily serve in the courtyard at its altar, which they may see, touch, and approach. The Levites and ritually clean Israelites may never see any of the area or furniture inside the tent but may only see the outer altar without approaching it or touching it. Ritually unclean Israelites and all non-Israelites may not see the outer altar nor enter into the opening of the courtyard which is covered with a curtain that is constructed from the same material as the curtain at the doorway of the tent (Exod 26:36; 27:16). Moreover, the outer altar is covered and hidden from everyone's sight when it is in transit, as is the other furniture (Num 4:1–20). Although the Levites carry the tabernacle and its belongings, yet they do not touch them but only carry them by poles inserted in them or on other means of transportation. Since the altars, lampstand, and table are covered, it is impossible for the Levites to approach them to perform any ritual acts at them. Thus even in transit the taboos of sight, touch, and approach remain in effect. See also Knohl, *Sanctuary of Silence*, 152–53.

67. The Hebrew word for wilderness is מִדְבָּר. It may be understood as an uninhabited land (BDB 184) or, more significantly, an inaccessible region and demonic realm that is the counter location to the most holy place at the tabernacle (Kleinig, *Leviticus*, 341–42).

68. See Haran, *Temples and Temple Service*, 176; Olyan, *Rites and Rank*, 50–62.

69. See Olyan, *Rites and Rank*, 15–27.

The Theological Purpose of the Daily Divine Service 197

Tabernacle's Most Holy Place	Tabernacle's Holy Place	Tabernacle's Holy Courtyard	Israelite Camp Common Area (Transitional?)	Outside Camp Common Area	Nations' Abode Common Area	Wilderness Common Area
Ritually Clean	Ritually Clean	Ritually Clean	Ritually Clean	Ritually Clean	Ritually Unclean	Ritually Unclean

Figure 26. Holy and common, unclean and clean locations.

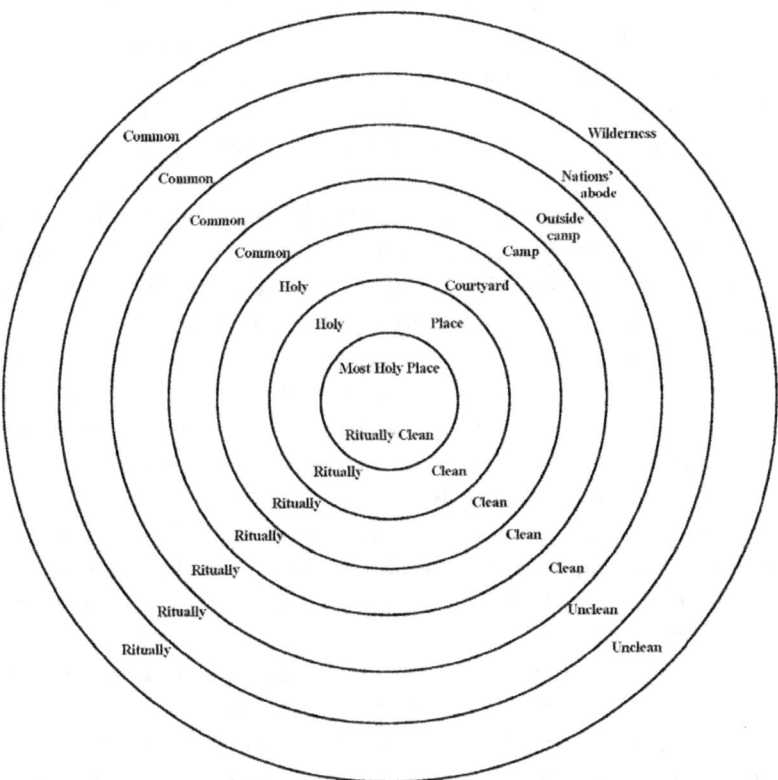

Figure 27. The centrality of the most holy place in the system of ritual locations.

CONCLUSION

Ancient Israel's entire ritual system is built on the foundation of the daily divine service. All of the individual offerings as well as the public weekly, monthly, and yearly offerings are enacted in coordination with the public daily offerings. For the ritual system to function properly and to accomplish the purposes for which the LORD institutes it, the rites in the daily divine service must be enacted in their correct sequence. By establishing the ritual order of the daily divine service, I have attempted to advance the field of scholarship that focuses on the practical order of Israel's main rites and the sequence of activities within its ritual system.

Due to the specific focus of this book other questions about the order of Israel's ritual system have been left unanswered. Further scholarship may clarify at what point in the daily service other offerings are performed. When in the daily divine service are the individual offerings, such as peace, sin, guilt, burnt, and grain offerings, presented and placed on the altar? What is the order in which Israel's other public offerings occur within the daily service, such as the corporate weekly, monthly, and yearly offerings? Are any or all of these additional offerings enacted before, during, or after the public daily burnt offering? Would they be offered between the morning and evening services and, if so, could they be offered at any time of the day? The answer to these and other related questions goes beyond the scope of this book.

The LORD institutes all of the rites in the daily divine service to function within the ritual system to achieve his purposes through them. He establishes the fire rite for the priests to perpetuate his holy fire at the tabernacle, so that his presence is maintained in the fire on the altar in the midst of the Israelite camp. Through the presentation rite the LORD ensures that the materials for the offerings are brought to him in preparation for their placement on the altar fire, so that he may accept the Israelites through their offerings. The blood rite prepares the victim to be smoked up on the altar fire, and most importantly, have its blood splashed against the sides of the altar to make atonement for the entire community of Israel, so that they may be purified from ritual uncleanness. In the incense rite the high priest, as Israel's representative, brings the entire community to God and bears their guilt with his ornate vestments into the tent of meeting, so that the LORD may sanctify them through the most holy incense. The burning rite produces the sweet aroma which is pleasing to both the LORD and his people whom he sanctifies and to whom he shows his favor through it. In the blessing rite, the LORD manifests his gracious presence at the altar and blesses the Israelites as he dwells among them. The LORD feeds his priests the most holy food from his table in the meal rite to sustain them in their service to him each morning and evening. The LORD institutes each of the rites in the daily divine service and establishes which agents do what acts with the specific materials at the proper times in their designated locations so that he may perpetuate his presence at the tabernacle, accept the Israelites through their offerings, purify them from their guilt, sanctify them to share in his holiness, and bless them by manifesting his presence to them continually through the ritual system.

A further examination of the Pentateuch would shed light upon the function of other kinds of offerings within the ritual system. How do the individual peace, sin, guilt, burnt, and grain offerings function in relation to the daily service and what does the LORD do to the individuals who offer them? What are the specific functions of the weekly, monthly, and yearly public offerings and what theological purposes do they serve? Do the individual offerings have any effect upon the entire community? Is an individual's responsibility for his own actions or condition alleviated through the public offerings? Do some kinds of offerings merely purify or sanctify, or do they accomplish some other purpose as well? Since the daily burnt offering is *public* and corporately affects the community of Israel every day, questions about an individual's status before the LORD or about the purposes of other kinds of public and individual offerings have not been addressed here. These questions require further investigation in the light of these findings about the function of the daily service.

The LORD established the daily divine service together with the rest of the ritual system for ancient Israel so that he may dwell at the tabernacle in the midst of his people. If the Israelites desecrate or defile his sanctuary, then the LORD will destroy them, depart from his tabernacle, and no longer dwell with them as their God. The LORD, however, has provided a way for him to continue to dwell among his people by instituting the daily divine service. Through the system of ritual agents in the daily service the LORD protects his holiness from desecration and defilement, which would occur by the encroachment of unauthorized agents. The LORD purifies and sanctifies the Israelites as the priests perform the rites of the daily service through the system of ritual acts. By authorizing the system of ritual materials in the daily divine service, the LORD provides the means through which he purifies and sanctifies his people. The LORD operates through the system of ritual times to accomplish a safe rite of passage for the community of Israel from night into day every morning and from day into night every evening, as well as from month to month and year to year. Most significantly, on each of these occasions he brings them from ritual impurity to a state of holiness. The LORD institutes the system of ritual locations to designate the places through which the priests and Israelites may safely come into his presence for their benefit. The LORD safeguards his presence among his people as these sub-systems function organically in coordination with each other to protect them from his wrath by daily purifying them from their ritual uncleanness and sanctifying them. The LORD institutes the daily divine service of ancient Israel so that he may dwell among his people as their gracious God.

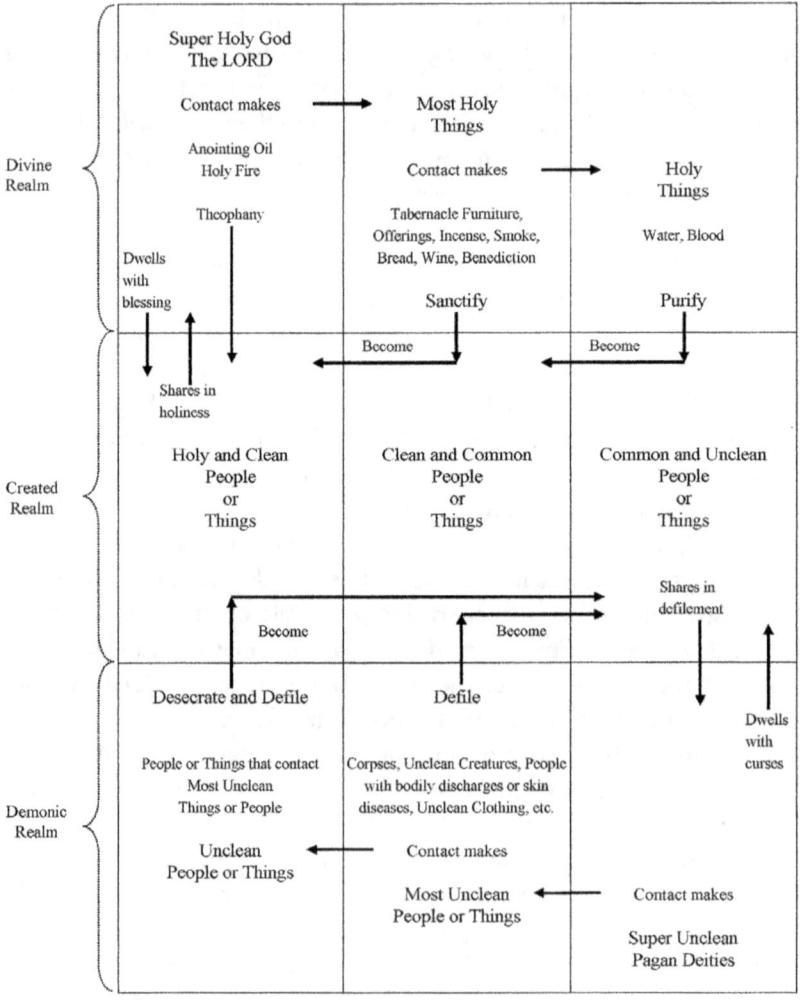

Figure 28. The daily system of purification and sanctification from desecration and defilement.

SUMMARY OF FINDINGS

In the present study I have analyzed the rites and ritual activities of ancient Israel's daily divine service by examining the prescriptive and descriptive texts in the Pentateuch to determine the service's practical order, ritual function, and theological purpose. My analysis has ascertained the probable order of the daily divine service and concludes that it is comprised of seven rites that are conducted in a specific sequence in the morning and in the evening every day. The functions of the seven rites have been discovered by researching what ritual acts are performed by which ritual agents with what ritual materials at what ritual times and in what ritual locations. The LORD's institution of each of the seven rites has shed light on their theological purposes, what God accomplishes through them. I have determined that the theological purpose of the entire daily service is for the LORD to purify his people from their ritual impurity and sanctify them by his dwelling among them as their God. The Pentateuch has provided sufficient evidence to conclude that ancient Israel's daily divine service is instituted by the LORD with the rites that are enacted in a practical order with their specific ritual functions so that God can work through them for the benefit of his people.

Bibliography

Aalen, Sverre. "רוֹא." In *Theological Dictionary of the Old Testament*, edited by G. Johannes Botterweck and Helmer Ringgren, 147–67. Vol. 1. Translated by John T Willis. Grand Rapids: Eerdmans, 1974.

Ashley, Timothy R. *The Book of Numbers*. New International Commentary on the Old Testament. Grand Rapids: Eerdmans, 1993.

Austin, John L. *How To Do Things with Words*. Cambridge: Harvard University Press, 1962.

Bailey, Lloyd R. *Leviticus-Numbers*. Smyth and Helwys Bible Commentary. Macon: Smyth and Helwys, 2005.

Bartelmus, R. "חָתַף." In *Theological Dictionary of the Old Testament*, edited by G. Johannes Botterweck, et al., 173–91. Vol. 12. Translated by Douglas W. Stott. Grand Rapids: Eerdmans, 2003.

Baxter, W. L. *Sanctuary and Sacrifice: A Reply to Wellhausen*. London: Eyre and Spottiswoode, 1896.

Bell, Catherine. *Ritual: Perspectives and Dimensions*. New York: Oxford University Press, 1997.

Beyse, K. M. "דִימְתָ." In *Theological Dictionary of the Old Testament*, edited by G. Johannes Botterweck, et al., 690–94. Vol. 15. Translated by David E. Green. Grand Rapids: Eerdmans, 2006.

Birkholz, Mark William. "A Matter of Life and Death: Priestly Service and Priestly Gifts in Numbers 18." MTh Thesis, Australian Lutheran College, 2005.

Blackman, Philip, ed. *Mishnayoth: Moed* 2. Translated by Philip Blackman. New York: Judaica, 1963.

———. *Mishnayoth: Order Kodashim* 5. Translated by Philip Blackman. 1964. Reprint, Gateshead: Judaica, 1983.

Block, Daniel I. *The Book of Ezekiel: Chapters 25–48*. New International Commentary on the Old Testament. Grand Rapids: Eerdmans, 1998.

Brichto, Herbert. "On Slaughter and Sacrifice, Blood and Atonement." *Hebrew Union College Annual* 47 (1976) 19–55.

Brown, Francis, S. R. Driver, and Charles A. Briggs. *Hebrew and English Lexicon of the Old Testament*. 1907. Reprint, Peabody: Hendrickson, 1979.

Budd, Philip J. *Leviticus*. New Century Bible Commentary. Grand Rapids: Eerdmans, 1996.

———. *Numbers*. Word Biblical Commentary. Waco, TX: Word, 1984.

Caquot, A. "שָׁבַד." In *Theological Dictionary of the Old Testament*, edited by G. Johannes Botterweck and Helmer Ringgren, 128–31. Vol. 3. Translated by John T. Willis, et al. Grand Rapids: Eerdmans, 1978.

Cassuto, Umberto. *A Commentary on the Book of Exodus*. Translated by Israel Abrahams. Jerusalem: Magnes, 1967.

Clements, Ronald E. "טָחַשׁ." In *Theological Dictionary of the Old Testament*, edited by G. Johannes Botterweck, et al., 563–66. Vol. 14. Translated by Douglas W. Stott. Grand Rapids: Eerdmans, 2004.

Coffman, James Burton. *Commentary on Leviticus and Numbers: The Third and Fourth Books of Moses*. Abilene: ACU, 1987.

Cole, R. Dennis. *Numbers*. The New American Commentary. Nashville: Broadman & Holman, 2000.

Craigie, Peter C. *The Book of Deuteronomy*. Grand Rapids: Eerdmans, 1976.

Danby, Herbert, trans. *The Mishna: Translated from the Hebrew with Introduction and Brief Explanatory Notes*. Oxford: Oxford University Press, 1933.

Douglas, Mary. *In the Wilderness: The Doctrine of Defilement in the Book of Numbers*. Sheffield: JSOT, 1993.

———. *Leviticus As Literature*. Oxford: Oxford University Press, 1999.

———. *Purity and Danger: An Analysis of the Concepts of Pollution and Taboo*. London: Routledge and Kegan Paul, 1966.

Dozeman, Thomas B. *Commentary on Exodus*. Grand Rapids: Eerdmans, 2009.

Eberhart, Christian. "A Neglected Feature of Sacrifice in the Hebrew Bible: Remarks on the Burning Rite on the Altar." *Harvard Theological Review* 97.4 (2004) 485–93.

Edersheim, Alfred. *The Temple: Its Ministry and Services As They Were at the Time of Jesus Christ*. 1874. Reprint, Grand Rapids: Kregel, 1997.

Eichrodt, Walther. *Theology of the Old Testament*. Vol. 1. Translated by J. A. Baker. Philadelphia: Westminster, 1961.

Eising, H. "רָכַז." In *Theological Dictionary of the Old Testament*, edited by G. Johannes Botterweck and Helmer Ringgren, 64–82. Vol. 4. Translated by David E. Green. Grand Rapids: Eerdmans, 1980.

Elaide, Mircea. *The Sacred and the Profane*. New York: Harper & Row, 1957.

Fabry, Heins-Josef. "הִחָנְמ." In *Theological Dictionary of the Old Testament*, edited by G. Johannes Botterweck, et al., 407–21. Vol. 8. Translated by Douglas W. Stott. Grand Rapids: Eerdmans, 1997.

———. "וּבְרָק." In *Theological Dictionary of the Old Testament*, edited by G. Johannes Botterweck, et al., 152–58. Translated by David E Green. Vol. 13. Grand Rapids: Eerdmans, 2004.

Feliks, Yehuda. "The Incense of the Tabernacle." In *Pomegranates and Golden Bells: Studies in Biblical, Jewish, and Near Eastern Ritual, Law, and Literature in Honor of Jacob Milgrom*, edited by David P Wright, et al., 125–49. Winona Lake: Eisenbrauns, 1995.

Freedman, David N., and Jack Lundbom. "רוּד." In *Theological Dictionary of the Old Testament*, edited by G. Johannes Botterweck and Helmer Ringgren, 169–81. Vol. 3. Translated by John T. Willis, et al. Grand Rapids: Eerdmans, 1978.

Friedrich, Gerhard. "salpigx, salpizw, salpisthj." In *Theological Dictionary of the New Testament*, edited by Geoffrey W. Bromiley, 71–88. Vol. 7. Translated by Geoffrey W. Bromiley. Grand Rapids: Eerdmans, 1977.

Gane, Roy. "'Bread of Presence' and Creator-in-Residence." *Vetus Testamentum* 42 (1992) 179–203.

Gane, Roy, and Jacob Milgrom. "בָּרַךְ." In *Theological Dictionary of the Old Testament*, edited by G. Johannes Botterweck, et al., 135–48. Vol. 13. Translated by David E. Green. Grand Rapids: Eerdmans, 2004.

Gennep, Arnold van. *The Rites of Passage*. Translated by Monika B. Visedom and Gabriella L. Caffe. London: Routledge and Kegan Paul, 1960.

Gerstenberger, Erhard S. *Leviticus: A Commentary*. Translated by Douglas W. Stott. Louisville: Westminster John Knox, 1996.

Gilders, William K. *Blood Ritual in the Hebrew Bible: Meaning and Power*. Baltimore: Johns Hopkins University Press, 2004.

Gorman, Frank H. *Divine Presence and Community: A Commentary on the Book of Leviticus*. International Theological Commentary. Grand Rapids: Eerdmans, 1997.

———. *The Ideology of Ritual: Space, Time, and Status in the Priestly Theology*. Sheffield: JSOT, 1990.

Gray, George Buchanan. *A Critical and Exegetical Commentary on Numbers*. New York: Scribner's Sons, 1906.

Grimes, Ronald L. *Ritual Criticism: Case Studies in Its Practice, Essays on Its Theory*. Columbia: University of South Carolina Press, 1990.

Hachlili, Rachel. *The Menorah, the Ancient Seven-Armed Candelabrum: Origin, Form, and Significance*. Leiden: Brill, 2001.

Hamilton, Victor P. *Exodus: An Exegetical Commentary*. Grand Rapids: Baker Academic, 2011.

Hamp, Vinzenz. "אֵשׁ." In *Theological Dictionary of the Old Testament*, edited by G. Johannes Botterweck and Helmer Ringgren, 418–28. Vol. 1. Translated by John T. Willis. Grand Rapids: Eerdmans, 1974.

Haran, Menahem. "The Priestly Image of the Tabernacle." *Hebrew Union College Annual* 36 (1965) 191–226.

———. "The Shining of Moses' Face: A Case Study in Biblical and Ancient Near Eastern Iconography." In *In the Shelter of Elyon: Essays on Ancient Palestinian Life and Literature in Honor of G. W. Ahlstrom*, edited by W. Boyd Barrick and John R. Spencer, 159–73. Sheffield: JSOT, 1984.

———. *Temples and Temple Service in Ancient Israel*. 1985. Reprint, Winona Lake: Eisenbrauns, 1995.

———. "Uses of Incense in the Ancient Israelite Ritual." *Vetus Testamentum* 10 (1960) 113–29.

Harrison, Roland Kenneth. *Numbers*. The Wycliffe Exegetical Commentary. Chicago: Moody, 1990.

Hartley, John E. *Leviticus*. Word Biblical Commentary 4. Dallas: Word, 1992.

Hausmann, J. "חָלַס." In *Theological Dictionary of the Old Testament*, edited by G. Johannes Botterweck, et al., 258–65. Vol. 10. Translated by Douglas W. Stott. Grand Rapids: Eerdmans, 1999.

Houtman, C. "On the Function of the Holy Incense (Exodus XXX 34–38) and the Sacred Anointing Oil (Exodus XXX 22–23)." *Vetus Testamentum* 42 (1992) 458–65.

Hummel, Horace D. *Ezekiel 21–48*. Concordia Commentary. St. Louis: Concordia, 2007.

Jenson, Philip Peter. *Graded Holiness: A Key to the Priestly Conception of the World*. Sheffield: JSOT, 1992.

Kapelrud, A S. "לִילְךָ." In *Theological Dictionary of the Old Testament*, edited by G. Johannes Botterweck, et al., 182–85. Vol. 7. Translated by David E. Green. Grand Rapids: Eerdmans, 1995.

Kavanaugh, Aidan. *Elements of a Rite: A Handbook of Liturgical Style*. Collegeville: Pueblo, 1982.

Keil, C. F. *Commentary on the Old Testament in Ten Volumes*. Vol. 3. Edited by C. F. Keil and F. Delitzsch. Translated by Andrew Harper. Grand Rapids: Eerdmans, 1983.

Kellerman, D. "הלע." In *Theological Dictionary of the Old Testament*, edited by G. Johannes Botterweck, et al., 96–113. Vol. 11. Translated by David E. Green. Grand Rapids: Eerdmans, 2001.

Kiuchi, Nobuyoshi. *Leviticus*. Downers Grove, IL: InterVarsity, 2007.

———. *The Purification Offering in the Priestly Literature: Its Meaning and Function*. Sheffield: JSOT, 1987.

Kleinig, John W. "The Blood for Sprinkling: Atoning Blood in Leviticus and Hebrews." *Lutheran Theological Journal* 33 (1999) 124–35.

———. *The Glory and the Service: Worship in the Old Testament*. Fort Wayne: Concordia Theological Seminary Press, 2003.

———. *Leviticus*. Concordia Commentary. St. Louis: Concordia, 2003.

———. *The Lord's Song: The Basis, Function and Significance of Choral Music in Chronicles*. Sheffield: JSOT, 1993.

———. "Sharing in God's Holiness." *Lutheran Theological Review* 8 ½ (1996) 105–18.

———. "Witting or Unwitting Ritualists." *Lutheran Theological Journal* 22 (1988) 13–22.

Klingbeil, Gerald A. *Bridging the Gap: Ritual and Ritual Texts in the Bible*. Winona Lake: Eisenbrauns, 2007.

———. *A Comparative Study of the Ritual of Ordination as Found in Leviticus 8 and Emar 369*. Lewiston: Mellen, 1998.

Knohl, Israel. *The Sanctuary of Silence*. Minneapolis: Fortress, 1995.

Knoppers, Gary N. *1 Chronicles 10–29*. The Anchor Yale Bible. New Haven: Yale University Press, 2004.

Kornfeld, W. "שדק." In *Theological Dictionary of the Old Testament*, edited by G. Johannes Botterweck, et al., 521–26, 527–30, 543–44. Vol. 12. Translated by Douglas W. Stott. Grand Rapids: Eerdmans, 2003.

Lang, B. "רפכ." In *Theological Dictionary of the Old Testament*, edited by G. Johannes Botterweck, et al., 288–303. Vol. 12. Translated by David E. Green. Grand Rapids: Eerdmans, 1995.

Levine, Baruch A. "The Descriptive Tabernacle Texts of the Pentateuch." *Journal of the American Oriental Society* 85 (1965) 307–18.

———. *In the Presence of the Lord: A Study of Cult and Some Cultic Terms in Ancient Israel*. Leiden: Brill, 1974.

———. *Leviticus: The Traditional Hebrew Text with the New JPS Translation*. Philadelphia: Jewish Publication Society, 1989.

———. "Lpny YHWH—Phenomenology of the Open-Air-Altar in Biblical Israel." In *Biblical Archeology Today, 1990: Proceedings of the Second International Congress on Biblical Archeology*, edited by Avraham Biran, 196–205. Jerusalem: Keterpress Enterprises, 1993.

———. *Numbers 21–36: A New Translation with Introduction and Commentary*. Anchor Bible. New York: Doubleday, 2000.

Levine, Baruch A., and William W. Hallo. "Offerings to the Temple Gates at Ur." *Hebrew Union College Annual* 38 (1967) 17–58.
Maimonides. *The Code of Maimonides: The Book of Temple Service*. Edited by Julian Obermann. Translated by Mendell Lewitts. New Haven: Yale University Press, 1957.
Meyers, Carol L. *The Tabernacle Menorah: A Synthetic Study of a Symbol from the Biblical Cult*. Missoula: Scholars, 1976.
Milgrom, Jacob. *Leviticus: A Book of Ritual and Ethics*. Minneapolis: Fortress, 2004.
———. *Leviticus 1–16: A New Translation with Introduction and Commentary*. Anchor Bible 3. New York: Doubleday, 1991.
———. *Leviticus 17–22: A New Translation with Introduction and Commentary*. Anchor Bible 3. New York: Doubleday, 2000.
———. *Leviticus 23–27: A New Translation with Introduction and Commentary*. Anchor Bible 3. New York: Doubleday, 2001.
———. *Numbers*. JPS Torah Commentary. Philadelphia: Jewish Publication Society, 1990.
———. *Studies in Cultic Theology and Terminology*. Leiden: Brill, 1983.
———. *Studies in Levitical Terminology: The Encroacher and the Levite: The Term Aboda*. Berkley: University of California Press, 1970.
Milgrom, Jacob, et al. "תְּרוּמָשׁ." In *Theological Dictionary of the Old Testament*, edited by G. Johannes Botterweck, et al., 72–78. Vol. 11. Translated by David E. Green. Grand Rapids: Eerdmans, 1998.
Mitchell, Bill. "Leviticus 24:6: The Bread of the Presence: Rows or Piles?" *The Bible Translator* 33 (1982) 447–48.
Mitchell, Christopher W. *The Meaning of brk "To Bless" in the Old Testament*. Atlanta: Scholars, 1987.
Noth, Martin. *Leviticus: A Commentary*. Translated by J. E. Anderson. Philadelphia: Westminster, 1977.
Oeming, M. "רָכַשׁ." In *Theological Dictionary of the Old Testament*, edited by G. Johannes Botterweck, et al., 1–5. Vol. 15. Translated by David E. Green. Grand Rapids: Eerdmans, 2006.
Olyan, Saul M. *Rites and Rank: Hierarchy in Biblical Representations of Cult*. Princeton: Princeton University Press, 2000.
Porter, Joshua Roy. *Leviticus*. Cambridge Bible Commentary. Cambridge: Cambridge University Press, 1976.
Propp, William H. C. *Exodus 19–40*. Anchor Bible. New York: Doubleday, 2006.
Rad, Gerhard von. *Old Testament Theology* 1. Translated by D. M. G. Stalker. New York: Harper, 1962.
Rainey, Anson F. "The Order of Sacrifices in the Old Testament Ritual Texts." *Biblica* 51 (1970) 485–98.
Rattray, S., and Jacob Milgrom. "בָּרַךְ." In *Theological Dictionary of the Old Testament*, edited by G. Johannes Botterweck, et al., 148–52. Vol. 13. Translated by David E. Green. Grand Rapids: Eerdmans, 2004.
Ringgren, Helmer. "קָקַח." In *Theological Dictionary of the Old Testament*, edited by G. Johannes Botterweck and Helmer Ringgren, 139–47. Vol. 5. Translated by David E. Green. Grand Rapids: Eerdmans, 1986.

———. "שדק." In *Theological Dictionary of the Old Testament*, edited by G. Johannes Botterweck, et al., 527, 530–43, 544–45. Vol. 12. Translated by Douglas W. Stott. Grand Rapids: Eerdmans, 2003.

Rodriguez, Angel Manuel. *Substitution in the Hebrew Cultus*. Berrien Springs: Andrews University Press, 1979.

Sarna, Nahum M. *Exodus*. JPS Torah Commentary. Philadelphia: Jewish Publication Society, 1991.

———. *Exploring Exodus: The Origins of Biblical Israel*. New York: Schocken, 1986.

Schwartz, Baruch J. "The Prohibitions Concerning the 'Eating' of Blood in Leviticus 17." In *Priesthood and Cult in Ancient Israel*, edited by Gary A. Anderson and Saul M. Olyan, 34–66. Sheffield: JSOT, 1991.

Searle, Mark. "Ritual." In *Foundations in Ritual Studies: A Reader for Students of Christian Worship*, edited by Paul Bradshaw and John Melloh, 9–16. Grand Rapids: Baker Academics, 2007.

Sendrey, Alfred. *Music in Ancient Israel*. New York: Philosophical Library, 1969.

Sendrey, Alfred, and Mildred Norton. *David's Harp: The Story of Music in Biblical Times*. New York: New American Library, 1964.

Simian-Yofre, Horacio. "סִינַי." In *Theological Dictionary of the Old Testament*, edited by G. Johannes Botterweck, et al., 589–615. Vol. 11. Translated by David E. Green. Grand Rapids: Eerdmans, 2001.

Stainer, John. *The Music of the Bible: With Some Account of the Development of Modern Musical Instruments from Ancient Times*. 1914. Reprint, New York: De Capo, 1970.

Stuart, Douglas K. *Exodus*. New American Commentary 2. Nashville: Broadman and Holman, 2006.

Tigay, Jeffrey. *Deuteronomy*. JPS Torah Commentary. Philadelphia: Jewish Publication Society, 1996.

Trudinger, Peter L. *The Psalms of the Tamid Service: A Liturgical Text from the Second Temple*. Leiden: Brill, 2004.

Turner, Victor W. *The Ritual Process: Structure and Anti-Structure*. Ithaca: Cornell University Press, 1969.

———. "Social Dramas and Stories about Them." *Critical Inquiry* 7.4 (1980) 141–68.

Weinfeld, M. "הִתְנַמ." In *Theological Dictionary of the Old Testament*, edited by G. Johannes Botterweck, et al., 407–21. Vol. 8. Translated by Douglas W. Stott. Grand Rapids: Eerdmans, 1997.

Wellhausen, Julius. *Prolegomena to the History of Israel*. Edinburgh: Adam & Charles Black, 1885.

Wenham, Gordon J. *The Book of Leviticus*. New International Commentary on the Old Testament 3. London: Hodder and Stoughton, 1979.

Whiston, William. *The New Complete Works of Josephus*. Revised and expanded ed. Grand Rapids: Kregel, 1999.

Yarden, Leon. *The Tree of Light: A Study of the Menorah, the Seven-Branched Lampstand*. Ithica: Cornell University Press, 1971.

Zimmerli, Walther. *Ezekiel: A Commentary on the Book of the Prophet Ezekiel*. Hermeneia: A Critical and Historical Commentary on the Bible. Edited by Frank Moore Cross and Klaus Baltzer. Translated by Ronald E. Clements. Philadelphia: Fortress, 1983.

Index of Ancient Sources

OLD TESTAMENT

Genesis

1:14–16	138n300
17:16	165n405
22:10	106n148
24:1	165n405
27:10	165n405
32:21	116n187
37:31	106n148
48:18	92n91

Exodus

3:2	72, 138
4:16	167n415
7:1	167n415
12:5	94n99
12:6, 21	106n148
12:7–8	116n187
12:10	171
12:14, 17	4
12:14, 17, 42	4, 5
12:24	4
13:20–22	154
13:21–22	72, 83, 138
14:18–21, 29, 31, 53	116n187
14:19–20	79n47
15:15, 30	116n187
16:9	32n25
16:16–18, 20, 27, 30	116n187
16:32–33	4
16:33	194
19:9–18	83
19:11–20	72
19:12–24	84
19:16–25	70n5
19:17	84n60
19:18	70n5
19:20	84n60
19:21, 24	84n60
19:24	84
20:7	166, 167
20:11	157n377
20:18–21	70n5
20:21	84n60
20:24	164, 167
20:26	152n356
22:7	15
22:31	195n61
23:12	157n377
23:20	165n405
23:25	165n405
24:4	84, 84n60
24:11	96n109
24:12–17	1
24:15–18	83, 84n60
24:17	155n368
24:18—31:18	1
25:2, 6	126
25:6	130n245, 131n252
25:8	183, 187
25:13–15, 27–28	98n124
25:21–37	128n235
25:22	84n60, 189n36
25:23	46n60, 134
25:24	134n280
25:26	123
25:26–28	134

Exodus (continued)

25:29	46n60, 47, 47n64, 51n75, 87, 121n200, 124n217, 129n240, 129n241, 132n259, 136, 147
25–30	3
25:30	46, 69n2, 123, 123n214, 124n216, 128, 136, 139n303
25:31	45n56
25:32–33	135
25:34–36	135
25:37	123
25:37–38	135, 135n285
25:38	46n59
25:39	135
26:1–30, 36–37	195
26:31–33	195
26:33	151n350
26:33, 34	151n350
26:35–36	128n234
26:36	98n121, 196n66
27:1	149n345
27:1–8	78, 78n41
27:3	109n162
27:6–7	98n124
27:9–18	195
27:16	98n121, 196n66
27:20	69n2, 122n207, 123n212, 131
27:20–21	122, 123, 123n210, 125, 136
27:21	4, 45, 122n208, 127, 194
28	48, 71n8, 145n327
28:1	49n67, 86n66, 126n225
28:1–2	89
28:2	132n260
28:2–38	126
28:4	132
28:6–12	124
28:6–14	133
28:7–12	140
28:9–12, 21, 29	139n303
28:9–13	149
28:12	48
28:12, 15, 29–30, 35, 38	132n262
28:12, 29, 30, 35, 38	125n221
28:12, 29–30	141n310
28:12, 29–30, 35	48
28:12, 29–30, 35, 38	129n243, 194
28:13–29	124
28:15	140n307
28:15–30	133, 140
28:16–17	37
28:29, 30, 38	125n221
28:29, 35	151n350
28:29–30	48
28:29–30, 38	69n2
28:30	124, 140n307
28:30, 38	105n141
28:31–35	124, 133, 149
28:33–35	48, 155
28:35	140, 141n310, 155n365
28:35, 43	56n89, 56n91
28:36	150n346
28:36–38	48, 124, 132, 140, 154
28:38	100n125, 116n185, 146n330, 149n344, 154n361, 157, 180, 183n19, 184n20
28:39	100n127, 133
28:39–43	77
28:40	132n260
28:42–43	28, 43, 52
28:43	4, 5, 48, 49n67, 53n81, 71, 71n8, 74, 129, 136, 142n312, 151n350, 152
29	38, 39, 93, 143n314, 178, 179n6
29:1–37	34, 35
29:3–4, 8, 10	86n66
29:4, 10–11	32
29:4–9	29, 29n15
29:5–9, 29–30	62
29:6	150n346
29:9	4, 5
29:10, 15, 19	93n93
29:11, 16, 20	106n148
29:12, 16, 20	110n162
29:15–16	103
29:16	37
29:16–17	38
29:17	39, 104
29:18, 25, 41	169n424
29:21	119n193
29:25	50n70
29:28	4, 169n422
29:30	56n89, 56n91
29–30	149
29:30	151n350
29:31–32	173

29:31–34	62	30:10, 31	4
29:33, 35–37	117	30:12–16	116n187
29:33, 36–37	116n187	30:17–21	70, 70n7, 71n7, 187n32
29:34	172	30:18	137
29:36	117	30:18–21	77, 129, 142n312
29:37	74n22, 78n40, 98n124, 139n304, 175n449	30:19–20	47, 48, 49n67
29:38	33, 94n99, 143n315	30:20	28n13, 43, 52, 56n89, 56n91, 169n424
29:38, 42	69n2	30:20–21	28, 29n14
29:38–39	50, 87n70, 110, 189	30:21	4
29:38–39, 41	142	30:22–29	98n124, 156, 187
29:38–40	152	30:22–38	135n285
29:38–41	34, 94	30:24	151n350
29:38–42	1, 50n69, 51, 152n353, 172	30:26–29	186
29:38–43	55	30:28–29	110n163
29:38–44	156n371, 156n372	30:29	139n304, 174, 175n449
29:39	78n45, 150	30:30–21	74
29:40	51n74, 95, 95n107, 131, 143n319	30:34–36	129, 130
		30:35	130
29:40–41	34n33, 50, 51, 95, 143, 143n317	30:36	47, 124n217, 138, 139n304, 156, 156n371
29:41	155, 157, 157n378	31:11	122, 130n245, 151n350
29:42	4, 54, 54n84, 92n90, 97, 98n123, 142n313, 143	31:13	184
		31:13, 16	4, 5
29:42–43	55, 189n36	32:30	116n187
29:42–44	90	34:6–7	184
29:43	54n84, 154, 155, 155n369	34:9	115n183
29:43, 45	143	34:25	106n148
29:43–44	155	34:29–35	165n406
29:43–46	183	35:8, 14, 28	123, 131n252
29:44	145, 146n330, 156	35:8, 15, 28	130n245
29:45–46	157, 178, 187	35:12–13, 15–16	98n124
30:1	133	35:13	123n215
30:1, 9, 35–37	122	35:14	123
30:1–9	122n203	35:15	122
30:2	134	35:19	151n350
30:4–5	98n124, 134	35:24–25	134
30:6	136n295	36:1, 3–4, 6	151n350
30:6, 36	136, 189n36	36:8–34, 37–38	195
30:7	130n245, 145n327	36:35–36	195
30:7–8	1, 45, 49n67, 122, 122n208, 125, 127, 135, 136, 146n333	37:4–5, 14–15, 27–28	98n124
		37:16	51n75, 124n217, 129n240, 129n241, 136, 147
30:7–9	130, 131n257		
30:8	4, 45, 69n2, 121n201, 194	37:25–29	122
30:8, 21	4	37:29	130n245, 135n285
30:9	47n64, 131n257, 133n277, 152, 152n352	38:1–7	78n41
		38:3	109n162
30:10	5, 184n20	38:5–7	98n124

Exodus (continued)

38:8	97
38:9–18	195
38:24–27	151n350
39:1, 41	151n350
39:22–26	133
39:23	141n311
39:27, 29	133
39:30	150n346
39:35, 39	98n124
39:36	123n215
39:37	123, 131n252
39:38	122, 130n245
40:1–35	3
40:12, 14	86n66
40:15	4
40:20	98n124
40:20–28	136
40:22	137
40:22–23	46
40:22–28	128n234
40:23	123n215
40:23, 25	194
40:24	137
40:25	123
40:26	136
40:26–27	122, 122n203
40:26–29	43
40:27	130n245, 146n333
40:30	137
40:30–32	129
40:31–32	28, 28n13
40:32	28n13, 43
40:34	83n57
40:34–37	83
40:34–38	1
40:38	83

Leviticus

1	37n37, 39, 40, 40n45, 40n46, 71n10
1:1	1
1:1–2	82n55
1:1–17	2, 34
1–2	35, 51
1:2	78n40
1:2–3, 5, 10, 13–15	86n66
1:2–6, 9–14	179
1:2–13	87n69
1:3	32, 100n125, 142n313, 157n373
1:3, 10	87n71
1:3–4	93, 100
1:3–9	39n43
1:3–13	34
1:4	34, 89, 90, 92n91, 94n99, 100n126, 116n187, 157n374
1:5	39, 87n71, 97, 97n121, 107, 187n32
1:5, 8, 11	161n390
1:5, 11	37, 38n40, 105, 106n148, 106n149, 110n162, 111, 194
1:5–6	104, 108n154
1:5–6, 9, 11–13	106
1:6	39, 40n45
1:7	74n22, 78
1:7, 12	26, 71n10
1:9, 13	104
1:9, 13, 17	169n424
1:10	33n29
1:10–11	103
1:10–13	173
1:11	38n40, 97n121, 98n122, 106, 111, 152n356
1:12, 17	50
1:13	98n122
1:13, 17	158n378
1:14–17	93n92
1:15	32n25
1:16	27n5, 31n23, 80, 80n54, 152n356, 173
2	34, 168n420
2:1, 4, 8, 11–14	86n66
2:1, 15	87
2:1–2	124n218, 143, 179
2:1–16	93n92, 143n317
2:2, 9, 12	158n378
2:2, 9, 16	131n257
2:2, 16	95
2:2–3, 9–11, 16	169n424
2:4	172
2:4–7	60, 172
2:5	96n111
2:8	32n25, 98n124
2:10	168n418

2:11	60n106, 148n339, 152	5:25 [6:6]	69n2
2:13	40, 87, 95, 104, 104n140, 108n158, 109n161	5:26 [6:7]	116n187, 194
		6	28
3:1, 3, 6–7, 9, 12, 14	86n66	6:0–10 [16–17]	171
3:1, 7, 12	32n25, 194	6:1, 7 [8, 14]	158n378
3:1–2, 6–8, 12–15	179	6:1 [8]	72
3:1–2, 7–8, 12–13	93	6:1 [8]—7:38	18
3:2	187n32	6:1–6 [8–13]	26, 27, 31, 69, 70n7
3:2, 8, 13	37, 38n40, 106n148, 110n162	6:1–11 [8–18]	172
3:3, 5, 9, 11, 14, 16	169n424	6:1–16 [8–23]	3, 35, 51
3:5	26n3, 50	6:2, 5 [9, 12]	150
3:5, 16	158n378	6:2, 5–6 [9, 12–13]	69, 182n16
3:11	175n453	6:2, 7, 13 [9, 14, 20]	146n330
3:11, 16	175n453	6:2, 7, 13, 15 [9, 14, 20, 22]	145
3:17	4, 5	6:2 [9]	72, 73, 79n49
4:1–21	40n46	6:3, 5 [10, 12]	73
4:3, 5, 16	88n76	6:3 [10]	71, 75
4:3, 14	86n66	6:3–4 [10–11]	28, 79
4:3–5, 14–16, 22–25, 28–30, 32–34	93	6:4 [11]	60n104, 61, 71, 76, 80, 196
4:4, 15, 24	194	6:5 [12]	50, 71, 71n10, 78, 145n329
4:4, 15, 24, 29, 33	106n148	6:6 [13]	69n2, 78
4:5–7, 16–18, 25, 30, 34	110n162	6:7 [14]	32n25, 87, 88, 89, 90, 96n111
4:6	38n40, 151n350	6:7 [14], 13–14 [20–21]	86n66
4:6–7, 17–18	194	6:7–8, 12–15 [14–15], 19–22	92
4:7	130n245	6:7–8 [14–15]	87n69, 145n329
4:7, 18	97	6:7–11 [14–18]	143n317, 168, 168n420, 170
4:7, 18, 25, 30, 34	38n40	6:7–16 [14–23]	91n86, 93n92
4:12	80n54, 196	6:8 [15]	50, 87, 95, 143, 145n328
4:12, 21	146n333	6:8–9 [15–16]	60
4:20, 26, 31, 35	115n183, 116n187	6:9, 19 [16, 26]	173
4:27–35	179	6:9 [16]	60, 60n107, 60n108, 88n76, 143, 171, 173
4:30	187n32	6:9–10 [16–17]	60, 172
4:31	158n378	6:9–11 [16–18]	172
4:35	169n424	6:10 [17]	168n418, 169, 171, 175n452
5:6, 10, 13, 16, 18	116n187	6:10–11 [17–18]	169n424, 170, 174
5:7–10	93n92	6:11, 15 [18, 22]	4
5:8	86n66	6:11 [18]	4, 106n148, 169, 169n422, 175n452
5:9	110n162	6:12–13 [19–20]	35n34
5:10, 13, 16, 18, 26	115n183	6:12–15 [19–22]	88, 89
5:11–13	93n92	6:12–16 [19–23]	51, 96, 97n119
5:12	169n424	6:13 [20]	87n69, 88n76, 89, 96, 96n114, 144n321
5:13	168n418		
5:14–19	93n92		
5:15	151n350		
5:22 [6:3]	173		

Leviticus (continued)

6:13–14 [20–21]	144
6:14 [21]	91, 91n86, 96, 144
6:15 [22]	4, 100n128, 126n225, 144n324, 145, 169n422
6:15–16 [22–23]	96, 144
6:16, 23 [23, 30]	151n350
6:16 [23]	40n46
6:18 [25]	194
6:19 [26]	173n442
6:20 [27]	151n350, 175n449
6:23 [30]	110n162, 156n371
7:1–7	93n92
7:2	106n148, 187n32
7:2, 14	110n162
7:3, 8–9, 11–14, 16, 18, 25, 29, 33, 35, 38	86n66
7:5, 25, 30, 35	169n424
7:6	151n350, 168n418, 170n428, 173n442
7:8	40, 104n138
7:9	96n111, 172
7:15–18	171
7:19	186
7:19–21	183n19
7:30	86n66, 194
7:33	39n44
7:34	4, 103n134, 169n422
7:36	4, 5
8	29n15, 35, 38, 171n431, 178, 179n6
8:1–4	32
8:6, 13, 18, 22, 24	86n66
8:6–13	29
8:7–13, 30	62
8–9	3, 37n37, 39, 93
8:9	150n346
8:12	88n76, 154n360
8:14–15, 18–19, 22–23	93
8:15, 19, 23	106n148
8:15, 19, 24	110n162
8:15, 34	117
8:19	37, 38n40, 103, 105
8:19–21	38
8:20, 21	104
8:21, 28	158n378, 169n424
8:26–27, 29	194
8:28	50n70
8:30	38n40, 75n28, 88n76, 119n193
8:31	173, 173n447
8:31–32	62, 172
9	37n37, 42n51, 56n88, 82, 89n77, 117
9:2, 4, 21	194
9:2, 9, 15–17	86n66
9:2–6	35
9:4	72n15
9:5	32, 32n25, 195
9:6	72n15
9:7	117
9:8, 12, 15, 18	106n148
9:8–9, 12, 15–16	117
9:9	39n44
9:9, 12, 18	110n162
9:12	105
9:12, 16	103
9:12–14	38
9:14, 17	50n70
9:14, 30	104
9:15	117, 117n190
9:16	34
9:16–17	35
9:18	37, 38n40
9:22	161n392
9:22, 24	160n387
9:22–23	55, 160
9:22–24	42
9:23	84
9:23–24	154n362, 166, 181, 182n16
9:24	69–70, 83, 83n57, 138, 161, 168
10	89n77
10:1	76n33, 130n249
10:1, 19	86n66
10:1–2	30, 70
10:1–2, 15, 17, 19	194
10:1–16	126n225
10:3	32n25
10:4, 17–18	151n350
10:6	115n179
10:9	4, 5
10:10	74n26, 119, 186
10:12	171, 173
10:12–13	60n108, 151, 168, 173
10:12–13, 15	169n424

10:13–15	169n422	16:21	93n93, 93n95
10:14	196	16:23–24	29
10:15	4	16:24	53n81, 118n192, 148
10:16	146n333	16:24, 34	118
10:17	103n134, 116n185, 116n187	16:27–28	146n333
10:17–18	173n442	16:29, 31, 34	4, 5
10:18	151n350	16:29, 34	5
11:32, 36, 47	186	16:29—17:11	118n191
12:7	32n25, 86n66, 194	16:29–31	118n191
13–15	126n225	16:30	118
13:59	186	16:31	118n191
14:1–9	187n32	16:32	118n191
14:5–6, 13, 19, 25, 50–51	106n148	16:34a	118n191
14:10–32	187n32	16:34b	118n191
14:11, 12, 16, 18, 23–24, 27, 29, 31	194	17	118n191
14:12	86n66	17:1	118n191
14:13	151n350	17:1–2, 10, 13, 15	105n143
14:14–17	117n188	17:1–9	112n172
14:40, 41, 45	196	17:1–11	103
14:57	186	17:2	105, 105n145, 106n145, 118n191
15:1–27	187n32	17:3	106n148
15:8	186	17:4	86n66, 118n191
15:14–15, 30	194	17:4–6	97
15:28–33	187n32	17:5	118n191
15:31	119, 195n61	17:5, 6	105n142
16	118, 118n191	17:6	158n378
16:1, 7, 10, 18, 30	194	17:6, 11	110n162, 112n172
16:2	84n60, 195	17:7	4, 5, 118n191
16:2–3, 16–17, 20, 23, 27, 33	151n350	17:8	103n133, 113n173
16:4	29	17:10	113n173
16:4, 24	74, 148n342	17:11	37n38, 103n132, 103n133, 103n134, 103n135, 103n136, 105, 106, 107, 107n152, 110, 111, 113, 113n173, 114, 114n175, 116n187, 117, 118n191, 183, 187n32, 190
16:5–6, 11, 17, 24	118n192		
16:6, 9, 11, 20	86n66		
16:6, 11, 15, 24, 30, 33–34	184n20		
16:10, 21–22, 26	196		
16:11, 15	106n148	17:11, 14	113n174
16:12	30, 76n33, 124n217, 130n245	17:15	186
16:12–15	195n66	19:5	100n125
16:13	194	19:13, 20	183n19
16:14	38n40	19:22	115n183, 116n187, 194
16:14–15, 18	110n162	19:26–28	15
16:15–19	118, 119n193	20:3	151n350, 166, 186
16:16, 18	118n192	20:6	15
16:16, 18–20	184n20	20:8	184
16:19	156n371	20:25	186
16:20–22	90	21	126n225

Leviticus (continued)

21:1—22:16	170, 180n10
21:6	186
21:6, 8, 17, 21	86n66
21:6, 8, 17, 21–22	75n31, 175n453
21:6, 21	169n424, 175n453
21:8, 15, 23	184
21:16–23	170, 170n428
21:17	4, 5
21:17–25	33n29
21–22	75
21:23	151n350
22:2, 15, 32	186
22:2, 32	166
22:3	4, 5
22:4	186
22:7, 11, 13	175n453
22:9, 16, 32	184
22:17–25	91n86, 91n87, 95n101
22:17–30	100n125
22:18	91n87, 105n145
22:18, 20–22, 24–25	86n66
22:19–20	100n125
22:19–21, 29	100n125
22:21, 29	100n125
22:22, 27	169n424
22:25	75n31, 175n453
22:28	106n148
23	57, 189n36, 190
23:4, 37, 44	189n36
23:8, 16, 18, 25, 27, 36–37	86n66
23:11	100n125
23:11, 20, 28, 40	194
23:13, 18	158n378
23:13, 18, 25, 27, 36–37	169n424
23:13, 18, 37	51n76
23:14	5
23:14, 21	5
23:14, 21, 31, 41	4
23:14, 21, 31, 41, 43	4
23:21	5
23:31	5
23:41	5
23:41, 43	5
24	13n18
24:1–4	127, 136
24:1–9	3
24:2	123, 131, 138n300
24:2–3	123n210
24:2–4	122n207, 123
24:2–4, 8	69n2
24:2–8	126
24:3	4, 45, 138n300, 145n327
24:3–4	125
24:3–4, 6, 8	194
24:4	45, 45n56
24:5–7	128
24:5–9	46, 46n60, 128, 131, 136, 139n303, 141
24:6	134n280
24:6–7	124
24:7	46, 47n61, 131n257
24:7, 9	169n424
24:8	123, 123n214, 126
24:9	4, 151n350, 168n418, 169n422, 173n442
24:14	93n93, 93n95
24:30	5
27:3, 25	151n350
27:9, 11	86n66
30–33	107n151

Numbers

1:51	98n124, 180
1:53	115n179, 180
3:2–4	126n225
3:4	76n33, 194
3:4, 6	86n66
3:6–7, 9	179
3:7–8, 41, 44, 11–12	179
3:10	100n127
3:10, 38	98n124, 180–81
3:23, 29, 35, 38	180
3:28, 31–32, 47, 50	151n350
3:38	128n234
4:1–20	196n66
4:6, 8, 11, 14	98n124
4:7	51n75, 123, 123n214, 123n216, 124n217, 129n241, 134n284, 147
4:9, 16	123
4:12, 15	151n350
4:14	109n162
4:16	130n245, 144n323, 151n350
4:20	84n60

5:1–4	195n61	10:9–10	194
5:8	116n187	10:10	57, 57n93, 57n95, 57n96,
5:9, 16, 25	86n66		160n386, 163, 163n399
5:16, 18, 25, 30	194	10:11–36	161n393
5:25	32n25	11:20	32n25
6:11	116n187	11:22	106n148
6:14, 16	86n66	14:14	32n25
6:16	32n25	14:16	106n148
6:16, 20	194	14:19–20	115n183
6:22, 27	54n83	14:37	195
6:22–27	3, 54, 181	15	95n108
6:23	160	15:2–7	87
6:24	165	15:3, 7, 10, 13–14, 24	158n378
6:24–26	55n86, 55n87	15:3, 13–14, 25	169n424
6:24–27	159	15:3–10	151n349
6:25	161n392, 165	15:4, 7, 9–10, 13, 27, 33	86n66
6:25, 26	166n414	15:5	151n349
6:26	165	15:5, 7, 10, 24	51n76–52n76
6:27	160, 164, 164n403	15:10	148n339, 169n424
7	46n61	15:14, 15	4
7:2–3, 10–12, 18–19	86n66	15:14–15, 21, 23, 38	4
7:3	195	15:15	4
7:12–83	43	15:15, 25, 28	194
7:13, 19, 25, 31, 37, 43, 49, 55, 61,		15:25, 28	116n187
67, 73, 79, 84, 85	109n162	15:25–26, 28	115n183
7:13, 19, 25, 31, 37, 43, 49, 55, 61,		16 and 17	179n4
67, 73, 79, 85–86	151n350	16:1–34	179
7:14, 20, 26, 32, 38, 44, 50, 56, 62,		16:5, 9–10, 17, 35	86n66
68, 74, 80, 84, 86	124n217,	16:6–35	130n249
	129n240	16:7, 16–17, 38, 40	194
7:89	82n55, 84n60	16:17	32n25
7:89—8:4	138n300	16:22	115n179
8:2–3	123, 125	16:40	32n25, 146n333
8:5–21	179n6	16:41–50	179
8:9–10	86n66	16:46	76n33
8:10, 12	93n93	16:46–47	183n19
8:10–11, 14–19	179	16:46–50	130n249
8:10–11, 21	194	17:3–4	86n66
8:12, 21	116n187	17:4	189n36
8:19	151n350, 180	17:7	194
8:22	179	17:11	115n179
8:24–26	179n5	17:11–12	116n187
9:7, 13	86n66	17:13	98n124
9:10	4, 5	18	178
9:15–23	161n393	18:1	116n185
10:1–10	3, 57, 161n393	18:1–5	180
10:2	162	18:1–7	179
10:8	4, 5, 57n94, 161	18:2, 15	86n66

Numbers (continued)

18:2–4, 6	179
18:3, 5, 16	151n350
18:3–7	98n124
18:5	115n179
18:5, 7	180
18:6	179
18:7	181
18:8	4
18:8, 11, 19	169n422
18:8, 11–12, 19	103n134
18:11, 19	4
18:17	110n162, 158n378, 169n424
18:19	40n47, 104n140, 194
18:20	169n421
18:22–23	179, 179n4
18:23	4, 5, 180
19	187n32
19:3	106n148
19:4	110n162, 187n32
19:5–6, 8	146n333
19:9	196
19:10, 21	5
19:19	186
20:3	195
20:25–28	126n225
26:53, 55–56	169n421
26:61	76n33, 86n66, 194
27:5	86n66
27:5, 21	194
27:18, 23	93n93
27:23	93n95
28:1–2	86, 87, 90
28:1–3	90
28:1–8	2, 3, 34, 51, 57n96, 88, 92
28:2	75n31, 78n40, 80n52, 86n68, 92n90, 97, 101, 160n386
28:2, 6, 8	155
28:2, 24	175n453
28:2–3	87n69, 90, 93
28:2–3, 6, 8, 13, 19, 24	169n424
28:2–8	87n69
28:3	86n68, 87, 88, 96, 96n114
28:3, 6	69n2
28:3, 11, 19, 26–27	86n66
28:3–4	33, 50, 94, 110, 150
28:3–7	91n86
28:3–8	50n69, 142
28:4	75n31
28:4–8	87
28:5	95
28:5, 8	50, 143, 143n317
28:6, 8, 13, 24, 27	158n378
28:7	34n33, 51n74, 95, 96n108, 131, 151, 151n350, 151n351, 152
28:7–8	51, 143
28:7–10	95
28:9, 12–14, 30–21, 28–29, 31	52n76
28:9–39	2
28–29	57, 57n96, 86, 86n67, 86n68, 189n36, 190
29:2, 6, 8, 13, 36	158n378
29:3, 4, 9–10, 14–15, 18, 21, 24, 27, 30, 33, 37	52n76
29:6, 13, 36	169n424
29:8, 13, 36	86n66
29:39	57n96
30:6, 9, 13	115n183
31:6	151n350
31:36	169n421
31:50	86n66
31:50, 54	194
32:20–22, 27, 29, 32	195
35:25, 28	140n305
35:29	3n5
35:31–33	116n187

Deuteronomy

	57
1:34	115n179
1:45	195
4:10	195
4:19	169n421
5:11	167
5:15	157n377
6:25	195
7:13	165n405
9:3	155n368
9:7–8, 19, 22	115n179
10:6	126n225
10:8	56, 56n89, 56n90, 56n91, 161n388, 194
10:9	169n421
10:17	154

12:1–28	103n136
12:2–5	164n402
12:3, 5, 11, 21	164
12:5, 21	166n412
12:7, 12, 18	195
12:12	169n421
12:15, 22	186
12:20–27	112n172
12:23	113n174
12:27	103n136, 110n162, 112n172
13:16	144n322
14:23, 24	164
14:23, 26	195
14:24	165n405
14:27, 29	169n421
15:20	195
15:22	186
16:11	195
16:15	165n405
18:1	169n424
18:1, 8	169n421
18:7	194
18:9–11	15
19:17	195
21:5	56, 56n89, 56n90, 56n91, 161n388
21:8	116n187
23:14	195, 195n65
24:4, 13	195
26:2	164
26:5, 10, 13	194
27:7	194
29:10, 14	195
29:19	115n183
29:26	169n421
29:27	115n179
32:9	169n421
33:8	122n204
33:10	43, 122, 122n204, 144n322
34:9	93n93, 93n95

Joshua

18:1	6
18:10	6
19:51	6
23:1, 25–26	6
24:17	165n405

Judges

16:29	92n91
18:31	6
21:19	6

1 Samuel

1:3	6
2:13–17	6
2:28	122, 122n205
3:3	123
4:1–22	83n57
7:9	144n322
21:6	123n215
30:23	165n405

2 Samuel

7:1–16	83n57

1 Kings

3:4	6
4:22	95n103
7:48	123n215
8:1–13, 62–66	6
8:64	179n4
9:3	166n412
11:36	166n412
12:27	6
14:21	166n412
18:22–39	70n3

2 Kings

18:21	92n91
21:4, 7	166n412

1 Chronicles

	123n211
6:48–49	56n90
6:49	6, 42, 122, 183n19
9:31	92n89
9:32	123n215
16	58n97
16:6	58

1 Chronicles (continued)

16:39	6
16:39–40	6
16:40	58
16:42	58, 58n98
21:29	6
22:19	6
23	56n90
23:13	56, 56n89, 56n91, 57, 122, 160n387
23:29	92n89, 96n111, 123n215
25:1–3	56n90
25:1–6	56n90
28:16	123n215
28:17	147
29:22	96n109

2 Chronicles

	44n53, 123n211
1:3–6, 13	6
2:3	123n215
2:4	6, 44, 122
3:1	6
4:6	110n163
4:9	179n4
4:19	123n215
4:20	123
5:7–14	6
6:1	83n57
6:14	179n4
6:20	166n412
7:1–3	83n57
7:1–11	6
7:7	179n4
7:12	83n57
12:13	166n412
13:11	42, 122, 123
20:5	179n4
26:18	122
29:6–9	75n30
29:7	44, 122
29:16	179n4
29:18	123n215
29:25	179n4
29:27	123
29:28	59n102
29:34	40n45, 179n5
29:35	6
30:1, 15	6
30:17	179n5
33:7	166n412
35:11	40n45

Ezra

1:2–11	6
3:2–6	6
6:9	40n47, 110n164
6:22	6
7:22	40n47, 110n164

Nehemiah

3:31	33n28, 91n88
10:28–39	6
10:29	6
10:33	123n215, 144n323
10:34	27n9
10:35	74n22
10:35 [34]	78n40
13:31	27n9, 74n22

Job

1:10	165n405
14:4	186
42:12	165n405

Psalms

19:8	138n300
19:15	100n125
23:4	79n47
50:8–13	154
50:9–13	80n52
51:19	144n322
90:8	138n300
91:5	79n47
104:20	79n47
107:10	79n47
141:2	44

Ecclesiastes

9:2	186

Isaiah

5:17	94n99
6:3	175n452
6:4	139n301
6:6	46n59
9:2	79n47
10:17	70n5
19:6	70n5
25:6–8	96n109
30:27, 33	70n5
31:9	70n5
33:14	70n5
56:7	100n125
60:2	79n47

Jeremiah

6:20	100n125
19:14	179n4
23:1–4	94n99
26:2	179n4
36:10	179n4

Ezekiel

4:3	96n111
10:5	179n4
16:13, 19	95n103
20:12	184
20:39	186
22:26	186
34:1–31	94n99
37:28	184
40:17, 20, 31, 34, 37	179n4
40:39–42	111n168
42 and 44	61n113
42:1, 3, 7–9, 14	179n4
42:1–14	173n447
42:13	62
42:13–14	62
42:14	61, 62, 76n35, 171n432
42:20	186
43:15	79n49
43:24	41, 109n161, 110n164
44:16	75n31
44:19	61, 76n35, 179n4
44:23	119n194, 186
46:19–20	173n447
46:20–22	179n4

Daniel

8:11–13	4n8, 142n314
11:31	4n8, 142n314
12:1	142n314
12:11	4n8

Hosea

4:16	94n99

Joel

2:17	173n447

Amos

2:7	186
5:19	92n91

Micah

3:3	40n45

Malachi

1:7, 12	80n51

APOCRYPHA

1 Maccabees

1:22	123n215
4:49–50	122
4:50	123
4:51	123n215

2 Maccabees

1:8	123, 123n215
10:3	123, 123n215

Sirach

26:17	123
50	58

Sirach (continued)

50:1–11	155
50:5–11	139n302
50:5–21	6, 44, 57
50:6–10	139n301
50:13–21	59
50:15	152n354
50:19–23	160n387
50:20	54n83

ANCIENT JEWISH WRITERS

Josephus

Jewish Antiquities

3:227	41n47

Philo

Laws

1:171	42

RABBINIC WORKS

Maimonides

Code

6:1–6	7

Mishnah

	8

Tamid

	7

1–2	28, 30, 78n44
1:3	90n80
1:4	30, 45n57
2:3	76n34
2:3–5	74n22
2:5	30
3:1, 6	45n57
3:1, 9	126n226
3:2	78n44
3:4	33n30, 91n88
4:1	37n36, 37n39
4:2	40n45, 110n163
4:3	40n47, 41, 52, 104n140
5:2, 4	126n226
5:5	31
5:6—7:3	44
6:1	76n33, 123
6:1–3	122, 126n226
7:2	54n83, 55n85, 59, 161n388, 166n410
7:3	7, 51n73, 52, 58, 146n331

Yoma

	29n17
1:8—2:2	28n10
3:2–4	30n19
3:3	42

Zebahim

5:4	36n36
12:3–4	40n46

NEW TESTAMENT

Revelation

4:8	175n452

Index of Subjects

Aaron
  authority of, 89n77
  bearing the judgment for all, 105n141
  burning incense in his fire pan in the camp, 130n249
  as first high priest, 126n223
  Moses as God to, 167n415
  performing the blood rite in the inaugural service, 105
  speaking the benediction, 161n389
Aaron and his sons
  blessing the Israelites, 160
  entering into the tent of meeting, 49n67
  maintaining the fire on the altar, 73
  ordination of as priests, 29
  referring to the high priest and the regular priests, 88n76, 145n326
Aaronic benediction. *See* benediction
Abihu. *See* Nadab and Abihu
acceptance, 100n125, 100n126
alcoholic beverages from vine fruits, 152
almond tree, imagery of, 135n288
altar for burnt offering. *See also* incense altar
  blood cleansing, 118
  blood splashed on all sides of, 111
  called the holy place, 152
  constructed of acacia wood overlaid with bronze, 78n41
  correlating with the base of Mount Sinai, 83–84
  east side of, 80, 98
  functions at the tabernacle, 79
  hidden from everyone's sight when in transit, 196n66
  hiding from Israel's view all of the ornate vestments of the high priest except the plate on his turban, 149n345
  located in the courtyard at the entrance to the tent of meeting, 84, 151
  as the most important piece of furniture at the sanctuary, 111n171–12n171
  north side of, 111
  priests sounding the trumpets over, 163
  removing lit coals from, 76
  as the table of the LORD, 80n51
  utensils associated with, 78
animal blood. *See* blood
anthropological rituals analysts, influence of, 12
anthropological system, 186, 188, 190
anthropologists, developed ritual analysis, 19n26
appeasement payment, atonement as, 115n180
appointed times, 57–58, 86, 92n90, 160n386, 189n36
Ark of the Covenant, 12, 83n57, 121, 138n300
ash heap, 77n39, 80, 80n54
ashes
  holiness of, 77n36

224   Index of Subjects

ashes *(continued)*
  removal from the altar, 26, 27, 27n6, 28, 71, 75, 78n44
  as a significant material, 77
  washing before clearing, 29n14
atonement. *See also* Day of Atonement
  on the altar for the burnt offering, 111–12, 114n176, 183
  as an appeasement payment, 115n180
  aspects of, 116n187
  daily appeasing God's wrath, 115n179
  expiating the community of Israel, 115
  Hebrew words for, 113n175–14n175
  LORD establishing the practice of, 103n135
  purifying the altar for burnt offering, 117
  reconciliatory aspect of, 115n180
  resulting from offerings, 14
  rite of, 44n55, 114, 117
  as a ritual purification, 117
  in three simultaneous ways, 114
  using the blood for, 107n153
  as the way the LORD cleanses his people, 183
atoning power, in the altar, not in the blood, 113n174
authority, of regular priests tied to the high priest, 73n18

banking, a fire, 78n42
barriers, established to safeguard holiness, 193
"beaten pure olive oil," 131, 131n252
beer, forbidden on the altar, 95n108
before the LORD, designating the area to the east side of the altar, 98n123
bells. *See* golden bells
benediction
  accomplishing what the LORD intends, 159n380
  announcing that the LORD is present, 166
  in front of the altar, 163n400
  granting God's blessing, 159
  invoking the name of the LORD three times, 164–65
  meaning of the phrases of, 165n404
  performative utterance commanded by God, 159n380
  performing, 53
  sanctifying the lay people, 85n63
  spoken only by the high priest, 160n387
  threefold structure of, 164n404–65n404
biblical ritual scholars, analyzing ritual acts, 12
bipartite courtyard, theory of, 173n447
blemishes, disqualifying animals from being offered, 33n29, 91n87, 95n101, 100n125
blessing
  bestowing a gift from the LORD, 54n82
  coinciding with the manifestation of the divine fire, 56
  coming after the burnt offering, 55, 57
  conveying goodwill, 159n381
  in different contexts, 165n409
  following the sounding of the trumpets, 58
  granting substantial gifts and material blessings, 165n405
  by the high priest wearing the gold plate, 55n85
  proclaiming of, 54
blessing rite
  announcing the presence of God, 176
  blessing the Israelites, 198
  composed of two ritual acts, 53
  different from the other rites in the daily divine service, 158–68
  divine institution of, 159–60
  priests sounding the silver trumpets before, 67
  ritual activities enacted in, 59
  ritual function of, 160–64

ritual locations of, 163
summary of, 164, 167–68
theological purpose of, 164–67
blood
  applied to the altar, 103n133, 112n172
  atoning for the lives of God's people, 115n181
  collecting as the purpose for killing the lamb, 106n149
  in the daily divine service, 102
  disposal of, 39, 102–3, 107
  draining from an animal, 106n148
  excluded from human use, 107n152, 113n174
  of grapes, 152n354
  making atonement, 113n174, 115
  as not holy or most holy, 119n193
  powerful in animistic societies, 102
  presentation of, 39, 39n44, 107
  purifying the altar and the priests, 117
  purifying the Israelites vicariously through atonement, 186
  ransoming the Israelites from death, 116n184
  as a ritual material, 109–10
  from a sin offering, 156n371
  splashed against the sides of the altar, 36, 37n36, 66, 103n132
  substituted for the Israelites transfering their sins to the sanctuary, 114n175
  substituting the life of the lamb for the lives of the Israelites, 116, 183
blood rite
  allowing the priests to enter into the LORD's presence, 120n198
  carried out regularly at the sanctuary, 103n136
  cleansing sins and uncleanness, 120
  consisting of five enactments, 41
  described, 36–41, 102–21
  divine institution of, 102–4
  enactments performed in, 102
  forgiveness resulting from, 115n183
  identical in both the morning and evening service, 66
  not sanctifying, 119n193
  occurring at the break of day and just before nightfall, 110–11
  occurring before the theophany in the inaugural service, 117
  preparing the lambs to be placed on the altar, 176, 198
  for the priests at their seven-day ordination, 117n188
  relation to the three ritual spheres, 120
  ritual function of, 104–13
  ritual location of, 112n172
  of the sin offerings compared to burnt offerings on the Day of Atonement, 118n192
  summary of, 112–13, 120–21
  theological purpose of, 113–20
boundaries, 137n296, 193, 195
bowls. See bronze bowls; golden bowls; silver bowls
brackets, in scripture references, 1n2
bread, without leaven lasting longer, 60n106
bread, cakes, and wafers, offering of presented with the animals, 35
bread and wine, on the table in the incense rite, 131
bread of God, 175n453
bread of the presence
  as both regular bread and daily bread, 124n216
  changing every Sabbath, 123n214, 128n238
  connection with burning incense, tending/lighting the lamps, and the drink offering, 136
  considered an offering by fire to the LORD, 47n61
  eaten by the priests, 47n61
  eaten in the morning meal rite on the Sabbath, 168n418
  gaining significance from the LORD's presence in the holy place, 128n239

bread of the presence *(continued)*
   mentioned in texts both within and outside the Pentateuch, 123n215
   removed and then eaten by the priests, 128
   sitting at the golden table for a week, 46, 123, 138
   in two piles of six loaves each, 46, 46n60, 131, 141
bread offering of the high priest, 17–18, 35
   burned on the altar for burnt offering, 96, 144, 144n322, 147
   enacted by his son, 145, 145n328
   having no immediate effect for Israel or the other priests, 100n128
   as the last offering of the day sent up in smoke on the altar, 51n72
   made from grain, 144n321
   no one eating any portion of, 88n74
   offered daily, 88n76, 144n321
   placed upon the memorial portion of the cereal offering, 51
   preparation of, 91, 91n86, 92n89, 96n112
   presentation of, 36, 88, 88n76
   stages of, 88n74
breastpiece of judgment
   containing Urim and Thummim, 140, 140n307
   fabricated from the same material as the ephod, 132–33
   like outer armor, 141n311
   names written and fastened over the heart of the high priest, 140n308
   stones with the names of the twelve tribes, 141n310
bronze bowls, used for splashing the blood, 109n162–10n162
burning rite, 44n55
   allowing the LORD to meet with his people, 176
   at the altar, 153
   completing God's acceptance of Israel, 157
   consisting of a sequence of ritual activities, 53
   divine institution of, 142–44
   identical in the morning and the evening, 67
   peculiar among religions in the ancient world, 142
   primary ritual acts of, 144
   producing a sweet aroma, 198
   ritual function of, 145–53
   smoking up the offerings, 50–53
   summary of, 153, 158
   theological purpose of, 153–58
burnt offerings. *See also* individual burnt offerings
   at an appointed time, 57n96
   burned up completely, 2
   categories of, 2–3
   consistent procedure for, 37
   distinctions between, 11
   divinely instituted, 142–43
   killing and flaying to remove the skin, 104
   making atonement on the Day of Atonement, 118n192
   materials for presented before materials for the cereal offering, 35
   not making atonement for the sanctuary, 118n192
   offered every day of the year, 2
   Pentateuch authorizing, 17
   performed throughout generations, 142
   prescription for, 50n69
   procedure for preparing, 34
   public performing a different function than private, 20
   regular burnt offering as, 143n315
   smoking up a soothing aroma to the LORD, 50n70
   three main stages of, 157
   transmitted to God through fire, 155n368
   trumpets sounded over every day, 58

camp, of Israel, 81, 195n61
censers, offering incense in, 122n205
central rites, of the daily divine service, 20, 21, 36–53, 66

Index of Subjects   227

cereal and drink offerings, portions for, 52n76
cereal offering
  accompanying the daily burnt offering, 51n76, 143n316
  baking, 60, 171, 172
  bread from eaten in a holy place, 173
  distinguished from private cereal offerings, 143n317
  divinely instituted, 143
  eaten at the meal rite, 168
  experiment that recreated, 147n335
  ingredients of, 60, 95
  inseparable part of the daily burnt offering, 144n321
  legislation for, 143n317
  made into unleavened loaves and eaten, 60n107, 171
  as most holy, 60n108
  offered in the form of fine flour, 60
  only a token portion is burned, 50–51, 144, 146–47
  presentation of, 34, 35, 36, 87, 87n71
  priests eating the remaining portion of, 60, 170n426
  producing an intense cloud of aromatic smoke, 147
  salting of, 109n160
chiastic arrangement, emphasizing atonement, 118n191
clean things and people, becoming defiled, 186
coals
  for burning incense on the inner altar, 30, 43n52, 75, 75n32, 76n33
  kindled in preparation for adding new wood, 75
  lighting the lamps in the holy place every evening, 76
  remaining on the altar, 28n11
  removing in the morning service, 31
column of smoke, as theophany, 154
common realm, priest entering into, 76

common things, holy things not coming into contact with, 61n112
communal offerings, as divine gifts to humans, 11
communities, ritual acts constituting and maintaining, 20n35
comprehensive rites, of purification and sanctification, 187n32
concluding rites, 20, 21, 53–63, 67
contagious aspect, of holiness, 61n112
contagious holiness
  God alone as an agent of, 148n342–49n342
  key to understanding, 175n449
  related to the tabernacle furniture and offerings, 139n304
containers, sitting on the table representing the twelve tribes of Israel, 129n240
corporate rites, of purification and sanctification, 187n32
courtyard
  area outside as common, yet ritually clean, 195
  holiness of, 98n121
  between its entrance and the tent, 194
  as least holy, 195n65
  restrictions on accessing, 179
  theory of a bipartite, 173n447
created realm, illustrated, 200
critical scholarship, on the divine service, 8–11
crown, of the high priest, 183n19

daily bread offering of the high priest. *See* bread offering of the high priest
daily burnt offering. *See* burnt offerings
daily cereal offering. *See* cereal offering
daily divine service
  as an act of God upon humans, 11
  analyzing parts of to determine functions, 16
  authorized and instituted by God, 15

daily divine service *(continued)*
  blood rite, 41
  centrality of, 1–2
  conducted across the generations in ancient Israel, 6
  consisting of two presentation rites, 87n69
  evidence for the perpetual enactment of, 5–6
  exact order and sequence of each part of, 25
  following a set order of seven rites, 23n41, 24–67, 64–65, 67, 201
  foundation of, 3–6
  foundational to and integrated with all of the other occasional rites, 17
  including an incense rite, 39
  instituted by the LORD, 201
  instituted for perpetual observance, 4
  interrelated components of, 15
  LORD as the primary agent in, 72
  materials for presented to the LORD, 88–89
  methodology for interpreting, 19
  ministry of, 56n91
  organization of this study of, 17–18
  parts intended to be performed perpetually, 3–4
  parts of, 24–25
  perspectives of scholars on, 7
  practical order of, 66
  priests sounding the trumpets over the burnt offering in, 58
  of purification and sanctification from desecration and defilement, 200
  purifying and sanctifying the Israelites, 178
  reassembling, 2
  reconstructing, 17, 44n55
  regular parts of, 70n6
  as the regular rite, 21
  required to be performed regularly, 4–5
  ritual function of, 68–177
  sequence of the meal rite in, 62–63
  sequence of three main ritual enactments in, 56–57
  stages of, 20
  stages of the analysis of, 22–23
  summary of scholarship on, 6–17
  theological purpose of, 16
daily drink offering. *See* drink offering
daily offerings. *See* offering(s)
daily passage of time, foundational to the entire ritual calendar, 190
daily reconsecration, necessity for, 156n370
darkness, danger and evil of, 79n47
David, 83n57
Day of Atonement. *See also* atonement
  blood of the sin offerings taken into the tent of meeting sanctifying the altar, 156n371
  blood rites on, 118n192
  high priest disposing blood from all of the public offerings, 105
  high priest washing his entire body, 148, 148n342
  manipulation of blood on, 117–18
  outer altar as the most holy place to burn incense on, 76n33
  purgation rites on, 118n192
  rites removing the impurities of the Israelites, 184n20
  ritual performance of, 29
  scapegoat on, 116n185, 184n20
  special vestments of the high priest on, 148n342
declaration, hand placing as, 93n95
defects. *See* blemishes
demonic realm, illustrated, 200
demons, existence of, 14
deputy, of the high priest, 55, 126, 126n225
descriptive texts, 3, 18, 24
developmental analysis, 10
dish, Hebrew word for, 134n282
dishes, for the piles of bread, 134
divesting, removing holiness from the priest, 76
divination, Old Testament opposed to, 15
divine fire. *See also* fire rite

on the altar for burnt offering,
    72n14, 150
banking, 78n42
burning continually, 79–80
burning up the entire animal with
    all burnt offerings, 26
came out from before the LORD
    at the inaugural service, 70n3,
    82, 83
connecting the outer altar with the
    inner altar, 127n230
as doorway to the spiritual realm,
    155n368
emanating from the presence of the
    LORD in the tent of meeting, 83
falling from heaven at the dedication of the temple in Jerusalem,
    83n57
or fire of God, 70, 182n16
God appearing as, 70n4
hidden from the Israelites, 154n362
illustration of the LORD's presence
    in, 185
for the incense rite, 30, 130, 138
maintaining, 26–27, 66, 79
as the most important ritual thing
    in the daily service, 187n33
necessary for the entire ritual system, 78, 182n17–83n17
necessity to keep burning, 27n8,
    69–70, 69n2, 182
renewing each morning and maintaining in the evening, 79
sanctifying food for the priests, 84
as a significant material, 78
signifying God's approval of Israel,
    73n21
smoking up the incense for Israel,
    138
taken from the altar for burnt offering into the tent of meeting, 138
on the top of Mount Sinai, 72n15
turning all of the offerings into
    smoke, 150, 155
divine fire-cloud, prevented the Egyptians from harming Israel, 79n47
divine institution
    of the blessing rite, 159–60
    of the blood rite, 102–4
    of the burning rite, 142–44
    of the fire rite, 69–71
    of the incense rite, 121–25
    of the meal rite, 168–69
    of the presentation rite, 86–89
divine realm, illustrated, 200
divine service. *See* daily divine service
drink offering
    accompanying all burnt offerings,
        51n76
    after the placement of all the other
        ritual materials, 52n77
    altar for burnt offering and ground
        at the tabernacle sanctified by,
        156
    brought out from the holy place,
        147
    in the burning rite, 143
    daily divine service including,
        47n64
    described, 34n33
    inseparable part of the daily burnt
        offering, 144n321
    not poured on top of the burnt
        offerings on the altar, 148n339,
        151n349
    poured out, 51–52, 52n79,
        143n319, 147, 148, 151,
        151n350, 151n351–52n351, 152,
        152n353, 152n354, 152n356
    presentation of, 34, 36, 87
    stored and prepared upon the
        golden table, 121n200, 129,
        131n255
    vessels used for pouring out, 51n75
    of wine or fermented beverage, 18,
        51n74, 95
"dynamistic" understanding, of the
    world, 10

elevation offering, 86n66, 107n151
encampment, by the Levites, 180
encroachers, killing of, 180n8
entrails and lower legs, washing of,
    104, 108, 108n157
entrance, to the tent of meeting, 97,
    98n124, 194, 194n58, 195n62

Index of Subjects

ephah, size of, 95n103
ephod, 133, 141n311
evening service, sequence of rites, 65
evil powers, God controlling through ritual acts, 14–15
exchange, of Israel's impurities for God's holiness, 184n20
expiation, 115n182
exterior of the tent of meeting and its opening on the west side of the altar, as a boundary, 195

face of God, 165n406
fear, LORD's fire as cause for, 70n5
fermented beverage
   Hebrew word for, 95n108
   not burned on the altar fire, 150, 152
fermented substances, usually associated with impurity, 95n107
filling of the hands, of the priests, 62n115
fire and presentation rites, preparing for the rites that come after, 25
fire offering, 169n424
fire pans, 28, 78, 135
fire rite. *See also* divine fire
   conducted every morning and every evening, 31, 78, 79n46
   described, 25–32
   divine institution of, 69–71
   as the foundation for all of the rites in daily divine service, 31, 69–85
   maintaining the holy fire at the tabernacle, 176
   maintaining the presence of the LORD, 84
   perpetuating holy fire, 198
   preceding the presentation rite, 26
   priest putting on his sacred vestments before going near the altar, 61n109
   ritual function of, 72–82
   sequence for, 27n7, 31
   summary of, 85
   theological purpose of, 82–85
firewood. *See* wood
flaying, 40, 40n45, 108

flock animals, locations for slaying, 111n167
flour, 59n103, 92n89, 95n103
font, 137, 151
food. *See also* holy food; most holy food
   for the people becoming holy, 84n63
   for the priests becoming most holy, 84n63
"food of God," 175
for acceptance, expressing divine favor or disfavor, 100n125
forgiveness, 115n183
formal ritual activity, 22n40–23n40
formulaic ritual texts, 18n24
formulaic texts, 18
fragrant incense
   burned before the LORD, 127
   coming out to the outer altar with the high priest, 155
   composition of, 130
   pleasing smell of, 139n302
   producing a thick cloud of smoke, 139n301
   sanctifying the people, 139n304
frankincense
   burning of from the bread of the presence, 46n61, 47, 47n61, 124n218, 130n250
   in the cereal offering, 95
   distinguished from fragrant incense and from regular frankincense, 131n257
   as an essential part of the bread, 124n218
   omitted from all kinds of cooked grain offerings, 147n336
   as part of the cereal offering, 87, 87n72
   placed on each of the two piles of bread, 46, 123–24, 128, 131
functionalist definitions, of ritual activities, 23n40

Garden of Eden, tree of life in, 135n288

gems, mounted on the breastpiece, 132, 133
generations, legislation for future, 3–4
glory cloud
    divine fire from, 182n16
    entering the most holy place, 84
    relation with the silver trumpets, 161n393
God. *See also* LORD
    as an agent of contagious holiness, 148n342–49n342
    doing something to or for his people through the divine service, 16
    gaining no benefit from the offerings of the Israelites, 142
    having no need for food and cannot be bribed, 154
    manifesting himself to the earthy realm through fire, 155n368
    placement of blood from the offering on the altar propitiating, 114–15
    redefining all natural systems of purity and impurity, 116n186
    as super holy, 175n452
    working through the rites for the benefit of his people, 201
gold, of finest quality, 134n278
golden altar. *See* incense altar
golden bells
    attached to the hem of the high priest's robe, 48, 133
    heard by the Lord and the Israelites, 149
    jingling, 140, 141
    people hearing, 149–50
    protecting feet and legs, 141n311
    protecting from death, 141n310
golden bowls, containing the fragrant incense, 46n61, 124n217, 134
golden containers, as part of the table's appurtenances, 129n240
golden menorah. *See* menorah
golden pitchers, 134, 147, 147n338
golden plate
    on the front of the high priest's turban, 139–40, 149n344, 154
    functioning as a helmet, 141n311
    originally called shiny thing, 150n346
    words appearing on, 124n220–25n220
    with the words "YHWH's holiness" fastening to the turban, 132
golden ritual vessels, used in the tent of meeting, 46n61
golden table
    accessories for, 129n241, 134
    for the daily incense rite, 134–35
    oil for the lamps and wine for the drink offering stored on, 47
    ritual activities performed at, 128
grain offering, following the burnt offering, 33n27
grapes, alcoholic liquid from, 96n108
griddle, for baking, 96n111
guard duty, of the Levites, 179n5, 180n8
guarding or watching over, 165n405
guests, for the meal rite, 170
guilt and sins of the Israelites, absorbed by the sanctuary and its furniture, 184n20
guilt offerings
    food from eaten in the morning meal rite on the Sabbath, 168n418
    serving expiatory functions, 100n125

hand. *See also* placing a hand
    leaning, 92n91
    placing on several kinds of individual offerings, 93
hearth, Hebrew words for, 79n49
Hezekiah, 44
hide of the daily burnt offering. *See also* skin of the lamb
    devoid of any ritual significance, 108n156
hides, burning outside the camp, 40n46
high priest. *See also* ornate vestments of the high priest; priest
    acting on behalf of Israel, 139n303
    anointed on his head, 88n76

Index of Subjects

high priest (continued)
  approaching the ark on the Day of Atonement, 195n66
  assisted by priests in the tent of meeting, 49n67
  authority of, 72n13, 73
  bearing on his shoulders the names of Israel, 48
  bearing responsibility for all of the offerings presented by the Israelites, 100n127
  bearing the guilt of all Israel before the LORD, 140, 140n305, 149n344, 180, 183
  bearing the names of the twelve tribes of Israel over his heart, 140
  blessing the congregation from the front of the altar in the courtyard, 161, 163, 184
  contracting super holiness, 148n342
  designating another priest to do something in his stead, 73
  enacting the incense rite and all of its ritual activities, 126
  entering the most holy place of the tabernacle, 84n60, 194
  functioning as an icon or image of God, 154
  functioning in a royal capacity, 154n360
  heard by God and by the peole, 155n364, 155n365
  LORD promising to meet with and speak to, 55
  needing a deputy to serve on his behalf, 126n225
  needing the light of the lamps to conduct the incense rite in the evening, 128
  not sounding the trumpets, 161n390
  performing all of the ritual acts, 121, 136n294
  performing the blood rite, 105
  performing the presentation rite, 89
  placing his hand on the head of the lamb, 33–34, 33n31–34n31, 89, 89n78, 92, 92n91, 93n95, 94
  presenting his daily bread offering, 88, 89, 100
  raising his hands to the level of the golden plate on his head while announcing the blessing, 55n85
  representing the LORD to Israel and representing Israel to the LORD, 73n18, 90, 149
  responsible for supervising the entire divine service, 73n17, 146, 180
  responsible for the burning rite, 146n330
  ritual agent of the incense rite, 125–26
  as the ritual head of the priests, 75n28
  seen as if superimposed over the smoke rising from the altar, 167n416
  serving as a mediator by bringing Israel into the presence of the LORD, 176
  special and normal vestments, 61n111
  successor to, 126n225
  viewing as a royal figure, representing the LORD, 150n346
  washing before donning his ornate vestments, 48, 53, 129
  washing his entire body before entering the most sacred area of the sanctuary, 29n18
  washing the most holy fragrant incense and soil from his hands and feet, 149
  washing with water before donning the special vestments on the Day of Atonement, 29
  wearing his ornate vestments for the burning rite, 52, 53n81
  wearing ornate vestments in the daily incense rite, 124, 129
  wearing the ephod, breast piece, robe, and turban with the gold

plate over the regular vestments, 48
wearing the golden crown with the divine name inscribed on it, 154, 154n361, 183n19
wearing the names of the twelve tribes on his shoulders, 140
high priest's successor, ritual functions performed by, 145n328
hin, size of, 95n104
holiness
    areas and grades of, 84n60
    belonging to YHWH, 125n220
    contagious aspect of, 61n112
    grades of, 175n452
    imparted to the Israelites, 183
holy altar, ritual purification necessary for approaching, 74
holy and common locations, illustrated, 197
holy and the common
    distinguishing between, 74n26, 187n34
    influencing the ritual status of the Israelites, 119
holy anointing oil, consecrating priests and vestments, 75
holy crown, golden plate as, 150n346
holy fire. *See* divine fire
holy food. *See also* food
    compared to most holy food, 171n430
    eating, 60, 172n441
    not directly communicating God's holiness, 84n63
holy garments. *See* vestments
Holy Holy Holy, God's threefold designation as, 175n452
holy place
    designation of, 60n108
    for eating the bread from the daily cereal offering, 151
    inside or near the tent of the meeting, 151n350
    as less holy, 195n65
    LORD meeting with priests in, 194

holy things
    desecrated by contact with unclean people or things, 186
    having the power to convey holiness, 139n304
    sanctifying things or people, 174n449–75n449
holy water, 186, 187n32. *See also* water
"honey," defined as fruit honey or nectar, 148n339

illocutionary speech act, intending a certain force, 159n380
impurity, 116, 186n26
inaugural service
    Aaron performing the blood rite at, 105
    blood rite before the theophany at, 117
    divine fire came out of the tent of meeting, 43, 83
    lay Israelites seeing the holy fire only at, 154n362
    performance of two blessings in, 55
    theophany following the benediction at, 166, 166n413
incense
    atonng for the Israelites' guilt, 183n19
    burning, 39, 42, 44, 45, 121–22, 121n201, 127, 129, 133
    cleansing the air of stench, 127n231
    kept in containers on the table, 47
    manifesting the presence of the LORD, 176
    as most holy, 156n371
    placing before the LORD prior to the burnt offerings, 43
    protecting the high priest and removing Israel's unintentional corporate sins, 184n20
    sanctifying the assembled congregation and the entire camp of Israel, 139
    unauthorized fire for burning provoking God's wrath, 30

incense altar. *See also* altar for burnt offering
  as the closest ritual location to the ark, 136
  description of, 133–34
  LORD meeting with the high priest at, 136n295
  not containing enough live coals, 30
  offerings allowed, 152n352
  removing ashes from and adding burning coals to, 45
  smoking up incense, 133n277
incense rite, 121–42
  bringing the entire community to God, 198
  components of, 121–22
  as a crucial part of the daily service, 49
  divine institution of, 121–25
  enacted in the morning and in the evening every day of the week, 135
  as the intermediate or liminal stage of the service, 191
  made up of a sequence of ritual acts, 49
  maintaining the bread of the presence and the lamps inside the tent of meeting, 176
  as the most central rite, 42–49
  performed for the benefit of the Israelites, 126n227
  performing before or after the burnt offering, 42–43
  removing the burning coals for, 30
  ritual function of, 125–37
  ritual locations of, 137
  summary of, 137, 141–42
  theological purpose of, 137–41
incorporation postliminal, rites of, 191n47
individual burnt and peace offerings, presentation of, 17
individual burnt offerings, 2, 33n31, 37n37
individual offerings, spontaneity of, 8–9

individual rites, of purification and sanctification, 187n32
initial rites
  of the daily divine service, 20, 21, 25–36
  sequence of the ritual activities for, 66
inspection
  of the lambs, 33
  of materials for offerings, 91, 91n86, 91n87, 91n88
Israel
  camp of, 81, 195n61
  comparing with lambs, 94n99
  consecrated by the glory of the LORD, 156n369
  purification and sanctification of, 185
  receiving the LORD's blessing, 73n20
  status in relation to the stages of the divine service, 193
Israelites
  accepted by the LORD, 140
  accessing the courtyard with the accompaniment of Levites, 179n4
  as agents in the fire rite, 73–74
  as beneficiaries of the blessing rite, 161
  benefiting from the ritual acts, 146
  bringing oil for burning in the lamps, 123n212
  bringing wood for the divine fire, 74n22
  caught between the holy presence of God and the ritual impurity of Sheol, 119n197
  grumbling against Moses and Aaron, 179
  having communion with God through the holy food, 85n63
  hearing the sounding bells on the high priest's robe, 154–55
  limited access to the courtyard, 179n4
  the LORD manifesting himself to, 54n84, 83

the LORD purifying and sanctifying, 187
meeting with the LORD in the appointed place at the appointed time, 189n36
moving from a status of ritual impurity to ritual purity, 183
needing to be sanctified, 190
not entering the tent of meeting, 142
not permitted to touch the altar, 98n124
placing a hand on several kinds of individual offerings, 93
presenting the public offerings, 90
protecting from destruction, 178
providing clear olive oil for the lamps, 123
providing materials for presentation, 90, 90n81
requirements for, 5
as ritual agents in the blood rite at the sanctuary, 105, 106n145
seeing the holy fire only at the inaugural service, 154n362
seeing the smoke from the offerings, 154
smelling the sweetness of God, 139
supplying the oil for the lamps, incense for the altar, and flour for the bread, 126, 126n227

jugs, 134, 134n285

kipper acts, on the Day of Atonement, 118n192
Korah, rebellion instigated by, 130n249, 179

laity. *See* Israelites
lamb(s)
all pieces of placed on the burning coals on the altar, 146
burned and sent up in smoke on the alter for burnt offering, 50, 142
preparation of, 66
presentation of, 33, 34, 36, 87, 87n69
priest placing a hand on. *see* placing a hand
representing Israel, 94, 94n99
securing the LORD's atonement vicariously for Israel, 93–94
slain in the blood rite, 106–7
unblemished yearling males, 94–95
lamps
burning throughout the night, 138
daily maintenance of, 45, 122–23, 122n207, 127
giving light throughout the night in the holy place, 138
illuminating the area at night time, 128n235
kept burning from evening until morning, 45
lighting, 45
lit from the fire taken from the altar for burnt offering, 76n33
olive oil for, 131
providing for the LORD's "sense of sight," 127n233
symbolic functions of, 138n300
lampstand, associated with the word of the LORD, 138n300
Law of Moses, 8
laying/placing a hand, distinguished from hand leaning, 92n91
leaven, 60n106, 148n339
legislative texts, 18
Levites
bearing the guilt of the Israelites, 179
carrying the tabernacle and its belongings, 196n66
doing guard duty, 180
drawing God's wrath upon themselves for any unauthorized encroachment, 180n7
limited access to the courtyard on specific occasions, 179n4
LORD set apart to serve him and to bless in his name, 56
mediating between the Israelites and the priests, 179

Levites (continued)
  never seeing the tent of meeting, 196n66
  not ordained or consecrated like the priests, 179n6
  not permitted to touch the altar, 98n124
  pronouncing blessing, 56n90
  specific duties of, 56n90
  work at the tabernacle from age twenty-five to age fifty, 179n5
Levitical barrier, between the Israelites and the tabernacle, 182
Levitical choir, song sung by, 56n90, 59n102
libation vessels, part of the accessories for the golden table, 129n241
light of the lamps, burning with the fire of God, 138n300
liminal stage, of the service, 191
linen undergarments, 77, 77n38, 132n261
linguistic terminology, explaining a theory of ritual analysis, 23n41
locutionary speech act, 159n380
LORD. See also God; YHWH
  accepting both the materials and the entire community of Israel, 100
  accepting his people and cleansing then from their sins, 157n374
  accepting the Israelites through their offerings, 157
  accepting the temple of Solomon, 83n57
  accessible through the fire at the altar, 84
  appeared in glory to all Israel in the fire, 72n15
  appeared to Moses in the form of fire, 82
  appearing in wrath if not treated as holy, 70n5
  authorizing incense to be burned, 122
  authorizing Moses to ordain Aaron and his sons, 72n13
  authorizing the daily maintenance of the lamps, 122–23
  authorizing the offerings, 90n83
  authorizing the priests to pronounce the blessing, 160n384
  blessing Israel, 164, 165–66, 181
  causing his name to be remembered, 167
  cleansing the Israelites from their ritual impurities, 118
  commanded Aaron to distinguish between the holy and the common, and between the unclean and the clean, 119
  commanded Moses to construct two silver trumpets, 160
  commanded Moses to implement the fire rite, 72
  consecrating and keeping his priests holy, 175
  "consuming" his food through his fire on the altar, 80
  daily revealing his presence, 184
  declaring his ownership of Israel in the benediction, 164n401
  desire to meet with his sinful, unclean people, 119n195
  determining what is ritually clean and ritually unclean, 116n186
  dwelling among the Israelites, 157, 158n378, 181, 199
  exchanging Israel's impurities for his holiness, 183–84, 184n20
  feeding his priests the most holy food, 128n239, 169, 198–99
  giving the blood on the altar to make atonement for all of the Israelites, 103, 113
  granting material well being to his people, 165n406
  granting peace to Israel, 165n407
  guarding from desecration and defilement, 178
  imparting benefits in the blessing, 165
  initiating the blessing, 160n384
  as instituting agent of the blood rite, 106

instituting all of the rites in the daily divine service, 198
instituting the blood rite, 106n146
instituting the fire rite, 69, 70–71, 85
instituting the incense rite, 126–27
as the main agent in the blood rite, 106n146
as the main agent in the rite of presentation, 90
making atonement for his people, 120
manifesting himself, 154, 155, 158, 194
meeting with and speaking to Moses or the high priest and the sons of Israel, 54n84
meeting with his people through the fire on the altar, 79n47, 84n61
meeting with Israel through the fire on the altar, 70n3, 154, 185
not commanding that the temple be constructed, 83n57
not eating food, 175
operating through the system of ritual times, 199
opposition to the rule of from other supernatural forces, 14
as a personal being, 167n415
placing sins on the scapegoat, 184n20
presence at the top of Mount Sinai, 72n15
present in the fire at the outer altar, 182
protection from the dangers of the night, 79n47
punishing Israel because the priests failed to perform their duties, 75n30
purifying and sanctifying his people, 183, 201
purposes accomplished through the fragrant incense, 138–39
receiving his offerings as they ascend to him in smoke, 101n129
releasing the Israelites from their sins, 115
residing in the most holy place inside the tent of meeting, 82n55
revealing his glory in the fire on the altar for burnt offering, 72
revealing his gracious presence visibly and audibly, 166
revelations to Moses on Mount Sinai, 1
as a ritual agent in the blessing rite, 161
as a ritual agent in the incense rite, 127n228
sanctifying and keeping holy his name, 164n402, 166
sanctifying his priests through the meal rite, 174
sanctifying the Israelites, 139, 155, 183, 198
sanctifying the most holy offerings, 187
serving by making offerings on the outer altar, 57
serving the priests as their host, 170
sharing his most holy food, 80n52, 101
shining his face, 161n392
signaling that the Israelites are dear to his heart, 140
speaking to Moses, 54–55
supplying the offerings for the altar, 101
wine reserved for, 96n109
LORD's rest, Hebrew words associated with, 157n377
luminaries, lamps as, 138n300

magic, 14, 15
Maimonides, 7
males, lambs required to be, 33, 94n100
materials. *See* ritual materials
meal rite
concluding the daily divine service, 168–76
divine institution of, 168–69

Levites *(continued)*
  including other kinds of grain offerings, 168n418
  involving the consumption of the most holy food from the public cereal offering, 170
  as the last of the concluding rites, 59–63
  location of, 174
  priests eating the most holy food, 67
  providing for the priests with food, 169, 176–77
  ritual function of, 170–74
  summary of, 174, 176
  sustaining the priests, 199
  theological purpose of, 174–76
meals
  locations for eating by the priests, 173n447
  Pentateuch giving few details about, 25
meaning, of ritual acts, 68
meat, producing smoke, 50n70
meat offerings, 87n71
mediation, illustrated, 181
mediators, agents serving as, 179
memorial portion, of the cereal offering, 147n334
menorah
  accessories for, 135, 135n285
  as the holder of the lamps, 135n286
  lamps taken down and then set back up on, 45n56
  located on the south side of the holy place, 136–37
  as part of the incense rite, 123
  seven lamps on, 135
  symbolic significance, 128n235
  tending the lamps on, 128
  tongs and fire pans accessory to, 46n59
Mishnah, 7
moral responsibility, Pentateuch emphasizing, 10
morning and evening offerings, 51n73, 190
morning and evening services, 25

morphology, of a language, 23n41
Moses
  as the archetypal priest, 126n223
  authority of, 89n77
  commanding the priests to cook and eat the food from their ordination offerings, 62
  LORD appearing to, 82
  LORD's revelations to on Mount Sinai, 1
  no distinct role in the fire rite, 72n12
  performing the blood rite in the ordination service, 105
  representing every high priest or his deputy, 55
  setting up the incense altar and burning incense, 43
  shining/radiant skin on the face of, 165n406, 167n415
  washing priests with water before dressing them in their vestments, 29
most holy food. *See also* food
  cannot be taken outside of the holy grounds of the tabernacle, 171n430
  location of the consumption of, 151n351
  prepared in a certain way, 170
  for the priests, 84n63
  priests eating as a sacred meal, 168
most holy offerings, compared to holy, 60n105
most holy place, 193–94, 195n65, 197
most holy smoke, sanctifying the priest, 156
most holy status, of the cereal offering, 60n108
most holy things, 175n449, 186
Mount Sinai, 1, 70n5, 83
"my food," LORD calling regular offerings as, 80n52

Nadab and Abihu, 70, 70n3, 70n5, 76n33, 130n249
name of the LORD, 164n403, 166, 166n412

Index of Subjects   239

narrative scholarship, on the daily divine service, 7–8
narrative texts, 18

offerers
  lambs securing God's approval and acceptance of, 94n96
  removing impurity and sin from, 115n180
offering(s)
  accomplishments of, 9
  allowed on the inner altar, 152n352
  brought to the tabernacle and inspected, 91
  burned on the altar and smoked up by the holy fire, 150
  categories of, 32n27
  deriving holiness from the holy fire, 168n419
  function of other kinds of, 199
  as a kind of banquet, 96
  laying a hand on, 93n92
  made from flour, 143n316
  as obligatory acts of atonement, 8
  Pentateuch authorizing other, 17
  presenting to the LORD, 32–36, 86n66, 90, 92n90, 99, 157n373
  saving aspect of, 10
  sending up in smoke, 67, 146n333
  serving as gifts to God, 13
  soothing scent of, 80n52, 155
  as unique in more than one way, 142
  various kinds of, 51
  wood for the divine fire as, 78n40
olive oil
  from beaten olives, 95n104, 131
  for the lamps, 123n212, 131, 134n285
onyx stones, fastened to the shoulder pieces of the ephod, 133
order
  of the daily service, 22, 24
  of presentation, 32–33
ordination service, 29, 35, 37–38, 62
ornate vestments of the high priest, 132n260, 132n261
  accomplishing different ritual purposes, 129
  in the blessing rite, 162
  comprising ritual acts, 12
  constituting ritual activities, 49n68
  described, 124
  functioning like military armor, 141n311
  of greater significance than the vestments of the regular priests, 48
  in the incense rite, 132, 139
  involving three ritual activities, 125n221
  manifesting God and his gracious appearance to his people in the burning rite, 149
  revealing the presence of the LORD, 166–67
  ritual acts accomplished by, 127n228
  as ritual appurtenances, 124n219
  worn as a ritual activity, 48
outer altar. See altar for burnt offering
outer room, inside the tent as the holy place, 194
outward act, affecting the physical existence of people, 11
ownership, 33n31, 93n92, 93n95

pagan cultures, lay people having access to idols, 121
pagan deities, 14, 101n129, 186n26
pagans, serving their deities, 175–76
pails, carrying ashes outside the camp, 78
Passover in Egypt, 94n99
peace, declaration of, 55n87
peace offerings, 26n3, 39n44
Pentateuch
  as a canonical template for the enactment of the divine service, 6
  categories of ritual sources, 18
  categories of texts, 3
  defending the Mosaic authorship of, 9
  evidence from like a mosaic, 24

Index of Subjects

Pentateuch *(continued)*
    never prescribing when the priest must bless the people, 25
    prescriptive and descriptive passages in, 18
    presenting the daily service in pieces, 2
    ritual sections in, 3
    superseding any notion of magic, 10
    as a systematic categorization of offerings, 9
"people of holiness," in the camp of Israel, 195n61
perlocutionary speech act, 159n380
perpetual due, 169, 169n422
perpetual legislation, for the Israelite laity, 5
perpetual observance, of the ritual calendar, 5
perpetual ritual provisions, 4, 4n7
perpetual ritual statutes, 4, 4n6
pillar of fire and cloud, 82–83, 155n368
pitchers. *See* golden pitchers
placing a hand
    on the animal's head, 33–35, 33n31–34n31, 89, 89n78, 92, 92n91, 93n95, 94
    designating ownership of a quadruped, 93
pomegranates, attached to the hem of the high priest's robe, 48
postliminal state, of rites of passage, 191
pragmatics, of a language, 23n41
preliminal state, of rites of passage, 191
preparatory ritual acts, not an end in themselves, 190n43
prescribed spoken words, in the blessing rite, 158–59
prescriptive texts, 18, 24
presence of God, manifested as the divine fire, 70n3
presentation
    of animals coupled with the hand placing, 93n93
    as the mode of offering to other deities in the ancient Near East, 101n129
    of offerings, 92, 157
    order of, 32–33
presentation rite
    conducted on behalf of the LORD, 90
    consisting of a sequence of enactments, 36
    daily offerings brought to the LORD in, 85–102
    described, 32–36
    divine institution of, 86–89
    locations significant in, 97
    not identical for the morning and evening services, 66
    in preparation for placement on the altar fire, 198
    providing the materials for the daily service, 176
    ritual function of, 89–99
    ritual materials used in, 94
    ritual times of, 96–97
    theological purpose of, 100–101
priest. *See also* high priest; priests
    adding wood to the altar before carrying the ashes outside the camp, 28
    carrying the ashes to a ritually clean location outside the camp, 27
    changing his clothes and taking the ashes outside the camp, 71n11
    cutting the lamb's throat through the main artery, 37n39
    offering a burnt offering keeping the hide for himself, 40
    performing duties in the holy place, 18
    performing the ritual activity, 26n4
    preparing the carcass for its placement on the altar, 104
    removing sacred vestments before carrying the ashes out of the sanctuary, 76
    washing hands and feet and putting on vestments in the morning presentation rite, 35–36

priesthood, instituted to serve on behalf of Israel, 5
priests. *See also* regular priests
   announcing the blessing together, 54n83
   blowing the trumpets, 59n102
   consuming the bread of the presence on the Sabbath, 47n62
   depending on the offerings of the Israelites for their livelihood, 169
   distinguishing between the holy and the common, 74n26
   eating the most holy food, 59n103, 63n116, 168, 172n441, 173n447
   enacting duties of the fire rite, 71
   encroachment of unauthorized, 180n10
   exclusive control of the blood, 117n189
   inspecting the sheep, 33
   maintaining the divine fire on the altar, 26, 70, 73n16, 79n47, 182n16
   making the bread for the daily bread offering of the high priest, 90n80
   not wearing sacred vestments to carry the ashes outside the tent of meeting, 61
   performing a mediating role, 90n82
   with physical defects, 170n428
   placing the name of the LORD upon the Israelites, 54, 164n403
   presenting the daily cereal offering to the LORD in front of the altar, 87
   providing for the livelihood of, 4n7
   receiving no portion of the land, 169n421
   regular not consecrated like the high priest, 75n28
   relation between the initial vesting of and the eating of the food at their ordination, 62n115
   removing sacred vestments, 60–61, 63, 171
   removing the ashes from the offerings of the previous day and adding wood to the altar for burnt offering, 26
   removing their vestments and carrying the ashes outside the camp at the morning service, 71
   requirements for, 5
   ritual duties of compared to Levites who are not priests, 56n90
   safeguarding God's holiness and protecting the people from the deadly consequences of desecration, 187n34
   sanctified, 156, 191
   sounding the trumpets, 53, 57–58, 57n94, 58n98, 59, 160, 160n385, 163, 163n399, 184
   splashing the blood of the lamb against the four sides of the altar, 157
   standing together with the high priest as he announces the benediction, 161n388
   washing hands and feet, 28, 42, 47, 52, 52n80, 70–71, 70n7–71n7, 91, 148
   washing prior to the fire rite, 74
   washing their entire bodies prior to vesting themselves for service at the temple in Jerusalem, 30
   wearing vestments, 48, 62
primary prescriptive source, consisting of Exod 25-30 as the foundational regulation, 3
private burnt offerings, distinguished from public daily burnt offering, 39n43
prophesying, by the Levites, 56n90
prophetic texts, contained in the prophets, 18
propitiation, placating God's wrath, 114n178–15n178
public divine service, establishing the Israelites as a priestly community, 9
public offerings
   categories of, 86n67
   performed on behalf of the entire community of Israel, 90

Index of Subjects

public offerings *(continued)*
    prescribed for other regular occasions, 2
    presenting at appointed times, 87n68
    presenting to the LORD, 86
pure gold plate/diadem, considered part of the high priest's turban, 132n261
pure table. *See* golden table
purgation rites, on the Day of Atonement, 118n192
purification
    corporate and individual means of, 186n32
    LORD's means of illustrated, 189
    occurring through the holy things in the daily service, 186
    resulting from the blood rite, 119
    rite of cleansing from ritual impurities, 117n190
    rites for individuals not involving holy substances, 187n32
    rites of passage, 192
purity and impurity
    as contagious, 119n196
    having to do with order and disorder, 116n186

red heifer, ashes of, 187n32
regular burnt offering
    distinguished from a burnt offering, 142n313
    established as the daily burnt offering, 143n315
    first enacted at the installation of the priests, 142n314–43n314
regular priests. *See also* priests
    assigned no ritual function in the holy place inside the tent, 125n222
    guarding against the encroachment of the Levites, 180
    holy only as long as they wear the vestments, 75n28
    mediating between the Levites and the high priest, 180
    not having free access to the holy place, 195n66–96n66
    performing a secondary role in the corporate blood rites, 105
    performing most of the acts in the presentation rite, 89
    primarily serving in the courtyard at its altar, 196n66
    serving as "deputies" of the high priest at the incense rite, 126n226
    serving the high priest, 180
    sounding the trumpets, 161, 161n390
    vestments of, 132n260
relationship, between the animal's life and human lives in the blood rite, 116n185
rites
    ascertaining the function of, 22
    conducted in a specific sequence, 15–16, 198, 201
    defined, 1n3
    dramatic structure of, 19n34
    examining prescriptive and descriptive texts about, 19n26
    functioning in relation to other rites, 20
    functioning similar to a language, 23n41
    meaning and functions of, 16
    origin of, 1
    proceeding with a set sequence of ritual activities, 25
    signifying something beyond themselves, 13
    typological and symbolical meaning of, 8
rites of passage
    divided into three subcategories, 191n47
    involving states of being as well as stages in the ritual process, 191n47
    movement from night into day understood as, 79n46
    specific, 190
    stages of, 19, 191, 192, 193

Index of Subjects   243

ritual, defined, 1n3
ritual acts
   associated with wearing the ornate vestments, 124–25, 124n219, 125n221
   in the blessing rite, 161–62
   in the blood rite, 106–9
   in the burning rite, 50, 146–50
   carried out daily at the tabernacle, 1
   conducted every day inside the holy place, 12
   detailed descriptions of, 7
   enacted to accomplish a purpose, 68
   ensuring the endurance of what they teach symbolically, 13
   in the fire rite, 74–77
   in the incense rite, 127–29
   interaction of similar to syntax, 23n41
   in the meal rite, 59, 171
   meaning of, 68
   as mediums of divine power, 11
   as multi-faceted, 13
   order of within the divine service, 15
   placing into broad categories, 11
   in the presentation rite, 91–94
   before the presented materials are burned on the altar for burnt offering, 43
   serving collective needs, 23n40
   stages of, 20, 27n6
   system of in the daily divine service, 182–85
   warding off demonic powers, 14
ritual agents
   of the blood rite, 105–6
   of the fire rite, 72–74
   of the incense rite, 125–27
   at the meal rite, 170
   ordained to perform the burning rite, 145–46
   participating in the blessing rite, 160–61
   of the presentation rite, 89–90
   system of in the daily divine service, 178–82
ritual analysis
   of the divine service, 69
   interpreting how rites function socially, 20n39
   as a methodology, 19–21
ritual biblical scholars, analyzing rites, 12
ritual bridge, between heaven and earth, 194n59
ritual calendar, 5, 189
ritual function
   of the blessing rite, 160–64
   of the blood rite, 104–13
   of the burning rite, 145–53
   of the fire rite, 72–82
   of the incense rite, 125–37
   involving, 22
   of the meal rite, 170–74
   of the presentation rite, 89–99
ritual impurity, 15, 74n24
ritual law, 10, 123n209
ritual locations
   for the blessing rite, 163
   for the blood rite, 111–12
   for the burning rite, 151–53
   for the fire rite, 79–81
   for the meal rite, 173–74
   for the presentation rite, 97–99
   related to burning the fragrant incense, 136–37
   system of in the daily divine service, 193–97
ritual materials
   of the blessing rite, 162
   in the blood rite, 109–10
   of the burning rite, 150
   of the incense rite, 130–35
   of the meal rite, 171–72
   of the presentation rite, 94–96
   presented to the LORD at the tabernacle, 92, 99
   preserving the fire in the daily divine service, 77
   ritual status of changing from common to holy, 92n90
   system of in the daily divine service, 185–89

ritual ordinances, commanded to be kept ceaselessly, 4
ritual scholars, engaging in ritual analysis, 19
ritual spheres, relation of the blood rite to, 120
ritual status, of the entire camp of Israel, 195n61
ritual structure, dealing with, 22
ritual symbol, described, 22
ritual system
  of ancient Israel built on the foundation of the daily divine service, 198
  consisting of everything related to the divine service and sub-systems, 20–21
  consisting of sub-systems, 23n41
  developments coinciding with history, 10
  functioning ethically, 14
  integrative approach to analyzing, 15
  as multi-dimensional, 21
  observing throughout the generations, 4
  Old Testament ideas on, 11
  ritual scholars appreciating, 16
ritual times
  for the blessing rite, 162
  for the blood rite, 110–11
  for the burning rite, 150
  for the fire rite, 78–79
  for the incense rite, 135–36
  for the meal rite, 172
  for the presentation rite, 96–97
  system of in the daily divine service, 189–93
ritual washing. *See also* washing
  connection with ritual vesting, 28, 47–48, 70n7–71n7
  symbolizing purification from disease, death, and corruption, 77n37
ritually unclean Israelites and all non-Israelites, not seeing the outer altar, 196n66

sacred, exclusive to impure, 119n194
sacred and the profane, as contagious, 119n196
sacred fire. *See* divine fire
sacred meal, as the final rite, 63
sacred vestments. *See also* vestments
  anointed with the holy anointing oil, 61
  never worn anywhere except within the confines of the tabernacle courtyard, 61n109
  priests wearing, 28, 71, 91
  required for eating the most holy food, 63n117
sacrificial meal, in which the high priest blesses the congregation and the sacred food is eaten, 44n55
salt
  acting as a preservative and a seasoning, 109n159
  added to all grain offerings, 87
  added to the cereal offering, 87n72
  adding to all offerings, 40n47–41n47, 104n140
  offerings dashed with, 104
  supplies kept at the sanctuary, 110n164
salting
  all of the parts of the lamb, 40–41, 109, 110
  of fragrant incense, 130
  of the incense, 130n248
  of offerings, 109n160, 109n161
sanctification
  brought about through the series of ritual acts, 190
  LORD's means of illustrated, 189
  not performed in the blood rite, 119n193
  of priests, 175
  rites of passage, 192
sanctuary, distinguished from the two holy locations inside the tent of meeting, 151n350
sash, of the high priest, 133
scapegoat, on the Day of Atonement, 116n185, 184n20

Index of Subjects 245

seasoning, salt functioning as, 109n159
second courtyard, outside the entrance to the sanctuary in Jerusalem, 179n4
secondary prescriptive material, 3
semantics, of a language, 23n41
sense of smell, role in the ancient world, 127n231
separation preliminal, rites of, 191n47
serving, distinguished from burning incense and announcing the blessing, 57
shadow of death, protection from, 79n47
Sheol, ritual impurity of, 119n197
shining face, of the LORD, 165n406
shoulder pieces, names on, 140n308, 141n310
shovel, removing ashes from the altar, 78
silver bowls, bronze bowls distinguished from, 109n162–10n162
silver trumpets. *See* trumpets
sin offerings
   food from also eaten in the morning meal rite on the Sabbath, 168n418
   only making atonement for the sanctuary, 118n192
   presentation of blood from, 39n44
   serving expiatory functions, 100n125
sins, destroyed by the super holiness of the LORD himself on the Day of Atonement, 184n20
skin of the lamb, 50n71, 104, 104n138, 108, 108n56
skinning lambs. *See* flaying
slaughtering, meaning to cut the lamb into its pieces, 37n39, 108, 108n154
slaying
   distinguishing from slaughtering, 108n154
   of the lambs not holding any special ritual significance, 106n149

referring to the ritual killing of the lamb, 37n39
smoke
   accompanying the high priest in the courtyard, 139n301
   from the burnt offering having sanctifying power, 156n372
   correlating with the cloud and the presence of the LORD, 162n393
   LORD appearing to the Israelites as, 70n5
   making, 146n333
   as the manifestation of the presence of the LORD, 55n85
   production of, as the central purpose of the daily divine service, 147
   revealing the presence of the LORD to the Israelites, 138–39, 184
   sanctifying the tent of meeting and the altar for burnt offering, 155–56
   setting both God and Israel at rest, 157
smoking up of a ritual substance, qualifying a ritual act as an offering for God, 147n333
solar and lunar cycles, regulating the ritual calendar, 21
Solomon, 44, 83n57
sons of Aaron, sounding the trumpets, 161
sorcery, Old Testament opposed to, 15
span, length of, 132n267
speech acts, types of, 159n380
spiced incense, taken from the golden bowls, 124n217
spices, 130, 130n245
splashing blood on the altar
   happening prior to burning incense and smoking up the offerings, 111
   making atonement, 120
   as most ritually significant, 37
   against the sides of the altar, 104, 107
spoken ritual enactment, blessing rite as the only, 159

statute forever, sounding of the silver trumpets as, 57n94
super holiness, 148, 148n342, 187
super holy God, making things most holy, 175n452
superior holiness, describing God's preeminent sanctity, 187n35
sweet aroma, signifying the LORD's pleasure and acceptance, 157n375
symbolic definitions, of rites, 23n40
symbolic significance, attached to the ritual act, 11
symbolic value, of ritual acts, 13
syntax, of a language, 23n41
system of purity, aiming to curb the free will of the Israelites, 13
system of ritual locations, 197, 199–200
systematic approach, 10, 20, 20n39
systematic method of ritual analysis, 21

tabernacle
    correlation with Mount Sinai, 84, 84n60
    furnishings imparting holiness to the priests, 156
    ground plan for, 81
    LORD's plans for constructing, 1
    as a portable Mount Sinai, 83n58
    rites performed inside as more holy, 12
table, altar for burnt offering as, 75n31, 80, 80n51, 80n52
taboos
    associated with the ritual use of blood in ancient Israel, 113n174
    of proximity, touch, and sight, 178
    regarding sight, touch, and approach, 195
    of sight, touch, and approach, 195n66
Tamid, 7, 142n314
temple in Jerusalem, 44, 58–59, 61, 62
tent of meeting, 99, 118, 189n36
terror, of the night, 79n47
theological and anthropological systems, combination of illustrated, 188
theological meaning, of offerings, 10
theological purpose
    of the blessing rite, 164–67
    of the blood rite, 113–20
    of the burning rite, 153–58
    of the daily divine service, 22, 178–201
    of the fire rite, 82–85
    of the incense rite, 137–41
    of the main parts of the system of ritual acts, 185
    of the meal rite, 174–76
    of the presentation rite, 100–101
theological ritual analysis, 19
theological system, 186, 188, 190
theophany of the LORD, 154, 166, 166n413, 184, 185
throne room, of God, 194
Thummim. See Urim and Thummim
time, Hebrew word for, 189n36
token portion, of the cereal offering, 147n334
tongs, 46n59, 135
transition liminal, rites of, 191n47
"tree," of the lampstand burning in the holy place, 138
tree symbolism, of the menorah, 135n288
tribes of Israel, high priest bearing the names of, 12, 133
trumpets
    announcing the presence of the LORD, 166
    in the divine service, 57n93
    heralding the presence of a king or his representative, 162
    relating thematically to the LORD's presence, 162n393
    relation with the glory cloud, 161n393
    signaling for the congregation to prostrate themselves, 59n102
    sounding, 53, 57–58, 58n98, 59, 160, 160n385, 161, 161n390, 163, 163n399, 184

Index of Subjects   247

uses of, 160n385
tunic, of the high priest, 133
turban, of the high priest, 48, 132
twelve loaves, representing the twelve tribes before the LORD continually, 128n239–29n239
twelve tribes, names engraved on the onyx stones, 133

unauthorized encroachment, 180, 181
unauthorized/strange fire, for burning incense, 76n33
unblemished, lambs required to be, 33
unclean and clean locations, illustrated, 197
unclean and the clean, 119, 187n34
unclean persons, incurring God's wrath, 115n179
underworld, blood used to invoke the powers of, 102
unleavened bread or cakes, cooked portion of the cereal offering as, 60n107
Urim and Thummim, 48, 133, 140n307
utensils, associated with the altar, 78

veil, in the tent for meeting, 195
vessels
  for the drink offerings, 47n64
  used for preparing any grain offering, 171–72
vesting
  of Aaron, 29n15
  before eating, 62
vestments. *See also* ornate vestments of the high priest
  basic, 48
  consecrated at the ordination of the priests, 62n115, 74–75
  covering the priest with God's holiness, 74
  divine command for the priests to wear, 71n8
  ordained by God, 126n224
  priests taking off as a final act of the divine service, 60

remaining in the sanctuary, 61n111, 76n35
  as the royal garments of the LORD, 141n311
  transmitting holiness, 61

washing. *See also* high priest, washing by; priests, washing by; ritual washing
  entrails and lower legs of the lamb, 108
  preceding any of the ritual activities in the fire and presentation rites, 47
  by the priests at the tabernacle, 30
  purifying the hands of each priest, 74
  before putting garments to minister, 29
  related to maintaining the fire rite at the temple in Jerusalem, 30
  in the rite of ordination, 29
water. *See also* holy water
  for cleaning the entrails and lower legs of the lamb, 110
  purifying hands and feet, 77
  sources of for washing, 110n163
  washing the parts of the animal, 98n122
wheat flour mixed with oil and salt, offering of, 17
wilderness, Hebrew word for, 196n67
wine
  associated with the best foodstuff, 96n109
  from the drink offering as most holy, 156n371
  poured on the side of the altar, 150
  presenting before the LORD, 87–88
  ritual use of, 95n107
  sitting on the table, 131–32
  storage of, 147n338, 148n339
wood
  adding to the altar for burnt offering, 26, 26n2, 27, 28, 50, 71, 71n10, 76, 78n44
  kinds used for the holy fire, 76n34

wood *(continued)*
   laity supplying for the fire, 74, 74n22
   as an offering, 27n9, 74n22, 78n40
   providing fuel for the divine fire, 77–78
words of blessing, 159–60, 159n380, 167n416
work of the Levites, 179n5

yearlings, lambs required to be, 33
YHWH. *See also* LORD
   invoking in the Aaronic benediction, 164–65
   "YHWH's holiness" on the golden plate, 48, 125n220, 149, 150, 154n361

Zion, LORD's fire in, 70n5

www.ingramcontent.com/pod-product-compliance
Lightning Source LLC
Chambersburg PA
CBHW050346230426
43663CB00010B/2011